You, _____, have a great

future because you understand that

success is a process — not an event.

# Praise for Zig Ziglar

"Zig Ziglar's unique mastery of the skill of instilling hope enlightens the hearts and minds of millions, freeing them to become all they can be."

— Peter Lowe, President and CEO, Peter Lowe International

"Zig Ziglar's electrifying speeches draw long standing ovations and leave audiences spellbound with enthusiasm."

—*Purpose Magazine*

"No one stirs the motivational embers with more power than Zig Ziglar."

—*Selling Power Magazine*

"The world is filled with motivational speakers with exciting, compelling messages, but few offer the perspective and balance Zig Ziglar does. By applying his down-to-earth message, and by utilizing his principles, in six years my advances have jumped from $10,000 to over $300,000."

—Debbie Macomber, Author

# Praise for Zig's Books and Training Tapes

"Success doesn't happen overnight. It takes patience, time, and a little guidance. Let *Success For Dummies* by Zig Ziglar unlock invaluable secrets that can guide you on your road to success."

—John C. Maxwell, Author, Speaker, Founder of INJOY, Inc.

"Zig Ziglar's 'Strategies for Success' training program, combined with our people using the cassette tapes in their cars, dramatically reduced the turnover of personnel in our three tire stores, where turnover is traditionally high. Since turnover is very expensive, we know the program does not 'cost' anything — like other wise investments, it pays dividends."

—Dave Goodnight, Advantage Goodyear Service

"The Zig Ziglar Training Program was instrumental in helping Tri-City Hospital become one of the Top One Hundred Hospitals in America. In the process, we were able to reduce mortality by 20 percent, cost of discharge by 16 percent, and increase our return on equity by 58 percent. Our employees have become better people, better partners, and better parents. Our CEO stated, 'Of all that I have accomplished here at Tri-City in the past eight years, I consider making the Ziglar training course part of our employee training to be my most successful endeavor.'"

—Dr. Bob Price, Chaplain and Trainer

"In the medical world, very few physicians will deal with more than one or two patients who have the 'Borderline Disorder' — a malfunction of the limbic system. In my career, I have treated over 1,400 'borderlines' with overall excellent results. I use medications like Prozac, as do other physicians, but I also insist my patients read positive thinking books and listen to motivational tapes. Zig Ziglar's books and training tapes are my favorites — the patients who learn what Zig teaches do the best. The results speak for themselves."

—Leland M. Heller, M.D.

"Speaking from a personal benefit and professional observation point of view, Zig Ziglar's 'Born to Win' seminar, as well as his 'Strategies for Success' training program, are life-changing experiences. He uses what I call a 'cognitive behavioral approach' to change attitudes as well as behaviors. He is straight-talking, easy to understand, entertaining, and his work is based on sound psychological principles. His training is logically organized and represents an optimum segmentation of material organized around core concepts to drive the points home and facilitate maximum learning. At the same time he breaks the material up into subjects so they don't run together in the learning process. Benefits to my patients have been substantial, especially three who suffer from Borderline Personality Disorder and were suicidal. As a result of applying these principles, my psychiatric practice has reached the point where my waiting list for new appointments is over seven months. I can't endorse this training material strongly enough."

—Louis B. Cady, M.D.

 TM

# References for the Rest of Us!®

## BESTSELLING BOOK SERIES

Do you find that traditional reference books are overloaded with technical details and advice you'll never use? Do you postpone important life decisions because you just don't want to deal with them? Then our *For Dummies*® business and general reference book series is for you.

For Dummies business and general reference books are written for those frustrated and hard-working souls who know they aren't dumb, but find that the myriad of personal and business issues and the accompanying horror stories make them feel helpless. *For Dummies* books use a lighthearted approach, a down-to-earth style, and even cartoons and humorous icons to dispel fears and build confidence. Lighthearted but not lightweight, these books are perfect survival guides to solve your everyday personal and business problems.

> **"More than a publishing phenomenon, 'Dummies' is a sign of the times."**
>
> — *The New York Times*

> **"A world of detailed and authoritative information is packed into them..."**
>
> — *U.S. News and World Report*

> **"...you won't go wrong buying them."**
>
> — *Walter Mossberg, Wall Street Journal, on For Dummies books*

**Already, millions of satisfied readers agree. They have made For Dummies the #1 introductory level computer book series and a best-selling business book series. They have written asking for more. So, if you're looking for the best and easiest way to learn about business and other general reference topics, look to For Dummies to give you a helping hand.**

Wiley Publishing, Inc.

# by Zig Ziglar

**Foreword by Lou Holtz**

**WILEY**

Wiley Publishing, Inc.

## Success For Dummies®

Published by
**Wiley Publishing, Inc.**
111 River Street
Hoboken, NJ 07030
www.wiley.com

Copyright © 1998 by Wiley Publishing, Inc., Indianapolis, Indiana

Published by Wiley Publishing, Inc., Indianapolis, Indiana

Published simultaneously in Canada

No part of this publication may be reproduced, stored in a retrieval system, or transmitted in any form or by any means, electronic, mechanical, photocopying, recording, scanning, or otherwise, except as permitted under Sections 107 or 108 of the 1976 United States Copyright Act, without either the prior written permission of the Publisher, or authorization through payment of the appropriate per-copy fee to the Copyright Clearance Center, 222 Rosewood Drive, Danvers, MA 01923, 978-750-8400, fax 978-646-8700. Requests to the Publisher for permission should be addressed to the Legal Department, Wiley Publishing, Inc., 10475 Crosspoint Blvd., Indianapolis, IN 46256, 317-572-3447, fax 317-572-4447, or e-mail permcoordinator@wiley.com.

**Trademarks:** Wiley, the Wiley Publishing logo, For Dummies, the Dummies Man logo, A Reference for the Rest of Us!, The Dummies Way, Dummies Daily, The Fun and Easy Way, Dummies.com, and related trade dress are trademarks or registered trademarks of John Wiley & Sons, Inc. and/or its affiliates in the United States and other countries and may not be used without written permission. All other trademarks are the property of their respective owners. Wiley Publishing, Inc., is not associated with any product or vendor mentioned in this book.

For general information on our other products and services or to obtain technical support, please contact our Customer Care Department within the U.S. at 800-762-2974, outside the U.S. at 317-572-3993, or fax 317-572-4002.

Wiley also publishes its books in a variety of electronic formats. Some content that appears in print may not be available in electronic books.

*Library of Congress Cataloging-in-Publication Data:*

Library of Congress Control Number: 97-81234
ISBN: 0-7645-5061-6

Manufactured in the United States of America

10 9 8

1O/SV/QW/QU/IN

# About the Author

**Zig Ziglar** (Dallas, TX) is an internationally known authority on high-level performance. He is chairman of the Ziglar Training Systems, which is committed to helping people more fully utilize their physical, mental, and spiritual resources. His I CAN course has been taught in more than 3,000 schools, and hundreds of companies use his books, tapes, and videos to train their employees. Zig has traveled more than 5 million miles throughout the world as a speaker and lecturer. He addresses over 300,000 people every year at the Peter Lowe Success Seminars and at businesses, sales organizations, schools, and church groups. He also reaches countless numbers through television and radio appearances. Zig is the author of several bestselling books, including *Zig Ziglar's Secrets of Closing the Sale, Raising Positive Kids in a Negative World, See You at the Top,* which has sold over 1.5 million copies, and his two most recent books, *Over the Top* and *Something to Smile About.* He also develops and markets training audio and video cassettes and other motivational and selling tools for worldwide distribution. His works have been translated into 32 different languages.

# ABOUT IDG BOOKS WORLDWIDE

Welcome to the world of IDG Books Worldwide.

IDG Books Worldwide, Inc., is a subsidiary of International Data Group, the world's largest publisher of computer-related information and the leading global provider of information services on information technology. IDG was founded more than 25 years ago and now employs more than 8,500 people worldwide. IDG publishes more than 275 computer publications in over 75 countries (see listing below). More than 60 million people read one or more IDG publications each month.

Launched in 1990, IDG Books Worldwide is today the #1 publisher of best-selling computer books in the United States. We are proud to have received eight awards from the Computer Press Association in recognition of editorial excellence and three from *Computer Currents'* First Annual Readers' Choice Awards. Our best-selling *...For Dummies*® series has more than 30 million copies in print with translations in 30 languages. IDG Books Worldwide, through a joint venture with IDG's Hi-Tech Beijing, became the first U.S. publisher to publish a computer book in the People's Republic of China. In record time, IDG Books Worldwide has become the first choice for millions of readers around the world who want to learn how to better manage their businesses.

Our mission is simple: Every one of our books is designed to bring extra value and skill-building instructions to the reader. Our books are written by experts who understand and care about our readers. The knowledge base of our editorial staff comes from years of experience in publishing, education, and journalism — experience we use to produce books for the '90s. In short, we care about books, so we attract the best people. We devote special attention to details such as audience, interior design, use of icons, and illustrations. And because we use an efficient process of authoring, editing, and desktop publishing our books electronically, we can spend more time ensuring superior content and spend less time on the technicalities of making books.

You can count on our commitment to deliver high-quality books at competitive prices on topics you want to read about. At IDG Books Worldwide, we continue in the IDG tradition of delivering quality for more than 25 years. You'll find no better book on a subject than one from IDG Books Worldwide.

John Kilcullen
CEO
IDG Books Worldwide, Inc.

Steven Berkowitz
President and Publisher
IDG Books Worldwide, Inc.

**Eighth Annual Computer Press Awards ≥1992**

**Ninth Annual Computer Press Awards ≥1993**

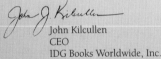

**Tenth Annual Computer Press Awards ≥1994**

**Eleventh Annual Computer Press Awards ≥1995**

IDG Books Worldwide, Inc., is a subsidiary of International Data Group, the world's largest publisher of computer-related information and the leading global provider of information services on information technology. International Data Group publishes over 275 computer publications in over 75 countries. Sixty million people read one or more International Data Group publications each month. International Data Group's publications include: **ARGENTINA:** Buyer's Guide, Computerworld Argentina, PC World Argentina; **AUSTRALIA:** Australian Macworld, Australian PC World, Australian Reseller News, Computerworld, IT Casebook, Network World, Publish, Webmaster; **AUSTRIA:** Computerwelt Osterreich, Networks Austria, PC Tip Austria; **BANGLADESH:** Data News; **BELARUS:** PC World Belarus; **BELGIUM:** Data News; **BRAZIL:** Annuário de Informática, Computerworld, Connections, Macworld, PC Player, PC World, Publish, Reseller News, Supergamepower; **BULGARIA:** Computerworld Bulgaria, Network World Bulgaria, PC & MacWorld Bulgaria; **CANADA:** CIO Canada, Client/Server World, ComputerWorld Canada, InfoWorld Canada, NetworkWorld Canada, WebWorld; **CHILE:** Computerworld Chile, PC World Chile; **COLOMBIA:** Computerworld Colombia, PC World Colombia; **COSTA RICA:** PC World Centro America; **THE CZECH AND SLOVAK REPUBLICS:** Computerworld Czechoslovakia, Macworld Czech Republic, PC World Czechoslovakia; **DENMARK:** Communications World Danmark, Computerworld Danmark, Macworld Danmark, PC World Danmark, Techworld Denmark; **DOMINICAN REPUBLIC:** PC World Republica Dominicana; **ECUADOR:** PC World Ecuador; **EGYPT:** Computerworld Middle East, PC World Middle East; **EL SALVADOR:** PC World Centro America; **FINLAND:** MikroPC, Tietoverkko, Tietoviikko; **FRANCE:** Distributique, Hebdo, Info PC, Le Monde Informatique, Macworld, Reseaux & Telecoms, WebMaster France; **GERMANY:** Computer Partner, Computerwoche, Computerwoche Extra, Computerwoche FOCUS, Global Online, Macwelt, PC Welt; **GREECE:** Amiga Computing, GamePro Greece, Multimedia World; **GUATEMALA:** PC World Centro America; **HONDURAS:** PC World Centro America; **HONG KONG:** Computerworld Hong Kong, PC World Hong Kong, Publish in Asia; **HUNGARY:** ABCD CD-ROM, Computerworld Szamitastechnika, Internetto online Magazine, PC World Hungary, PC-X Magazin Hungary; **ICELAND:** Tolvuheimur PC World Island; **INDIA:** Information Communications World, Information Systems Computerworld, PC World India, Publish in Asia; **INDONESIA:** InfoKomputer PC World, Komputek Computerworld, Publish in Asia; **IRELAND:** ComputerScope, PC Live!; **ISRAEL:** Macworld Israel, People & Computers/Computerworld; **ITALY:** Computerworld Italia, Macworld Italia, Networking Italia, PC World Italia; **JAPAN:** DTP World, Macworld Japan, Nikkei Personal Computing, OS/2 World Japan, SunWorld Japan, Windows NT World, Windows World Japan; **KENYA:** PC World East African; **KOREA:** Hi-Tech Information, Macworld Korea, PC World Korea; **MACEDONIA:** PC World Macedonia; **MALAYSIA:** Computerworld Malaysia, PC World Malaysia, Publish in Asia; **MALTA:** PC World Malta; **MEXICO:** Computerworld Mexico, PC World Mexico; **MYANMAR:** PC World Myanmar; **NETHERLANDS:** Computer! Totaal, LAN Internetworking Magazine, LAN World Buyers Guide, Macworld Netherlands, Net, WebWereld; **NEW ZEALAND:** Absolute Beginners Guide and Plain & Simple Series, Computer Buyer, Computer Industry Directory, Computerworld New Zealand, MTB, Network World, PC World New Zealand; **NICARAGUA:** PC World Centro America; **NORWAY:** Computerworld Norge, CW Rapport, Datamagasinet, Financial Rapport, Kursguide Norge, Macworld Norge, Multimediaworld Norge, PC World Ekspress Norge, PC World Nettverk, PC World Norge, PC World ProduktGuide Norge; **PAKISTAN:** Computerworld Pakistan; **PANAMA:** PC World Panama; **PEOPLE'S REPUBLIC OF CHINA:** China Computer Users, China Computerworld, China InfoWorld, China Telecom World Weekly, Computer & Communication, Electronic Design China, Electronics Today, Electronics Weekly, Game Software, PC World China, Popular Computer Week, Software Weekly, Software World, Telecom World; **PERU:** Computerworld Peru, PC World Profesional Peru, PC World SoHo Peru; **PHILIPPINES:** Click!, Computerworld Philippines, PC World Philippines, Publish in Asia; **POLAND:** Computerworld Poland, Computerworld Special Report Poland, Cyber, Macworld Poland, Networld Poland, PC World Komputer; **PORTUGAL:** Cerebro/PC World, Computerworld/Correio Informático, Dealer World Portugal, Mac*In/PC*In Portugal, Multimedia World; **PUERTO RICO:** PC World Puerto Rico; **ROMANIA:** Computerworld Romania, PC World Romania, Telecom Romania; **RUSSIA:** Computerworld Russia, Mir PK, Publish, Seti; **SINGAPORE:** Computerworld Singapore, PC World Singapore, Publish in Asia; **SLOVENIA:** Monitor; **SOUTH AFRICA:** Computing SA, Network World SA, Software World SA; **SPAIN:** Communicaciones World España, Computerworld España, Dealer World España, Macworld España, PC World España; **SRI LANKA:** Infolink PC World, PCaktiv, Windows World Sweden; **SWEDEN:** CAP&Design, Computer Sweden, Corporate Computing Sweden, Internetworld Sweden, it.branschen, Macworld Sweden, MaxiData Sweden, MikroDatorn, Natverk & Kommunikation, PC World Sweden; **SWITZERLAND:** Computerworld Schweiz, Macworld Schweiz, PCtip; **TAIWAN:** Computerworld Taiwan, Macworld Taiwan, NEW ViSiON/Publish, PC World Taiwan, Windows World Taiwan; **THAILAND:** Publish in Asia, Thai Computerworld; **TURKEY:** Computerworld Turkiye, Macworld Turkiye, Network World Turkiye, PC World Turkiye; **UKRAINE:** Computerworld Kiev, Multimedia World Ukraine, PC World Ukraine; **UNITED KINGDOM:** Acorn User UK, Amiga Action UK, Amiga Computing UK, Apple Talk UK, Computing, Macworld, Parents and Computers UK, PC Advisor, PC Home, PSX Pro, The WEB; **UNITED STATES:** Cable in the Classroom, CIO Magazine, Computerworld, DOS World, Federal Computer Week, GamePro Magazine, InfoWorld, I-Way, Macworld, Network World, PC Games, PC World, Publish, Video Event, THE WEB Magazine, and WebMaster; online webzines: JavaWorld, NetscapeWorld, and SunWorld Online; **URUGUAY:** InfoWorld Uruguay; **VENEZUELA:** Computerworld Venezuela, PC World Venezuela; and **VIETNAM:** PC World Vietnam. 3/24/97

# Publisher's Acknowledgments

We're proud of this book; please register your comments through our online registration form located at www.dummies.com/register.

Some of the people who helped bring this book to market include the following:

*Acquisitions, Development, and Editorial*

**Senior Project Editor:** Pamela Mourouzis

**Acquisitions Editor:** Mark Butler

**Permissions Editor:** Heather Heath Dismore

**Copy Editors:** Christine Meloy Beck, Gwenette Gaddis

**Editorial Manager:** Colleen Rainsberger

**Editorial Assistant:** Darren Meiss

*Composition*

**Project Coordinator:** Cindy L. Phipps

**Layout and Graphics:** Cameron Booker, Lou Boudreau, Linda M. Boyer, J. Tyler Connor, Angela F. Hunckler, Todd Klemme, Brent Savage, M. Anne Sipahimalani, Deirdre Smith, Ian A. Smith, Rashell Smith

**Proofreaders:** Sandra Profant, Christine Berman, Rebecca Senninger, Janet M. Withers

**Indexer:** Anne Leach

---

*Publishing and Editorial for Consumer Dummies*

**Diane Graves Steele,** Vice President and Publisher, Consumer Dummies

**Joyce Pepple,** Acquisitions Director, Consumer Dummies

**Kristin A. Cocks,** Product Development Director, Consumer Dummies

**Michael Spring,** Vice President and Publisher, Travel

**Brice Gosnell,** Associate Publisher, Travel

**Suzanne Jannetta,** Editorial Director, Travel

*Publishing for Technology Dummies*

**Richard Swadley,** Vice President and Executive Group Publisher

**Andy Cummings,** Vice President and Publisher

*Composition Services*

**Gerry Fahey,** Vice President of Production Services

**Debbie Stailey,** Director of Composition Services

# Dedication

This book is dedicated to Dave Anderson and Gordon Thayer, Native Americans who overcame great obstacles to achieve great success. And to P. C. Merrell, Dr. Emol Fails, Dr. Adrian Rogers, and Bob Colombe, all of whom take pride in their Native American heritage. They have been good friends and have inspired me in my career and my family and spiritual lives.

# Author's Acknowledgments

As always, when a work the size of *Success For Dummies* is released, you can rest assured that a number of people were heavily involved, so I'm indebted to many. First, I want to thank my friend Lou Holtz for his willingness to write the foreword for me. I've been a friend and a fan of Lou's for a long time and his enthusiastic support is very meaningful.

Undoubtedly, I will leave out some who were important to the project, but I must start with my editor, who is my youngest daughter. Julie Ziglar Norman is an absolute delight to work with. She has enormous energy, has great insight, is an exceptionally hard worker, and her major interest is helping me to produce the very best possible book. In this editorial process, she and I have been grateful to work very closely with the editorial staff at Wiley, consisting for this book primarily of Pam Mourouzis, Christy Beck, and Gwenette Gaddis. I also want to thank Barbara M. Terry for her work on the audio manuscript of *Success For Dummies*.

My mentor and friend Fred Smith provided invaluable concepts and suggestions, which I've used throughout the book. Dr. Leland Heller and Dr. Louis Cady are physicians who periodically visit with me via mail and telephone, giving me unique insights, which contributed to the value of the book. Ditto for Rabbi Daniel Lapin, whose biblical wisdom is always refreshing and helpful. My fellow speaker and writer Tony Jeary was kind enough to share much of his research and made valuable contributions, as did authors Joe Batten, Lawrence L. Fargher, Rodney Weckworth, General Colin Powell, and Sir John Templeton. Writers and publishers such as the Economic Press, William Arthur Ward, Dr. J. Allan Petersen, Sidney Harris, *The Executive Speechwriter Newsletter,* and *The Speaker's Source Book* by Glen van Ekeren contributed significantly.

I want to acknowledge my daily local newspaper, *The Dallas Morning News,* as a constant source of information, as well as national publications, including *USA Today* and *The Wall Street Journal.* In addition, I received much theological help from my own pastor, Dr. Jack Graham, and another close friend, Dr. James Merritt. Dr. John Maxwell, John West, and Dr. Jay Strack were also helpful. From a health and exercise point of view, Dr. Forest Tennant, Jr., and Dr. Kenneth Cooper were important factors in dispensing accurate information that will benefit many.

And then there are the two indispensable ones. The Redhead, my bride of over 50 years, exhibited the patience of Job as she pleasantly tolerated my impossible speaking and writing schedules. Additionally, she carried even more of the family, church, and social responsibilities than usual and still had the time and energy to give me the love and support that I need and cherish.

Truly a critical player, Laurie Magers, my executive assistant for over 20 years, was the connecting link between my editor, Julie Ziglar Norman, and me. Her capacity to handle my busy travel schedule and take care of the countless phone calls involving all the facets of our business still amazes me. Add to those responsibilities the fact that she input all the text of this manuscript — with the countless changes, corrections, insertions, and deletions — into the computer, and her performance was truly incredible. Her last five months have been the busiest of her 20-year tenure, and she handled them professionally and with grace.

Lastly, I'd like to thank Oliver Nelson, a division of Thomas Nelson Publishers, for granting me permission to reprint the "benchmarks of success" from my book *Over the Top.*

# Contents at a Glance

# Table of Contents

# Foreword

*T*o have the privilege of contributing to Zig Ziglar's book *Success For Dummies* is one I truly cherish. Zig could have selected many other individuals who are more gifted than I and obviously possess literary skills superior to mine. However, he could not have selected anyone who is a bigger fan of his than I am. Let me simply express my feelings about Zig as a writer, motivator, and friend — *he is the best.*

The year was 1977, and my life was very discombobulated. I had just resigned from the New York Jets and felt like an utter failure. I had relocated my family to Arkansas, and my father had died of a heart attack in the interim. Even though to an outside observer I appeared to have my life together, I was really floundering. I had lost all direction with my life, and the future didn't appear bright. I did the only thing I knew to do in this difficult situation, and that was to pray to God for guidance. As Zig says, "God doesn't send you a fax telling you what to do, but if you are headed down the wrong path He won't give you any peace of mind."

We purchased a home from an extraordinarily nice couple who were relocating because of a job change. The former owner could tell that something was bothering me, and within a few weeks, he sent me six tapes of a presentation that Zig Ziglar had recorded for his new employer. I didn't know who Zig Ziglar was, so I really didn't have a strong desire to listen to the tapes. One day I had to drive to Little Rock to recruit an athlete. It was a three-hour drive one way, so I decided to listen to the tapes. I listened to one tape of Zig and was hooked.

I could hardly wait to get back in the car to continue listening. He was the most interesting speaker I had ever heard, and his message contained so much common sense! The more I listened to the tapes, the more motivated I became. I found myself to be exceptionally happy and motivated to conquer the world every time I listened to the tapes. I nearly wore them out because I listened to them so much.

Our Arkansas football team was facing a tremendous challenge that year, but they responded very positively. Our final season record was 11 wins and only one loss. Prior to playing Oklahoma in the Orange Bowl, we had to suspend three athletes who had scored 78 percent of our touchdowns. We were a 24-point underdog going into the game, but we were fortunate to win the game 31-6. It was a miraculous season, and I credit much of our success to Zig Ziglar and his tapes. I am certain Zig had no idea what a positive influence he had been in my life at such a critical time, but I assure you that the above story is true.

After listening to the tapes, I hit the bookstores in search of all the books Zig Ziglar had written. Not only did I read everything I could that he had written, but I studied them religiously. His book *See You at the Top* is the best book I have ever read on self-improvement. I not only underlined it but outlined it as well to make certain I had absorbed the maximum amount of knowledge contained in it. I thought it was so good that I insisted my children read the book. When they had a special request that I thought was reasonable, such as going away for summer camp or some comparable desire, I would inform them that their request might be permissible only if they read Zig's *See You at the Top* and then discussed it intelligently with me. It was one of the smartest things I did for my children. I noticed a marked improvement in their attitudes after reading it. The reason I did this was I didn't want my children to be overly influenced by their peers. Reading *See You at the Top* exposed them to a realistic and positive approach to problems in life.

Several years ago, I received the ultimate compliment from Peter Lowe, who conducts Success Seminars in various cities around the country: He asked me to speak on the same program with Zig Ziglar. We both arrived at the site on the evening before the engagement, and Zig asked my wife and me to have dinner with him. It was a great evening, and Zig was as positive, entertaining, and motivating as he was on tapes and in his books. It is highly unusual when a person can speak so eloquently and freely to 20,000 people and still hold the attention of two people during a dinner conversation. Zig Ziglar has the ability to do this. I have spent many hours with Zig over the years, and I can testify that not a single time have I been disappointed in his conduct or attitude. He is the same on the stage as he is off the stage. He has impressed me with his talents and abilities, but I have found that he also makes great preparation in everything he does. *Success For Dummies* reflects not only his talents and abilities, but his preparation as well.

While at Notre Dame, I asked Zig to come and speak to our football team. He was once again outstanding. I have always tried to expose our football team to positive people, and Zig was at the top of my list.

The only thing that will change you from where you are today to where you want to be tomorrow is the books you read, the people you meet, and the dreams you dream. *Success For Dummies* will definitely change you for the better. As you perhaps know, Zig has written several bestsellers, such as *Secrets of Closing the Sale, Raising Positive Kids in a Negative World, Confessions of a Happy Christian, See You at the Top,* and *Over the Top.* I feel especially honored to write the introduction for what I think is his best book, *Success For Dummies.* Now that I've looked at the title for this book a little closer, I get the funny feeling Zig had a different reason for asking me to contribute to it. In any event, I am proud to call Zig Ziglar my friend because he, like this book, is *the best.*

— Lou Holtz, Former Head Football Coach, University of Notre Dame

# Introduction

Most people think of success in relation to business and financial wealth, but I propose that you aren't truly successful until success permeates your entire wheel of life. The seven spokes of that wheel are

- ✔ Career
- ✔ Family
- ✔ Financial
- ✔ Personal
- ✔ Mental
- ✔ Physical
- ✔ Spiritual

Because you must achieve some degree of success in each area before you can experience the true satisfaction of genuine success, *Success For Dummies* covers success in every area (or on every "spoke") of life.

## What Is Success?

Success is many things to many people. Here are a few signs of success:

- ✔ Success is closing the door to your office at the end of the day with a smile of satisfied contentment crossing your face. It's knowing that you did a good job and that those who interacted with you had a positive experience.

- ✔ Success is looking forward to getting home and seeing the people you love. It's being mentally and emotionally free to share yourself with them and to be interested in them. Success is being loved by the people you love.

- ✔ Success is sitting down to pay the bills and knowing that you have enough money to cover them, this month *and* next month. It's knowing that you have taken measures to ensure the financial security of your family in the event of your demise.

- ✔ Success is knowing where to turn when it seems that there's nowhere to turn. Having a spiritual life is akin to eating food and drinking water. It's necessary!

- ✔ Success is having interests or hobbies to call your own. It's things that you personally anticipate doing again and again. Having interests gives you joy and peace.

- ✔ Success is waking up in the morning and feeling good. It's knowing that you eat right and exercise regularly and that you do everything you personally can to ensure continued good health.

- ✔ Success is turning out the lights, slipping under the covers, and thinking to yourself, "It just doesn't get much better than this!" It's whispering a prayer of gratitude to your Creator before you fall into a deep, restful sleep.

# What Success Isn't

And here are a few things that success is *not:*

- ✔ Success isn't calling home from work for the fourth time this week, apologizing because you're going to miss dinner with the family again.

- ✔ Success isn't hurrying into the house and hiding behind closed doors or the television set because "After the day I've had, I need my space!"

- ✔ Success isn't having all the riches in the world and still trying to figure out how to have *more* of all the riches in the world.

- ✔ Success isn't physically going to a worship service and mentally writing a to-do list for when you get home.

- ✔ Success isn't all work and no play.

- ✔ Success isn't burning the candle at both ends and living on a diet of food that's delivered through little windows.

- ✔ Success isn't spending mental energy figuring out how to explain why your project isn't going to come in on time, why you have to miss your child's school play, why you can't pay the bill in full as you promised, why your eyes are red and your blood pressure is going through the roof, why you're canceling your golf game, and why you just don't find any joy in living.

Success is directly related to having a balanced life. If any one area is out of sync, all the areas of your life suffer. This book shows you how to find balance. Like walking a beam, balance comes with confidence derived from putting one foot in front of the other. When you first mount the beam, your arms flail around wildly, seeking the position that stabilizes your body. After you're able to stand quietly on the beam, you focus on taking the first step. Your mind goes over a mental checklist of things to remember: "Keep your eyes up, arms extended, and concentrate. . . ."

After reading this book, you'll have a complete mental checklist of what you need to do to be successful in walking this beam called life.

# How Relationships Play an Important Role in Success

Throughout this book, I emphasize success in relationships. Research indicates that relationships are the key to success in health, prosperity, happiness, hope, and virtually everything of significance in life. My friends who do a great deal of counseling tell me that nearly 100 percent of all the counseling they do is the direct result of relationship difficulties between husband and wife, parent and child, employer and employee, teacher and student, neighbor and neighbor, sibling and sibling, and so on.

The inability to have good relationships has escalated dramatically in the last 30 years. Modern American society has become rude, mannerless, and self-centered; its philosophy has become "Hooray for me, to heck with you, I'm going to do it my way. I'll win through intimidation. I'm going to look out for Number One, and I'm going to do it now." That philosophy quite accurately depicts a miserable human being. I personally have never met a happy, self-centered person, and I bet that you haven't, either.

Misery is the only emotion left for people who have alienated everyone around them. Manipulating and intimidating people, disregarding their needs, and always putting yourself first makes you a lonely person. People who have trouble fostering relationships spend a lot of time alone, and, quite simply, lonely people are miserable people.

## Seeing the relationship philosophy in action

I want to establish a relationship philosophy via a little scenario that takes place on a Friday afternoon at about 5:00. In this particular case, the husband has been out of town all week and is now walking to the front porch, heavily laden with luggage and a bulging briefcase. He doesn't want to set everything down to ring the doorbell or to get out his keys, so he kicks the door to get his wife's attention. He doesn't just kick the door lightly; he kicks it in frustration and anger and, in the process, damages the door.

His wife, upon hearing the commotion, rushes to the door, opens it, and is startled to see her husband standing there. Without setting down his belongings, he delivers this oration: "I'm late because I've been to a meeting, and I'm really glad I was there. I learned some things that really bug me. I learned, for example, that there are a number of rights around this house that I have not been getting, and as a matter of fact, I've made a list of those rights. The first thing you and I are going to do is sit down and talk, because I'm telling you right now, there are going to be some changes made around here!"

When he finishes, the wife responds: "Well, Buster, I didn't go to a meeting. I didn't need to. And I haven't written a list. I didn't need to do that, either. It is burned indelibly into my own mind. There are some rights around here that I haven't been getting, so you come on in and we'll have that talk, because I agree with you that there are going to be some changes made, and you're not going to like most of them!"

Can't you just imagine the delightful, loving, romantic, exhilarating weekend that followed this encounter? Don't you just know that on Monday morning, husband and wife left home charged up with renewed excitement and determination to go out and change the world, to make it a better place to live?

## *Action, take two*

Now change the scenario slightly. On the same front porch on the same Friday afternoon, the same husband walks to the porch, heavily laden with his luggage and bulging briefcase. He doesn't want to set down his things to ring the doorbell or use his key, so he gently taps the door with his foot. His wife opens the door. As she does, he looks at her and begins his oration: "Sweetheart, I apologize for being late, but I'm delighted to be here now. I'm late because I went to perhaps the most important meeting of our lives. In this meeting, I learned some things that really bother me. I have learned, for example, that in all probability I have not been meeting the needs that you have as my wife. Before I even unpack, I would like for us to sit down and talk. I would like for you to tell me what I can do to become the kind of husband that you deserve to have and that you thought you were getting when we married."

In response, the wife says, "Actually, I've been very happy as your wife. From time to time, I've wondered if I have been meeting all the needs you have as my husband. I think it's a wonderful idea to sit down and talk."

This story needs no elaboration, does it? It's astonishing what happens in your life when you move from being a self-centered individual to pleasing the other person. This idea is true not only in marriage, but also in customer relationships, work relationships, teacher/student relationships, politician/ constituent relationships, and so on. As I show you throughout *Success For Dummies,* this principle applies to every walk of life. This book centers on the philosophy that I illustrate in this Friday-afternoon scenario, namely that you can have everything in life you want if you will just help enough other people get what they want.

# About This Book

This book is designed to answer your questions about success in the order you want them answered. Sure, I wrote it from one end to the other, but it's written in such a way that you can turn to any section, in any chapter, in any order you like, and never feel that you missed a lick. Start in the middle (which puts you at about Chapter 12) and find out about preparing for the future and determining how to grow spiritually. Or start at the end and be inspired by ten motivational gems. It's your book, it's your life, and you know what is most important to you. The absolute best advice I can give you is to *start now!*

# Foolish Assumptions

I assume that you're reading this book because you want more out of life. You want success! This may not be the first self-help book you have purchased, and I sincerely hope that it won't be the last.

If your motivation for buying this book was to increase your income, that's good, because this book can help you do so. If your motivation was to improve your family relationships, it can help you do that, too. If your motivation for wanting this book was to find direction, you'll definitely get lots of that. Maybe your kids are giving you fits and you know that child-rearing is not your forte; help is here.

Maybe your marriage relationship is in a bad state, or your spiritual life is one big, black void. Maybe you're completely happy and just want to stay that way. You're in the right place if you said, "Hey, that's me!" to any of the reasons that I stated. Keep reading to see results!

# How This Book Is Organized

This book is divided into six parts, and each part is further divided into chapters. The following sections explain what you can find in each part.

## Part I: All About Success

This section delivers a success formula that you can apply to your life right now, with astonishing results! It details the foundational attitude, skills, philosophy, and objectives that result in success when they are developed on a foundation of good character.

I cover in depth the part that relationships play in your success, happiness, health, prosperity, security, peace, and spiritual life. How to improve your relationships and, in effect, improve all areas of your life is spelled out for you.

If you have ever stumbled over what success means for you personally, this part of the book may rivet your attention. It covers all the hallmarks of success — find out which hallmarks you already possess!

## Part II: Getting Motivated

If you aren't sure what motivation really is, this section gives you a comprehensive understanding of not only what it is but also how to get it, and how to get it back time and time again.

## Part III: Putting Together a Strategic Plan

Maybe you're good at just about everything except making a plan and getting organized. This section helps you to evaluate what you want out of life. Then it shows you how to develop a plan for the goals you want to achieve and looks at several ways that you can go about achieving them.

## Part IV: Your Goals in Life

I include in this section detailed instruction on goals that deal with the spokes on the wheel of life. Physical health, mental growth, spiritual growth, friendship goals, husband/wife goals, parental goals, career goals, and societal goals are all covered. You can read about how to improve your relationships with your family, your friends, your employer or employees, your Creator, and yourself.

# Part V: Moving Onward and Upward

Your greatest assets in life are the people with whom you have relationships. In this section, you can find out how to call on the people who care about you. Their input can help you to develop realistic goals that you can believe in and accomplish. The journey to success cannot be made alone!

You probably didn't know that success is a habit. In this part of the book, I also establish habit as a desirable trait to develop, and I explain in great detail the way to get the habit.

# Part VI: The Part of Tens

I call this the "quick-read" section. It's full of fun, interesting information and stories. Uncover the ten benchmarks of success, read the stories of ten successful individuals, find out which ten things to incorporate into any success strategy, and enjoy ten motivational gems that help you start your day off right.

Read the *whole* book and get your relationships, and consequently your life, headed in the direction of *success*.

# Icons Used in This Book

Throughout the book, I place icons in the margins when I want to point out a particularly noteworthy piece of information, a memorable quote, or an inspiring story. Here's what each of those icons means:

Next to this icon, you can find tips for improving your life at home, with your spouse and your children.

This icon points out ways in which you can increase your success in your job or career.

Look for this icon if you're searching for ways to improve your relationship with the one you love.

This icon highlights information about making your personal success better, whether in relation to your mental life or your spiritual life.

This icon directs your attention to actions that can help you gain greater success.

Make note of the information next to this icon; this stuff is important!

This icon marks gems of knowledge that come from wise men and women throughout the ages.

When I include a story to inspire you or to demonstrate a message, I mark it with this icon.

This icon marks anecdotes and opinions from my own life — all 70-plus years of it!

# Where to Go from Here

Before you begin your journey into *Success For Dummies,* spend some very important time with yourself and contemplate what success means to you. As you read the different sections, see how they line up with the concepts that you believe to be true. Take notes and reread sections that you find especially meaningful. Keep highlighter pens of different colors nearby to make relocating special information easy.

You can start anywhere you like, but I suggest that you read the first chapter to get the formula for success right away. Keeping the formula in mind is helpful as you consider the different areas of your life and how the formula applies to each and every one. Follow the suggestions in this book, and I'll see you at the top!

# Part I
## All About Success

"A large part of our success is based on our ability to resolve conflicts before we get to work."

# In this part . . .

What is success? Maybe you think that success is only about monetary gain. Maybe you feel that you're successful only if you are at the top of your field. But, as you'll discover in the pages that follow, I believe that success involves much more than money and prestige.

I believe that "being successful" means having a balance of success stories across the many areas of your life. You can't truly be considered successful in your business life if your home life is in shambles. You can't have great success in your home life if your financial life is unsuccessful — you'll always have stress about your finances, and you'll miss wonderful times with your loved ones.

This part of *Success For Dummies* focuses on the basics of the seven areas of life that I feel are important for balanced success: career, family, financial, personal, mental, physical, and spiritual.

# Chapter 1

# The Success Formula

## In This Chapter

▶ Discovering the elements of the success formula: attitude, skills, philosophy, objectives, and character

▶ Finding out about success in your personal, family, business, physical, mental, spiritual, and financial lives

▶ Putting the success formula to work for you

*W*hat is success? The answer depends on who's responding to the question. There are as many definitions of success as there are people. With that idea in mind, I want to do a little generalizing and then talk about my formula for accomplishing this elusive thing called success.

Success involves every facet of life: your relationships with others, your ability to make it in the business world, the health that you need to preserve, and the happiness that you enjoy. It also involves a security that goes well beyond financial security; I'm talking about the security of knowing that you have the love, trust, and support not only of family but of friends and associates as well.

Don't misunderstand me: Success *does* include a degree of financial prosperity. (Money isn't the most important thing in life, but it's reasonably close to oxygen on the "gotta have it" scale.) To be candid, I like the things that money can buy: houses, cars, clothes, vacations, and so on. I don't need to be super-rich, but I do have a great need not to be poor; I've been there and done that. I remember the days of buying gasoline 50 cents at a time, falling desperately behind in my rent, and losing a car because I couldn't pay for it.

In addition to the financial prosperity that I just mentioned, success to me means success at home, success in my profession, and success with my friends and associates. It also means peace of mind, which is part of the spiritual aspect of life (covered extensively in Chapter 12) that I enjoy through my faith.

The question is, what can you do to achieve this balanced success that involves your personal, family, and business lives as well as your physical, mental, and spiritual well-being, with a recognition of the need for financial prosperity? The formula that I outline in the following section is a great place to start.

# Finding the Formula for Success

Over the years, I have developed a formula that has helped me achieve what I consider to be success. Throughout *Success For Dummies,* I refer to various parts of this formula, which begins with the right mental attitude and includes adding the right skills and the right philosophy, finding direction, and building on a foundation of character.

## Developing the right mental attitude

Your journey toward success will flow more smoothly if you ride the "right" attitude all the way to the top. "I think I can" beats "I can't" every time. A can-do outlook on life helps you to achieve goals in record time and make friends and lifelong business associates along the way. Everyone enjoys being around someone who is a solution-finder and who looks for the good instead of the bad in everything.

Here are some important points about attitude to keep in mind:

✔ You need to have the right attitude toward your family, friends, and associates. An attitude of acceptance, forgiveness, love, kindness, respect, and consideration goes a long way in any relationship, including those with family members, friends, and business associates.

✔ You need to have an accepting, open-minded attitude toward your personal growth and education. The world changes constantly; as they say, "Change is inevitable — except from a vending machine." Unless you change with it, you're destined for mediocrity at best.

If you don't stay abreast of the knowledge brought about by modern technology, the trends in the marketplace, and the discoveries in the field of health improvement, you will be left far behind or, at best, will experience only a portion of the progress that you're capable of experiencing. Having the desire to stay familiar with these changes and being open-minded about them ensures your continued success well into later life. (Some people are so narrow-minded that they can look through a keyhole with both eyes at the same time. Others are so cynical that they still think somebody pushed Humpty-Dumpty.)

✔ You need to have a positive yet cautiously realistic attitude toward your own abilities and yourself. Knowing your capabilities and being realistic about your possibilities are starting places for success. For example, your chances of being a rocket scientist are slim if you flunked fifth grade math twice, so spending several years in college taking every course you need to be a rocket scientist but avoiding the math classes until the last semester is the same as planning to fail. Unrealistic expectations are the seedbed of depression. If you gained 20 pounds over the last three years, believing that you can lose all 20 pounds in three or four weeks is setting yourself up for a letdown. That goal just isn't realistic.

You should, however, be far more positive than negative. You can undermine your success just as easily by setting your sights too low. If you set out to lose one pound a month, for example, the slow pace will eventually cause you to lose hope, interest, and enthusiasm. That's one of the reasons I believe that counselors and mentors are an important part of the mix that makes the success formula work. The most popular and successful weight-loss programs combine sensible eating, exercise, and the help of mentors or counselors. Everyone needs help in setting realistic goals, especially in areas where they have previously suffered setbacks. Then they need encouragement and motivation to hang in there until they reach those goals. (I cover mentors more extensively in Chapter 2.)

✔ You must have a sensible attitude toward positive thinking. I'm amused on some occasions and frustrated on others when I hear someone say that "Attitude is everything" or that "With positive thinking, you can do anything." Careful analysis forces you to realize that this idea is simply not true. For example, Reggie White, the All-Pro defensive end for the Green Bay Packers, is an upbeat, optimistic, enthusiastic, highly motivated positive thinker, but with him at 300 pounds, those assets would do him absolutely no good if he decided that he could change careers and make it as a jockey. He would almost have to carry the horse across the finish line, wouldn't he?

I, too, am a positive thinker, and I love the game of golf. But, being over 70 years old and carrying a 16 handicap, I'd be hard-pressed to make the PGA Tour (except maybe as an extra to entertain or inspire the other golfers), no matter how positive I get.

Another reason you must take a cautious approach — or even a skeptical approach, on occasion — is that blind optimism can make you a target for victimization. Some people take the concept of "being positive" out of context and try to apply it when it simply doesn't fit. If your car breaks down, for example, taking the positive approach and assuming that the individual who stops to help you has only good intentions is foolhardy in this day and age. To believe everything that everybody says and to think that everybody's motives are honest is taking naïveté to the absurd. Unfortunately, this world includes charlatans who see a person with a warm, positive, open attitude as an easier mark than a person who is cautious.

You need to understand that what the "right" attitude — positive thinking that's tempered with a dose of realism — really does is permit you to use your own abilities. And those abilities are awesome! When you recognize, develop, and use what you have, positive thinking is enormously effective.

## Adding the right skills

Your attitude is enormously important; it enables you to accomplish amazing things. But without the right skills, you're limited in what you can do, regardless of your attitude. An enthusiastic salesperson with the right attitude can achieve a degree of success in selling a good product — sometimes even considerable success. But this individual can't realize his or her full potential without being thoroughly trained in the product and understanding something about the people with whom he or she is dealing.

Salespeople must have good people skills and be able to answer the questions that prospective customers ask. Without those skills, they miss a high percentage of the sales that they should be making. If salespeople know that their prospects have the money to buy and that their product fills a specific need, but they miss sales because they can't answer prospects' questions, frustration, disappointment, and the obvious lack of income that results can ultimately put those salespeople out of business.

In a similar vein, many enthusiastic, highly motivated, upbeat people don't have a clue how to operate today's high-tech equipment. Others don't know how to deal with people effectively in a changing world. As a result, they can have limited success, at best. Many people love the field of auto mechanics, for example. But if they don't have the education or the intelligence to understand the computers that are used in today's automobiles (which have more computer power than was available to astronauts on the first trip to the moon!), they can't advance very far in this high-tech industry.

In short, without the skills to go with the right attitude, your success ceiling is predetermined, and it isn't especially high. Remember, motivation always precedes education. The person with the right attitude and the right skills can become more successful than ever before because competition for good-paying, skilled jobs continues to decline.

## Having the right philosophy

The third part of the success formula is to have the "Golden Rule" philosophy. I state it like this:

> You can have everything in life you want if you will just help enough other people get what they want.

## Education suffers due to lack of interest

Unfortunately, many of today's high school students are not really interested in developing the skills that they need to make the success formula work. The March 3, 1997, issue of *USA Today* reported a serious generation gap between what Baby Boomers were interested in and what young people today are interested in.

For example, 64 percent of Baby Boomers were interested in preparing for a career, compared to only 54 percent of students today. Doing well in school was important to 83 percent of Baby Boomers, but only 37 percent of students today find it important. An active social life, however, was important to 60 percent of Baby Boomers, versus 80 percent of students today.

Unfortunately, these statistics indicate that as high-tech gets even higher-tech and interest in preparing for a career diminishes, businesses are going to encounter serious shortages of qualified people for rewarding jobs and careers. Statistics like these are one reason I continually share with audiences that the opportunity for success has never been greater than it is today. The need is great, but many people are not preparing to meet that need.

I hasten to add that this philosophy isn't a feel-good theory; it's a highly practical approach to your overall success. Life is not a series of isolated chambers; directly and indirectly, all aspects of life — personal, business, and so on — are interwoven. Your physical, mental, and spiritual lives are connected, and all these areas impact the financial aspects of your life.

Over the years, I've identified that everybody, regardless of where they live and what they do, wants the following eight things in life:

- ✔ To be happy
- ✔ To be healthy
- ✔ To be at least reasonably prosperous
- ✔ To be secure
- ✔ To have friends
- ✔ To have peace of mind
- ✔ To have good family relationships
- ✔ To have hope

A study reported in *USA Today* identified something interesting about employees in the workplace. Employers were asked, "What do you think your employees want most?" The employers responded that #1 was good wages, #2 was job security, and #3 was the chance for promotion. However, in those same locations, the employees rated good wages as #7, promotion as #12, and job security as #13.

What the employees said that they wanted was #1 interesting work, #2 appreciation for work done, and #3 a feeling of being in on things. You can pretty well sum up those responses by saying that employees wanted to be treated as equals, or at least as fellow human beings.

Here's an interesting fact: The U.S. Department of Labor says that 46 percent of the employees who voluntarily quit their jobs do so because they don't feel appreciated. In addition, I read the research of a consultant who said that 93 percent of the employees he queried told him that when they completed a difficult task under special assignment from an employer, the employer never said anything to them about it — no "good job" or "thank you for your effort" — nothing. That's unfortunate because the cheapest and most effective motivation in the marketplace is simple but sincere recognition for extra effort.

Now, if the employer provided a climate where the work was interesting, expressed appreciation for the work done, and helped employees feel as if they were in on things, doesn't it make sense that the employer would have happier, healthier, more secure workers? This atmosphere would affect the employees' relationships at home and at work and give them hope that their futures will be even better than their past. Put these things together and you have more productive workers. And employers pay more productive workers more money, which makes those employees more prosperous.

At this point, you may be thinking, "But what about the employer?" Well, research indicates that employers want loyal, productive employees and a growing, profitable business. By providing their employees with what they want, employers get exactly what they want: loyal, productive employees and a growing, profitable business.

## Finding your direction

You can have the right attitude, the right skills, and the Golden Rule philosophy, but if you don't have a game plan for life, you will ultimately become a "wandering generality." You must have a planned direction if you're going to utilize your attitude, ability, training, and philosophy to the fullest.

No one attempts to build even a doghouse without a plan, nor does anyone attempt a vacation without some sort of plan — even if it's as simple as "We're going to drive to the Grand Canyon." Yet most people never learn how to develop a plan of action for their lives. As a result, most people spend years in occupations or professions that they chose at someone else's suggestion, or because others were doing it, or because it was easy or available, or perhaps because they had "nothing else to do."

TRUE STORIES

# A classic example of the Golden Rule philosophy

A classic example of how the "get what you want by helping others get what they want" approach works is the results that a major automaker got when it came out with a new design. This design necessitated the construction of new plants and the retooling of existing ones. Before making these changes, management asked the employees who would actually be building the new vehicles whether they had any ideas for making the assembly lines more effective. The workers had dozens of marvelous ideas. After all, the person turning the wrench knows more about the way it really works on the assembly line than the engineers who designed the wrench.

First, the employees explained that when they had to go down the steps into the pit to work on the underside of a car, they sometimes slipped and fell, injuring themselves. Why not raise the assembly line so that they could simply walk underneath the car to work on it?

Second, they suggested that the assembly line be tilted in their direction so that they wouldn't have to do so much bending over. Leaning over to work on the assembly line put undue hardship and stress on workers' backs.

The results were truly spectacular. Medical expenses decreased dramatically. Productivity escalated. Quality of work improved substantially. The workers had been treated properly — they were "let in on things," they were listened to, and their suggestions were followed. Management was delighted with the results, and stockholders were ecstatic.

These good results came about because management gave the employees something that they not only wanted but also badly needed. Giving employees what they need isn't "coddling"; doing so is simply meeting management's responsibility and creating a win/win situation.

The following sections talk a little about forming your game plan for life. You can find much more information about setting goals in Part IV of this book.

### Knowing where you want to go

As I report in my book *Over the Top,* research conducted by David Jensen of UCLA proves that people with a goals program earn more than twice as much money as those without goals. In addition, they are also happier and healthier and get along better with the folks at home. I'm of the very strong opinion (not based on scientific research, but from years of observation) that these people also have more friends, more peace of mind, more security, and more hope for the future. These factors contribute to a longer and more rewarding life — I've never met a depressed individual who had specific, long-range goals and a plan of action to reach them.

For example, most golfers want to lower their score, but they never specifically set lowering their score as a goal or develop a plan of action for doing so. Regularly, I hear people say that they would like to have more friends, but they don't make it a specific goal, nor do they develop a plan of action for making friends. Others want a new home but haven't specifically set that new home as a goal or developed a plan of action to make it happen. People may fail to plan because they've never been taught to do so, or they may not even have heard of goal-setting.

One classic example of what happens when people learn the skills of goal-setting and aspire to do something about their goals involves a janitor at a hospital in Texas. He had been with the hospital for 21 years and had never owned a home. Perhaps he hadn't given the idea of buying a home much thought because he felt that he didn't have enough money. However, in my "Strategies For Success" training program, which the hospital provided, he discovered how to set goals. He didn't get a raise, but he did buy a house. My question to you is this: Do you think that today, because the hospital taught him how to set goals, he is a happier, more loyal, more productive employee? The answer is obvious, isn't it?

Another example is Tony Greiner. A superb golfer, Tony had been a PGA member for more than 15 years, but he had never made a hole-in-one. When he and I talked about goals, Tony realized that he had never seriously thought about setting such a goal for himself. But less than two months after setting a hole-in-one goal, bingo! He made one.

### Expecting to get where you want to go

To accomplish any objective, you have to plan and prepare for it — then you have a legitimate reason to expect it to happen. Expectations play a major role in success in any field of endeavor.

A survey I read recently reported that one thing that was constantly on the minds of nearly two-thirds of people was good relationships with the people they love. A few years earlier, a study revealed that almost 100 percent of people felt that the most important thing in their lives was their relationships with their families. Yet when the group from the former survey was asked what they were doing to improve those relationships, what was their plan of action, most of them answered noncommittally, "Well, you know, we're just so busy. . . ." That answer doesn't make sense, but, unfortunately, that's reality for "wandering generalities." Reality also says that because they don't *plan* to have better relationships or take the time to *prepare* for better relationships, they don't *expect* to have better relationships.

I'm an avid golfer. I almost run a fever when I head for the golf course. When given an opportunity to play a top course, I don't sleep soundly the night before. Like me, most golf enthusiasts genuinely love the game. Ask typical golfers, even those who shoot 100 (that's not great), whether they love the game, and their enthusiastic answer is yes. Ask them whether they'd like to improve their scoring, and 100 percent of them say yes. Yet I challenge you to go to a driving range or warm-up area on any golf course and watch the way they practice. Most of them hit the ball as far as they can, regardless of which club they're using. They do so despite the fact that two-thirds of golf strokes are taken within 60 yards of the hole; nearly half of those strokes are taken on (or almost on) the green with a putter. They take great pride in how far they can hit the ball, although every good golfer and teaching pro repeatedly tells them that the surest and fastest way to score better is to spend more time practicing the finesse or "touch" shots around the green and putting on the green. Sadly, these golfers honestly believe that they want to improve their scoring, yet the approach they take will never enable them to achieve that end.

If you really want to improve your golf score or your relationships, you must be honest with yourself and properly plan and prepare. Then, and only then, can you expect to achieve the desired results.

*Success For Dummies* is designed to inspire you to make the plans necessary to get the things you really want in life. After you make your plans, little things that would have previously stumped you won't get in the way. It's a proven fact: It's easier to get there when you know where you're going!

## Keying in on character

You can have millions of dollars and not, by any stretch of the imagination, be considered successful by those who know you. The reason is simple: You can make millions of dollars without having character. Character is the fifth and final part of the success formula. Without it, the best attitude, the strongest skills, the most concrete philosophy, and the most worthwhile objectives mean nothing. Not a single one of the prior four parts of the success formula would matter. Drug dealers, smut peddlers, and con artists may accumulate considerable financial wealth and acquire the things that money can buy, but they are never truly successful because without character, they can acquire few, if any, of the things that money can't buy. Unfortunately, the same thing can be said about some businesspeople, politicians, athletes, attorneys, physicians, movie and TV stars, and so on.

People with integrity do the right thing. When you have integrity, you have nothing to fear because you have nothing to hide. In doing the right thing for the right reason — and again, I'm speaking of your personal, family, and business lives — you experience no guilt and no fear. With those two albatrosses of fear and guilt removed from your back, it's much easier to travel farther, faster, and higher.

# Putting It All Together

Because so much of this book is built around relationships, I encourage you to examine the formula as a whole:

> The right attitude, plus specific skills, plus the right philosophy and the right objectives, all built on a character base, enables you to have winning relationships with friends, family, associates, and members of the community at large.

I reference this formula numerous times throughout this book, so you may want to dog-ear this page. Reading the remainder of this book is the first step toward putting this simple success formula to work. Building a foundation of skills, devising a personal philosophy that you can live with and live by, determining your objectives, and sticking to your principles in every walk of your life all help you maintain an attitude that keeps you ready for the challenges that life is sure to throw your way.

A catcher in a baseball game would be hard-pressed to catch a fastball without his sturdy, form-fitting, shock-absorbing catcher's mitt. Similarly, life is a game of hardball. You hold in your hands a "mitt" that can help you "catch" all the finest things in life. Use it!

# Chapter 2

# The Relationship Role

### In This Chapter

▶ Creating a relationship philosophy

▶ Understanding how relationships impact your personal, family, and business lives

▶ Exploring the role that relationships play in your physical, mental, and spiritual lives

▶ Building winning relationships

*W*hy is *Success For Dummies* centered around relationships? Because if you asked 1,000 people what they want most in life, I can assure you that "happiness" would be near the top of everyone's list. Ask those same people what they think would make them happiest of all, and the over-whelming majority would say, "Having wonderful relationships with the people I love."

I challenge you to check your own record. You'll probably find that if you're getting along well with the most important people in your life — that is, the people you love — you are basically a happy person. This is true almost regardless of the status of your bank account or your position on the corporate totem pole.

On the other side of the ledger, if you're *not* getting along well with the people you love, it still doesn't make any difference how many bucks you've got in the bank or whether you're the CEO of a Fortune 500 company or a wealthy entrepreneur. You still are not a happy person.

This chapter identifies the part that relationships play in your overall success in life. Of the eight things everybody wants (explained in Chapter 1), six of them — happiness, health, prosperity, security, peace of mind, and hope — depend, to a large degree, on relationships. The other two — friends and good family relationships — *are* relationships. Keeping in mind that you can't be happy or completely successful if you don't have good relation-ships, I deal with relationships in every phase of life — not just with family and friends, but also with God, the people you serve, and the people who serve you: your neighbors, employees, employer, and the people who work at the grocery store or sandwich shop, to name a few.

# Defining Your Most Important Relationship: The One with Yourself

As you look at the part that relationships play in your life, think about yourself. What is your relationship with yourself? Do you like who you are? If not, what are you doing about it? I frequently say that you have to *be* before you can *do,* and *do* before you can *have.* Through this book, I want to help you get better acquainted with who you are and share with you some things that you can do to grow to like yourself better.

Your ability to get along with other people is an indication of who you are and how you feel about yourself. You have to *be* the kind of person with whom you and others are comfortable. The more you respect yourself, the higher the standards you set, and the greater your integrity, which enables you to *do* the right things. When you do the right things, you're more likely to *have* good relationships with others and more success in general.

Chapters 6, 7, 8, and 9 help you get to know and like yourself better. After you make your way through those chapters, I sincerely believe that you will have all the information you need to be your own person, make the right choices, and do the right things so that you can have the good things that life offers.

# Looking at Your Family Relationships

Your relationship with your family also plays a major role in your success. One of the most comprehensive studies of success that I know of was done on the 1949 graduates of the Harvard Business School. This graduating class, the first from the business school, consisted entirely of men, most of whom had served in World War II.

Laurence Shames wrote a book called *The Big Time* about these men, and a CNN news story that aired in August 1994 was devoted to them. To give you a measure of their success, one man in five could be counted a millionaire, almost half were CEOs, chairmen, or COOs of their companies, and two-thirds of them remained at one company for their entire working career. That's incredible!

What accounts for their outstanding success in such large numbers? Here are a couple of their answers:

- ✔ They had wives who supported them in their endeavors — intelligent women with whom they talked and shared ideas and who offered feedback that was extremely helpful.
- ✔ They built their personal, family, and business lives on integrity.

In other words, they worked to build and maintain good relationships. With those relationships firmly in place, they were able to achieve great success in their careers.

## Love gives what it has

Fair is fair: You've heard about the supportive wife; now look at the supportive husband. My friend Don Johnson from Germantown, Tennessee, producer of the incredibly beautiful "Afterglow" music tapes, shares a story sent to him by Judy Rogers in Westerville, Ohio. I quote her letter verbatim:

"In the fourth year of his layoff from his job, Dad gave Mom a dishwasher for Christmas. You have to understand the magnitude of the gift. Our old house had its original wiring and plumbing, and neither could handle the required installation. There was no spot in the small kitchen for such a large appliance. And we hadn't even been able to meet the mortgage interest payments for over six months.

"But Dad hated the thought of washing dishes; he would rather do anything else. And Mom had undergone major surgery that spring, a radical mastectomy for breast cancer, and found it difficult to do any work requiring the use of her arms.

"No large box appeared, no new plumbing or wiring was installed, no remodeling of the kitchen occurred. Rather, a small note appeared on a branch of the Christmas tree, handwritten by Dad:

"'For one year I will wash all of the dirty dishes in the household. Every one.'

"And he did. He really did!"

Yes, Judy's dad gave out of his abundance — an abundance of love, care, time, and concern — because he could see that his wife needed his help. If someone tried to recognize Judy's dad for his deed, he probably would react like the little guy in the next story.

## *"I done it for love"*

Margaret Baillargeon reports in the Christmas 1996 issue of *Catholic Digest:*

"Richard, at age seven, was the second-youngest of nine children. While he never lacked attention, he nevertheless had his little chores to do around the house. One Saturday afternoon, three days before Christmas, my mother was in her usual rush to get everything done. She asked Richard to go upstairs and polish her Sunday shoes. After awhile Richard brought down the shoes, obviously proud of the job he had done. Mother was so pleased that she reached into her purse and handed him a quarter. A quarter was quite a treasure, especially three days before Christmas, but Richard looked puzzled. He took the money, picked up the shoes, and quietly went back upstairs. In a few minutes, mother rushed up to change her clothes. As she slipped her feet into the shiny shoes, her right foot hit a lump in the toe. She was half-annoyed and hurriedly pulled out a wad of paper. She unwrapped it and out fell a quarter. Written in a seven-year-old scrawl were the words, 'I done it for love.'"

The best things that happen to you, and the best things you do, are done "for love." That's why I say that good family relationships motivate you to higher levels of success. Success really does begin at home.

# Improving Your Business Relationships

In the business world, relationships are an integral part of success or failure. Most people don't know that when Thomas Edison's laboratory and factory burned down, he was 67 years old and carried no insurance. Before the ashes were cold, Henry Ford handed Edison a check for $750,000 with the words "no interest" written on it. He also included a note saying that if Edison needed more, he would have it.

Many people were surprised by Ford's generosity, but one reason he gave Edison the money probably went back to an incident that took place many years earlier. Edison was working on an electric car and had built batteries that made it viable to a point. He heard that a young man named Henry Ford was working on a gasoline engine, so he went to see him and asked him many questions. Ford answered those questions thoroughly and carefully. At the end of the interview, Edison said to Ford, "Young man, I think you're on to something. I encourage you to continue in your pursuits." Later, Ford said that these words of encouragement from the most highly respected inventor in the United States meant a great deal to him. He obviously continued in his pursuits.

Throughout this book, I share examples of how people built the kind of relationships in their business careers that enabled them to achieve and attain the heights of success.

## *Be a superstar*

Business relationships play a major role in the security and productivity of every individual involved, as well as the growth and success of the company. I'm fascinated with the research done by Bell Laboratories, a high-tech company. These figures do not hold true for all companies, but the concept is true.

Bell Laboratories discovered that out of every 100 employees in a typical organization, approximately 5 of them are misplaced. They're hard-working, intelligent, and cooperative, but for some reason they simply do not fit into the culture or the company mission. Of the remaining 95, approximately 88 are good, solid employees — honest, productive, dependable, loyal, and so on. The remaining 7 are superstars who are far more productive than the 88 good, solid workers on the payroll. Actually, they are eight times as productive, which is an incredible figure. Their value is dramatically higher because they not only know and love their jobs but also are constantly "on the grow."

These seven superstar employees are team players to the nth degree and are a team-building, unifying force, which increases company production tremendously. They get along well with other employees, have bought into the company's mission, and are excited about what they do. Their value comes from the fact that they make an honest effort to know and understand the roles that others play in the company.

These superstars take advantage of break time, lunchtime, and the early morning hours, as well as a few minutes after work, to acquire information and cement relationships with people above and around them, developing team spirit.

These superstars also make it a point to be available when someone comes to them seeking information or inquiring about techniques or procedures at which they excel. They patiently and cheerfully share information and, in the process, make the company more productive. As a result, the people they teach make more progress, qualify for promotions and raises, and enjoy a better reputation within the company. The gratitude they feel for their benefactors bonds them to these superstars and builds team spirit. Superstars who build others move up in the ranks and are extraordinarily valuable to the company — job security at its best. You truly can have everything in life you want if you will just help enough other people get what they want.

# He got his promotion

When I met Darrell Wood, I was impressed with his pleasant friendliness, the rapport that he had established with his staff, and the quiet, businesslike approach that he took to his job at Luby's Cafeteria in Plano, Texas. Over the next three years, we became friends. Recently, he introduced me to one of his assistant managers and then said, "Unfortunately, he's got too much ability to stay permanently in this position, so I will be losing him pretty soon." My response was, "Darrell, you're not going to be 'losing him'; you're going to be taking another step up the management ladder, because I can assure you that leadership in any company that has any kind of future is always looking for people who develop leaders."

After hearing my comment, Darrell smiled and said, "Yes, I know that is true. And I've been very fortunate inasmuch as I've had the privilege of promoting a number of people." I determined to check back with Darrell regularly on this event. Less than two months later, he gave me the good news that he had been invited to join management at the home office, a significant promotion.

That's exciting, but look at what has happened to the associates he has worked with. In just two and a half years, eight associate managers and assistant managers worked at his store. All of them were promoted to higher levels of responsibility. Three managers and five associate managers are now working at other units. One of the hourly employees also has moved into the management training program.

Darrell is proud of and grateful for his accomplishments. It's also evident that his leadership beliefs, which follow, are the foundation upon which he has developed his people and moved them into better positions:

- Provide an environment in which people can succeed.

- Have defined and reachable goals.

- Understand what your people's talents are.

- Make sure that everyone understands you and the task you have set out for them. Leave no "gray areas."

- Commit time and effort to all projects.

- Be a cheerleader for everyone you come in contact with.

- Understand that success is internal, not external — believe in what is right, and stay true to your plan.

- Have goals for the individuals who work for you. Where do you want them to be in six months, one year, and so on? Let them know your expectations.

- Set the attitude for the entire building — your employees mirror you and your attitude.

- Talk up the positives. Recognize and correct the negatives, but don't dwell on the negatives.

As you examine Darrell's leadership beliefs, you notice immediately that his major focus is developing his associates so that their future includes a leadership position.

# Manage your frustration

An informative article by John Sheridan in the November 7, 1994, issue of *Industry Week* quoted Professor Robert E. Bidwell of the University of Dayton's School of Business. Bidwell said that people are not trained to handle frustration, despite the fact that frustration is a daily event for most of us.

Bidwell contends that "the inability to manage frustration has a greater impact on productivity and quality than intelligence, energy, vision and creativity put together," and that "frustration creates a cascading or domino effect." He believes that a manager's staff makes the manager successful, yet by dumping his or her frustration downward, a manager "contaminates the environment of the people he depends on to make him successful."

The solution starts with effective communication, which you build by performing consistently. You also need that old-fashioned quality of honesty. A manager develops trust by demonstrating integrity and a willingness to tell the truth, even when he "screws up." Bidwell says that a manager must admit, "We made a mistake. That policy was wrong. We're going to change it." That approach builds trust — a prerequisite for relationship-building.

Next, grow up, be mature, and understand that honey catches more flies than vinegar. Don't let your anger and frustration negatively impact the people around you. When you're feeling angry or frustrated, make it a point to do absolutely nothing. Sit down, take a deep breath, pause for a moment, recognize that you are upset, and understand that your anger can destroy you. Ask yourself what long-range difference the situation that made you angry or frustrated makes, and then answer this question: What can I do to turn my anger into a positive by doing something constructive instead of destructive?

A top executive at a major training and consulting firm says that he's convinced that cultivating partnerships is a key tactic for overcoming or preventing frustration. Partnering empowers the person in direct charge of production to make decisions and take action. Today, customers want speed at the point of service. They want to deal with people who can make decisions now. When employees are empowered to make those decisions, they gain a sense of partnership and responsibility. This principle works in the home, school, church, government, or Chamber of Commerce — anywhere.

Good communication reduces your frustration and makes it easier to build and maintain the kind of relationships that build profitable businesses.

## Remember that the next person you meet is important

A number of years ago, a young lady went to work for a large hotel chain and was doing quite well. Then she heard that the head of the chain was going to be a guest in the hotel the next day. She had never seen him, and she was nervous and uptight, so she asked other clerks if they had ever seen him. None of them had. She was really concerned that she might foul up if she checked him in.

The next evening, she got a call from the head of the chain, who said, "When I checked in this afternoon, you were so professional, so gracious and friendly, I am delighted to have you as a member of the staff." The interesting thing is that she never knew that he had checked in. She did not know until the phone call that he was the head of the chain. All day long, she had been treating every man who checked in as if he were the boss.

Why not treat everybody like Very Important People? Would it make a difference in your relationships with them? Would it improve your business and make you a lot of friends? The answers are obvious, aren't they?

## Make friends with (or get along with) your boss

Success in your job or your profession depends on your relationships with other people. It's true that your employer hires and keeps you on the payroll because of your productivity, but your relationship with your employer also affects your promotability.

Behavioral psychologists advise that you never forget that your boss is your boss. Your job is to do the work the way the boss wants it done. Your objective should be to do your job in a way that makes the boss's job easier. You're there to remove obstacles for the boss, not to *be* the obstacle. Your job security and opportunity for promotion often rest on your effectiveness in this function. Management frequently judges you by how well you get along with the boss, and that judgment can affect your progress. Working with or around a rotten boss teaches you how to set priorities, neutralize potentially explosive situations, and choose your moments.

Don't try to change the boss. There's only one person in the world you can change, and that's you. In studies conducted by the Center for Creative Research, Michael Lombardi, Morgan McCall, and Ann Morrison learned this: "Most successful executives had at one time or another a boss who was impossible. But they learned to deal with that impossible boss, get along with him, and acknowledged that it was the impossible boss that made it possible for them to develop tolerance and growth, overcome obstacles, and attain their positions of success."

Listen to what else they said: "These people helped them form their own best management techniques and procedures. They had seen an individual who was tough to deal with and they determined they were going to do it better. It helped them to acquire patience and to deal with conflicts constructively." The "bad boss" turned out to be a good teacher. The employees built the relationship rather than destroying it, learned from the experience, and benefited as a result. Wasn't that "bad boss" a friend in disguise?

# Understanding How Relationships Are Important Financially

In the financial world, again, success is largely built on relationships. Who you know and how well you know them can open doors. How many people you know (don't forget to include yourself) got jobs or advanced in their jobs because of who they knew? That translates into relationships. Maybe your mother has a friend whose husband worked with a guy in sales who called on a company that just happened to be looking for someone with exactly the job qualifications your mother told her friend you have. Her friend mentioned you to her husband, who vaguely remembered something, so he asked his wife, she called your mother, your mother called you, you called the company, and you got an interview and eventually the job.

There's nothing unusual about that scenario; it happens over and over again. Maybe your parents did business with the same banker for 40 years, and when you needed a loan, the banker approved your application based more on what he knew about the reputation of your family and the banking relationship they had than on your credit history to date.

Relationships are more often than not responsible for getting you jobs, which provide the income you need to buy your home from a real estate agent, who makes enough money off your home purchase to put a down payment on a Jaguar. The Jaguar salesperson puts her commission with the rest of the money she has been saving to start her own business, and life goes on. The relationships that people create when they do business with each other create income for everyone.

In my own case, my relationship with my wife has greatly benefited me financially. She pays the bills and keeps our budget in order. Had it not been for her, I fear that our financial condition would have, on many occasions, fallen into a disastrous state. We still had difficult times, but that wasn't because of the management of the money; it was because we had little money to manage!

I didn't marry her with the intention that she would be my financial advisor; I married her because I loved her. I only discovered her financial capabilities after I married her, and I consider her aptitude in that area a big bonus for me. Yes, all types of relationships have financial implications.

# Seeing How Your Physical, Mental, and Spiritual Health Affects Your Relationships

Health is critical to successful living. Physical health is considered most often by individuals because the results of being physically healthy or unhealthy are usually outwardly obvious. Ignoring poor physical health is difficult when signs of it appear in your mirror on a daily basis. By comparison, however, mental and spiritual health can have a much more dramatic impact on the success you achieve in relationships, and ill health in these areas is much more difficult to discern.

## Physical health and relationships

For the last 25 years, I have been a prolific reader, reading an average of about three hours a day. I have learned much from a number of sources. Admittedly, most of them are people I have not met, but many are people I do know, and knowing them has enabled me to build relationships and glean a great deal of information from them. My relationships with the people who write nutrition and exercise books, for example, have resulted in my physical health being much better.

Almost without exception, everyone believes that physical well-being has a direct bearing on relationships. When you're overly tired or extremely hungry, you're more likely to be irritable, impatient, and difficult to get along with. If you suffer from a lack of sleep, your energy level is affected, and you're more likely to be rude and thoughtless. These feelings create relationship difficulties wherever you are; they're unwelcome in the home, on the job, at school, in a social circle, and in a house of worship.

On the other hand, when you're feeling good and your energy level is high, you're far more likely to be enthusiastic, considerate, gracious, and kind. These moods make you far more acceptable and welcome wherever you go.

The lady in the next story (originally published in *The Book of Modern-Day Parables,* by Fulton Oursler) is a good example of what can happen when you're too tired and stressed out:

> A woman living in New York's elite Central Park South district had just about everything anyone could wish for — everything, that is, except a healthy child. Her 5-year-old daughter had been stricken with a life-threatening illness, and no one knew what to do. New York's finest physicians were stymied and unable to help, even though she spared no expense in trying to save her child. However, just when it seemed all hope was lost, the mother read in the *New York Times* of a prominent doctor from Switzerland who was coming to New York to lecture at the NYU School of Medicine.

> The mother instinctively believed that this doctor was the one who could save her child, so she began her relentless pursuit of him, calling, writing, and pleading for his assistance — but never a reply. Then, one rainy afternoon, while steeped in her personal misery, a short, portly, and very wet bearded man knocked on her door. "What do you want?" she demanded. "I beg your pardon," he began, "but I seem to have lost my way and would like to use your phone to call my driver, if I may. Do you mind?" "Well, I'm sorry," the woman replied in a stern voice, "but I have a very sick child and do not want her to be disturbed," and she closed the door. The following morning, she spied yet another article about the doctor she had so urgently sought to help her child, only this time the article included a picture of the man. Incredibly enough, it was the man she had closed the door on just the day before. What a difference it could have made if she had responded pleasantly by offering to make the call herself.

The story is repeated thousands of times each day when people close the doors of opportunity that come their way. Relationships cannot be built on rudeness and impatience. Be kind and nonjudgmental. Open your mind and heart, and treat people with courtesy and respect. Who knows what may happen?

## Mental health and relationships

From the perspective of success in mental health, Dr. Norman Vincent Peale's book *The Power of Positive Thinking* came at a critical point in my life. Although at that time we hadn't met, Peale certainly became a mentor to me. I never met Dr. David Schwartz, but his book *The Magic of Thinking Big* enabled me to set and reach higher goals and convinced me that, yes, I really can reach them. Today, my friend Fred Smith continually challenges me mentally, as do Dr. John C. Maxwell, my pastor Dr. Jack Graham, and a score of other people. My mental growth has been substantial because of my relationships.

Your mental health and growth may be strongly influenced by a friend who listens quietly while you rant and rave at the world. Maybe your pastor or spiritual counselor helps you stay mentally fit. Different types of relationships affect different levels of mental health. The important thing is to note that relationships do play a role here.

## Spiritual health and relationships

From a spiritual perspective, those families who regularly attend worship services — whether in a church, a synagogue, a mosque, a temple, or whatever — have happier, healthier marriages; fewer divorces; and fewer instances of suicide, drug abuse, or alcohol abuse. They also earn more money, which contributes to their financial success.

### He was good for her mental health

Two of the greatest prime ministers England ever had were Benjamin Disraeli and William Gladstone. Each man made enormous contributions to the British Empire and loyally served the throne. It's difficult to say who was greater, but they certainly were different.

The story is told of a well-known British lady who spent an evening seated next to Gladstone at a formal state dinner. She spent virtually all of the evening in discussion with him. A few days later, at another state dinner, she was seated next to Disraeli, and she spent most of that evening in discussion with Disraeli.

Someone asked her what she thought of the two men and what were the prime differences between the two. She responded that Gladstone was knowledgeable in a wide range of subjects, a deep thinker, and certainly a man who was capable of incredible achievements. She stated that, as a result of her conversation with Gladstone, she was convinced that he was perhaps the most brilliant man England had ever produced.

At that point, she paused and commented that after spending the evening talking with Disraeli, she was convinced that *she* was one of the brightest, wittiest, most knowledgeable people that England had yet produced.

My question is this: Which one of these men did this lady like best? If she had to follow one, which one do you think she would follow? As she discusses them with her friends, whom do you believe she talks most about? The answers are obvious, aren't they? Any time you show intense interest in another person, the individual upon whom you shower your attention thinks that you are a nice, bright person whom they would like to have as a friend.

Disraeli followed the greatest rule in human relationships when he recognized that you should imagine that everyone is wearing a sign around their neck that says, "Make me feel important." That's exactly what he did.

Sir John Templeton, one of the wealthiest people in the United States, says, "If we have not developed a reservoir of spiritual wealth, no amount of money is likely to make us happy. Spiritual wealth provides faith. It gives us love. It brings and expands wisdom. Spiritual wealth leads to happiness because it guides us into useful or loving relationships."

Speaking from personal experience, I can tell you that I have enjoyed even more of the good things in life since I started going to church regularly after forming a personal relationship with Jesus Christ on July 4, 1972. I immediately started attending worship services, where I received encouragement, instruction, and inspiration. I started studying my Bible, which provided me a road map for life. The Psalms and Proverbs contain a wealth of information on business and human relations. The books of John and Hebrews, as well as the rest of the Bible, are filled with faith, hope, love, and encouragement. As a result of putting those biblical principles to work, I now have complete peace of mind, and my wife and I enjoy a relationship that most couples only dream about. The same principles have bonded us with our children, their mates, and our grandchildren.

# Summing Up the Relationship Role

In looking over the physical, mental, and spiritual aspects of my life to this point, I can clearly see that what I've done with my life has been largely determined by the people I've met and the mentors I've chosen. In my corporate office, I display the pictures of 21 people who have influenced my life substantially over the years. The first picture on the wall is of my mother. She was my first role model and my first great teacher, and I have built my life on many of the things that she taught me as a child.

As you evaluate your own life, I'm confident that you, too, will remember the names of countless numbers of people who have made what you've done much easier and much more enjoyable.

Figure 2-1 graphically ties together all the areas of life that relationships cover.

The relationship philosophy of "You can have everything in life you want if you will just help enough other people get what they want" truly helps make living a joy. Understanding how relationships flow and how to make the relationships you're involved in the best they can be helps you to put others first. If you do, I can promise that you'll be the real winner in every sense of the word.

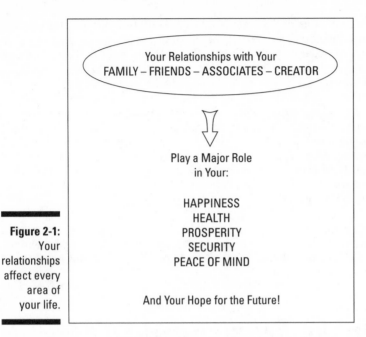

Your Relationships with Your
FAMILY – FRIENDS – ASSOCIATES – CREATOR

Play a Major Role
in Your:

HAPPINESS
HEALTH
PROSPERITY
SECURITY
PEACE OF MIND

And Your Hope for the Future!

**Figure 2-1:**
Your
relationships
affect every
area of
your life.

# Building Winning Relationships

After you recognize the vital role that relationships play in success, I hope that you take a look at your own relationships and think about how you can make them better. Winning relationships are built primarily on trust, mutual benefit, optimistic and uplifting attitudes, respect, and thoughtful consideration. The following information can put you in touch with all these qualities.

## Start with optimism

I'm truly fortunate because I am optimistic by nature. Dr. William Arthur Ward said:

"The doors of opportunity are open to the optimist. Gates of achievement swing wide for the person who sees infinite possibilities in the insignificant.

"Most folks would rather be around a person who sees hope in the future than one who sees nothing but trouble ahead. I'm talking about the kind of optimist who sees a solution in every problem, whose undying conviction is that everything in nature is ordered for the best and is adapted to produce the most good."

If you have a friend who, regardless of your help and encouragement, chooses to view life as a hopeless problem to be lived, you are well aware of how exhausting this friend's visits can be. Life is too short to spend your precious time trying to convince a person who *wants* to live in gloom and doom otherwise. Give lifting that person up your best shot, but don't hang around long enough for his or her bad attitude to pull you down. Instead, surround yourself with optimistic people.

## *Focus on the 'tudes of life*

With optimism as a foundation for winning relationships, look at some of the 'tudes of life. Concentrate on these 'tudes, and you'll build winning relationships everywhere:

✔ **Gratitude:** I mention this 'tude first because *the more you express gratitude for what you have, the more you have to express gratitude for.* You'll never find a happy person who isn't a grateful person, so gratitude is a marvelous place to start. And grateful people are fun to be around.

✔ **Attitude:** Psychologists have maintained for generations that attitudes are more important than facts. An attitude *with facts* (reasons for being optimistic), however, is tremendously rewarding and productive. Attitude is the determining factor in major accomplishments. Fortunately, attitude is something you can control, and in the process, you can build good relationships.

✔ **Magnitude:** You need to magnify the important things and reduce the magnitude of problems that seem insurmountable. "Don't make mountains out of molehills" is a wise observation that everyone would do well to observe, because it stabilizes relationships.

✔ **Latitude:** Latitude is a way of saying that you have the freedom to do virtually anything within the bounds of human decency and law. You have the latitude to be all that you can be and accomplish incredible objectives. Regardless of your ancestry, the circumstances of your youth, and so on, you have the latitude to move from where you are to where you want to be. And when you grant that latitude to others, you cement your relationships.

✔ **Multitude:** You face a multitude of challenges and opportunities every day, but when you concentrate on the challenges, you blot out life's opportunities. Just as you can hold a dime close enough to your eye to blot out the sun, when you concentrate on opportunities you blot out the challenges so that you can overcome them. Focusing on opportunities instead of challenges increases your attractiveness as a friend, family member, or business associate.

# Build relationships on trust and mutual benefit

All long-term relationships are built on trust and mutual benefit. Without trust, you can't have a good relationship; without "something in it for me," the relationship isn't going to be long-lasting. That doesn't necessarily mean that both parties in the relationship want the same things from the relationship, however.

An employer wants services in exchange for the money the employee wants from the employer. A friend may want to carpool with you to save money, while you are grateful for the conversation that you get to have on the way to work. There's no end to the number of trades that people make in their relationships every single day.

A classic example of trading different but mutual benefits is my relationship with my close friend and mentor, Fred Smith. Fred is the wisest man I've ever known and one of the greatest teachers I've ever had. My benefits from the relationship are substantial: He teaches me things that I use in my books, tapes, and lectures and, more important, in the personal, family, and business aspects of my life.

Your question may be, "What does Fred Smith get out of the relationship?" He says that he gets as much as I do because he knows that I genuinely appreciate what he's doing for me. Fred has repeatedly told me that he loves to teach and, in particular, loves to teach *me* because he knows that I use his teachings in my books, tapes, and seminars. His interest is in getting information to the people it can help. He's not concerned about getting credit; he has a higher agenda in mind.

Fred's relationship with himself is obviously a good one. It takes a great deal of confidence and maturity to put the "bigger" picture ahead of oneself. Knowing who you are, where you stand, and what you have to stand on goes a long way toward making you feel safe, strong, and confident in the multitude of relationships around which your life revolves.

# Heed the Ten Commandments of Human Relations

What can you do as an individual to make sure that your relationships are stable and solidly built? The Ten Commandments of Human Relations can work for you:

1. **Have unshakable integrity, a good attitude, and thorough knowledge of the skills necessary to do the job well.**

**2. Smile and speak to people.**

That's elementary, isn't it? It takes 72 muscles to frown, but only 14 to smile. And a smile is the first thing that you notice about others.

**3. Call people by name.**

You've heard this a thousand times, but personalizing your conversations really makes a difference.

**ZIG SAYS**

# Mentors benefit, too

It never occurred to me that mentors receive benefits from mentoring until I was 23 years old and living in Florence, South Carolina, selling waterless cookware. I had been struggling in the business for two and a half years when I attended a meeting that P. C. Merrell, a divisional supervisor for the cookware company I worked for, conducted. He really turned me on, and I began selling like a house afire.

The company I worked for, Wear-Ever Aluminum, held its National Booster Week the last week in August each year, and the field force was inspired to go all-out for that special week. I did just that, selling two and a half times as much as I had ever sold in a single week. Excited, I drove to Atlanta to rendezvous with my "mentor" and sales manager, who had brought me into the business.

I arrived in Atlanta at about 3:00 a.m. For the next two hours, I gave him a blow-by-blow description of everything I had said and done to accomplish my marvelous feat. He listened patiently to the worst case of "I-itis" in history, nodding his approval of everything I told him.

Finally, I came to the end of my story, and what I had done to my colleague suddenly hit me. Completely embarrassed, I apologized profusely for totally dominating the conversation and finally asked him, "How are you doing?" He looked at me and smiled and said, "Zig, don't give it a thought. I've enjoyed every

moment of your excitement as you shared with me your big week and the progress you're making. You have every reason to be pleased and even proud of what you've accomplished."

Then he paused for a moment and again with that little smile said, "But, Zig, let me tell you something. As excited as you are about what you've done, you're not nearly as excited about it as I am. Need I remind you that I'm the one who brought you into this business, put you through all the initial training, conducted those Monday morning sales meetings, and went out into the field and worked with you? I answered your questions when you were frustrated because of your lack of progress, and encouraged you when you were down. So, Zig, I feel that I've had a big hand in what you are now accomplishing. If you think what you have personally done is exciting, let me tell you something. You don't know what excitement is until you experience what I am now experiencing — watching someone I've worked with make it in a business that I love. Your day will come, but right now I'm enjoying my day."

That's quite a message. Real joy and happiness come far more from what you do for other people than from what you do for yourself. Along these lines, there are leaders who develop followers and leaders who develop leaders. You have a choice in that matter.

**4. Be friendly, helpful, and encouraging.**

If you meet somebody with a chip on his or her shoulder, the best way to get it off is to let him or her take a bow.

**5. Speak and act as if everything you do is a genuine pleasure.**

**6. Be genuinely interested in other people.**

You can like almost anybody if you really try.

**7. Be generous with your praise and careful with your criticism.**

Remember, the best thing to do behind a person's back is to pat it.

**8. Be considerate of the feelings of others.**

**9. Be of service to others.**

What counts most in life is what you do for others.

**10. Develop a good sense of humor.**

## See things from the other person's point of view

To build winning relationships, you need to understand the other person's perspective. Not only does a good quarterback study how to run an offense, but he also studies the defensive psychology and strategy as well. That way, he has a better feel for how to accomplish his objectives.

You also need to think like the other person thinks so that you can speak in understandable terms. I love the story of the doctor's wife who called a plumber because she was having trouble with a toilet. The plumber asked her, "What's the problem?" She said, "The toilet can't swallow." That was a language that they both understood. When you make yourself understood, you score points and build good relationships.

## Don't be a know-it-all

If you really want to build winning relationships, be careful not to become a know-it-all. Have you ever noticed how unpopular the people who have an answer for everything are? Doesn't make any difference what subject you bring up; they've got the answer. For example, I really blew it in this situation:

A few years ago, when doing an early-morning seminar, I greeted the young woman who was guarding the backstage door with a cheerful, "Good morning, how are you doing?" She said, "I'm not doing well. I hate to be here." I confidently, cheerfully, and arrogantly said to her, "Well, think about it this way. There are some people who don't have any kind of job doing anything, so maybe you'll feel better with that thought."

The young woman looked at me and said, "Look, I'm not ready for any of your 'positive thinking.' I'm having an extremely tough time." As I walked away, I thought to myself, "Boy! What a lousy attitude!" However, as I pondered it during the next few minutes, I realized that what she needed was some simple empathy, somebody to say, "Is there anything I can do?" or "I'm sorry things are not going your way."

I went back at the earliest possible moment to apologize to the young woman, but unfortunately, she was gone. That's one of the reasons I now talk a lot more about the "right" attitude than a "positive" attitude. In that particular incident, my relationship with that young woman and the possibility of my giving her any real encouragement later was destroyed because I was too intent on saying what I had to say and was not really empathetic to her problem.

Relationships are built on putting yourself in the other person's position. Try to imagine how others may feel, and you can deal with them more effectively and get along with them far better.

## Take time to be kind

Two thousand years ago, a Jewish scholar wrote, "Be ye kind one to another, tenderhearted, forgiving each other." To promote winning relationships, whether at home or on the job, you need to treat people like cows, as in the following story:

My dad died during the Great Depression when I was 5, so all of us kids did our part around the house. Our economic survival was built around five milk cows and a large garden. We sold the surplus milk and butter and many of the vegetables.

I was milking cows by the time I was 8 years old, and I can tell you from experience that cows don't always "give" milk — you have to fight for every drop! I can also tell you that the way you treat the cow has a direct bearing on the quantity and the quality of the milk she produces. If you speak harshly to her and treat her badly, two things happen: She gives less milk, and the milk may not be usable, because when she's upset, the milk she produces is often bitter and useless. (She may retaliate and kick you, too!)

I'm not suggesting that you need to kiss the cow, but speaking kindly to her and stroking her a time or two lets her know that you appreciate her efforts. (And it doesn't hurt to tell her that she has the four most beautiful legs you've ever seen.) My mother loved her cows and expected her children to love them and treat them well. As a result, we got maximum production from our cows, which gave us an extra bonus. After keeping a cow for two or three years, we raised her milk production so much that Mom was able to sell that cow for considerably more money than she paid for her. For us, that was a big plus.

Always treat people kindly, gently, and with respect and consideration. They'll respond favorably, and if they happen to be on your payroll, they'll work harder and be more productive. On the other hand, if you are unkind and speak harshly, they are unable to perform at their best. Kindness and consideration have many rewards, wherever you are and whatever you're doing.

## Pass it on

To build winning relationships, take a lesson from relay runners. The mile relay is one of the most exciting races in track. Much of the success depends not only on the speed of the runners but also on their skill in passing the baton from one runner to the next. Many times, the winner is determined by the smoothness and speed of the transfer.

That same principle works in life. You know how you feel when someone says something nice to or about you — it lifts your spirits and makes you feel good. If you make a habit of passing that feeling on to someone else by sincerely complimenting them for something they said or did, you'll be amazed at what happens: You feel even better about yourself, the other person is pleased, and winning relationships are established or reinforced.

For example, the country club that my wife and I belong to is truly great, with two beautiful golf courses and wonderful dining facilities. However, its major attraction is that the whole staff — beginning with Eldridge Miles, the head pro — treats us like long-lost siblings and gives us the distinct impression that they are always delighted to see us. They give that impression because they are real. The members feel a genuine bond with them.

I'm convinced that the major reason all these people are so nice is that Eldridge is always encouraging the internal customers (meaning the staff) and saying nice things to and about them, so the staff, in turn, treats external customers of the club the same way. I was very impressed with Chuck Bolden, the service director, the first day he was there because he takes exactly the same appraoch. A special event was taking place in the dining room, and I walked in looking for someone. When I didn't see who I was looking for, I turned and walked away. Chuck literally ran after me, caught me, and asked whether he could do anything to help me. I was impressed with that gesture, particularly because he had no idea who I was. In short, it wasn't name or face identification that prompted his action; it was a willingness to serve and an eagerness to help. Gestures like that build customer loyalty and winning relationships.

I can assure you that the people involved do not treat my family and me the way they do because we happen to have a reputation in the business world. Many others have said exactly the same things about the country club staff numerous times. Relationships are important — if you build relationships first, building a career, a marriage, or a business becomes much easier.

# Chapter 3

# The Hallmarks of Success

*In This Chapter*

▶ Looking at the characteristics of successful people

▶ Figuring out how to enhance these characteristics in yourself

*W*hat constitutes a successful businessperson, mate, parent, or individual? I believe that success is made up of the following characteristics:

- ✔ Conviction
- ✔ Commitment
- ✔ Hard work
- ✔ Love for what you do
- ✔ Integrity
- ✔ Character
- ✔ Consistency
- ✔ Persistence
- ✔ Discipline
- ✔ Heredity
- ✔ Environment
- ✔ Humor
- ✔ Luck
- ✔ Faith
- ✔ Passion
- ✔ Connections

These hallmarks of success are qualities that you learn and acquire over time. The degree of success that you experience is usually tied to the number of these qualities that you exercise in your life. No one begins life instantly knowing how to work hard, be disciplined, have a good sense of humor, be persistent, have integrity, and so on. In this chapter, I explain how the qualities work together and how to put each one to work.

The good news is that the qualities necessary to succeed in *any* area of life are similar in *all* areas of life. For example, a successful businessperson is an effective, hard worker. He or she has to duplicate those qualities in marriage and in parenting to be successful in those roles as well.

I believe that you're successful when you have some of the things that money can buy and all of the things that money can't buy. Dr. Jack Graham puts it this way: "Wealth is the total of what you have that money can't buy and death can't take away." In essence, success means that you're successful at home, on the job, and in the neighborhood; you're successful in the here and secure in the hereafter.

# Conviction and Commitment Come First

Success begins with the desire to be successful and the conviction that you can be successful. Then, and only then, do you make plans to reach that specific objective of achieving success. After you make plans, you must be willing to commit to them. But no responsible person makes a commitment until he or she has a reasonable plan of action to fulfill that commitment.

For example, I watched two of my daughters try to give up the habit of cigarette smoking. Over and over again, they put down the cigarettes just to pick them back up. It wasn't until they made a firm decision that they *wanted* to quit that they formed a game plan on how to go about it and then set a date to lay down the cigarettes once and for all.

Suzan, my oldest daughter, sought the help of her physician. She was given nicotine gum, a mild tranquilizer, and instructions to see the doctor once a week and call if she felt that she wanted to light up.

Julie, my youngest daughter, started telling everyone she saw that she was quitting smoking six weeks in advance of the date she had chosen. She then sent for literature and started a Nicotine Anonymous group that met once a week in her home. She wrapped silver duct tape around her last pack of cigarettes, wrote "God and I can do this" on the outside, and made a commitment that if she decided to have a cigarette, she *had* to get it out of *that* pack.

Both daughters were successful because they were first convinced that they needed to quit; they then developed the desire to quit and, after a lot of trial and error, made and committed to a workable plan to quit. Their plans were as different as they are, which makes another important point: Your goals have to be set by you, and you are the only one who can make a plan to reach them in a way that is both comfortable and natural for you. I have yet to meet anyone who quit smoking because their wife's, husband's, mother's, father's, doctor's, friend's, or child's goal was for them to quit.

Look at the hallmarks of success that both daughters had to employ to successfully give up the cigarette habit: hard work, conviction, integrity, consistency, faith, connections, character, commitment, discipline, humor

(I won't go into it here, but things got pretty funny sometimes), and lots of persistence — remember, they both quit *several* times before they were successful.

Regardless of the kind of success you are seeking, the hallmarks of success are essential to attaining that success. You can find the information you need on setting goals for acquiring those hallmarks of success and for every area of your life in Chapters 6 through 17.

# Hard Work Is a Must

Yes, hard work is necessary. In society today, many people are somewhat like the fellow who, when asked how long he had been working for his company, responded, "Ever since they threatened to fire me!" Unfortunately, too many people don't take their work seriously until their employment is endangered. The same may be true in your relationships with your mate and your children: Only when you get into trouble do you get serious about working to solve the problem.

Instead of waiting to be chastised for doing sub-par work and neglecting your responsibilities, why not apply yourself and remove that feeling of dread or impending doom from the corners of your mind? Set yourself free by giving your best in every situation.

## Marriage requires work

The hard-work principle also applies to maintaining your marriage. Suppose that your mate is critically injured in an accident and can no longer be your playmate, companion, and coparticipant in dancing, sports, swimming, travel, and other things that you love to do together. In order to be successful as a mate, you need to remember the commitment and the good times and understand that disasters or tragedies cause one of two things to happen: You either grow closer to each other, or you decide that you're not going to be a "sacrificial lamb" and jump ship.

Historically speaking, those folks who maintain and work at their commitment develop a new interest in activities that frequently enables them to grow even closer and serve as role models for their children, friends, and other members of the family. Keep in mind that you took each other "for better or worse."

Nothing is quite as satisfying as succeeding under difficult circumstances. If success is always a smooth ride, you may enjoy it, but you'll gain very little satisfaction from it.

## All hard work is hard work

Virtually everyone recognizes that you really have to work to be successful in your career, job, or profession. Unfortunately, many people don't understand that career mothers and household executives don't sit around all day and do nothing. The following vignette can help correct that misconception for those folks who still haven't gotten the message:

A man came home from work one evening to find his house in shambles. The beds had not been made, the kitchen sink was filled with dirty dishes, and the children's clothes, toys, and books were scattered throughout the entire length of the house. Besides that, dinner wasn't ready and waiting as it usually was.

"What in the world happened?" the man asked his wife when he saw the mess.

"Nothing, dear," she said. "Absolutely nothing. You are always wondering what I do all day long. Well, just take a look around you. Today, I didn't do it."

## *Parenting requires work*

When you brought your child into the world, you committed to being responsible for raising your child. If your child strays from the "normal" route and chooses what disappoints any parent — that is, to become a rebel, a drug user, or an alcohol abuser, or to involve himself or herself in other antisocial behaviors — what do you, the parent, do? Do you abandon your child and say, "I want no more to do with you," or do you remember your commitment and work at solving the problem and maintaining the relationship with your child?

A word of caution here: No parent takes full credit for every beautiful, loving, kind, superb thing that his or her child does. Nor should a parent take full responsibility for every bad thing the child does. You teach what you know is right, but you must remember that when children reach the age of accountability and you've taught them right from wrong, if they are out of sight, the choices they make are their own. If the child chooses to rebel and do otherwise, your feelings of guilt don't make you more effective as a parent. Instead, you work at bringing the child back into the fold, just as you would work at the company to bring it back into successful operation.

## Forty cents was a lot of money

I was raised during the Great Depression by a widowed mother with 11 living children, 6 of them too young to work. Things were tough financially. Five milk cows, some fruit trees, and a large vegetable garden provided most of our food. Each of us children did what we could to contribute: My brothers and I got part-time jobs in a grocery store, and my sisters worked in small department stores.

One of my responsibilities each morning was to tie each cow to a stake; take her to good, lush grass; and solidly pound the stake into the ground. At lunch time, I would move the cows to another spot with more good grass. One day, I was eager to get back to school and play a little softball before the lunch break ended. In my hurry, I improperly staked one of the cows. She got loose and invaded a nearby garden.

That afternoon, when I returned for the cow, I was confronted by a lady who was upset because of what our cow had done to her garden. I apologized profusely, promised to be more careful in the future, and headed home.

When Mom asked what had taken me so long, I told her what had happened, recounting my apology. My mother said to me, "Son, to apologize is one thing, but to pay for what you did is more important." We returned to the lady to make restitution. She estimated that the cow had eaten about eight bunches of turnip greens, valued at 5 cents a bunch, for a total of 40 cents. That 40 cents came out of my pocket.

That doesn't sound like much money today, but in my grocery store job I earned 5 cents an hour, so 40 cents represented eight hours of work. After that experience, when I staked the cows, I staked them well. I believe that's one of the most important lessons I ever absorbed. Because a parent's goal is to work himself or herself out of a job, parents must teach responsibility throughout childhood.

Sometimes it's not easy to apologize, begin again, admit error, take advice, be unselfish, keep on trying, be honest, profit by your mistakes, forgive and forget, think and then act, or shoulder deserved blame — but doing so always pays.

# *Loving What You Do Helps — But Loving Every Aspect of What You Do Isn't Necessary*

Periodically, some celebrity, speaker, or preacher makes the comment that the critical component to success in any area of life, particularly on the job, is to love what you do. Loving what you do is a marvelous plus, but people make too much of this idea in one respect: Some people take it too far and interpret it to mean that you should love *every phase* of what you do. That is not realistic.

You can have a marvelous career or a job that you love, but what happens when the company falls into financial difficulties, times get lean, you have to spend an inordinate amount of overtime at the office, you struggle with payroll, dissension enters the ranks, and tension fills the workplace? Do you jump out because work is now "no fun"? Hardly! You committed to a career, and if you love the company and your job and the potential is great, you tough it out so that you help the company reach its potential. (Possible exception: If a legitimate opportunity arises and you know in your heart that you are pursuing an opportunity and not just leaving a problem, then you're probably making a good career move.)

That's important because the basic problem with jumping ship with the first windstorm is that the next time a cloud appears on the horizon, you're more likely to jump ship again — and again. I speak from personal experience. After a slow start in sales, I experienced considerable success in sales and sales management for the next five years. At that point, I stopped growing — and started swelling. I became a critic and a malcontent, and for the next five years I chased the pot of gold at the end of the rainbow by making 17 career changes. I became a "wandering generality" — with disastrous results. Don't let it happen to you.

# Integrity Is Integral

Integrity is a hallmark of success that everyone can readily identify — even children, regardless of their age. This observation from Volume 12, Number 1, of the *Executive Speechwriter Newsletter* may make you think twice about the example you set for your kids before you criticize them for their behavior:

> "When I told my kids to clean their rooms, they took a closer look at the condition of my tools and possessions in the garage. When I told them that honesty was our family's greatest virtue, they commented on the radar detector I had installed in my car. When I told them about the vices of drinking and wild parties, they watched from the upstairs balcony at the way our guests behaved at our adult functions. Integrity is easier preached than practiced, and children are especially good at seeing the differences between what their parents preach and what their parents practice."

You also need to understand that integrity is transferable. The lessons you learn and use at home and in your marriage are the ones you transfer to your work. The kind of person you are determines the things you do, whether at home, on the job, or in social situations.

In seminars on being successful, former Notre Dame football coach Lou Holtz gives three basic guidelines to follow. These guidelines strengthen what I'm saying and apply equally on the job, with your mate, and with your kids:

> ✔ **Do what's right.** Be on time, be polite, and be honest; remain free from drugs; and if you have any questions, get out your Bible.
>
> ✔ **Do your best.** Mediocrity is unacceptable when you are capable of doing better.
>
> ✔ **Treat others as you want to be treated.** Practice love and understanding.

# Character and Consistency Pay

Maintaining your character demands that you be consistent in your actions, which back up your words. Most people would rather *see* a sermon than hear one preached any day.

Many years ago, Nathaniel Hawthorne expressed well the need for consistency in character when he wrote in *The Scarlet Letter,* "No man, for any considerable period, can wear one face to himself, and another to the multitude, without finally getting bewildered as to which may be the true."

Each of your actions is an indication of your character. When you buy a basket of peaches, tomatoes, or apples, the marketing capability of the merchant is displayed at the top. The merchant's *character* is displayed in the product found at the bottom of the basket. When the butcher shows a beautiful side of a steak or roast through clear plastic, but you get home and see that the other side is the one with all the fat and bone, you rightly feel that you have been taken — because you have. Unfortunately, the butcher just lost your trust and, many times, your business. Character really is a hallmark of success.

Consistency is one of the most important and stabilizing qualities that you can have. Author/speaker/minister Dr. Jay Strack said this in the September 9, 1996 issue of his weekly newsletter, *Desktop Devotions:* "Time changes things, sometimes drastically. Styles change, as do expectations, salaries, communications systems, styles of relating to people. But some things have no business changing, like respect for authority, personal integrity, wholesome thoughts, pure words, clean living, love for family and authentic servanthood. Character qualities are never up for grabs. Times must change, but character never."

You can't inherit character, but you can learn it and then demonstrate it. Ultimately, the measure of your character is not what you inherited from your ancestors, but what you leave to your children and descendants. Character on the job, with your mate, and in the home is constantly on display and builds good relationships. Conversely, lack of character destroys relationships and any chance for real success.

# Persistence Is a Must

Many roads and qualities lead to success, but sheer, dogged persistence is one hallmark that everyone can employ and use. Goethe put it this way: "Austere perseverance, harsh and continuous, may be employed by the smallest of us and rarely fails its purpose, for its solid power grows irresistibly greater with time."

Persistence, obviously, is not the only factor in success, but the intriguing thing about persistence is that the longer you persist, the more focused you become on the objective you pursue. Persistence enables you, through various experiences and failures, to uncover talents and develop a creativity that first astonishes you, then delights you, and finally brings you material rewards far beyond your initial expectations. People who quit when they encounter the first obstacle never develop the creativity that is the ultimate reward for keeping a commitment and persisting until you reach your objective.

When you encounter intolerable conditions or impossible situations, the very act of persisting forces you to ask yourself these all-important questions:

- ✔ Am I missing something?
- ✔ What other route can I take?
- ✔ Does my mentor have the answer?
- ✔ Have I overlooked the obvious?
- ✔ Can I accomplish this objective by taking shorter steps? By working harder? By setting time aside for the specific purpose of thinking about this problem and this problem alone?
- ✔ Should I literally walk away from it and take a long, quiet walk? (A walk is my favorite approach for overcoming obstacles.)
- ✔ Should I back away temporarily because, at this precise instant, the timing isn't right?

Asking these questions doesn't mean that you're abandoning your goal; it simply means that you're planning and preparing to reach the objective in a different way. Everyone has worked through this process in one form or another. You work and work on solving a problem with no results. Then, in essence, you "forget about it," only to have the solution suddenly pop out, clear as day. Actually, you didn't forget it. All the thought processes and experiences of your lifetime were quietly working internally, until one day an event, a word, a thought, or a comment taken out of context suddenly fit directly into the plan and — bingo! — your answer appeared. Let me remind you that the answer came because you persisted. You can take that character quality a long way.

ZIG SAYS

# Persistence: A personal example

My dream to be a speaker was born in 1952, when I heard Bob Bale speak in Florence, South Carolina. He gave me valuable direction, which I followed. However, it wasn't until 1968 that I was able to go full-time in the business, and it wasn't until 1972 that my career as a speaker really took off. In those intervening years, I was privileged to read a large number of excellent books and listen to outstanding speakers as I traveled countless miles driving to the "freebies" that I conducted. I also picked up examples, illustrations, and stories as I participated in a wide range of events.

During this period, my skills as a communicator slowly developed, and my experience produced real-life stories and lessons that I shared with audiences of all kinds and sizes. I spoke to civic clubs, Lions, Jaycees, Rotaries, schools, rehab centers, prisons, churches — to virtually any group who permitted me to share with them. I solicited feedback from those folks who were experienced in the field and who had my interests at heart. Through it all, I had some discouraging times when it seemed as though nothing was happening, but not only did I have the dream, but the dream had me. I can honestly tell you that not once did I ever contemplate abandoning the idea of being a full-time professional speaker. During those years, I continued to work in sales because, with a wife and four children, my first priority was to provide for them.

Folks may question the wisdom of pursuing my dream all those years. Often, the future didn't look especially bright. Regardless of how hard I tried to get speaking engagements, they seldom came. Even the "freebies" weren't all that easy to get. (Keep in mind that in the 1950s and early 1960s, the speaking business was minute in comparison to what it is today. The Chambers of Commerce and the Sales and Marketing Executives Clubs were virtually the only organizations who were sponsoring events, and only established speakers were invited to address audiences on the rare occasions where money changed hands.)

Along the way, I became obsessed with the idea that what I had to say was important, and that I could make a difference in people's lives. This idea was born as a result of words P. C. Merrell said to me — words that changed my sales career dramatically — and was reinforced by the fact that I was applying those principles in my own sales organization with outstanding results. So, although I had times of frustration and even discouragement, I never seriously considered giving up the dream.

In retrospect, I realize that the long delay was largely responsible for much of the success that I've enjoyed over the last 25 years. I was applying the principles on a real and everyday basis in my own sales life and in the lives of the people whose careers I was directing. I quickly found that the principles went far beyond the sales world. This revelation created a desire to discover more so that I could share more. Along this journey, I came to realize that the more I knew about my subject, the more creative I could be in my presentations. The more new ideas I acquired from others, the more useful my own ideas became, because truth forms a synergism. I was careful to seek truth and ethical principles as I built my career.

I believe that whatever your chosen profession, if you make a strong commitment and have a burning desire in your heart — combined with the conviction that you can make a difference — dogged persistence provides you the best insurance for success. Remember that persistence enables you to develop other skills as you go along, provided that you're always "on the grow" and are genuinely excited about benefiting the people you're dealing with.

# Discipline: Thinking to Get Ahead

Another hallmark of success that's necessary for success in business, with your mate, as a parent, and as an individual is a word that most people regard as negative, objectionable, or even dirty. I'm speaking of *discipline.* The word comes from the word *disciple,* which literally means "to teach." According to the *American Dictionary of the English Language,* discipline means "to instruct or educate; to inform; to prepare by instructing in correct principles and habits." More than anything else, it means to bring your mind under control. Discipline is something you do *for* yourself or others, not something you do *to* yourself or others — that's *punishment.*

Think about that definition for a moment. Isn't it an appropriate guideline for success in business, as well as at home with your mate and kids? Discipline teaches children rules and acquaints them with the importance of following the instructions and leadership of their manager and/or boss in years to come. And in the marketplace, until you know how to manage (that is, discipline) yourself, you can never successfully manage or lead others. One of my favorite observations is this:

*PEARL OF WISDOM*

> When you discipline yourself to do the things you need to do when you need to do them, the day will come when you can do the things you want to do when you want to do them.

In a nutshell, the way to prepare yourself for a profession and get ahead is through discipline. As a person who is fortunate enough to be doing the things he really wants to do, I can tell you that I am grateful for the discipline that I imposed on myself, which enabled me to persist in the pursuit of my dream when I was 45 years old, broke, and in debt.

Today, when more emphasis is placed on rights than on responsibilities, the discipline and character to accept responsibilities are welcome additions to the success formula. Discipline helps you get along better with your mate and raise the kind of kids that anyone would be proud to have.

# Heredity and Environment Play a Part

For years, psychologists have debated which is more important: heredity or environment. I remember well when one of my children brought in a less-than-spectacular report card, and I expressed displeasure with the poor performance. This child, who shall remain nameless, looked at me and asked with a smile, "Well, Dad, do you think it's heredity or environment?" (Yes, Parents, some questions really don't have escape-proof answers.)

> # Lessons from the military
>
> One of my favorite people, a man whom I've come to know through platform appearances and interchanges before he or I speak, is General Colin Powell, one of the most respected public figures in the United States. Here's his answer to the question, "What did you learn in the military?"
>
> He said that the first thing he found out was that everyone is at the same level (thanks to the uniform haircut given to all recruits). Other things he discovered were
>
> - To stand at attention and salute, which instills discipline and obedience
>
> - To march in step and function as a part of a team while taking individual pride as a team member
>
> - That not staying in step with the others brings undesirable consequences
>
> - That if he performed well, both he and his team were recognized
>
> Powell points out that basic training physically hardens recruits and makes them respect their own bodies, enabling them to perform better. He observes that the first week is generally so difficult and the drill sergeant so demanding that most recruits develop something akin to hatred for the sergeant. But the hatred fades quickly. By the second week of training, typical recruits are doing everything they can to please their drill sergeant. That's an amazing turnabout. Many recruits translate the discipline from the sergeant into love and caring for themselves, which is a new experience for some. The truth is, discipline is loving — just ask any parent. Discipline is essential to every individual and is crucial for teams. No unit can ever become a potent fighting force without discipline, and no life can be truly successful without it.
>
> The criteria for becoming a successful soldier, businessperson, mate, parent, or citizen are the same. You can function as a team member only after you've brought your personal life under control and found out how to "drill."

Some people get here with a few more cards in their mental deck, but I believe that every person is capable of doing incredible things — far more than he or she initially realizes. However, success does beget success, and your environment, combined with your heredity, is the determining factor.

According to a study done in Missouri, you acquire roughly two-thirds of your working vocabulary by age 3. Another study by psychiatrist Ross Campbell says that 80 percent of your character is formed by age 5, and 90 percent of your personality is acquired by age 7. (I think that I'm safe in saying that virtually everyone who reads this book is at least 7 years old.)

You may be thinking, "I came from a bad environment. Where does this leave me?" Answer: Your past still leaves you with a brilliant future — if you're willing to accept responsibility for making that future all that it can be.

# A Sense of Humor Helps — Especially When You Don't Feel Nice

Because winning relationships are hallmarks of your success with your spouse, children, associates at work, and social acquaintances, understanding why being nice and having a sense of humor can help is critical. Not to be nice in all areas can have serious and sometimes surprising repercussions, as the next story demonstrates:

A man and his wife were driving down the highway. He was going too fast, and she warned him that the highway patrol officers would be after him. He arrogantly said, "I'm only doing 70. They won't bother me." He increased his speed to 80, and again she warned him. This time, even more adamantly, he said, "Don't worry about a thing." About two minutes later, the siren of a highway patrol car could be heard clearly from the rear, so the man pulled over and rolled down his window.

When the patrolman approached the side of the car, the man, instead of meekly seeking mercy, began verbally attacking the patrolman, berating him for a couple of minutes before finally running down. The patrolman smiled and asked the driver's wife, "Ma'am, is your husband always this obnoxious?" She sweetly responded, "No, ordinarily he's very nice and pleasant. It's only when he's half-drunk that he does things like this."

You don't need much imagination to figure out what happened next, do you?

Seriously, though, learning to take things in stride and getting tickled when you could have chosen to get angry just as easily is to your advantage 100 percent of the time. If you can find the humor in otherwise distressing situations, you will enjoy life more fully, and you'll move past obstacles with relative ease.

# Luck: Is It Really a Hallmark of Success?

Some people observe that the harder they work, the luckier they get. Others spell *luck* with a P, because they believe that "pluck" determines one's luck.

My *1828 Noah Webster Dictionary* says that luck is "that which happens to a person; an event, good or ill, affecting a man's interest or happiness and which is deemed casual. . . . We never say in a literal sense that a plant has the 'luck' to grow in a particular place or a fossil has the 'luck' to be of a particular form. We say a person has the 'good luck' to escape from danger or the 'ill luck' to be ensnared or to suffer loss. He has had good luck or bad luck in fishing or hunting. Luck, or what we call 'chance,' 'accident,' 'fortune,' is an event which takes place without being intended or foreseen."

Unfortunately, during the last 30 years, the role that luck plays in life has been overemphasized. For many years, folks told their children that if they worked hard, told the truth, and saved their money, eventually things would turn out well for them. Now, many people are teaching their children by example (and with the help of the media) that if that approach doesn't work, they can buy lottery tickets and still get rich. Unfortunately, this attitude is creating quite a few gambling addicts — up more than 50 percent since the lottery took off about 15 years ago — not to mention the discouragement that is the traveling companion of false hope.

## Successful people work for their luck

Let me acknowledge that I feel that being at the right place at the right time is better than being the smartest person in town. However, I must add that most people appear at the right place at the right time not by luck but by design. They get what appears to be a big break, but in reality, they worked hard to get to where the big breaks come.

Having been in sales all my life, I have come to appreciate that success is determined more by effort than by luck. Occasionally, when I would hit the jackpot with a big sale or a large number of sales that came in a flurry, colleagues would accuse me of being lucky. However, my data showed that if I made a certain number of calls day in and day out, I'd get a certain percentage of appointments. Out of those appointments, I'd get a certain number of presentations. Out of those presentations, I'd get a certain number of sales. This formula didn't come out exactly every day or, for that matter, every week. But at the end of the month, I could tell you exactly how much business I produced per call, per display, and per sale — which meant that I could tell you what I had sold for the month. The figures were very consistent when I looked at them over the long haul.

## Consistency produces "lucky" results

The year I finished number two out of a sales force of over 7,000, not one week or one month did I finish in the top 20. But at the end of the year, I was number two. One reason was that I never shot a blank. Even while I was on vacation, I made a few calls so that I could keep the string going. Luck, in my book, is the direct result of consistent, organized, enthusiastic effort.

Wise folks have made these observations:

- ✔ Ralph Waldo Emerson said, "Shallow men believe in luck; wise and strong men in cause and effect."
- ✔ Calvin Coolidge said, "Those who trust to chance must abide by the results of chance."

✔ Goethe said, "Woe to him who would ascribe something like reason to chance."

✔ One of my favorite people, Barbara Bush, said, "You don't just 'luck into' things. You build step by step, whether it's friendships or opportunities." I agree.

# Faith

My faith is the greatest hallmark of success in my life. My faith involves my relationship with Christ, and since I began that relationship in 1972, my life has been infinitely better.

I hasten to add that my faith is not blind. I have carefully studied my Bible, and the research done on validating the Bible leads me to believe that it is truth. I find in the book of Proverbs the best information about business I've read, in the book of Psalms the best information about relationships I've seen, and in the book of John the most significant information about faith that I've encountered.

Is faith realistic? I let the following data speak to whether faith gets results:

Hospitals are beginning to recognize that spiritual well-being can be crucial to the healing process. In the early 1990s, the deputy director of a program for Veterans Administration hospitals that works to help doctors control costs and improve quality studied 700 coronary patients. The study tracked some of the most costly and complicated procedures, such as bypass operations, valve replacements, and open heart surgery. Also included in the study were veterans undergoing care for heart attacks and chronic heart disease.

One group of patients had daily visits by a chaplain. The other group of patients saw a chaplain for only minutes during their entire hospital stay. The study found that the patients who had the most contact with a chaplain were released from the hospital an average of two days sooner than patients who did not receive regular visits. The group visited by a chaplain also had fewer complications after surgery. The director of the study estimates that the cost of the chaplain visits was no more than $100 per patient. The savings from letting a patient go home earlier, however, amounted to as much as $4,000 a day.

I know many successful individuals. Many of them have done very well financially, not to mention in the other areas of life that affect happiness and well-being. Some of them have meager incomes but are rich in all the other areas of life that bring contentment and happiness. The common denominator? Faith.

My friends and acquaintances who enjoy success are of many different faiths, but all of them believe that they don't have the final word in how their lives play out. They know that they are not alone in their journey from birth to death, and this knowledge strengthens them for the trials that they face along life's way. Supporting the people you love and care about is far easier when you feel loved and cared about as well. That's why success seems to be standard for folks with faith. Life is so much more than money, and perhaps the greatest success of all is owning that little piece of knowledge!

# Developing Passion

My mentor, Fred Smith, says that passion for anything occurs at the moment you get a glimpse of the potential for the project, yourself, your mission, and so on. My objective in this book is to give you a glimpse of your potential, a glimpse of what you can do. When you get that glimpse, passion is born. And passionate people get things done.

Recently, my friend and colleague Tony Jeary asked me, "How do you develop passion?" I'd never been asked that particular question before, but as I started to think about it, I put together some thoughts that I believe are valid. The following steps take a look at how you develop passion:

1. **Analyze what you want in life and come up with a plan for reaching those goals.**

   Though passion can be brought on almost instantly by a life-changing event, it usually begins with a careful analysis of what you want in life. What is your direction? In short, what are your goals? After you clearly identify your goals (which Part III of this book can help you with), you develop a plan of action to reach those goals. When the plan makes sense, then and only then do you make the commitment to move ahead.

2. **Take steps toward your goals.**

   As your plans unfold, each step that you take toward your goals has a direct bearing on your excitement, enthusiasm, and confidence. As you enjoy little successes, your imagination (which I believe includes a picture of your future that you paint in your mind) explodes, and passion enters the picture. And when passion is full-blown, it's unlikely that you will abandon your objectives.

### 3. Use your head to direct the passion that develops.

Effective passion is a directed emotion that synergizes all your qualities to make a total you that is considerably greater than the sum of all those qualities. Some identify passion as "heart," because people with passion accomplish things that go beyond their physical and mental abilities. My personal conviction is that your heart is the dominant force, but your head provides the direction, brings the passion into focus, and provides the imagination that makes it happen.

Any study of history or current events reveals a multitude of stories about average people whose accomplishments have been extraordinary. You can give passion the credit. Take Bill Bates, a special teams player for the Dallas Cowboys, for example. Bates was considered too slow and too small to play in the NFL. He wasn't drafted but made the team as a free agent. For the last 15 years, he has been an invaluable member of the Cowboys' secondary.

He not only gives his all but also inspires the other players to do the same. He brings more than just his ability; he brings a commitment fueled with passion that makes him infinitely more valuable. The same approach to any job, profession, or other endeavor is the difference between survival and genuine success. Check the records: Whether it's in music, medicine, physics, science, academics, or athletics, the great ones have passion for what they're doing.

# Making the Right Connections

Many people are doing a great deal of networking these days, and that includes me. For years, you've heard people say, "You've got to have the right connections to get ahead," or that a person "had all the doors opened for him — no wonder he's making it big!"

The right connections can open doors, but what happens inside those doors is entirely up to you and your own persuasiveness and abilities. In my life, the people I work hardest to make connections with are the ones I can learn from, not the ones I may get an opportunity to sell something to. For more than a quarter of a century, my interest has been in finding people who have led lives of integrity and who know things that I need to know in order to accomplish my objectives. I get valuable information from magazines, newspapers, and books every day. However, on some occasions I need to talk with someone who can answer questions that arise at the moment. I can't always put my hand on the right book, recording, tape, or magazine, but I can always put my hand on the telephone.

**TRUE STORIES**

## Passion can save lives

A classic example of a person with a passion is Candy Lightner, who started Mothers Against Drunk Driving (MADD). Her daughter was killed by a drunk driver who escaped with little more than a slap on the wrist. She determined at that point to wage war against drunk drivers. An instant passion developed within her to make a contribution to society so that other mothers would not lose their children, husbands, and parents because of drunk drivers. She has been personally responsible for the passing of many laws and, consequently, the saving of many lives. I'm convinced that literally thousands of people are alive today — and healthy as well — because of Candy's passion.

Here are some of the people I rely on:

- ✔ **Psychologists and psychiatrists:** I have developed relationships with some truly outstanding psychologists and psychiatrists who guide me through the psychological minefields that abound in the world today. Through them, I ask questions and get psychological validation that what I'm about to speak, write, or record is sound.

- ✔ **Theologians:** I have built relationships with theologians who have thoroughly and carefully studied the Bible and how it applies to daily life. They believe it strongly and live by those biblical principles. I can call those people and get theological answers to dilemmas that everyone faces from time to time.

- ✔ **Physicians:** I've developed relationships with physicians who give me physiological answers when I'm dealing with the physical aspect of life.

Your relationships with people — the people you love, as well as the people at work, in the neighborhood, and in your social circle — have a strong influence on your future. As you read this book, you'll discover relationship skills that can help you to overcome inherited or environmental problems that you may have had as a child and can catapult you into the fast-forward category of life.

## Just what does money buy?

Because success is about much more than money, the question is, "What do I do with the other areas of my life after I become secure financially and have more than provided for my family?" When the hallmarks of success permeate your life, make sure that you maintain balance. The late John D. Rockefeller is an example of what happens when money is one's only objective.

In the process of becoming an oil baron, Rockefeller accumulated a vast fortune. Because of his drive, steamroller tactics, and long working hours, his health began to deteriorate while he was still in his 50s. He was a miserable human being from a physical and an emotional standpoint. He had no joy or happiness in his life.

Then he made a radical change in his approach to life: He started giving away the fortune he had amassed. His demeanor and drive changed from that of a driven man doing questionable things to earn money to that of an individual who genuinely wanted to help people.

In Rockefeller's day, a dime was worth considerably more than it is today. He was constantly passing out dimes everywhere he went. Distributing a fortune of countless millions of dollars in ten-cent lumps is impossible, but the joy from giving — particularly to children — completely changed every aspect of his life. Many of his millions were disbursed to significant charities. His health dramatically improved, his enjoyment of living increased substantially, and he lived to be well into his 90s. His life ultimately depicted the hallmarks of success. Yours can, too!

# Part II
# Getting Motivated

"Okay, you were depressed because you didn't win, but couldn't you have been happy enough about finishing second to pick up the $100,000 check?"

# In this part . . .

Success is a moving target. How you measure success changes as *you* change. This part of the book is the bedrock for understanding how motivation works, what your internal needs are, and how those needs affect your behavior. Look here for the lowdown on how to motivate yourself and others to attain success.

# Chapter 4

# Understanding How Motivation Works

*M*otivation is a powerful tool for success. The degree to which you can remain motivated and continue to make forward progress determines whether you realize the life goals that you establish. But the reward for being motivated isn't just raw goal-accomplishment. The accompanying benefits of being motivated are numerous — and they can change your life.

I'm going to open this chapter with the most motivating information of all: the rewards. When you fully understand these benefits of motivation, you can make motivating yourself a lifelong habit.

✔ **Creativity:** Motivated people think more clearly. They focus more intellectual resources on their current project, and the result is more creativity.

✔ **Energy:** People who are motivated actually need less sleep — not because they're on a constant adrenaline rush but because they possess a genuine, energizing excitement.

✔ **Flexibility:** Motivated folks have discovered that flexibility is a developed skill that doesn't depend on circumstances. When their circumstances change, they're more open to bending to deal with the situation rather than being rigid about an outcome.

✔ **Health:** People who have a positive feeling about their life and its potential have reason to get and stay healthy. They have experienced the difference in energy and healthfulness during nonmotivated times, and they prefer the motivated lifestyle.

✔ **Magnetism:** A motivated lifestyle is attractive, and motivated people have a certain magnetism. Others are naturally drawn to winners who are energizing by nature and habit.

✔ **Momentum:** Motivation is self-perpetuating. It gathers speed as it rolls along in offices, homes, and communities. Living out your motivation gets easier because it becomes a habit.

✔ **Multiplication:** Motivation is contagious — it spreads and multiplies. The people around the one who is motivated "catch" that motivation.

✔ **Recognition:** When people live out a motivated lifestyle, they stand out. Others respect them for their achievements, admire their spunk, and, because they want to be associated with winners, offer their assistance.

✔ **Optimism:** Motivated individuals have found out that optimism opens more doors than negativity. They have discovered a life pattern of finding the silver lining or the potential in any turn of events. They aren't thrown off course by change. They find the good in everything.

✔ **Productivity:** Motivated people get more done. They move with a spring in their step, and they attack tasks with enthusiasm. They move quickly, deliberately, and with a concern for maintaining a can-do attitude along the way.

✔ **Stability:** Folks with motivation are focused and are not easily distracted or dissuaded from their destinations. They are tuned in to the object of their motivation.

The little feeling of anticipation that you get while reading about the rewards of motivation is just an inkling of what motivation is. Keep reading so that you can find out what motivation is, how to get it, and how to keep it!

# Understanding What Motivation Is

Because using motivation to your advantage starts when you understand what motivation is, take a minute to consider the meaning of motivation. Being motivated means being ready to take action. You can know every detail of how to become successful, but you need to be ready to *act* on that knowledge in order to start your journey toward success.

# Looking at What Motivates People

Everyone is motivated, but not in the same way. How one person demonstrates motivation may be quite different from the next person. Some people are initiators, and others are "waiters." (Yes, even those folks who wait can be motivated.) Chapter 5 gives you more information about how to find what motivates you personally.

Everybody is motivated periodically or temporarily to do something worthwhile, to make a contribution, to be somebody, to move forward, and so on. The problem is that many people are motivated to do something so seldom or so sporadically that they take from society more than they contribute. The major difference between the givers and the takers is the consistency in their motivations. That consistency comes only with the development of the total person, starting with a character base.

All my life, I have tried to understand why people do the things they do. (And sometimes my greatest challenge is to figure out the motivating factors for my own behavior!) When I boil down all my observations into a couple of concepts that get people to *do* something, I come up with these two motivators:

- The desire for gain
- The fear of loss

All people have both motivators inside them, creating actions and reactions. One motivator may dominate some people most of the time — perhaps the difference is the "half-empty glass" or the "half-full glass" philosophy. But both motivators are valid reasons for actions and responses. For example, some people may take a job offer because of the travel involved, and others may reject the job for the same reason. Inside, they see either gain or loss as the outcome of the travel.

## The desire for gain

According to Rabbi Daniel Lapin in his book *The Jewish Edge,* four basic desires exist to motivate people:

- **"Gold" or wealth:** Nothing is wrong with wealth as a form of motivation, as long as it is *a* motivation and not *the* motivation. The desire for wealth is limiting in that if money becomes your major motivation, you fall short in many other areas of life. Wealth acquired as a result of your efforts and kept in balance with the rest of your life provides financial security and a certain peace of mind. Not having to worry about the bills and being able to enjoy some of the fun things in life is a good thing!

- ✔ **Power or strength:** This motivating factor also gives you a feeling of security and helps you feel good about yourself — if you have acquired that power by playing the game in an ethical manner. Power motivates many people to do such things as build companies that employ others or achieve high political office so that they can do good for themselves, their families, their community, their country, and their fellow man. Properly used, strength or power motivation is basic and wonderful.

- ✔ **Wisdom:** Wisdom is acquiring all the knowledge you can and then using that knowledge to make intelligent decisions. Because wisdom is the correct use of the truth in the knowledge you have, wisdom enables you to make good decisions and treat people in an ethical manner. Doing so gives you a legitimate chance to have plenty of friends, good family relationships, peace of mind, and the hope that the future is going to be even better.

- ✔ **Honor:** Unfortunately, in today's world people often forgo honor, confuse popularity with notoriety, and work to get the latter, with disastrous long-term results. Taking the "service" approach and doing the right thing gives you a realistic chance of being recognized, re-warded, and honored for the right reasons. Check the records, and you find that people who occupy prominent places of honor are men and women who have lived their lives with integrity and have been servants to scores of other people. Many times these people are dedicated parents, school teachers, small business owners, ministers in small churches, government workers, farmers — anyone who has simply used the other three motivating factors of wealth, strength, and wisdom in a completely ethical manner.

The bottom line is that people whose prime motive is contributing to others are able to do more for themselves with the extra energy and feeling-good-about-themselves attitude that results from helping others.

## *The fear of loss*

During World War II, the United States government initiated a life insurance program stipulating that the beneficiaries of any U.S. service person killed in action would be paid a $10,000 insurance benefit. Although this insurance was a marvelous idea, the government still had to do a sales job on the policy. A young lieutenant presented the life insurance plan to the troops, giving them all the intricate details and encouraging them to sign up. Not one volunteered. Finally, an old sergeant who had been around for a long time said to the young lieutenant, "Sir, let me talk to the troops. I believe they'll listen." The young lieutenant objected, stating that he had explained all the details and that the men simply were not interested. The old sarge, however, persisted and finally persuaded the young lieutenant to let him have a shot.

The sergeant's sales talk was short and very clear. "Gentlemen," he said, "if you get this insurance policy and you get killed, the government is going to send your family $10,000. If you don't get the policy and you are killed, the government is not going to send your family anything. Now, my question to you is very simple: Which of you do you think the government is going to put on the front lines first? The ones who get killed and cost the government nothing, or the ones who get killed and cost the government $10,000? You think about that." Need I tell you that 100 percent of the troops signed up for the policy?

Whether the story is true or just another GI tale, I'll never know. But this I do know: Fear motivation does work.

In most cases, however, fear motivation is short-lived, because you get over your fear. The fear of losing a job if you don't perform is sometimes, at least temporarily, effective at making you perform. Telling a 5-year-old that you're going to deny him television privileges if he misbehaves works to modify his behavior — at least temporarily.

It's been said that you should base your actions on love and not fear. Theoretically, that's true, but in practice it does not always work out that way. There are legitimate fears. Fear of ignorance causes you to seek an education, and fear of poverty makes you work. Fear of disease motivates you to practice healthy and sanitary living. Fear of losing your job inspires you to show up on time and do the best you know how to do. Fear of failing a class drives a student to spend extra time with the books. Fear of losing your family inspires you to be faithful to them, work hard for them, and show them love on a daily basis.

From time to time, I use the acrostic FEAR for *False Evidence Appearing Real.* However, if the evidence is real, healthy fear is essential for survival. You should have real fear in walking across a busy street without going to the corner. A fear of driving your car at excessive speeds under any conditions, but particularly where the visibility is poor or the streets are slippery, is legitimate. Legitimate fear for realistic reasons is not only natural but also desirable. However, don't allow fear to run rampant through your life, to the point where it becomes so devastating that it produces failure. The problem isn't getting rid of fear, but using it properly.

You must be able to distinguish healthy fears from unhealthy ones (such as worrying every time you hear a siren that a loved one has been in an accident). When you can do that, fear is a friend. Until you can do so, however, fear can be an enemy. Figure out what you should fear, and approach the rest with confidence.

# Nine things that people want to gain and are afraid to lose

Take a look at how these nine items relate to motivation and behavior:

**Respect:** People want to be respected for who they are and to be acknowledged for their uniqueness. A certain level of trust accompanies respect — you need people to honor your preferences as an indicator that they believe that you have thought through your opinions and values and have arrived at your own conclusions. Respect assumes that you are capable of discerning your own best directions for living and tells you that you are valuable.

**Reputation:** Reputation is a social need, one that is probably most familiar to folks in their "fear of losing" mode. The word *putation* comes from the implied act of "passing along" information. Your *re*-putation is from others passing along a report about you. The degree to which you are concerned about what people say about you, positive or negative, often motivates you to act in a way that gets you a good report rather than a bad one.

**Status:** Status is a compilation of respect and reputation, but it has an importance all its own. The need for status usually displays itself as a desire for gain. A higher status is usually in front of you or just outside your grasp, luring you to try a little harder and strive a little longer to attain it. Status may also be a measure of how good your reputation is and how much respect you have attained. Status is most certainly a taskmaster that beckons people to behave in certain ways with the promise of tangible rewards.

**Appreciation:** Everyone wants to be appreciated. Folks like to be noticed and liked for who they are and what they've done. People usually require appreciation from those folks who are closest to them; they want their inner circle of friends and family members to feel that they are essential. Respect, reputation, and status can be fabricated or faulty, even undeserved. But when you are *appreciated* by the people closest to you, you truly feel valuable.

**Power and influence:** If motivation has a dark side, then the need for power and influence is a prime candidate. Some people equate the ability to influence or control circumstances or people with self-worth. The need for power seems to be insatiable in some folks and can, if left unchecked, lead to oppressive actions against resistors. However, if you can be a servant and do things for the good of all, not just yourself, you can have a clear conscience in your position. Some politicians are able to operate that way; some have forgotten their position as public servants.

**Happiness:** Happiness has always been a need, but it can be elusive. In the past, people believed that they had a right to pursue happiness — the American Constitution even said so. Today, however, many people believe that they have a right to be happy, that society owes them happiness. For these people, the single-minded pursuit of happiness leads to behaviors that bring anything but happiness. Happiness is a choice that you can make regardless of resources or circumstances. But, no doubt, the pursuit of it motivates behavior.

**Joy:** Joy is the motivator that causes people to do the unexpected. The path to real joy is through contentment, gratefulness, and anticipation of life with all its twists and turns. Joy goes beyond happiness because it doesn't rely on a positive circumstance to elicit positive emotions or behaviors. What a different home or workplace you would have if the desire for joy motivated all behavior!

**Peace:** When I was younger, I really wanted happiness. The older I get, the more I look for peace. Some may see that change as a softening with age, but I see it as adopting wisdom and perspective in a world where failing to reflect gets people in trouble and causes them to alienate their friends and family.

**Love:** I saved the most powerful motivator for last. Oh, the things we do for love! Some people forsake heritage and honor; some serve strangers with untold sacrifice; and some commit heinous crimes so that their lovers accept them.

How does this list apply to you and the topic of motivation? One of these needs motivates you every minute of every day. If you want to motivate yourself, you must tap into the power of these needs and address them.

Get a sheet of paper and, starting with the first motivator, write down whether you have the respect of yourself. Define what respect means to you and how you can achieve respect. Move down the list, going through the process with each motivator. When you finish, you have a good idea of what you want and need to do.

# Finding Your Hot Buttons

The real key to motivation is to get into your mind and discover your hot buttons. You do things for your own reasons, not for other people's reasons. If you discover *why* you want what you want, then you can create and configure the motivation. The fellow in the next story succeeded in life because he did what *he* wanted to do. Read on:

At age 6, James Usher was holding onto his father's leg when his father was shot to death. At 14, James held his mother in his arms as she died after being sick for 11 months. She had been receiving welfare, social security checks, and food stamps. The month following her death, the checks and food stamps arrived, along with another check for James. He sent them all back to the government. James's six older brothers were upset with him, saying that the money was free and refusing to let him live with them unless he took it. James explained that the money wasn't free and that he would have to pay for it, in more ways than one, if he accepted it. He lived alone from that time on.

James, an African-American lad who was born in a barn and spent his early years in a small town in Mississippi, didn't know that he didn't have a chance in life. At 12, he was earning $160 a week cutting yards with his best friend, who lived across the street.

Despite the fact that his classmates voted him the least likely to succeed, this modest, bright, highly motivated, articulate young man now owns several businesses, is active in his church, is a motivational speaker and certified trainer, and gives speeches around the country. Because one of James's major concerns is the negativism permeating much of his race, years ago he chose the goal of becoming wealthy by age 35 so that he could devote the rest of his life to helping other people realize their dreams. Today, he provides scholarships for students and assists people who have financial needs. James Usher is an example to us all.

The question is, what motivated James Usher? His first motivator was his mother. As she was dying in his arms, the last thing she said to him was, "Make something out of yourself, James. Make Mama proud." Those words had a dramatic impact on him, and he determined to do exactly what his mother had urged him to do.

This story is the first tiny part of answering the question, "Is all motivation self-motivation?" James could have chosen to ignore his mother's words, but instead he chose to heed them and "make Mama proud." Had she not uttered those words of encouragement, whether he would have been able to do what he is currently doing and has already done is uncertain.

If James Usher can overcome his start in life — the early, tragic losses of his father and mother and overwhelming poverty — don't you *know* that you can do more, much more, with your own life?

# How Motivation Works

The bottom line for motivation is reward. Some kind of reward — whether it's a gain or a loss — is behind all behavior. The reward can be either positive or negative; I occasionally come across people who are motivated by a negative outcome. That kind of motivation may not be healthy, but it does dictate behavior.

The rewards for "right" behavior are well known, but you may seldom consider the rewards for "wrong" or "negative" behavior. For example, everyone knows that good grades are the reward for studying and that good health is the reward for eating right and exercising. But everyone has also, on occasion, noticed children behaving badly in order to get the attention they want. Once, when my daughter Julie was about 5 years old, she tried repeatedly to get her mother's attention while her mother was on the phone. In an angry fit of frustration, Julie set fire to some boxes in the utility room. I don't need to tell you that her mother didn't waste any time getting off the phone when those boxes went up in flames! Julie's reward for that behavior was the attention she wanted — and then some. I assure you that the "and then some" part was *very negative.* Consequently, Julie never set anything on fire again.

## Setting up incentive rewards

Rewards are important. For example, financial rewards motivate piece-goods production workers to be more efficient in what they do, work more consistently, and hone their skills. The incentive for preparing for old age inspires many people to set aside a certain amount of their income. In short, incentive motivation reflects the desire for gain.

Incentive motivation is the proverbial carrot in front of the horse. The promise is that something significant is going to come your way if you accomplish an objective. That something may be as simple as a mention in a newspaper column, recognition before your peers, or winning a trophy that has no value to anyone except you. I still have in my office a trophy that I won in 1962 for being the number-one salesperson in a national organization of over 3,000 people. That trophy has no value to anyone else, but to me it's a reminder that for one year, I was the most productive salesperson that the company had.

When Red Auerbach coached the dynasty-producing Boston Celtics, he carefully outlined each pregame talk. Auerbach took great pride in making every pep talk original. However, as legend has it, he found himself at a loss for words during the NBA championship one year. Auerbach turned to his star player, Frank Ramsey, and asked whether he had any words of wisdom for the team. Ramsey gave the invitation a little thought; then he approached the blackboard and wrote, "You win . . . $10,000! You lose . . . $5,000!" That incentive motivation was all the pregame pep talk the Celtics needed that day.

## Staying motivated with three stages of rewards

Three stages of rewards do the job of keeping people motivated:

- ✔ **The carrot:** The enticement of a reward gets you going. Just as a carrot dangling in front of a horse gets him moving, the promise of a payoff gets most people moving. You build your visions during this stage. When people hear of the potential, they buy in to the promise that awaits them.

- ✔ **Milestones:** The points at which you get smaller rewards for partial completion of a task or journey are the milestones. If you're doing well, you get an immediate payoff that encourages you to keep going toward the bigger reward at the end. If the carrot isn't working, you may never reach the milestones. Encouraging comments such as "I'm proud of you — keep after it" or "Three more steps and you're there" can make the difference at this point. Progress that is recognized and rewarded is likely to continue.

> ✔ **The prize:** The prize is the reward at the end for winning or completing the endeavor. It's the payoff that you were hoping for. Remember, if you set up a reward for someone, always follow through and deliver it. If you set up a reward for yourself, claim it and then enjoy it.

All three stages of the process are powerful tools for motivating yourself toward the success that you have defined for yourself.

My step-grandaughter, Jenni Norman Haecker, decided very early in life that she wanted to be an elementary school teacher — that goal was her carrot. Her milestones on the way to realizing her dream were graduating from high school and college. All along the way, friends and family encouraged her, and after she was presented her degree, we had a big party to celebrate. But the party wasn't her prize or reward; the job she now has teaching third grade in Watauga, Texas, is her prize for reaching her goal.

Jenni was motivated by her desire to be a teacher, so she took the necessary steps to reach her goal and collect her prize. You can use this process to accomplish results in your life as well.

# Defeating Demotivation

Demotivation is anything that deflates and discourages you anywhere along the path to your objective. For example, you are demotivated when you demand perfection of yourself or when an employer demands perfection from you. Demanding the *best* of yourself and having others demand it of you is fine, but demanding *perfection* is an impossibility and can only lead to disappointment and demotivation.

Demotivation can also occur when you're placed in a negative environment where "nothing is right" according to the folks around you, where you always have problems, where you never receive any hope or encouragement. That kind of environment definitely leads to demotivation.

Criticism, particularly steady criticism in large doses, is a demotivating factor. Over a period of time, criticism can make you feel that you're worthless because you "never do anything right." Being oversupervised or directed or getting the feeling that your parent, manager, or boss feels that you can't be trusted to do a good job demotivates you to an extreme.

Perhaps the most bizarre use of demotivation I have ever heard of was in a "motivational speech" delivered by Coach Bulldog Turner before the final game of the New York Titans. In 1962, this ill-fated team was playing in the now-defunct American Football League when the coach gave this "motivational" talk: "There won't be any New York Titans next year, so most of you are playing in your last pro game. Most of you aren't good enough to play anywhere else."

If you have played on a team, you probably agree that hearing words like Coach Turner's before you take the field undoubtedly results in a less-than-stellar performance. When the person who is supposed to inspire you to give your best effort tells you that he knows you're going to lose and that you're not good enough to play elsewhere, you feel demoralized. Folks in positions of authority are supposed to encourage you — not *discourage* you. Incidentally, after that magnificent send-off, the Titans got clobbered 44-10. I'm surprised that the defeat wasn't worse.

You also demotivate yourself when you do things that you know are wrong. Your self-disappointment gives you a feeling of worthlessness, and your self-talk is saturated with self-defeating words like "I'm no good. I never do anything right." In short, you beat yourself up and, in the process, you also de-energize yourself and become further demotivated.

Part of the solution is wrapped up in some advice that I gave to a young woman who was distressed because she had two failed marriages behind her. I said to her, "In your lifetime, you've made literally millions of choices and decisions. Two of them were wrong. Now let's concentrate on those decisions you've made that were right, emphasize the positive, and evaluate future decisions more carefully, taking extra pains to make certain your choices do not violate your own code of ethics."

This advice can work for you, too. Realize that your problems may be traced back to a poor decision on your part, but to overcome your problems, you must forgive yourself and move on. Focus on doing better the next time, not on dwelling on what you could have done better last time.

## Motivated or demotivated: Your choice

Some people are influenced from a negative perspective; instead of getting excited about finding solutions when they hear about a problem, they lose courage, motivation, and drive. Several factors contribute to this reaction. One factor comes into play when criticism is unfair or untrue. When a person receives undeserved criticism, he or she may lose hope, feel victimized, and want to throw in the towel.

The demotivation may come from the outside, but the choice as to how you handle the demotivating event definitely comes from the inside. You can let this kind of treatment make you bitter — or make you better. You can say, "It's not right! It's not fair! I'm going to get even!" Or you can choose to say "What can I learn from this?" and "I'll show them that their criticism was not only unfair and unjustified, but it simply had no validity."

## Associating with motivating people

The people you associate with — whether on the job or socially — can have a motivating or a demotivating effect on you. Some folks see life in a positive light and are natural motivators. If a positive person asks you how you're doing and you say, "Not well at all. I've had this cold for a week now," their response is something like, "I'm so sorry. I bet you'll be good as new and feeling better in no time!" A negative, demotivating person may respond by saying, "I know what you mean. A cold like that can sure ruin your week. If you're like me, it'll probably take you a whole month to get over it!"

You associate with some people not by choice but simply by circumstance. You can't choose your coworkers, for example; sometimes you have to do the best you can to work with and get along with them congenially. However, you don't have to associate with demotivating people at breaks, meals, or after-work social events. Find ways to remain cordial, but don't spend too much time with those people.

Instead, surround yourself with people who make you feel better about yourself, people who notice what's right and good instead of what's wrong and bad. Everyone has said on some occasion, "I just feel inspired; I feel better about myself and my future when I'm around so-and-so." In other words, choose to associate with people you want to be more like.

Attending worship services, educational seminars, and inspiring concerts; working with a mentor; and even going to athletic events can motivate you by association. You can absorb lessons at those events that make a substantial difference.

## Smiling and being verbally positive

Simple things, such as verbalizing positives or smiling at people and having them smile back at you, are some of the most effective motivational forces you can imagine. You *choose* to smile, which indicates that motivation is partly internal and that being motivated is your responsibility. Your negative actions and demeanor elicit a negative response; your positive actions and demeanor bring out a positive response. Your smile brings forth a positive reaction in virtually every case.

Seldom do I go to my church, club, company, or favorite restaurant that the impact of all my previous visits doesn't manifest itself almost immediately. When I walk in, I always greet people with "How ya doin'?" At this point, in all the places I just mentioned, most of the people there respond with a smile, "Better than good!" They know that I'm going to respond in the same way, and that phrase has become a habit with them. Those people and I are

---

## Greed is a demotivator

One of the misconceptions of life is that people who are money-hungry are the ones who end up with the money. Temporarily, this scenario may be true, but over the long haul, the exact opposite happens.

You probably remember the story of the goose that laid the golden eggs. The owner of the goose discovered a golden egg in the goose's nest. Each morning, another golden egg appeared. Instead of patiently waiting for the goose to lay an egg each day, the man foolishly killed the goose, thinking that he would find a mine of golden eggs inside. Of course, he didn't.

Most small children think that the story is interesting, and it is apparently designed to teach a lesson in patience. Adults consider it foolishness personified to believe that by killing a goose that lays golden eggs, you would get all the eggs at once, but this story that I heard on the radio is about a man who did exactly that.

A movie-theater manager in Korea was showing *The Sound of Music* to a packed house every time the doors to his theater opened. He greedily wanted to find a way for more people to see the movie so that he could make more money. He decided to shorten the movie by taking out most of the music.

I don't need to tell you what happened to the crowds. Those moviegoers wanted to see a good movie with great music. When they didn't get the music they wanted, they stopped giving the theater manager what he wanted: the profit he would have made if he had continued to deliver value.

When greed enters the picture, bad things happen — sometimes quickly, sometimes far down the road, but virtually always. On the other hand, if you always deliver value, you're the big winner in the long run.

---

better off because we exchange something of value — motivation from each other. We've come to expect and appreciate it. Again, I choose to do that, but my choice brings forth a more intimate interchange than would have taken place without our special greeting.

# Motivation: Temporary or Permanent?

The debate persists: Is motivation something that gets you excited for the moment and lets you down the next day, or can it endure for a long time?

I see the impact of motivation in people's lives every day. I get many letters and phone calls from people who say that for them, motivation has completely changed their lives. Yet other people say that motivation has had little impact on them.

At long last, Stanford University has provided the reason for the variance. A study at the university showed that only 5 percent of the people who buy into a concept are able to implement it; the other 95 percent don't have the resources to do so. Those few words created as much excitement in me as any single sentence ever has, because they made something crystal-clear: The books and tapes are the resources. That's why I get so many more letters from people who say that my books and tapes have changed their lives than I get from people who say that my speech changed their lives.

The next time you see an author who presents a philosophy or concept that you believe can enrich your life, I encourage you to take the following steps:

1. **Check out the author's credentials and see whether he or she can document the results you hear being touted.**

2. **If the evidence is solid, buy the book or tapes.**

Those books and tapes give you the resources you need to implement the concepts. When you take those steps, you make certain that the motivation you feel at the moment can survive the day and impact your future over the long haul. This book, as I hope you have already determined, is a valuable resource.

People who are concerned about their futures take the necessary steps today in the form of growing, learning, studying, and planning for their futures. This process generates enthusiasm and excitement about their futures, so they take the necessary action to ensure those futures. People who aren't concerned about their futures because they don't think they have futures are the ones who take no action. They drift along, singing the old Doris Day song "Que Sera, Sera," and they drift into their declining years without any excitement or, in most cases, without any resources to enjoy even the basics of life without depending on others.

It's interesting to note that these two groups of people live at the same time, possibly in the same area, and may work in the same job or profession. In short, it's not the absence of opportunity but the absence of motivation that is the problem for the second group. If you really think that you have no future, let me suggest that having a future is a matter of choice on your part. If you continue to read books like this one and start setting specific goals, you are doing something about your future. Your excitement (motivation) grows, and from that point on, you can develop the actions that dramatically enrich your future.

# Chapter 5

# You Can't Get Motivated Until You Know Your Motives

Motivation is an energizer that makes you friendlier, happier, and healthier. It clears your thinking, increases your creativity, stimulates you mentally, and uplifts you emotionally. A motivated person is more productive than an unmotivated person — sometimes dramatically so. Knowing what your motives are enables you to get motivated. If you don't know what you want and why you want it, you can't make a plan to get it. Sometimes other people tell you what you want, and for a while you may buy into their plans for you, but ultimately, if the motives driving you aren't your own, you lose interest in achieving the goal.

Unfortunately, motivation isn't necessarily permanent. But you can make it permanent if you create a habit of doing those activities that motivate you. "Easier said than done," you say? Well, this chapter is here to help you figure out what gets you going and what doesn't.

## Using the DISC System to Find Your Personality Type

You are a complicated and unique individual; many variables have directed your life to this point. But the following information about personal behavior preferences can help you along your journey if you understand how it applies to you. Knowing your behavior preferences helps you to identify what motivates you to make the choices you make. When you know what drives your choices, you can use that information to find your natural strengths and thus make choices that best fit your style. Staying motivated is considerably easier when you enjoy what you do, and customizing your job to your natural style is possible with the information that the DISC system gives you.

People's approaches to life fall into four basic categories, which the experts have labeled with a variety of titles. You may be familiar with the terms Choleric, Sanguine, Phlegmatic, and Melancholic. Or how about Driving, Expressive, Amiable, and Analytical? Or Red, Green, Yellow, and Blue? Each of these terms represents a basic personality type.

At Ziglar Training Systems, our tool of choice is the DISC program, which separates people's personalities into four categories:

- ✔ Directive, dominant person
- ✔ Interactive, influencing person
- ✔ Supportive, stable person
- ✔ Competent, cautious person

# Selling with DISC in mind

To give you one specific example of how you can use your understanding of personality types to create a win/win situation, look at how DISC is used in the world of selling:

- ✔ **High D:** If you're a High D selling to another High D, being yourself is important. If you're a High D selling to a High I, be prepared to socialize. Selling to a High S means that you must talk a little more slowly, share more information, be more deliberate, and not push. If you're selling to a High C, provide evidence — the proof and the facts.

- ✔ **High I:** If you're a High I selling to a High D, be businesslike. Don't initiate small talk. When selling to another High I, remember to ask for the order. When selling to a

High S, earn his or her trust; don't become overly friendly. Stick to proof and facts if you're dealing with a High C.

- ✔ **High S:** If you're a High S selling to a High D, show confidence. Provide social time if you're selling to a High I. When selling to another High S, be reassuring. If you're selling to a High C, use evidence and answer every question.

- ✔ **High C:** If you're a High C selling to a High D, concentrate on "what," not "how." When selling to a High I, hit the high points and spare the details. If you're selling to a High S, give him or her time to digest the information that you share. And if you're a High C selling to another High C, remember to take action.

We administer a personality profile test to all prospective employees of Ziglar Training Systems and to the people who attend our three-day "Born to Win" seminar because a personality profile substantially speeds up the self-discovery process. If you want to find out what motivates you, what you need out of life, and the best way to go about getting what you need, I strongly encourage you to take a personality profile test.

If you're interested in taking a personality profile test, call Ziglar Training Systems at 800-527-0306 and ask to speak to a sales representative. The tests cost from $19 to $40, depending on how in-depth they are.

So that you have a better idea of what each of the four profiles entails, let me elaborate on the basics of the DISC format:

- ✔ The **Directive** personality, which I refer to as the **High D,** wants authority, prestige, freedom, varied activities, difficult assignments, and challenges. When dealing with a High D, you need to provide brief, direct answers to his or her questions. Stick to the business at hand, ask "what" questions, and stress the logic of your ideas and approaches. Seek agreement on facts and ideas. If timeliness counts or sanctions exist, get those facts out into the open but relate them to end results or goals.

- ✔ The **High I** is called the **Influencer.** He or she wants social recognition, popularity, people to talk to, freedom of speech, control, and freedom from details — High Is like to work on their own. They seek favorable working conditions, recognition of abilities, and the opportunity to motivate and help others. When you're dealing with High Is, provide a favorable, friendly environment. Give them chances to verbalize their intuition as well as their ideas about people. Provide concepts backed by testimonials of experts for them to transfer talk into action. Allow time for stimulating and fun activities. If you're going to give details, put them in writing.

- ✔ The **High S** is the **Supportive, Stable** person who wants the status quo. These people are security-conscious and want to know the risks involved in any given situation. They want time to adjust, saying things like, "Don't put it down my throat too quickly. Tell me about it, let me absorb it, come back later, and we'll deal with it." They want identification with the group, appreciation, a structured work pattern, and a limited territory. Give them bounds within which they must work and an area of specialization. Provide a sincere, personal, and agreeable environment and have a direct interest in them. Ask "how" questions to get their opinion. Be patient in drawing out their goals. Present ideas or departures from the status quo in a nonthreatening manner.

- ✔ The **High C,** or the **Competent** personality type, wants evidence and accuracy — no sudden changes, an exact job description, a controlled work environment, the status quo, and a systematic approach to solving problems. These people are quality- and detail-oriented. Give them facts and figures and an opportunity to ask "why" questions. Recognize their specific skills and what they have accomplished. Present your ideas to them in a prepared and structured manner.

Even with these short descriptions, I'm sure that you have already determined the personality style that you most identify with. Keep your own style in mind as you explore the remainder of this chapter.

*Note:* The major purpose of my slipping in this information is not to teach you, because what you get out of it in one reading is minimal. Instead, I hope to convince you to begin studying personality types. If you recognize the four basic personalities and know how to relate to each one, you can deal more effectively with your mate, your children, your coworkers, your neighbors, your friends, and everybody else.

# *What Makes You Tick, and What Turns You Off?*

Knowing your basic personality type is the first step in determining who you are. Next, you need to use that information to figure out what makes you tick. One way to do so is to ask yourself, "What do I need?" Table 5-1 gives the simple answer for each personality type in the DISC system.

| Table 5-1 | Who You Are and What You Need | |
|-----------|------------------------------|-----|
| *If You Are a(n)* | *You Need* | *And an Environment That Is* |
| Directive, dominant person (High D) | Power and authority | Fast-paced, creative, with the authority to shape the environment, overcome obstacles, and get results |
| Interactive, influencing person (High I) | Acceptance; to be liked by others | Fun, fast-paced, with plenty of team activities |
| Supportive, stable person (High S) | Genuine appreciation and security | Steady-paced routine that sees tasks through to completion; plenty of harmony |
| Competent, cautious person (High C) | Respect; to be right in your opinions and work | Predictable, with careful planning and clear objectives and requirements |

You also need to think about what shuts you down or robs you of interest. Again, go to the DISC model and find the line that describes you in Table 5-2.

| Table 5-2 | Who You Are and What You Fear or Resist |
| --- | --- |
| *If You Are a(n)* | *You Probably Fear or Resist* |
| Directive, dominant person (High D) | Being taken advantage of |
| Interactive, influencing person (High I) | Loss of social recognition |
| Supportive, stable person (High S) | Loss of security and the unknown |
| Competent, cautious person (High C) | Criticism of your work or opinions |

Now that you know what makes you tick and what turns you off, consider your strengths. Ask yourself these questions:

✔ What things have helped me to be successful so far?

✔ What do I do that doesn't make me tired when I do it?

✔ What works for me?

✔ What do others say that I'm good at?

✔ When am I operating at my optimum levels?

Combining your strengths with your known personality style ought to ring some bells for you and give you direction. And when you have direction, being motivated is almost a natural state.

# What Do You Want Out of Life?

The question is, what do you really want out of life? Are you money-motivated or service-oriented? Knowing the answer to this question is part of knowing what motivates you and contributes to your happiness and success.

## Making money: A powerful motivator

Do you aspire to a big house, a healthy bank account, a big car, a home in the country, exotic vacations, expensive jewelry and clothing, and so on?

Those material ambitions are not necessarily wrong — if you pursue them with the right mindset. In many cases, numerous people benefit from one person's prosperity. For example, if you're an extraordinarily successful salesperson, selling useful goods or services, you put literally hundreds of people to work supplying those goods and services. However, if your method of acquiring those material goods is opening sweatshops, paying substandard wages, creating intolerable working conditions, and literally taking the joy of life and freedom from those on whose backs you're riding, you are pursuing those material ambitions with the wrong mindset.

If money motivates you, you probably don't want to pursue a career such as minister or elementary school teacher, because those types of careers are not particularly high-paying.

## Service: Helping others to grow

If your joy and excitement come from teaching and helping other people to grow, you find much satisfaction in showing others how to succeed in life. Just making lots of money won't satisfy you if you're service-oriented, because service-oriented people need to see how their money and their time at work can be of service to others.

Many service-oriented people have helped me to grow throughout my life. For example, my first-grade teacher taught me to read; my boss in the grocery store meat market taught me the beauty of free enterprise. My history teacher at Hinds Community College taught me to love history and to have compassion for other people. The owner of the Yazoo City, Mississippi, *Herald* taught me financial responsibility through the paper route she assigned to me. Every one of those people played a major role in my life, and I fully believe that they were so effective in helping me and others to grow because their motivation in life was service to others.

# Choosing Among the Types of Motivation

Motivation comes in many forms, and what motivates one person may not motivate the next person at all. In this section, I talk about some of the various ways to motivate yourself. Look for the carrot, the milestone, and the prize in each type (Chapter 4 tells you more about those stages of rewards), and think about which types may work for you personally.

# Gain motivation through personal growth

When you develop your skills, improve your thinking capacity, or increase your knowledge of topics, thus making you more valuable to yourself, your family, and your employers, you are acquiring assets that you can utilize throughout your whole life. Growth motivation has the additional benefit of making you feel good about yourself. That's a benefit because the way you feel about yourself has a direct bearing on the way you perform.

As a child, you felt good when you did well on a test, were promoted to the next grade, got elected class president, or received special recognition because you accomplished some worthy objective. You can get that same feeling as an adult by volunteering to head up a community project; by being the best salesperson, employee, spouse, or parent; or by coaching a team that your child participates on.

Personal growth requires commitment, goal-setting, and responsibility; you can't just say "I'm going to grow" and expect it to happen. But when you work to, say, acquire new job skills and are promoted or given a pay raise as a result, your confidence grows, and your feelings of self-worth increase.

Growth motivation feeds itself. Fortunately, *habit* enters the picture. When you get in the habit of reading, attending seminars, listening to educational tapes, and working with a mentor — all of which help you grow as an individual — your motivation is far more likely to become permanent.

# Be motivated by gratitude

One morning in Houston, I caught a taxi to a breakfast session before a seminar at which I was speaking. As I stepped into the cab, I greeted the driver with my usual enthusiasm, saying, "Good morning! How're you doing?" His answer was, "Praise God! I am in America!"

For the short ride to the facility, I heard one of the finest sales talks on America and free enterprise that I've ever heard. It was truly incredible! The cab driver told me about the joys of being granted rights that were precious to him, living in a free society, and having an opportunity to do what he wanted to do. When I inquired about his background, he told me that he was a health care professional from Nigeria, but he was far more excited about being a cab driver in the United States than a health care professional in Nigeria.

As I exited the cab, I thought to myself, "Isn't that something! The man was a white-collar professional back home and is a cab driver here, but he's far more excited about his freedom and opportunity here." I've often wondered why people who are born in a free-enterprise environment with unlimited opportunities have a tendency to take those opportunities and blessings for granted. Much to my regret, I didn't get his address to follow up on our conversation, but I'd lay odds that he is no longer driving a taxi. He probably is working toward owning the cab company or has been recruited by some professional to bring that same commitment, excitement, and enthusiasm to a better-paying career.

My immigrant friend quickly turned to motivator that morning. During our short taxi ride, his enthusiasm led him to give me some rules for success:

- ✔ Pay your bills. You got the goods or services, and you owe money for them, so pay for them.

- ✔ Obey the laws. Laws aren't made to cramp your style; they're intended to enable you and everyone else to live and operate freely and safely in a society that offers enormous rewards.

- ✔ Keep your eyes on God. God is in charge; He's the one who made you, and if you follow His example, you have the best chance for being successful.

- ✔ Run from lazy, crooked people. They get you in nothing but trouble, they're not good examples to be around, and you should avoid them at all costs.

- ✔ Make your workplace your home. When you start working somewhere, do so with the idea of being there forever, but perform as though your job is on a day-to-day basis. That way, the company has confidence in you and trusts you to do the right thing because they know that you don't want to foul up a home where you're going to spend many years.

- ✔ Love and honor your boss. He or she can be helpful to you, and you can be helpful in return — it's a two-way street. Most of the time, when you show the respect and honor due your boss, your boss is going to honor and respect you.

- ✔ Keep your promises. "If your word is no good, then eventually you're no good" — that's what my mama always told me. You have to be dependable so that people trust you. When you keep your promises and do your best on the simple things, you are inevitably rewarded with better jobs and better opportunities.

- ✔ Mind your own business. I suspect that if time hadn't run out, this point wouldn't have been the final one, but here it is: When you row your own boat, you don't have time to mind other people's business. And when you're doing a good job, your own business is really all the business you can handle.

Needless to say, this motivator was motivated by the cab driver who was excited about his dream and having the opportunity to live it. He had set his goal long ago. He was living his dream. He wasn't waiting until he could get into something better; he was performing with the opportunity he had. He was happy with what he had and was enthusiastically giving life his best shot. That, my friend, is marvelous preparation for a better tomorrow.

## Let activities motivate you

Walking, reading, traveling, praying, lifting weights, listening to music or motivational tapes, setting goals, finding something to laugh about — all these activities serve as their own kind of motivation. Get busy!

Each of these activities requires a decision to get involved and take physical action, reinforcing the idea that motivation is your responsibility. I often hear people say that they aren't motivated to do a particular activity. The rule is to go ahead and do it — and then you *are* motivated to do it. Feelings simply aren't dependable sometimes. If everyone waited until they felt like doing something, I'm afraid that most people's careers would be derailed early on.

One of my favorite examples of letting activities motivate you is people who are involved in organized sports. Many times, they don't feel like practicing when they go to practice. However, after they get involved in the athletic endeavor, they start feeling like practicing. Another example is reading. Reading certainly is a choice, yet the act of reading something exciting literally starts the flow of dopamine, norepinephrine, and serotonin, as well as the endorphins in your brain, according to Dr. Forest Tennant. These neurotransmitters physiologically energize you, so they are definitely motivators.

## Use humor to get motivated

A good joke book is a marvelous way to generate a good laugh. Or try reading a few comics each morning to get your day started. Laughter gets those neurotransmitters to flood your brain, which physiologically energizes and motivates you to get into action.

A number of years ago, according to legend, television and movie star/comedian Carol Burnett was getting out of a taxi when her coat accidentally got caught in the door. The driver, apparently in a hurry, pulled off without seeing Carol's plight. Fortunately for her, traffic was heavy and he couldn't go very fast, but she had to run hard to keep up with the cab and not be pulled down and run over. A passerby saw what was happening and alerted the driver to the emergency. The cab driver stopped, opened the door, and Carol was freed. The driver asked her, "Are you all right?" The winded but witty Carol replied, "Yes, I'm fine, but how much more do I owe you?"

Several months ago, I was on a call-in radio talk show, and a lady who was down in the dumps gave me a call. Her voice was sad, and she was almost crying as she lamented, "I am 55 years old, I have never done anything with my life, and it's too late now." I then said half-seriously, half-mockingly, in sort of a chastising tone of voice, "Ma'am, how old did you say you are?" She repeated her statement, "I'm 55 years old, I've never done anything, and it's too late now." I laughingly said, "Ma'am, you are just a spring chicken! As a matter of fact, does your mama know where you are?" With that, she broke out in spontaneous laughter, and for the next several minutes I was able to share some things with her that lifted her spirits.

Do I think that her spirits were permanently lifted as a result of that comment? No. But when I got the lady to laugh, she was willing to listen. When she was willing to listen, she was receptive to the next input in her mind, which was of a positive, instructional nature. I encouraged her to continue listening to uplifting information and inspiring music. I urged her to associate with people who have a good attitude, to get on an exercise program, to join the library and start a regular reading program, and so on. She agreed to do those things, which can help her attitude over the long haul. If a good, hearty laugh lifted this woman's spirits and caused her to laugh at herself (which is healthy) and take positive action, won't it do the same for you if you give it a chance?

## *Motivate yourself through misery*

The following story depicts self-motivation at its best:

My son-in-law, Richard Oates, had not really done a great deal with his life. He had tried desperately to succeed as a rock singer, but despite having genuine talent and a commitment to that objective, he was struggling for survival. One evening when he and my daughter Cindy were in Sacramento, Richard was scrounging around for quarters to feed the washing machine and dryer when a thought suddenly hit him: "I've got too much ability to be in this situation." Though he may not have acknowledged it at the moment, he was not just unhappy; he was actually miserable being where he was because he knew that he was capable of doing more.

The next day, Richard went to a small home builder and applied for a job. He was hired to sweep up and clean out just-completed houses. That first day, he did more than two workers normally did, and his employer asked him whether he knew anything about finishing (meaning the doors, windows, crevices, and so on). He replied that he did because he had worked with his stepfather as a carpenter. The next day, he did more finishing in one day than two workers generally did, and he was offered a full-time job. After a year, he realized that the size of the builder's operation limited his future. He applied for and got a job with one of the nation's biggest home builders. In a matter of about 18 months, he was a superintendent, doing an excellent job. His and my daughter's desire to live in Dallas moved them there, and today he's doing a marvelous job as the chief operating officer of Ziglar Training Systems.

I seriously doubt that Richard had that course of events as his objective when he was scrounging for quarters that night in Sacramento, but the important thing that his story shows about the success journey is that the trip starts with a thought that leads to action — *self-motivation!* When you do each task full-speed-ahead to the best of your ability, an amazing number of doors begin to open. His self-motivation then was spurred by his miserable circumstances. His self-motivation today is an intense desire to help as many people as possible by distributing personal growth and training programs, and he's doing a great job.

## Know that losing can — and should — be a motivator

At the end of the 1996-97 basketball season, Michael Jordan was the proud possessor of another MVP trophy for the championship series — the fifth time he had won that trophy. This accomplishment was fully as rewarding as the conclusion of the 1996 season, when he led the Chicago Bulls as they stormed through a record-setting season of 72 wins and only 2 losses. Then he was at his best during the championship games against Seattle.

Jordan had come back and had shaken off the rust that had accumulated during the 18 months he spent playing baseball in the minor leagues. However, there's more to the story. When he decided to rejoin the Chicago Bulls during the last portion of the 1994-95 season, he was confident that he would quickly return to form. On occasion, he did show flashes of brilliance on the court, but he struggled much of that season. His return to glory was thwarted by the Orlando Magic in the semifinals.

The disappointing experiences took their toll on Jordan, who said that those disappointments motivated him to bounce back. He even thanked the Orlando Magic for giving him the incentive. Jordan had learned that he couldn't just come back — he had to work harder than before he left. He used the adversity of defeat as a catalyst to train harder in the off-season. In the 1995-96 season, he was back on top of his game and was again the premier player in basketball.

# Smile

Generally speaking, the first thing you notice when you meet a person is the smile — or absence of a smile — on his or her face. Very few things influence for the good and give more encouragement than a sincere smile. English essayist Joseph Addison said, "What sunshine is to flowers, smiles are to humanity. They are but trifles, to be sure, but, scattered along life's pathway, the good they do is inconceivable."

Your smile can motivate the people who see it, and the smiles of others can motivate you. Your own smile can motivate you, too, and not just when you see it in a mirror. Put a smile on your face, even when you don't feel like smiling, and pretty soon that smile seeps inside and cheers you up. In radio broadcasting classes, students are told to smile when they talk into the microphone, even though the listeners can't see that smile, because talking with a smile on your face makes you sound more friendly and warm. Listeners can *hear* you smile.

Try deliberately putting a smile on your face, and you'll see. You may feel at first as though your smile is forced, but as people react favorably to your cheerful demeanor, their manner puts you in a good mood, and I think you'll find that your cheerful act becomes genuine.

# Draw motivation from completing tasks

Recently, my daughter Cindy and I were walking and, as always, having a wonderful time being together and sharing ideas. She told me that when she first started using a goals planner, she didn't like it, considered it a burden, and had a tendency to leave it behind. However, she said, over a period of time she began to realize that each time she checked off a completed task, she experienced a feeling of accomplishment and satisfaction that encouraged her to get busy on the next task. In short, accomplishment made her feel good about herself and prepared her to handle her next assignments more effectively. That's motivation, and it came from taking an action that she initially didn't want to take. The motivation started externally (I really encouraged her to use the planner), but the choice to continue taking that action was hers (internal).

# Motivate yourself by motivating others

Doing something for someone and then finding out that your action had a significant impact on that person's life is one of the truly great motivating factors. What can and should be even more motivating is knowing that sometimes the things you do that impact a person's life are so small that even you are unaware of them.

---

# Dress up and you'll feel "up"

The scene was a beauty contest at the Heritage Manor South Nursing Home in Shreveport, Louisiana. The youngest contestant was 67, the oldest 91. I was the escort for my sister-in-law, Eurie Abernathy, who was 73.

I've never been behind the scenes of a beauty contest before, but this one generated incredible excitement. At 4:00 p.m., the residents gathered for an early evening meal so that they could properly prepare for the 7:00 beauty contest. Promptly at 5:00, the 13 contestants headed for the beauty shop, where the resident beautician worked her magic. The ladies then retired to their rooms to dress in their best. Later, they gathered in the "holding room" to prepare for their grand entrance.

A feeling of anticipation ran through the room. Some of the contestants sat quietly; others were nervously laughing and talking with each other. Each time anyone commented on how beautiful they looked, the contestants glowed with delight. Who would win was the topic of much discussion.

Finally, the contest was on, and all too quickly it was over. Tremendous applause broke out when the winner was proclaimed. Everyone cheered for her as she accepted her bouquet of roses and made a speech. Then she sashayed up and down in front of the delighted guests, staff, and other contestants. All agreed that the evening was magnificent.

Big deal? You bet it was! For a moment, the participants relived their youth. Their obvious delight in being dressed up and made over was a real tonic to their spirits. Yes, humans really are social creatures. No matter what your age, recharging your engines socially helps cheer you up. Nothing shakes up the doldrums like a beauty contest or a family dinner party or a nice evening out. All work and no play truly does make you dull. So add a little sparkle to your life — dress up, laugh, or even giggle. Do it often, and it will not only make your day but also enrich your life.

---

Teaching someone a simple lesson can turn out to be a life-changing or enriching experience for that person. Someone taught Einstein that 2 + 2 = 4. Someone taught Johann Sebastian Bach the musical scale, and someone taught George Washington — and you — how to read.

### Passing it on motivates the motivator

John Howard Payne walked dejectedly through the streets of Paris toward the cold garret where he slept. Misfortune and sickness had overtaken him. Suddenly, a door opened and light streamed through. Into the arms of a man who stood upon the threshold leaped happy children and a wife beaming a welcome. The door closed. Darkness fell again. The incident had happened in a twinkling of an eye, but that night in his attic, tears streaming down his face in the candlelight, Payne wrote the song, "Home, Sweet Home." A simple incident in a time of distress proved to be an open door through which a splendid vision — the home that awaits you — could be seen.

When Payne was inspired by a simple but beautiful scene, he turned that motivation into immediate action and enriched the lives of countless others as well as his own. Try it yourself!

### Giving for motivation

When my daughter shared with me her success with a goals planner (see "Drawing motivation from completing tasks," earlier in this chapter), I was motivated, and from this exchange comes another lesson on motivation. When you give others sincere compliments for something they have done for you or indicate that their life has been an inspiration to you, you inspire them, just as Cindy inspired me. Motivation also comes from giving, especially when that giving makes the other person more effective in any area of life.

## Seek encouragement

Former Notre Dame football coach Lou Holtz tells the following story:

A fellow was driving on a slippery country road when he slid into a ditch. He walked to a farmhouse a short distance away and approached the old farmer, who received him warmly. When the motorist described his problem, the farmer said that he didn't know whether he could help the young man or not, but he would do what he could. He explained that his old mule, Dusty, was blind and somewhat hard of hearing. The farmer hitched up the old mule and hooked him to the frame of the car. Next, he got behind old Dusty and in a loud voice said, "Pull, Charlie, pull!" No response. Once again, in a loud voice he said, "Pull, Billy, pull!" Nothing. Then, in a still louder voice, "Pull, Sally, pull!" Not a move. Finally, he said, "Pull, Dusty, pull!" and Dusty proceeded to pull the car out of the ditch.

The grateful motorist, somewhat puzzled, asked the farmer, "You had only one mule and yet you called out to Charlie, Billy, and Sally, with no response. But the minute you called out to Dusty, he pulled the car out of the ditch. Why did you do it that way?"

The old farmer smiled and said, "Well, Dusty's getting a little old and doesn't believe he's as strong as he used to be. As a matter of fact, he's gotten downright negative, and if he'd thought he had to do it by himself, he probably couldn't have. But when he thought he had three other mules helping, he gave it his best shot and did it all himself."

The message in this story is twofold: One, you probably can do a great deal more than you realize. Two, a little encouragement from someone else helps you do even more.

## *Harness the best motivator: The Golden Rule*

The purest and most effective of all motives is the Golden Rule: Treat other people the way you want to be treated. You do so not because you're going to get benefits yourself, but because it's the right thing to do and because you want to do it.

I always express the Golden Rule in a slightly different way — namely, that you can have everything in life you want if you will just help enough other people get what they want. Understanding that this rule is a *philosophy* and not a *tactic* is extremely important. You don't say or do something for someone else with the expectation of that person returning the favor. Doing a favor in order to get a favor is manipulation, and manipulation simply doesn't work. Eventually, the victim of your manipulation feels deep resentment and avoids you at all costs.

Several years ago, I injured my knee while bowling and was left with a noticeable limp for several days. The night after my accident, I spoke in Omaha, Nebraska.

After my introduction, I went hobbling out on stage. The master of ceremonies put the microphone on me, and I could almost hear the audience thinking, "Look at how Zig is limping! He's hurt, but bless his heart, I bet he's going to do the very best he can!" Oh, I knew that I had the complete attention and sympathy of that audience!

I don't understand the therapeutic value of having a microphone attached to me, but my knee quit hurting when the microphone went on. For the next 60 minutes, I was up and down, stooping, squatting, entertaining, pleading, and instructing. I felt no pain and didn't limp during those 60 minutes. However, the moment I took off the mike and stepped down from the stage, my knee gave way and I fell.

What happened is simple: For 60 minutes, I concentrated on the audience. The instant I took the microphone off, I stopped thinking about my audience and started thinking about myself.

The message is clear: When you direct your motivation toward benefiting others, you're more effective than when you're thinking only about yourself. I felt good when I was concentrating on others; I fell when I turned my thoughts to myself. This is another way of saying, "You can have everything in life you want if you will just help enough other people get what they want."

# Part III
# Putting Together a Strategic Plan

The 5th Wave — By Rich Tennant

@RICHTENNANT

YEAR 1 - GET RESCUED
YEAR 2 - GET RESCUED!
YEAR 3 - GET RESCUED!! NOW!
(FOCUS MORE)
YEAR 4 - GET RESCUED
(SCREAM LOUDER!)
YEAR 5 - BUILD GOLF
RESORT

"My thinking has changed a little this year."

# In this part . . .

Armies never go into battle without a plan. Coaches don't send players into a game without a plan. Chefs don't begin preparations for a great meal without a plan. And you can't start down the road to success without a plan, either.

In this part of *Success For Dummies,* I help you formulate a personal plan for success. Chapter 6 walks you through figuring out what you *really* want, Chapters 7 and 8 discuss setting goals, and Chapter 9 deals with motivation — a central issue in putting together a good plan for success in your life.

# Chapter 6

# Deciding What You Want Out of Life: The Choices You Make to Get What You Want

*Y*ou are *what* you are and *where* you are because of countless choices that you've made during your lifetime. Each choice has an influence, however slight, upon your path in life. You can choose to be cheerful, or you can choose to be gloomy. You can choose to be rude, or you can choose to be courteous. You can choose to love your neighbor, or you can choose to hate your neighbor. You can choose to be sober, or you can choose to be drunk. You can choose to be an asset to society, or you can choose to be a detriment to society. You can choose to eat sensibly, or you can choose to indulge in unhealthy eating habits. You can choose to be prosperous, or you can choose to be broke. You can even choose to be mentally healthy, or you can choose to literally destroy your sanity. When you understand that every choice has an end result, you place yourself in a position to become successful in every area of your life.

Each choice that you make takes you either toward what you want in life or away from your heart's desire. The goal of this chapter is to help you identify whether you're on- or off-course, based on the decisions and choices you've made, and to get you heading down the right path if you aren't there already.

---

## Getting help from relationships

Probably in no other phase of life are your relationships as important as they are in the fulfillment of your dreams. Accomplishing all your goals without help is difficult, if not impossible. Along the way, you have to have help and encouragement.

In addition to encouraging relationships, you need those people who love you enough to deal with the difficulties you have and the faults and frailties that are a part of your make-up because you're a human being. Sometimes your severest critics are your best friends, because they challenge you. Often, negative people, who say that you can't, provide the inspiration that makes you persist until you get there. We all prefer people who encourage us in our dreams, but the combination of the two makes the difference.

---

In this chapter, you can find step-by-step guidance for finding out whether your dreams are reachable or even desirable. The answers you give to the questions you're asked determine the choices you make about how to proceed with your life plan. This question-and-answer process makes decision-making simpler than you've ever imagined.

# Taking Inventory

You are where you are right now because of the choices you have already made, so taking at look at the past helps you understand the true impact that choices have on your life. You should take inventory of everything you have and everything you've done that has any significance. These things happened because of a series of choices that were made *for* you as a child and *by* you as you matured.

## Asking yourself a question

What do you really want out of life? Reflecting on that question can save you an enormous amount of time and heartache. An extremely high percentage of college graduates end up in a field unrelated to what they majored in, which leads me to think that most people wander through their childhood, teenage years, and young adulthood with no clear concept of what they want to do with their lives. Many people pursue goals that are set or influenced by someone else, but pursuing those goals, if they aren't also *your* goals, doesn't produce maximum satisfaction or significant accomplishments. The sidebar "Was it his goal?" demonstrates this point well.

## Was it his goal?

Some time ago, I had the privilege of having dinner with a group that included former University of Georgia head football coach Vince Dooley and his wife, Barbara. Mrs. Dooley shared with me that the one thing she emphasized to her sons was that they must never think in terms of growing up to become coaches. Her husband had been a successful coach and athletic director, but he was away from his family much of the time.

The Dooleys' youngest son, Derek, became a lawyer and joined a prestigious firm at a lucrative salary. After a year, he announced that he had resigned his position and signed on to be a graduate assistant football coach at one-sixth of his law firm salary. His mother was particularly chagrined and found the news hard to believe.

However, Mrs. Dooley reported that, a year later, her son was literally bouncing all over the place and was the happiest he'd ever been. He explained to his parents that he had to resign from the law firm because he knew that in just two or three more years, the standard of living would have imprisoned him. He also knew that one day he would look back in regret at not having done what he really wanted to do.

Derek's move took character and courage, two of the most important qualities of success. My prediction: He's going to do "better than good" as a coach.

The beginning point for the momentous undertaking of figuring out what you want from life is a note pad, a quiet spot, and time to ponder the question at length. Think along the lines of "If I were absolutely certain that I wouldn't fail, and if I had all the resources necessary to get there, what would I really want to be, have, or do?" Let your imagination run wild, and permit no judgment to follow the impulses that you put on that piece of paper. List everything you can think of; I help you narrow down the list later.

Don't use money as your yardstick, but don't eliminate it as a desirable goal. Money is frequently the result of performance and service, but making money your prime goal influences other choices to a large degree.

## *Knowing that you gotta have a dream*

After you complete that long list, let it sit for a day or two or even a week. As you revisit the list, ask yourself these questions to help pinpoint which goal on that list is truly your prime ambition and dream:

- ✔ If I reach this prime dream, my major goal, will I be both happy and healthy?

- ✔ In my quest for this dream, will I still be able to have many friends and have good relationships with my family, friends, and coworkers?

- ✔ How secure will reaching this dream make me?

- ✔ Is this goal something I will love to pursue for a lifetime?

- ✔ What obstacles do I need to overcome to make my dream a reality?

- ✔ Am I dreaming this dream because I know that my parents or mate want me to do this particular thing, or will I pursue this goal because it really is my heart's desire?

- ✔ What can I work on now to enable me to fulfill these dreams? If I want to play first violin in a symphony orchestra, write novels, own my own business, become a physician, and so on, what are the first steps I must take?

- ✔ Whom should I seek as a teacher or mentor to help me reach this dream?

- ✔ What is the appropriate timeline for achieving this dream? (Or can I really set one?)

- ✔ Do I have the talent, knowledge, and discipline necessary to reach this particular goal?

Obviously, you need to use good judgment and common sense in the evaluation of your skills versus what you want to do. Let your imagination run wild when you make the initial list, but be honest with yourself now. Being realistic at this point saves you time and possible grief later.

Dreams are important, and you must have them to reach your full potential. First, you get the dream, and then the dream gets you. Always keep in mind the words of Anatole France: "To accomplish great things, we must not only act but also dream, not only plan but also believe."

## Deciding wisely

To make your dreams a reality and achieve the balanced success you seek, you must make good decisions. Because wise decisions are so vital to the fulfillment of your dreams, the rest of this chapter talks about the decision-making process. For example, if you desire to be a marathon runner, you should turn down the offer of a cigarette. If you want to be an FBI agent, you don't involve yourself in any illegal activities. If you want to be accepted at a particular college, you find out what its requirements are and decide to exceed them.

TRUE STORIES

# He knew what he wanted

A mother asked her small, quiet, thoughtful son an important question: "What would you like to be and do most of all?" I'm confident that she wasn't prepared for the answer she received. The young boy looked at his mother and said with conviction, "I want to be big and I want to be athletic."

His answer appeared to have one serious problem — namely, that his entire family was small in stature. So his mother was faced with a dilemma, which she met head-on. She explained the family tree to him and said that although he might not be able to do anything about being big, he could do a great deal about being an athlete.

For a long time, it appeared that his mother was wrong on the latter point, because this small, shy, introspective youngster was all thumbs. He was the last one chosen for pickup games, regardless of the sport. He was also the first one cut from the baseball, football, basketball, and soccer teams. When he was in the ninth grade, after one more failed effort, his coach took him aside and asked him why he continued to pursue the impossible dream; he simply wasn't cut out to be an athlete. Because he was such an excellent student, why didn't he concentrate on developing his skills in other areas and simply enjoy watching other athletes perform?

For most youngsters, this conversation would have dealt a devastating blow, but the youngster the coach was talking to was Merlin Olsen. Not only had he started to grow, but he was also developing the speed and coordination that enabled him to become an All-American high school football player and later, at Utah State, an All-American college defensive player. In addition, he graduated magna cum laude, was on the academic All-American team, and received virtually every award that can be granted an athlete.

As a professional football player, Olsen made the Pro Bowl 14 times. Those of you who aren't football fans may remember him for his roles in television's *Little House on the Prairie* and *Father Murphy.* Today, he is a highly respected member of a number of organizations, excels at public speaking, and has helped raise more than a billion dollars for the Children's Miracle Network.

Here's the message: Hold on to your dreams. Work hard at them like Merlin Olsen did, but keep in mind that at the foundation of your dreams lies the kind of person you are. The kind of person you are determines the height of your climb, and the depth of your belief is the determining factor in the realization of your dreams.

## Keeping your dreams

Your integrity, commitment, acceptance of responsibility, and willingness to take the necessary steps to fulfill your dreams reveal the kind of person you are at the very core of your being. Many people dream but are unwilling to take the necessary steps to realize that dream. Sir William Osler, one of the most prominent physicians of this century, put it this way:

"To know just what has to be done — then to do it — comprises the whole philosophy of practical life."

One of the steps toward realizing a dream is to have patience. Give your dream time, and you give it a chance to happen.

# Understanding the Decision-Making Process

At this exact moment, you are where you are because of the choices you have made in your life. Many of those decisions were relatively easy for you. You don't call a board meeting to decide whether to wear a tie or go casual for the day, nor do you sweat over whether to say hello to the next person you see. Yet every choice you make is a prelude to other choices, which are influenced by your initial choice.

Most choices — what you eat, the clothes you wear, the route you take to work, which shoe you put on first, and so on — are made by habit. Even tradition can make you base your choices on habit. Maybe you always spend $50 per family member for birthday gifts, so you spend that amount again this year, even though you missed work for two months due to illness and you're still trying to catch up on the bills. Being truly realistic about the choices you make means making *conscious* decisions. Life doesn't blossom by living it in rote fashion.

As choices become more difficult, you need to involve more thought in the process. Your experience; your position in the family, company, or community; and the consequences of the decision all weigh into how much time and thought you give the decision.

Bert Lawlor said, "Decision and determination are the engineer and fireman of our train to opportunity and success."

# *Knowing That Where You Stand Influences Where You Sit*

The position you occupy — whether in a company, in a family, or in any other relationship — has a direct bearing on the decisions you make. If you work in your company's marketing department, for example, you're probably gung-ho about any legitimate method of getting your product and/or business in front of the people who are in a position to buy. You may not be quite as cost-oriented in making decisions as the head of the accounting department is. That individual probably regards direct-mail advertising as an expense, whereas in marketing you regard it as an opportunity to generate income.

When you're confronted with a choice that affects not only you but also other people, the process becomes more complicated. Before making any decision that involves more than one person, get input from all sides. One decision you should make right up front is to be open-minded and empathetic to the other people's needs and desires. That decision enables you to get along better with the other people, bring balance to the process, and maintain harmony, which is important for achieving maximum effectiveness.

When a decision impacts a number of people who are part of your team, remember that decisions are more likely to be implemented effectively and enthusiastically when everyone on the team feels like an important part of that team. When possible, include the others in the process. If involving them is either impossible or impractical, understand that their acceptance of your decision depends on your credibility. If you have a track record of using mature judgment and doing what's right, your decision is more likely to be well received.

## How experience relates to decision-making

Your experiences *influence* your decisions but don't necessarily *control* them. For example, a set of twins had an alcoholic father. One of them became an alcoholic, the other a teetotaler. When both twins were asked why they did or did not drink, the alcoholic son said, "Well, what else would you expect? My father was an alcoholic." The teetotaler said, "Well, what else would you expect? My father was an alcoholic." Each had the freedom of choice, just as you have the freedom to choose thousands, even millions, of times in your lifetime.

You can't always depend on experience; sometimes you don't have any. The Pilgrims certainly didn't have any experience with the New World when they arrived there, nor did the first astronauts have experience in moon landings. As Laurel Cutler says, "There is no data on the future."

# Deciding in Advance When Possible

Many decisions can and should be made in advance. For example, in rearing our children, my wife and I decided that any conduct that was either illegal or immoral was not open for debate. Otherwise, just about everything was on the table for discussion. That decision saved considerable time and avoided contention.

Another decision that we made in advance was that we would not permit our children to do things that would put their lives in jeopardy. For example, one Friday evening, our son, who had just gotten his driver's license, wanted to go with a buddy to a football game roughly 90 miles from home. Our decision was no, but not necessarily because we didn't trust his driving skills, though his experience was limited. When we combined that fact with the fact that traffic is generally heavier and a higher percentage of drunks are on the highways on Friday nights, we didn't think that his going to the game was wise. We made the decision easily because we had formed the basis for the decision in advance. We assured him that his day would come, but not now.

Follow a simple rule: If you can take the worst and the potential gains are significant, take the risk. In this situation, we couldn't take the worst, and the potential gains were insignificant, so we didn't give the okay.

## Making principle-based decisions in advance

Here's another example of decisions made in advance: I was offered a chance to buy stock in a restaurant chain that was just getting started. The first three restaurants were phenomenally successful, and I could have bought ground-floor stock. My decision was easy, however, because I had decided in advance that I wouldn't invest in a business that sells liquor. I have seen too many tragedies occur as a direct result of drinking, so I chose not to take any part in furthering the alcohol business.

An anonymous speaker once said, "When one bases his life on principle, 99 percent of his decisions are already made."

## Heeding good advice from Harry Truman

When I think of Harry Truman, I think of his famous quote, "The buck stops here." Truman also said, "If you can't stand the heat, get out of the kitchen." He knew that, as president, he would receive a considerable amount of criticism — some justified and some unjustified. Truman felt that, despite the inevitable criticism, a leader has the ultimate responsibility to make the final decision.

TIP

## When you ask for advice, listen carefully

Some people follow their doctor's advice — and that's good — but patients do foul up. You may misunderstand instructions, too. Consider this tale, for example:

A 91-year-old man had an annual physical. Two days later, his doctor saw him strolling down Main Street with a young woman who couldn't have been a day over 75. They were holding hands and grinning from ear to ear when he spotted his doctor and said, "Thanks, Doc. I did what you said — find me a friendly mamma and be cheerful." "No," replied the doctor, "I said, 'You have a heart murmur and be careful.'"

Seriously, most people ask for advice on occasion and, even as they are being advised, start the picking and choosing process about what parts of the advice they'll take and what parts they'll leave behind. You don't have to take advice just because someone gave it to you, but understand that you're on your own when you choose to heed only portions of the advice you're given. If you see a road sign that indicates an S-shaped curve ahead and has the speed limit listed at 15 mph, and you decide to slow to 15 mph but drive in a straight line, you're in big trouble. Don't blame the advisor if you use only bits and pieces of the advice and it doesn't work for you.

Much of the world is indebted to Harry Truman because of the things he started. Winston Churchill called him "the man who saved Western civilization." Truman put a stop to traditional American isolationism. He pushed through the Marshall Plan to rebuild Western Europe after World War II. He made efforts to end segregation in the U.S. Armed Forces and federal civil service.

Truman had only a high school education, but he was a marvelous student, particularly of history. When Israel became a nation, the State Department advised him not to recognize it. The thinking was that Israel was a small nation surrounded by a hostile enemy, and recognizing the nation was imprudent for the U.S. However, Truman knew his history, and 11 minutes after Israel became an independent nation, he recognized its sovereignty. That took courage. You should realize, however, that he really made that decision long before Israel became a nation.

Truman also gave the go-ahead to drop the atomic bomb. Today, considerable controversy surrounds that decision, but the military unanimously felt that, as horrible as it was, using the bomb saved millions of Japanese and American lives. That decision also took courage, but most significant decisions take both initiative and courage. Truman had an abundance of both qualities — that's why history has been so kind to him.

Success and leadership demand that you make tough, important, and even controversial decisions — often in advance — if you expect to reach your full potential.

# Making Good Decisions

I'm amazed at how little thought is given to making decisions. How they are made, why they are made, and when they are made are often taken for granted. People expect to think seriously about decisions like marriage, having a child, or accepting a job offer that moves them hundreds of miles away from family, but they give little thought to the actual process of decision-making. Taking too much time to make a decision can be as harmful as never making the decision. Making decisions too hurriedly can also cause years of regret. You need to keep several points in mind as you make little decisions as well as life-changing decisions. The following sections walk you through the decision-making process.

## Thinking it through

If you allow yourself time to think the decision through to its possible conclusions, you ultimately make better decisions. Ask yourself the following questions:

- ✔ How would I feel if this decision appeared in tomorrow's paper?

- ✔ What impact will this decision have on my mate and children?

- ✔ Am I compromising my integrity with this particular decision?

- ✔ Is this decision consistent with my personal, family, corporate, or team goals?

- ✔ Will this decision take me closer to or further from my major objective in life?

- ✔ Am I making this decision under the influence of people who have a great deal to gain if I say yes (or no)?

- ✔ Are the people who are influencing my decision looking after my best interests or their own?

Answering those questions makes your decision a little clearer and more certain.

**CESS AT WORK**

# Making sure that a decision fits your long-term objectives

I'm frequently invited to join various organizations, usually with the promises that I "wouldn't have to do a thing" and that "the financial benefits would be considerable." Others have offered me opportunities to "get rich quick," but the methods, on occasion, were questionable. I've always declined those offers on the basis of our mission statement, too. Even if they were legitimate, if the method didn't fit with our mission statement, the answer was always an easy no. That decision — made in advance — has been a tremendous time-saver.

# Enduring temporary pain for long-term gain

We recently had to make a decision at our company that cost us several hundred thousand dollars and played havoc with our budget. However, the decision was a matter of integrity, so we really had no choice. The going was temporarily tough, but in a matter of months, things were back to normal. Shortly thereafter, the wisdom of the decision became even more obvious.

I personally know someone, who has asked to remain anonymous, who refused a promotion because she knew that her married boss was trying to make a move on her. Her refusal resulted in her one and only firing, but she has never regretted her decision. She did not compromise herself, she got an even better job, *and* she met her husband as a result of the job change. Good, logical decisions are rewarded with good end results.

## Weighing the benefits versus risks of decisions

When you're making decisions, one factor should always be paramount in your mind: What do you have to gain and what do you have to lose by saying yes? For example, at age 18, one of our daughters wanted to take up skydiving. Skydiving might have increased her confidence and been an exciting and perhaps even pleasurable experience — those are the positives. But what are the negatives? She could well have paid for those advantages with her life. With that risk in mind, we strongly discouraged her from skydiving, and she agreed and acceded to our wishes. What she had to gain from the experience compared to what we all might have lost made the decision an easy one.

## Depending on your faith

The most important question you need to ask in the decision-making process is "Will this choice or decision line up with my faith?" If a decision is extremely important yet very difficult to make, I ask God to give me wisdom in the matter, and then I ask my mentor as well as my theological advisors for their counsel. I also pray about the decision and ask what is to me the most important question: "What would Jesus do?" Please understand: I know that God isn't going to send me a fax and tell me exactly what I should do, but if I'm headed in the wrong direction, I know that He won't give me peace of mind concerning the issue.

I also strongly believe that in seeking God's wisdom and direction, folks with little or no formal education or resources can excel in their personal and work lives.

Eugene Peterson's *The Message* gives an eloquent picture of wisdom's benefits: "Wisdom is the art of living skillfully in whatever actual conditions we find ourselves. It has virtually nothing to do with information as such, with knowledge as such. Wisdom has to do with becoming skillful in honoring our parents and raising our children, handling our money and conducting our sexual lives, going to work and exercising leadership, using words well and treating friends kindly, eating and drinking healthily, cultivating emotions within ourselves, and attitudes toward others that make for peace. Threaded through all these items is the insistence that the way we think of and respond to God is the most practical thing we do. In matters of everyday practicality, nothing absolutely nothing, takes precedence over God."

## Listening to your feelings

Many times, you simply don't know what to do. You consider every angle, weigh all the facts, consult with experts, and even pray about the decision, and still no distinct answer comes. That's when you need to take a quiet walk and listen to your instincts. Many times, you instinctively know the right decision to make, particularly when making major decisions. I encourage you to act on those hunches.

An unknown author said, "A hunch is creativity trying to tell you something." Hunches, also known as *intuition,* are only recognized by those folks who listen to their feelings.

# My Decision-Making Process

Great golfers — those who win on the PGA Tour — establish a routine that they follow religiously before every shot. This routine relaxes them and gives them confidence that they will hit the shot well. Similarly, following a procedure before making significant decisions, whether you make them individually or with counsel, gives you confidence that you will make good decisions.

I go through this procedure and follow some basic rules every time I make a significant decision:

- ✔ If I'm really tired, I don't make significant decisions (except in emergencies). If someone is pressing me to decide something "right now," unless an immediate decision is critical, I say, "If I have to decide now, the answer is no. After I have had a chance to catch my breath and review the facts, there's the possibility it could be yes." Then I put the ball back in his or her court and ask, "Do you want my decision now, or should we wait?" Because he or she usually receives some benefit from my yes, that person always agrees that waiting is best.

- ✔ I like to determine the maximum benefit of a decision, assuming that everything goes my way. Then I ask, "Suppose nothing goes my way? Suppose this doesn't develop and materialize as I expect it to? What is my maximum exposure? What would I lose?"

- ✔ For significant business-related decisions (and these must be really big), I run them past our board of directors. These people are successful in their businesses and professions and have a considerable amount of knowledge, experience, and wisdom, all of which are musts in the decision-making process. I get their advice and follow their recommendations, with good results in most cases.

  If the decision is too minor to involve the board but I still want input, I get my family together to look at the pros and cons.

## Missing some of them is okay

Sometimes you have to sacrifice what you want to do for, or with, your family at the moment for their long-range benefit. The financial gain may be so significant that the family would be best served in the long-term by making the decision a financial one. A great deal can be said about the benefits of parents being at every Little League game, soccer game, school play, recital, and so on of their children. But if your family is struggling financially, attending a Little League game when a substantial sale is hanging in the balance or a promotion is staring you in the face is using poor long-term judgment. Don't ignore the fact that your long-term responsibilities are to provide for your family. On those occasions, you can miss that game, recital, or whatever without guilt.

However, if you find that you're *always* deciding in favor of the business, the long-term family price is too high. I'm careful to note any trends in my decision-making, and if the financial consideration starts to win too often, then the decision goes to the family, almost regardless of the financial benefits that may come my way. Common sense and mature judgment are in order.

In my own life, the business choice almost always won for too long. But many years ago, I became sensitive to what was happening and started making better, more balanced decisions, particularly as they related to weekends with the family.

✔ I like to pray about my decisions. I ask God to help me see the truth of my motives and to lead me in the way I should go. If I'm about to make an unwise decision, I simply don't have peace about that decision, and I consequently act on that feeling of unease. I ask myself, "How will this decision affect all the areas of my life — personal, family, career, financial, physical, mental, and spiritual?" Obviously, not all decisions affect all areas, but if the decision involves a financial reward but also carries considerable family sacrifice, for example, I think carefully as to whether what I give up is compensated for by what I gain.

# Prioritizing Your Decisions

Some decisions are considerably more urgent than others. Although many time- and labor-saving devices are available today, prioritizing your time and decisions is more important than ever. To succeed in the family or on the job, you need to prioritize in order to "keep the main thing the main thing."

A fascinating example of prioritizing is the following story from the *Executive Speechwriter Newsletter,* Volume 9, Number 4, about author and diplomat Clare Booth Luce.

> Luce told of her visit with John F. Kennedy when he was in the White House. She was known for her forthrightness and straightforward manner. She said to President Kennedy, "Mr. President, you must get the Soviets out of this hemisphere." They talked for a few minutes, and then the phone rang and the president left the room.
>
> Kennedy came back very excited and said, "I got my textile bill passed! Now, what were you saying, Clare?" Luce responded, "Mr. President, there are many great men remembered in our civilization. Of one man, they said He went to a cross and died so that all men's sins may be forgiven. Of another man, they said he went in search of a new route to an old world and founded a new world. Of another it is said that he took up arms against his mother country and with a motley army of rebels defeated the greatest military power on earth to found a new nation. And of another it is said that he had to hide in the dark of night as he came into Washington, and grieved for four years that the nation might be half-slave and half-free. Mr. President, of none of these great men was it said, 'He got his textile bill passed.'"

## Doing the right thing takes priority

In the early 1990s, hundreds of people were taking the state bar exam in Southern California. During the course of this demanding exam, a man had a seizure. Two individuals immediately went to his assistance. They administered CPR, called for paramedics, and attended to the man until the paramedics arrived. Their total time investment was 40 minutes. When the time allotted for the exam ended, they requested an extension because they had invested 40 minutes with the gentleman who was in dire need of assistance. The supervisor in charge ruled that no exceptions would be made, that the two had acted out of choice, and that, consequently, they would be judged accordingly. The state bar senior executive backed this decision.

Where have common sense and compassion gone? Did the supervisor think that the test-takers should have let the gentleman die? Realistically, you can't make regulations to cover every unexpected event. That's where common sense, good judgment, and compassion must enter the picture.

In many cases, a higher calling takes precedence over just going by a set of written rules. I recognize that we must have laws, but the higher law I'm talking about is a simple one that says, "Do the right thing." These two test-takers did the right thing, and if they never received their licenses to practice law in California, they could still live with themselves for possibly having saved the life of a fellow human being. On occasion, doing the right thing brings about temporary loss, but over the long haul, it puts you well ahead of the game. Doing the right thing is always the right thing.

I keep a daily list of items that I must deal with. You may find, as I have, that writing down what you need to accomplish enables you to see what needs to be tended to first. Everyone has have-to-do items and optional items on his or her list. Some things need to be accomplished by very specific deadlines, and those items are most easily identified when you make your list.

Oftentimes, the small, nagging things throw the biggest kinks in your day. Those are the items that you want to put off and skip over as you complete item after item on your list. However, giving the little things a place on your list helps you with follow-through and keeps you from feeling dread when you remember what you should have done. Write it down, prioritize, and breathe easier every day. I do.

# Forming a Plan of Action

After you make choices, you need a plan of action with which to implement your decision. Making a plan of action brings on more decisions about who should be in charge and what steps are involved. Continue making these smaller decisions until you develop a plan of action that you sincerely believe will succeed.

Be entirely honest with yourself and ask, "Do I have the courage to follow through? Do I have a double agenda? Am I making this decision because I want to look good, or will it benefit the company and/or the people involved?" If you legitimately care about the people your decisions affect, you ask these questions, because people really don't care how much you know until they know how much you care — about them. If you find that your motives are wrong, be prepared to back down from your decision or to live with feelings of guilt. If you find that you don't have the courage to follow through, even though you know that you should, visit with your mentor and get the support you need so that you can do what you know is right.

# Doing the Best You Can With a Decision You're Stuck With

Sometimes you don't have a choice: A decision has been made, and you must live with it. For example, say that you are promoted to manager at your company, and the previous manager had committed to constructing a new four-story office building. You ascertain that the building should be at least six stories tall, but the foundation is already in place, and construction for the first floor is complete. At this point, you can't add two floors because the foundation can't support them. Your choice, then, is to make the best of the situation and maximize the use of the four stories.

Or maybe your mate has accepted a job promotion that requires your family to move out of state. You know that the promotion is best for the family, but you regret and even resent having to leave family, friends, and a job you love. You can make the move miserable for everyone, or you can make the best of it. Either way, you end up in another state.

# Remembering That Even Bad Decisions Can Lead to Good Things

Keep in mind that you're free to choose, but the choices you make today determine what you will be, do, and have tomorrow.

Periodically, I'm asked what I would do differently if I had it to do over. I pondered that question on many occasions, and then one day I heard a woman respond to that same question. She said, "I would not do anything differently because if I did, I might not be where I am — and I really like where I am."

I'm grateful that I overheard the conversation because I realized that I feel the same way. I really like where I am. I have wonderful relationships with my wife, children, grandchildren, and in-laws, and I enjoy remarkable health. This is not to say that I haven't made mistakes, because I certainly have, particularly during those first years of marriage and child-rearing. Some of those mistakes were extremely foolish, yet many of them aimed me directly at where I am at this moment. That's an exciting and comforting feeling.

The important thing is not to follow one poor decision with another. Many times, people do exactly that: They deny the original mistake or try to cover it up, even to the extent of lying about it. That strategy isn't wise; it simply leads to a series of bad decisions. That's one of the reasons I write about the importance of integrity in Chapter 3. Integrity demands that you do the right thing so that you have fewer things to apologize for, explain away, or regret. Instead, cut your losses as quickly as possible after making a poor decision. Think through the situation and then make good choices, followed by any necessary corrective action. In other words, make the new decision based on where you are at this moment in an effort to solve the problems that the poor decision brought about.

# Why you behave the way you do

I conclude this chapter with some ideas that I encourage you to read carefully, because they explain the irrational behavior of intelligent people from time to time. Understanding these concepts helps you see how you may make irrational decisions — because you automatically reject information or knowledge that causes you to feel hurt or emotional pain. I hope that you turn back to this section and reread it from time to time, because it can help you understand why you make or made certain decisions. That understanding helps you make better decisions in the future.

Rabbi Daniel Lapin, a scientist trained in logic, explains why, despite all the evidence, intelligent people make questionable — and even foolish — decisions. *Cognitive dissonance* is the culprit, he says. Cognitive dissonance means that you choose to reject data that conflicts with an emotional position you hold. Everyone has laughingly said, "Don't confuse me with the facts! I've already made up my mind." Rabbi Lapin uses this example to validate his point.

Tests conducted in psychology departments of many universities demonstrate cognitive dissonance over and over. The rabbi references one test in particular, one that involves getting a group of people into a room, half of whom just purchased a brand-new automobile. These people think that they're waiting for an experiment for which they volunteered, but really they're being monitored in the waiting room. As they wait, they thumb through magazines. What they don't realize is that the magazines have been doctored and put there for a purpose. They contain far more than the usual number of automobile advertisements. The subjects are watched to see whether those folks who just bought a new car behave differently than those people who have not yet purchased one.

The study revealed that the people who just bought a new Volvo, for example, read only the Volvo ads, because nobody who just purchased a new car wants to discover that they could have done better by buying another make.

If a friend just bought the same model of car that you have, you may ask, "How much did you pay for it?" He gives a figure quite lower than the one you paid. You doubt it very seriously and tell your mate and friends, "He paid more for it than that!" Your mind and soul reject information that hurts. That's an important principle in understanding yourself and making better, more logical decisions.

# Chapter 7

# Focusing on Needed Goals

- - - - - - - - - - - - - - - - - - - - - - - - - - - - - - - - - - - - - - - - - - - - - - - - - - -

## In This Chapter

▶ Working the factors chart to assess where you are

▶ Understanding what goal-setting can do for you

▶ Making the commitment to take action now

▶ Deciding which goals are most important to you

▶ Forming a game plan for your life

▶ Going through the goal-setting process

- - - - - - - - - - - - - - - - - - - - - - - - - - - - - - - - - - - - - - - - - - - - - - - - - - -

*W*hen I do small seminars, I use a number of overhead transparencies. I always have the projector completely out of focus when I show the first image, and without appearing to notice the problem, I talk to the audience for a couple of minutes. It's interesting to watch all the people who point their fingers at the overhead in a friendly manner, informing me that I have a problem. At that point, I tell the audience, "Chances are good that roughly 100 percent of you believe that my overhead is 'all fouled up.'" They laugh. I've actually had people come onstage before I make that statement, heading for the projector to "help me out."

I then say, "Actually, the overhead is not all fouled up; it's out of focus. Many people's lives are very much like this overhead projector — simply out of focus. Their lives go in a dozen different directions and, as a result, they seldom accomplish their major objectives in life."

Genius has been described as the "ability to focus on one thing at a time." A study conducted at a leading university followed a group of gifted students with extremely high IQs. Of the students who accomplished significant feats, all of them were able to do so not because of their high intellect but because of their ability to focus on the objective at hand.

Most people wear many different hats. Chances are excellent that you are, in one form or another, pursuing financial resources to support yourself and your family. You are undoubtedly interested in spending time with your family and friends. In addition, you no doubt want to find out more about yourself, your life, and how to accomplish your objectives. You recognize that you need to take care of yourself physically, and wanting to rest and relax along the way is perfectly natural. You also want to be a good neighbor and contribute to society.

All those desires are natural and good, but you simply can't focus on all of them simultaneously. The objective is to focus on *what you're busily engaged in doing at the moment.*

For example, I know someone whose objective was to "get healthy." In order to do that, she needed to quit drinking alcohol, stop smoking, lose 35 pounds, and start an exercise program. She got healthy, and it only took her 11 years. What — 11 years? Yes, getting healthy is a process, and she had to start at the beginning. The alcohol had to go first. Had she tried to quit smoking while she was still drinking, the alcohol would have lowered her resistance to the urge to smoke, and she would have smoked. She had to quit smoking before she could lose weight and get in shape, because she had a hard time breathing when she exercised, and past attempts at quitting smoking taught her that she would gain weight. She quit smoking with the knowledge that she would gain weight but that she would lose it as soon as she got used to not smoking. A year passed before she was ready to exercise and lose weight. Two years later, she had lost her weight and was feeling good about herself. She had focused on breaking one habit at a time, and she methodically worked through her long-range plan for good health. Had she tried to change any two or more major areas at the same time, she would have "short-circuited" from the stress, and failure would have been imminent.

To be successful in life, you need to learn to work toward one major objective and juggle two to three short-range to mid-range goals at a time. This chapter shows you how to do just that. I show you how to identify the areas of your life that need and deserve the majority of your attention, and how balancing your life makes you better at everything you do.

# Knowing Where You Are and Where You Want to Go

Direction is important. If you don't know where you want to go, you'll probably end up somewhere you don't want to be. The often-told story of swimmer Florence Chadwick illustrates this point:

On her first attempt to break the record for swimming the English Channel, Chadwick encountered heavy seas. Fortunately, she had trained in the cold Atlantic Ocean, was in peak condition, and was prepared to do battle with the huge waves and chilling temperature.

In addition, her trainers were alongside her in a boat. They greased her body to help provide protection from the cold and gave her hot soup from a thermos. In short, she had many things going for her on her quest.

All her planning and training, however, didn't include what to do when a heavy fog set in. As the fog descended, her vision seemed limited to no more than a few feet, the water seemed to get colder, the waves seemed to get higher, and she began suffering from cramps in her arms, legs, feet, and hands. Her muscles screamed in pain, and although she was close to shore, she finally gave up her valiant effort and asked her trainers to take her aboard the boat.

Later, reporters asked her why she gave up when she was such a short distance from shore. Her answer was simple: "I lost sight of my goal. I'm not sure I ever had it firmly in mind."

The message is clear: You may not encounter a physical fog as Florence Chadwick did, but having a clear mental picture of the goal before you start is critically important. This approach enables you to see through those unexpected "fogs." When you set goals, visualize those goals, and work toward those goals, you have a far, far better chance of reaching those goals.

By the way, Florence Chadwick did exactly that and later accomplished her objective, becoming the first woman to swim the English Channel.

# You're not lost — you just need directions

The following story comes from author Dennis Kimbro in Volume 11, Number 4, of the *Executive Speechwriter Newsletter:*

"One day a traveler in a remote country town, convinced that he was on the wrong road, came to a halt in a village. Calling one of the villagers to the car window, he said, 'Friend, I need help. I'm lost.'

"The villager looked at him for a moment. 'Do you know where you are?' he asked. 'Yes,' said the traveler. 'I saw the name of your town as I entered.'

"The man nodded his head, 'Do you know where you want to be?'

"'Yes,' the traveler replied, and named his destination. The villager looked away for a moment. 'You're not lost,' he said, 'you just need directions.'"

Many of us are in the same position as that traveler. We know where we are — sometimes disappointed, dissatisfied, and experiencing little peace of mind. And we know where we want to be — at peace, fulfilled, and living life abundantly. Like the traveler, we are not lost — we just need directions.

It doesn't take much to find the high road to success, but to reach it, you need an agenda for the present. You need directions for today. *You need a purpose.* Listen to the advice that the president of Lincoln University gave to a group of incoming freshmen: "Your life can't go according to plan if you have no plan!"

# *Get a checkup from the neck up*

For years, one of my favorite expressions has been "We all regularly need a checkup from the neck up." Unfortunately, the checkups that most people give themselves are fairly limited, which is one reason why people too often fail to see their true potential. With that caution in mind, I encourage you to slow down and make the following checkup as thorough as possible — this evaluation doesn't have a time limit. Whether the checkup takes you five minutes or five hours is of little importance; the results are what you're interested in.

The purpose of this checkup process becomes clearer as you go along: You simply must know where you are if you're going to get where you want to go. You must have a starting place. After you complete the checkup, you can look at the wheel of life (see Figure 7-1) and measure whether your life is in balance and whether you're on your way to getting more of the things that money can buy and all of the good things that money can't buy (see Chapter 3 for more information about this definition of success).

On a scale of 1 to 5, with 1 being an area needing much improvement and 5 being an area needing no improvement, rate yourself on these charts. Mark each item carefully, because these are the key factors in each goal-setting area of your life. If a factor does not apply to you, simply write **n/a** (for not applicable) in the space provided. In the space provided for Other, list any significant items that apply to you that are not listed. You will know them automatically. For example, if you have asthma, you can list your condition in the physical section and rate how you take care of yourself in relation to that condition. List your achievements as well as the areas in which you may earn a low score.

| *Physical* | *Rank* | *Financial* | *Rank* |
|---|---|---|---|
| Appearance | | Proper priorities | |
| Regular checkups | | Personal budget | |
| Energy level | | Impulse purchases | |
| Muscle tone | | Earnings | |
| Weight control | | Living within income | |
| Diet and nutrition | | Charge accounts kept current | |
| Stress control | | Adequate insurance | |
| Endurance and strength | | Investments | |
| Regular fitness program | | Financial statement or "bottom line" | |
| Other | | Other | |

| Spiritual | Rank | Mental | Rank |
|---|---|---|---|
| Believe in God or a higher power | | Read/listen to motivational material | |
| Involvement at place of worship | | Associate with uplifting people | |
| Share faith with others | | Positive outlook | |
| Prayer | | Happy most of the time | |
| Religious study | | Stable moods | |
| Inner peace | | Contentment | |
| Other | | Other | |

| Family | Rank | Personal | Rank |
|---|---|---|---|
| Relationships with parents | | Recreation | |
| Relationships with siblings | | Friendships | |
| Relationship with mate | | Community involvement | |
| Relationships with children | | Hobbies | |
| Relationships with extended family | | Quiet time | |
| Spend time with family | | Growth time | |
| Enjoy time with family | | Consistent life | |
| Make family a priority | | | |
| Other | | Other | |

| Career | Rank |
|---|---|
| Challenged | |
| Happy | |
| Chance to advance or grow company | |
| Growing in career knowledge | |
| Continuing education | |
| Goals program in place | |
| Are where you want to be | |
| Other | |

Now circle every item that you scored 2 or less so that you can easily see which areas need improvement. Look at your scores in each area and determine what number is your average. (If you're like most people, two numbers will dominate each section.) Use the number that you have the most of for your score. Keeping the results of this chart in mind, complete the wheel of life (see Figure 7-1). Starting with your score on the mental spoke, draw a line clockwise to your score on the spiritual spoke and continue all the way around the wheel of life. Is your circle big and round? Lopsided? Extremely small? The visual aid of the wheel tells you instantly how balanced your life is. The closer you are to having a full-sized, rounded circle, the better balanced you are.

What you learn about yourself and your life from the wheel can help you as you complete the procedure for qualifying your goals, listed later in this chapter.

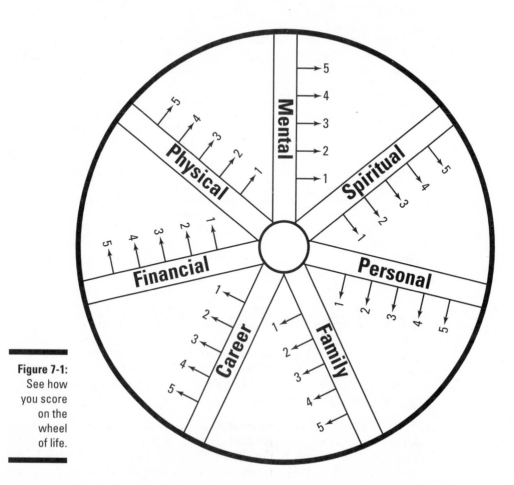

**Figure 7-1:**
See how you score on the wheel of life.

## *Make sure that you really want to become what you think about*

An article in the May 24, 1995, *Dallas Morning News* stated that ex-British leader Harold Wilson had died in his sleep. By coincidence, on that date, I picked up a book entitled *Creative Responsibility* by Thomas Sikking (a book that I have owned since 1980) and read a rather interesting excerpt concerning goals.

Sikking tells the story of an 8-year-old English boy who wanted to be the Prime Minister of England. He imagined himself as the Prime Minister and even had his picture taken as a schoolboy standing in front of Number Ten Downing Street. Becoming Prime Minister was not only his goal, but he could also envision himself as Prime Minister of England — and yes, his name was Harold Wilson.

Somebody once said that you become what you think about. As evidenced by Harold Wilson's story, there's certainly an element of truth in that saying. Understand that your *thinking* determines your *actions,* and your *actions* determine your *rewards.* When you don't set specific and conscious goals, says Sikking, that which you think about most of the time becomes your goal, and you're always a success — even if you succeed at being a failure. And when you fantasize about the negative things in life, you paint mental images that you will have a tendency to work toward and eventually become.

A student who fears failing a test has a better chance of failing than a student who is confident about passing. Think about it: Both students probably base their feelings about the test on facts. The student who fears failure probably hasn't done the work that he needed to do, such as organizing his notes or studying, so he thinks, "What's the use? I'll probably fail anyway." The confident student has done all the things mentioned and knows that she has studied enough to make a good grade on these tests.

# Understanding the Power of Goals

The power of goal-setting is that setting concrete goals enables you to go beyond first base. It's one thing to want something to happen but quite another to actually set a goal to make it happen and work toward that goal in a conscious, dedicated manner.

You may think to yourself, "I've tried that goal-setting stuff before and it didn't work." Most people agree that goals are important; some can even give you a list of their goals. But the majority stop there, never taking action toward those goals. Until you clearly list your goals *and* have a written plan attached to them, you aren't a goal-setter or a goal-achiever — *yet.*

Maybe this story will help to convince you how important goals are.

A dream of all golfers is to have a hole-in-one. That was one of my dreams for many years. However, despite the fact that on two occasions I came within one inch of having that hole-in-one, I never really consciously lined up for a shot thinking, "I want to get that hole-in-one." I thought in terms of hitting a good shot, swinging like I should, and getting the ball close to the pin, but I never thought in terms of knocking the ball right in. Then one day I got a letter from my friend Tony Greiner, who had been a PGA assistant pro for many years. Although he had seen several of his friends get holes-in-one, he had never gotten one himself. But in 1994, he said, he realized that he should include everything on his "wild idea list," including a hole-in-one. Less than 30 days after writing it down as a goal, he got his hole-in-one!

As I read what Tony had done, in the back of my mind I started thinking, "You know, that should be a specific goal of mine, too." I took considerably longer than Tony to realize my goal, but on August 11, 1997, playing at the Greensboro (North Carolina) Country Club, the length of the uphill shot was 147 yards, but in the hole the ball went! I can't describe the feeling of ecstasy that came over me when that ball went into that cup. Now, every time I line up on a par three, I'm thinking, "Hole-in-one." I've been playing golf for 45 years, and I don't know exactly when I'm going to get that second hole-in-one, but I have an idea that I won't need another 45 years to do it!

# Taking Action Now!

A psychologist surveyed 3,000 people and asked them, "What do you have to live for?" More than 90 percent were simply enduring the present and waiting for something to happen — for their children to grow up, until they could afford a trip, or for someone to die. Most of them were waiting for tomorrow, forgetting that all you ever have is today because yesterday is gone and tomorrow never comes.

The sad thing about this survey is spelled out in one word: *waste.* What an incredible waste of time, talent, ability, and potential!

One of those immutable laws of physics says that a body at rest tends to remain at rest until and unless some internal or external force acts upon it. If you wait for an external force to act upon you, you may be waiting forever; that external force may never come. That's why you need to take the bull by the horns, seize the moment, decide what you want out of life, develop a plan of action, and pursue that plan until something positive happens. Even if you fail to accomplish the objectives you set, you are infinitely better off in the seeking than you can possibly be in the waiting. If you're thinking that you don't have the desire to *do* anything, I suggest that you read Chapters 4 and 5 on motivation.

Before you finish this chapter, I hope that you will decide that "tomorrow" has finally arrived and that today you will begin the process of setting and achieving your goals. The beginning is the most important step of all. Obviously, you can't finish something that you never start. Today, I encourage you to move from the role of "gonna-doer" to the role of "I'm doing it, and I'm going to do even more." The goal-setting process enables you to become the goal-setter and goal-reacher that all successful people are. The beautiful thing is that this goal-setting process works regardless of what your goal is. And because it works on all goals, it enables you to achieve the balanced success that everybody wants but that most people only dream about.

# Setting Your Priorities

The number of goals to be, do, and have is limitless, so learning how to prioritize which goals are worth your time and attention is very important. The following list can help you do so.

1. **Identify everything that you want to be, do, or have. (I cover this process in Chapter 6.)**

2. **After 24 hours, ask yourself why you chose each item. If you can't articulate in one sentence why a goal is significant and appropriate at this time, delete that goal from your list.**

3. **Ask yourself, "Do the goals I have show balance?"**

   If not, eliminate the out-of-balance goals.

4. **Ask yourself these five questions:**

   • Is it really my goal?

   • Is it morally right and fair to everyone involved?

   • Will it take me closer to my long-range objectives?

   • Can I commit myself to start and reach this goal?

   • Can I see myself reaching this goal?

   *All* these questions must have a yes answer.

5. **Give each goal this final test of the basic eight wants in life:**

   • Will it make me happier?

   • Will it make me healthier?

   • Will it make me more prosperous?

   • Will it increase my security?

   • Will it help me make more friends?

- Will it give me more peace of mind?

- Will it improve my family and other relationships?

- Will it increase my hope for the future?

Often, you're not aware of the importance of some of the choices you make until years later, but that doesn't alter the fact that it's always the right time to prioritize and make the right choice. Author Glen Van Ekeren said, "When you know what your values are, making decisions becomes easier."

One of life's ironies is that many parents work overtime or even take second jobs in order to provide their families with more of the "good things" in life. However, study after study has revealed that when given the choice, the children for whom Mom and/or Dad are working so hard would prefer more of their parents' time. In other words, the most precious gift that parents can give is themselves. Your presence says more than a thousand presents ever can.

# Crossing Your Bridges Before You Come to Them

Author Bruce Barton said, "I do not like the phrase 'never cross a bridge until you come to it': It is used by too many men as a cloak for mental laziness. The world is owned by men who cross bridges in their imaginations miles and miles in advance of the procession. Some men are born with more imagination than others, but imagination can, by hard work, be cultivated. Not by mere day-dreaming, not by lazy wondering, but by hard study and earnest thought."

Barton is talking about having a game plan for life. If events aren't planned, they seldom take place. Folks who start each day with no objectives in mind too often end the day with nothing accomplished. This doesn't mean that you should follow a 24-hour-a-day work schedule; allow *some* flexible time in your schedule for personal growth, family, recreation, exercise, reading, and so on. However, if you're going to meet your responsibilities in life, you need to have a plan of action, and that plan of action should include dedicated study, earnest thought, and specific, predetermined objectives. A plan like that gives you a balanced life.

# Getting SMART About Your Goals

First, take a look at how simple goal-setting really is. The acrostic SMART (supplied by an unknown author) shows you how easy it is to identify a goal.

✔ **The S stands for *specific*.** Write down every goal you have and put boundaries around it so that you will know when you have achieved that goal. Saying "I'm going to be a better manager," "I'm going to be a better parent," "I'm going to get a better education," or "I'm going to get a new house" simply isn't effective. You must *specifically* and *clearly* identify your target. The more details you give, the more likely you are to get excited about your goal and develop the passion that enables you to focus on reaching that target.

If you decide that you are going to be a better parent, for example, you must determine "better than what." Better than being too tired after work to spend time helping with homework? Better than being impatient and yelling at the children over every little thing? Better than never saying "I love you"? You can see that this procedure doesn't get to the solution quickly enough. Instead, decide to spend time with your child, be patient, and hold your tongue — except when it comes to saying "I love you." Get specific!

✔ **The M stands for *measurable*.** Not every goal is measurable. For example, you can't specifically measure how much your self-esteem has improved, although you may know and feel that it has improved. However, putting measures on a goal helps you to realize at any moment where you are in pursuing that goal. For example, if your goal is "I want to be a better parent," how can you know when you have reached "better"? Instead, write some smaller, specific steps that move you toward the larger goal of becoming a better parent. You can set up steps such as the following:

- I will tuck my children into bed lovingly and carefully every night this week and spend those last few minutes talking with them.

- At breakfast, I will be careful not to be uptight or grouchy. Instead, I will be pleasant and cheerful and assure my children that today is going to be a good day.

- This week I will spend at least one hour in one-on-one time with each of my kids, doing something that each child particularly enjoys.

At the end of the week, give yourself a checkup to determine whether you've completed each particular step. If you successfully reach your mini-goals each week for several weeks, you will see measurable progress toward your larger goal. (Yes, you have become a better mom or dad.)

The more effectively you can measure a goal, the more likely you are to complete the goal because progress itself is a tremendous encourager. Even though you can't see progress by the day, you will by the end of the week — or certainly by the end of the month.

✔ **The A stands for *attainable*, and the R stands for *realistic* (meaning that the goals are out of reach but not out of sight).** Many people set goals that are completely out of reach, whereas others set them so low that they represent no challenge. Both approaches are unrealistic. Many people knowingly set impossible goals so that they have a built-in excuse for not achieving those goals. This practice is clearly self-defeating. You must have a realistic chance of reaching a goal, combined with a belief that you will reach it, in order for it to have long-range motivational impact.

For example, because weight loss is on the minds of more than two-thirds of the people in the United States — and well it should be — people often fall victim to empty promises, such as "lose 30 pounds in 30 days without getting hungry and without exercising!" That goal isn't realistic. You didn't gain that weight in a month, and you're not going to lose it in a month. Permanent weight loss comes only with a change in lifestyle.

I was on that weight-loss roller coaster for 24 years before I understood that the problem was my lifestyle. I spent too much time on the couch, too much time at the dinner table, and not enough time exercising. My weight-loss goals, though temporarily attainable, were permanently destined to fail because I expected to take the weight off quickly and keep it off permanently without an exercise program. However, when I realized that I was able to get into a smaller suit after every ten pounds of weight loss, I was motivated to lose the ten pounds so that I could "justify" the purchase of a new suit. That goal was realistic and attainable, and I accomplished it in 1973. Because my lifestyle changed, the weight remains off.

✔ **The T stands for *timely*.** You need an accomplishment-point if the goal can be measured in that way. Formulate a plan of action with a deadline that enables you to measure your progress in incremental steps — as I did by aiming to lose ten pounds at a time.

Simply determining that you will, say, clean out the garage by a specific date helps you to claim the time that you need to accomplish the goal. You may choose to spend two hours each Saturday for the next six Saturdays or spend an entire Saturday on the project. Name the increments according to your needs. Make your goals fit your lifestyle.

## You can't do it for 'em

You can't set goals for other people. (The exception is a small child who has not reached the goal-setting stage yet. Setting goals for small children should be done pleasantly and cheerfully as a fun thing rather than a "gotta-do" thing.) When you try to set a goal for your children to go to college, for example, you're working on something that is impossible for *you* to achieve. However, if you plant the seeds of that goal in your children's minds, talk about it regularly, and encourage them in their studies and commitments, the odds that they will attend college go up dramatically.

Similarly, you can't set a goal to change your coworkers. However, when you change yourself, chances increase substantially that they will change also.

List things that you can do to give yourself cause to celebrate — losing five pounds by your high school reunion, making four more sales calls, getting along with a negative coworker, and so on. Anything that gives you a sense of accomplishment has a positive impact on you. Even though you can't measure all goals, you *can* measure the progress you have made toward them.

# A Process That Works

Before you decide whether a single goal fits into your goals program, you should work that goal through this eight-step process.

*Note:* This process can take considerable time — but it can save you much time and frustration by eliminating goals that are not for you at this time and helping to identify what you need to focus on now.

## Step 1: Set a goal that's SMART

As explained in the preceding section, your goal must be SMART: specific, measurable, attainable, realistic, and timely. Remember:

- ✔ Some goals must be big.
- ✔ Some goals must be long-range.

✔ Significant goals must be broken down into smaller parts to ensure daily accountability. (For example, if you want to lose 50 pounds this year, you can break that down to a goal of 4 pounds a month or 1 pound a week and then figure out how many calories you need to cut out or burn off to achieve that weekly weight loss.)

✔ You should set no more than four goals to work toward on a daily basis.

✔ You should seek divine guidance and direction on each goal.

## Step 2: Identify what's in it for you

People often fail to reach their goals because they concentrate on the costs rather than the benefits. "If I lose the weight," they reason, "I'll have to give up this and do that." Or "If I quit smoking, I know that I'll gain weight and be miserable and difficult to get along with."

Instead of concentrating on the negatives, think of the benefits that you're going to enjoy. As you set goals, make a list of the tangible rewards that will be yours when you reach each goal. Each time you begin to ask yourself whether pursuing a goal is worth the effort, simply take out the list of benefits and read them aloud again.

## Step 3: List the obstacles that stand between you and your goal

You need to identify obstacles in order to be realistic and avoid being surprised. People have shared with me many times that they had no idea that pursuing such-and-such a goal was going to be so demanding, require so much effort, take so long, and involve so many unexpected pitfalls. Careful planning in advance eliminates much of this disappointment, but you must understand that you can't always see the roadblocks ahead. That's why commitment, attitude, responsibility, and focus on the benefits remain constant necessities. Patience is also extremely important. Just remember that by keeping yourself focused (there's that word again!) on the goal, you can see the benefits and not just the obstacles.

Very few people get excited about obstacles. A mammoth traffic jam when you're in a big hurry or a bad cold just before a long-planned vacation doesn't create excitement in your life. Disappointments or setbacks of any kind are seldom viewed with enthusiasm. Yet those very difficulties should generate excitement, if for no other reason than that overcoming obstacles makes you strong and enables you to soar to greater heights.

In some cases, the obstacle actually speeds your move upward. For example, an airplane lifts from the ground faster and moves higher more quickly when it lifts off *into* the wind. Air is the only obstacle that a bird in flight typically faces, yet without the air, the bird falls to the ground instantly. Some birds (most notably the eagle) ride air currents to as high as 10,000 feet with no effort of their own other than to extend their wings.

If you recognize your ability, spread your wings, and take advantage of the air currents (obstacles) around you, you may be able to fly higher and accomplish more in the process. For example, how many people do you know who have been fired or laid off and ended up in a position far more enjoyable and better paying than the one they left?

A prophet of old says that problems produce patience, patience produces persistence, persistence produces character, character produces hope, and hope produces power — and power is what you need to accomplish your objectives. The goal-setting process gets you motivated, which releases that power to accomplish your objectives.

## Step 4: Seek counsel and guidance

You may need a counselor of some kind to carefully identify what skills are required to reach your goal. Seeking guidance also helps you along the way because a counselor can help you carefully prepare a plan of action for dealing with obstacles.

For example, when I was overweight, I sought the advice of my physician, Dr. Ken Cooper, to find out exactly how much weight I needed to lose and to find out about a sensible exercise and eating schedule. My daughter sought the advice of a counselor at college to determine the best way to reach her educational goals.

## Step 5: Consider who can help you

Being able to achieve your objective starts with your family and, in many cases, extends to include your coworkers, your boss, or your mentor. You need to carefully identify friends who can be encouragers — people to whom you are close enough to share your goals and who can check your progress and encourage you. These actions enable you to maintain your focus and keep your eyes on the goal itself. You'll find that some goals are absolutely impossible without the direct help of friends. The man in the next story can testify to that!

A man's barn floor was inundated with 29 inches of water because of a rising creek. This Nebraska farmer recognized that he had a substantial problem, but he also believed that he could find a solution. His objective was to move his entire 17,000-pound barn to a new foundation 143 feet away.

The man's son devised a latticework of steel tubing and nailed, bolted, and welded it on the inside and the outside of the barn. To this framework, he attached hundreds of handles. Then the man invited 344 volunteers to pick up his barn and move it to the new foundation.

Actually, the process was reasonably simple. After just one practice lift, the volunteers slowly walked the barn up a slight incline to the new foundation. Interestingly enough, each volunteer had to lift less than 50 pounds, and moving the barn to its new foundation took only three minutes.

Two great lessons come from this little story:

- ✔ A considerable amount of thought and preparation on the parts of the man and his son set the stage. They had to have a specific, workable plan of action. (See Step 7.)

- ✔ What one or two people would have found impossible, the community found relatively simple. Teamwork goes a long way to solve many problems.

The next time you encounter a difficult situation that you can't handle alone, think about these two principles and put them to work.

## Step 6: List the skills and knowledge required

I'm quite sure that the man wrote out a list of things that would have to be done to move his barn. He probably included in that list who had the skills and knowledge to do each task. Lucky for him, his son had the skill and knowledge necessary to weld handles onto the barn and the mathematical capabilities to know how many handles were needed and how far apart they needed to be placed. This step is necessary when you enlist others to help you achieve your goal.

## Step 7: Develop a plan of action

How are you going to incorporate all the preceding steps and bring them together so that you have a specific plan of action to overcome the obstacle, enjoy the benefits, develop the skills, and work with the people involved? The plan must be specific; you must have a commitment to reach that objective; and you must have a daily checklist so that you know what you're doing toward reaching that goal. Weekly and quarterly checklists help you to be certain that you're making progress on your mid-range and long-range goals and that you're not getting sidetracked along the way.

## Step 8: Set a deadline for achievement

A goal without a deadline is nothing more than a good intention. You must set a start time and a finish time for every goal that you set; you wouldn't be setting the goal if you had already done the things that you needed to do to achieve it. Without a time frame, it is too easy to procrastinate, especially on the goals that take months or even years. Plan your completion date, and when you arrive there with your goal accomplished, reward yourself.

# Rewarding Yourself for Accomplishing a Goal

You need to give yourself a reward of some kind when you reach your objective. Getting yourself a new suit of clothes or spending a weekend with your mate in a nice hotel or resort may be an enticing reward. If finances are tight, consider an evening out, a day off, or a drive in the country — just make sure that the reward is one that you thoroughly enjoy. It doesn't cost much to rent videos and pop a little popcorn. Or check out a book from the library and reward yourself with uninterrupted reading time. Take a long, relaxing, hot shower or bubble bath. Light candles, put on soft music, and light a fire in the fireplace. Pamper yourself — you've earned it. Regardless of your budget, you can find ways to reward yourself. (In my case, a good reward is a round of golf.)

A lot of thought and effort goes into creating a workable goals program for yourself, but you will be rewarded in many wonderful ways if you discipline yourself to follow your plan to achieve your goals. After you make goal-planning a part of your life, you'll wonder how you ever made it from one year to the next without a program. Direction determines your destiny.

# Chapter 8

# Be Positive: Getting Started Toward Your Goals

- - - - - - - - - - - - - - - - - - - - - - - - - - - - - - -

## In This Chapter

▶ Staying positive when everything looks bleak

▶ Using the talents that you've been given

▶ Pursuing your goals with hope

▶ Daring to do the unusual

▶ Knowing that failure is a short step toward success

▶ Identifying the ultimate success attitude

- - - - - - - - - - - - - - - - - - - - - - - - - - - - - - -

**S**o you've figured out what you want in life, you've set specific goals, and you're ready to work toward those goals. Now what? I've written this chapter to help you start off on the right foot, with the right attitude. Stories about individuals who have overcome the odds encourage you to move toward your dreams. And reading these types of stories helps you to understand that when bad things happen or you suffer a setback, you are temporarily delayed, not finished. Seemingly negative things become the teachers that help you to be the best you can be.

# Be Positive That You Need and Want to Achieve a Specific Goal

According to William James, the father of American psychology, the attitude that you have in approaching an objective is the single most important factor determining whether you reach that objective. I like what Bishop Fulton J. Sheen said about how attitudes relate to goals: "When we walk towards the light, the shadow will always follow, but when we walk away from the light, the shadow is always in front of us."

In other words, as you walk toward the light of success (that is, the lure that draws you toward doing something significant), the shadows (your fears) grow dimmer and dimmer because every step gives you confidence that you can accomplish your objective. However, if you turn your back and refuse to use your abilities by setting worthwhile objectives, each step you take away from the light (the goal that you know you want to set) makes the shadow grow larger, longer, and more ominous. The fear grows that not only will you not succeed because you didn't set one objective, but also that you'll be too fearful to attempt future objectives. Those who don't set goals and plan their futures seldom have futures that are in line with their capabilities. Even more important, failure to plan indicates that non-goal-setters are not *really* interested in their futures.

Sheen is on to something — he's absolutely right. Discouragement is a tremendous factor in the lives of many people, particularly those who strive with all their might and see little progress toward a worthy objective.

---

# I am a winner . . .

. . . because I think like a winner, prepare like a winner, and perform like a winner.

. . . because I set high but attainable goals, work toward those goals with determination and persistence, and never stop until I reach them.

. . . because I am strong enough to say "No!" to those things that would make me less than my best, and to say "Yes!" to the challenges and opportunities that will make me grow and improve my life.

. . . because total commitment is my constant companion, and personal integrity is my lifetime mentor.

. . . because I am learning to avoid the tempting shortcuts that can lead to disappointment, and the unhealthy habits that could result in defeat.

. . . because I have a well-earned confidence in myself, a high regard for my teammates and coworkers, and a healthy respect for those in authority over me.

. . . because I have learned to accept criticism, not as a threat, but as an opportunity to examine my attitudes and to improve my skills.

. . . because I persevere in the midst of obstacles and fight on in the face of defeat.

. . . because I am made in the image and likeness of my Creator, who gave me a burning desire, a measure of talent, and a strong faith to attempt the difficult and to overcome the seemingly impossible.

. . . because of my enthusiasm for life, my enjoyment of the present, and my trust in the future.

— William Arthur Ward

Everyone faces discouragement. My friend and mentor Fred Smith observes that, from time to time, everyone enters periods of "darkness." He makes the analogy that you are in darkness while driving through a long tunnel in the mountains, but you are making progress toward the light. The key word in that last sentence is *progress*. Even though a curve in the tunnel may prevent you from seeing the light, you have every reason to believe that light is not far ahead.

Fred points out that you should never lose sight of the good in a bad experience. He says that in weaving a beautiful tapestry, the dark threads are needed to bring out the full beauty of the pattern that's formed by the lighter threads. He also observes that you don't develop perseverance in good times — only during tough times. Understanding this lesson is important.

The next time you're discouraged, don't stop — you're making progress, and light is just around the corner. Use your time in the darkness to increase your knowledge, and your progress will come faster and be more certain.

## He dreamed the impossible dream

Everyone, from time to time, dreams the impossible dream. And that's all that too many people do with their lives — they simply dream. I believe that every youngster who picks up a golf club today has dreams that are exploding all over the place. This is particularly true because of Tiger Woods, who is by every yardstick available one of the most remarkable athletes ever to hit the American scene. His influence is phenomenal, and his success is truly outstanding.

However, I'm convinced that the story of Robert Landers is equally remarkable. He's pot-bellied, has long sideburns, and plays with a wide stance and a strong right grip. He holds his hands high and away and uses about a three-quarter swing. (That's not the way the PGA golf pros teach the game.) However, in 1995, he qualified for the PGA Seniors Tour while wearing tennis shoes, $2 pants, and no glove, carrying a $20 golf bag and a $70 set of clubs.

Although Robert's future is unpredictable, what he has already accomplished is amazing. This homespun phoenix, at age 50, sprang from the ashes of a back injury, poor equipment and facilities, and no training to astonish golfers around the world by qualifying for the Seniors Tour. His feat is even more remarkable when you understand that only one of every 350,000 or so amateur golfers makes the regular PGA Tour. Almost without exception, these golfers have taken many lessons, have state-of-the-art equipment, and have access to excellent practice facilities. Most of them have been groomed from childhood by outstanding teachers and have had years of competitive experience.

There are lessons that you can take from Robert Landers' experience:

- ✔ Dreams can and do come true. Landers was faced with a choice: Do something with his life or do nothing. He decided that if he practiced where he was, with what he had, he could develop a competitive game. He went for his dream.

- ✔ Landers was an awfully hard worker. Almost regardless of how he felt and how tired he may have been, at the end of each day he hit 150 to 300 golf balls. As a golfer, I can tell you that's a lot of shots.

  Because Robert was operating on a financial shoestring, and hitting that many balls at the driving range costs a good deal, I'm sure that you're wondering, "So where did he hit those golf balls?" In his own pasture. Using a mismatched set of clubs (no two of which were alike) and practice balls that had long ago seen their better days, he hit shots literally anywhere in the pasture that he could, including over his cows. He also hit balls over the barn.

Without ever having taken a lesson, Robert developed a style that suited him. The fact that he made the Seniors Tour is a tribute to his persistence and to the incredibly hard work schedule that he pursued. In the process, he faced a certain amount of ridicule, but what other people thought about what he was doing and his possibilities made no difference to him. He marches to the beat of his own drum — and that's not a bad beat to follow.

Where will Robert go now? Nobody knows. But I'm convinced that he's going to have a lot of fun and will remain the same kind of person that he is today. I hope so; having a genuine American folk hero is really neat. Go for it, Robert — and the same to you, Dear Reader.

Incidentally, if you share Robert's dream of making it to the PGA Tour, or even if you just want to lower your handicap, Gary McCord's *Golf For Dummies* (published by IDG Books Worldwide, Inc.) is must-reading for you!

## *Persistence really pays*

America has produced thousands of "you'll never make it" stories — tales of people who overcome tremendous odds to become successful. These stories appear in print regularly, and almost every day I see individuals who have lived these stories. One of the most amazing tales is that of Bobby Griffin from Bristol, Virginia:

At age 17, Bobby dropped out of the ninth grade and was told that he would never make it. His trip through life hasn't been easy, but it has certainly been one of the most exciting trips that I've ever heard about. His life truly demonstrates what persistence, hard work, commitment, and faith can accomplish.

As a young man, Bobby persuaded his dad to buy a service station and let him run it. The station wasn't an overwhelming success; running it was a real struggle. Then, in 1950, Bobby won a trip, and he and his wife, Frieda, stripped the service station's cash register of funds to buy gasoline and went to Sarasota, Florida. While in Florida, they spotted a beautiful convertible in a used-car lot. When Bobby started to step in for a test drive, the salesman stopped him because he had sand on his shoes. Then the salesman placed a piece of cardboard on the floor mat to protect it, and Bobby sat down in the car.

At that moment, Bobby had a crazy idea: Why not sell cardboard floor mats to automobile dealerships? Everybody thought that the idea was hilarious. He became the butt of countless jokes. He believed, however, that he had a good idea. He persuaded a manufacturer to produce 10,000 floor mats for him, but after he saw the 10,000 mats, he decided that they really should be red, so he hand-colored all 10,000 sets with a sponge and red paint. Then Bobby set out to make his fortune.

For the next few weeks, he lived in his car, going from town to town, facing rejection after rejection. Finally, he had another idea: sell the floor mats to banks printed with advertising and let the banks give the mats to car dealerships. The only problem with this great idea was that banks weren't buying it. His funds were running lower and lower. Frieda, a loving and supportive wife, was growing weary of constantly juggling finances and running the service station herself.

Then — BINGO! — a banker in Nashville told Bobby that he should "forget this crazy idea and go back to running his service station." However, the banker was willing to order 500 mats, provided that Bobby guaranteed that the banker would like the mats when they were delivered. At that point, Bobby was so desperate that he agreed. He sent the mats, and for the next three months, he heard nothing. His finances and the hardship of travel were taking their toll, yet his newfound faith simply would not let him quit.

His persistence paid off — just in the nick of time. Bobby's wife was strongly encouraging him to drop the project when he got the most welcome news imaginable. The Nashville banker sent him a check for the 500 mats and an order for more, including an endorsement. Bobby Griffin was on his way. The government later issued him the two patents on the floor mats that he had requested earlier.

Today, Bobby Griffin is a wealthy, generous man who gives away scholar-ships and helps numerous charities. He travels and shares his story with others. Yes, persistence and belief in an idea rewarded Bobby. Chances are good that they can do the same for you.

## *You can expect to win if you have a plan*

A classic example of facing impossible odds is a story about Digger Phelps (author of IDG Books Worldwide's *Basketball For Dummies*). In 1974, he was Notre Dame's basketball coach, and his team was preparing to meet the perennial national champion UCLA Bruins in a contest in South Bend, Indiana. UCLA was the overwhelming favorite. The gamblers had taken the game off the boards because everyone knew that Notre Dame didn't have a chance. Everybody, that is, except Digger Phelps and his team.

He prepared his players in an unusual way. On Monday after practice, he had his team go to the ends of the court and cut down the nets from each goal. If you know anything about basketball, you know that the only time players cut down the nets is when they've just won a significant game involving a championship or a victory over a heated rival. On Tuesday at the end of practice, the players again went down to the ends of the court and cut down the nets. They repeated that action on Wednesday, and by Thursday those players had become downright good at cutting down the nets. By Friday, they brought down the nets with true professionalism. Saturday afternoon, when the game was over and UCLA had gone down in defeat, the Notre Dame players cut down the nets with even more passion. They had accomplished their objective.

Obviously, I'm not saying that cutting down the nets was the reason Notre Dame won the game, but consider this: Those players got to cut down the nets after the big game because all week long, they had planned to win. All week long, they had prepared — in practices filled with enthusiasm and hard work — to win. All week long, as they cut down the nets, they were establishing more and more firmly in their minds that, yes, they really were going to win and that when they did, they would take this action. That's sound preparation.

Whatever your objective, plan to win, prepare to win, and then you can legitimately expect to win.

# *Make the Best of What You Have*

People who misjudge their abilities and don't recognize that they have certain limitations are sad to witness. They invest their lives in pursuing an objective that they have limited talent to accomplish. Many people who are following certain success rules — such as desire, direction, and foundational qualities of character — and who have many other wonderful attributes simply don't have what it takes to reach a specific objective.

Personally, I want nothing more than I want to be able to sing. I frequently get compliments on my speaking voice and am often asked if I do any singing. But the reality is that I can't carry a tune and have no sense of musical timing. When they were young, my own children asked that I not sing in church. I have to carefully watch the choir perform songs that include hand-clapping; otherwise, I would clap at the wrong time. Years ago, I recognized that I can't sing but I can talk. Perhaps you fit into a similar situation.

Antonio, the hero of the following story (which I received in a letter from Dr. Donald E. Wildmon, president of the American Family Association), certainly shared my frustration:

Antonio was a lad who lived in Cremona, Italy, during the 17th century. Cremona was a musical town where great acclaim was bestowed on those who could sing or play an instrument. As Antonio walked through the streets of Cremona with his friends, he listened to their beautiful voices. Unfortunately, although Antonio wanted to join the others in making music, his friends called him Squeaky Voice when he tried to sing. He tried to play the piano and the violin, but his skills were limited. The only thing he could do really well was whittle on a block of wood with his knife.

One day, while sitting at the edge of the street, whittling, watching, and listening to three of his friends play and sing beautiful songs, he noted that the people passing by frequently dropped coins into their hands to reward their efforts. One gentleman stopped longer than any of the others and even asked them to repeat a song. When they finished, he dropped a coin into the hand of one of the singers and then moved on down the street. Much to their shock, the boys discovered that it was a gold coin, which was quite a bit of money to give a street singer. But the man who gave it could afford to do so. His name was Amati, and he was identified as the greatest violin-maker in all of Italy.

That evening at home, Antonio thought about Amati and decided that he, too, wanted to become a violin-maker. The next morning, Antonio went to Amati's home and persuaded him to let him be his apprentice. For many years, Antonio studied with the master, and in due time his work became known throughout the world.

Antonio's last name was Stradivari. To this day, musicians still make music from his violins, which now sell for dollar amounts well over six figures. History doesn't record whether Antonio continued to gripe and complain because he didn't have the talent to sing. I suspect that he became quite happy using what talent he had. As a matter of fact, I would venture to say that he was grateful for it.

The message is clear: If you don't have the talent you want, use the talent you have. Focus on what you *can* do rather than on what you *can't* do.

## Succeeding "in spite of"

"The only disability in life is a bad attitude," said figure skater Scott Hamilton in the *Rocky Mountain News* in reference to his diagnosis of testicular cancer.

Some people succeed despite apparently insurmountable handicaps. One of my favorite stories (which I read in the September 30, 1995, issue of the *Dallas Morning News*) is that of Tony Melendez, who has thrived despite some tremendous handicaps — he was born without arms.

Tony wanted to become a priest but was denied that privilege because some functions in the priesthood require the use of arms. This setback was disappointing, but he has never let disappointments stop him.

He first started playing the guitar at age 16. Most of the time, he plays the guitar while seated in a chair with the guitar on the floor. He strums the strings with his feet and plays notes with his toes. He says that most of his early public appearances were at weddings and funerals, but over a period of time, as his skill and reputation grew, he began to enjoy the religious pieces he'd been playing. Tony says, "Christian music goes beyond just a romantic love song, but brings a gentleness, goodness, and hope that is significant."

He's had some incredible highlights in his career. He played in 1987 in his hometown of Los Angeles for guest of honor Pope John Paul II. After Tony finished his song, the Pope bounded from the elevated stage and kissed him. Melendez says that he was completely overwhelmed. Since then, he has had the privilege of playing before the Pope on three other occasions.

Tony writes much of his own music, but his entire life is not just in music. He and his wife have adopted a little girl named Marisa.

The message is clear, isn't it? When you look at what you have and use it to the fullest extent of your ability, you discover that you're not that concerned about what you don't have.

## Know That You Can Be a Great One

The heading above this paragraph contains the words that one of my early mentors, P. C. Merrell, said to me when I was struggling so hard to survive in the world of selling. His belief in me had a dramatic impact on my life. Many people have gone much further in life than they thought they could because *somebody else* thought they could.

As I was reading and thinking about the following quote from writer Zane Grey, I realized that he struck a chord that virtually anyone can relate to because it opens the doors of hope and possibility. I encourage you to read it slowly and contemplate it. As you look at the words he has put together, I believe you'll understand that you've already done most — if not all — of the things that he talks about. The fact that you've already done these things indicates that you can repeat them, which says to me that not only can you be a great person, but that you're already on the way to becoming a great person.

"These are the tests of true greatness — to bear up under loss, to fight the bitterness of defeat and the weakness of grief, to be a victor over anger, to smile when tears are close, to resist disease and evil men and base instincts, to hate hate and to love love, to go on when it would seem good to die, to seek ever the glory and the dream, to look up with unquenchable faith to something ever more about to be. These things any man can do and so be great."

# *High Hopes Help People Persevere*

If you're going to attain your goals, you must be willing to stretch and reach for your goals. The questions, "How much should I stretch? "How long should I reach?" and "What does it take to hang in there?" often arise, though.

An article that I read recently makes fascinating and exciting observations about hope. It says that people who have a great deal of hope claim to have more mental energy and have more clearly set, personally challenging goals. These folks understand that obstacles are a part of the goal-reaching process, and they focus on succeeding rather than on what may be keeping them from succeeding. Because they are better equipped to cope with life's difficulties and see past them, they are happier, healthier, and experience less stress.

Individuals with hope actively pursue their objectives, but that hope needs fuel — and the fuel is encouragement. Encouragement can come in the form of praise and recognition from friends, family, and employers. It can also come from books, seminars, and recordings. For long-range objectives, hope is especially critical, and it's something that the person who is willing to stretch seeks. Finding encouragement when you need it to keep going is your responsibility.

The article emphasizes that hope involves more than just wisdom and optimism. The author says that having hope can ensure your success in achieving goals, but being intelligent only assures that you have a *chance* of reaching those goals. The conclusion of the article is fascinating: that hope is counterproductive if your intent in seeking to fulfill your goals is to harm or take away from others in some way. What I think the author means is that you can't ride the success or happiness train on the backs of others. Taking the honest approach to reaching your goals makes the trip more fun, and you get there with a clear conscience and no regrets.

# Dare to Do the Unusual

Every coach, regardless of the sport, wants to coach winning teams. Good coaches also want to prepare their athletes for the game of life. Many of them take different approaches as to the best way to do so. Some of these approaches are unique and against the current thinking — but they still work.

## Taking an unusual approach

John Gagliardi's unusual approach to coaching football has been very successful. Only Eddie Robinson of Grambling University has coached more winning football games than Coach Gagliardi. At the end of the 1997 season, St. John's University, a small Catholic school with roughly 1,600 students, had notched 337 collegiate victories under the tutelage of Coach Gagliardi. They won national small school titles in 1963, 1965, and 1976 and have been to the Division III semifinals on four other occasions, the last in 1994.

Coach Gagliardi doesn't put his athletes through exhaustive calisthenics, nor do they tackle or run wind sprints or laps in practice. Weight-lifting isn't mandatory, and the players call the coaches by their first names. They don't spend long hours watching game films or doing anything else connected with football — their practices are limited to about 90 minutes.

This unusual coach started in 1943 as a 16-year-old, when his high school coach was drafted into the military and his teammates picked Gagliardi to coach them. They won their league championship that year, and the school hired him back. Ironically, he says that his high school coach taught him a great deal. He points out that whatever his coach did, he does the opposite. He says he observed that, most of the time, hard scrimmages kept the players banged up. He believes that because most of his players have been tackling since fourth grade, they already know how to tackle.

Coach Gagliardi has his team practice plays at full speed and believes that execution is everything. He prepares his team by putting together clips of their best plays from the Saturday before and then running that film for them on Mondays. He says that showing the players what they did right is the best way to teach.

Unusual, yes — but as Frederick Klein points out in his *Wall Street Journal* article of September 20, 1996, this kind of coaching works for John Gagliardi. Maybe this coach is on to something!

## Pursuing an unusual goal

Many people have dreams of success that are, to say the least, out of the ordinary. Most of these folks don't pursue those dreams simply because they are concerned about how it will look and what people will think. "A person in that position . . . why would he do that? Why would she do this?"

For example, I'm certain that many municipal court judges in the United States would be extraordinarily reluctant to do what a judge in Minnesota chose to do, but he obviously didn't care what others thought. The judge had always had a dream, and he recently fulfilled that youthful ambition. He became a newspaper carrier with a four-mile route after his doctor recommended regular exercise to treat his heart condition.

The judge's story intrigues me for several reasons:

- ✔ If you need to exercise (and all of us do), why not go for a "two-fer" (see Chapter 7) and make it profitable?

- ✔ Taking on the paper route shows that he still has that youthful feeling, which he's enjoying by living a long-cherished dream.

- ✔ When he collects for the paper, he is brought face-to-face with the way other people live and the way they deal with their financial challenges on a daily basis.

- ✔ Having a customer complain because the paper landed in the flower bed or a mud puddle must be sobering for a judge. And don't you wonder how he would handle a customer who was irate because the paper was late or didn't arrive at all? As a former paper boy, I can tell you that "nice" people can really let off a lot of steam when the paper boy falls below 100 percent in meeting his commitment.

All in all, I believe that this judge's paper route makes him a better judge, a better person, and probably a better family man. Those are pretty good advantages for making exercise both fun and profitable.

# Understand That Failure Is a Short Step Toward Success

One of the first things that I came to know as a rookie salesman was that every prospect who says no brings me that much closer to one who says yes. Salespeople are taught — and rightly so — that they actually are paid every time they make a call, regardless of what the prospect says. Each salesperson has an average. Some are highly skilled and experienced and may sell to one prospect out of three. Others may be just getting started and lack the "natural ability" or skill, and they may sell to only one out of ten. However, if you take the average sale, figure your commission on that sale, and divide it by the number of your average (by ten, for example, if you sell to one out of ten on the average), you realize that you are "paid" every time you make a sales call, regardless of the result. The effect of this averaging on your attitude is amazing — you're inspired to keep making those sales calls. With averages in mind, most salespeople would laughingly say after being turned down, "Man alive, this is exciting! I'm now one step closer to success!"

The same principle works in every area of life. In most cases, people who are remarkably successful have also encountered more than their share of failures.

## *Knowing where you are*

As Chapter 7 explains, reaching any destination, or plotting a course for reaching any destination, is difficult if you have no idea where you are at the moment. However, many people try to go places and have no idea where they are at many stops along the way. Look at two specific examples:

- Research proves that, everything else being equal, a salesperson who keeps records on *why* he did or did not sell to a prospect sells substantially more merchandise than the salesperson who doesn't keep records. However, a salesperson who knows not only what happened but also why it happened and *how he can utilize that information to his benefit* sells considerably more. Knowing the "why" makes it possible to take care of the "how," lessening the salesperson's inclination to kid himself about why results aren't better.

- Evidence shows that you lose weight faster and keep it off longer if you keep a detailed written account of exactly what you eat and the circumstances under which you eat. You must remember to write down everything, even what you ate on the run or while standing up, while you were in the coffee shop, or when you stopped by a friend's desk and picked up a goodie that was there for the taking. By keeping this diary, you never kid yourself about "not eating a thing."

Regardless of what you're doing, understand that if you know what you want and have a plan of action to get there (see Chapter 7 for help in coming up with a plan), you're far more likely to make more sales, lose that weight, get that education, move up the corporate ladder, and so on.

# Knowing where you're going

Not only must you know where you are when you start, but you must also plot your course as you go. Airline captains must know where they started, but they also must constantly plot their course and stay in contact with the ground personnel and with other aircraft in the air; otherwise, disaster awaits them.

You may not be faced with that type of disaster, but you can rest assured that your personal, family, and business lives are on a collision course with failure if you don't regularly assess where you are and what progress you're making.

I love the story of the battleship captain who was plowing through high seas when his radar picked up an obstacle a few miles ahead. He radioed the captain of the craft and told him that his craft was in the captain's plotted course and that he should change his course. The response came back, "No, you need to change your course." Again the captain sent a message, identifying himself and the fact that he was the captain of a battleship, and saying that for the other man's own good, he should change his course. The response came back, "I am a lighthouse. You should change your course." In other words, you must know where you are and where you're going or you'll end up a wreck!

In your journey to the top, you have to change course on occasion because you can't know all the nuances, obstacles, and circumstances that may arise. That's why flexibility and checking up on where you are as you go are so important. Checking up on yourself requires discipline because when things are going well, you may assume that they always will — and that's when you encounter disastrous situations. Just remember that you can discipline yourself and change your course of action to prevent being disciplined by others. Discipline is an important quality that you must have in order to achieve your potential and have any shot at greatness.

Isabel Moore said, "Life is a one-way street. No matter how many detours you take, none of them leads back. Once you know and accept that, life becomes simpler because then you know you must do the best you can with what you have, what you are, and what you have become." Spending time and emotional energy wishing that things were like they used to be is a complete waste of time. Where you are and how you plan to move forward from there are the questions you need to ponder.

# Develop the Ultimate Success Attitude

One morning as I was preparing to dress, I walked into the closet and chose among several pairs of slacks. Then I did the same thing to choose a shirt and socks to match. As I made my selections, my memory took me back to my childhood in Yazoo City, Mississippi. In those days, the Sears & Roebuck catalog was a mainstay in many rural areas and small towns. I distinctly remember once ordering a pair of slacks and a few weeks later ordering a sport coat. Much to my delight, the coat and slacks were a perfect match. In my mind, I had just gotten a big bonus, because now I not only had a pair of slacks that I could wear with other jackets and a coat that I could wear with other slacks, but I also got a suit in the bargain!

As I reflected on this memory, I chastised myself slightly for not expressing gratitude more often for all the things that have happened to me since childhood. Similarly, I encourage you to develop a daily gratitude list. When you awaken in the morning, express gratitude for the fact that you did awaken and that you're in a house, so you aren't homeless. If you're in a bed, express gratitude for that. If the weather outside is cold or hot, express gratitude for a temperature-controlled room. Express gratitude for the clothes and shoes that you wear and the breakfast that you eat. Try it for just a week and see what happens.

Go down the list of all the things you have to be grateful for that day — you'll be amazed at how much better your day starts. And if the day starts right, you have a good chance of it going well all day. Why not express gratitude on your way home for the job you just completed? Develop that *attitude of gratitude* for what you have — including your talents and abilities — and you take a giant step up the success ladder.

Cicero said, "Gratitude is not only the greatest of virtues, but it is the parent of all the others."

# Chapter 9

# You're Not Making Progress — Now What?

● ● ● ● ● ● ● ● ● ● ● ● ● ● ● ● ● ● ● ● ● ● ● ● ● ● ● ● ● ● ● ● ● ● ● ● ● ● ● ● ● ●

## In This Chapter

▶ Knowing what to do if your plan to reach your goals just doesn't work

▶ Forgiving your parents, your family, yourself, and others

▶ Understanding the power of words

▶ Using mistakes to move forward

● ● ● ● ● ● ● ● ● ● ● ● ● ● ● ● ● ● ● ● ● ● ● ● ● ● ● ● ● ● ● ● ● ● ● ● ● ● ● ● ● ●

**S**uppose that you're like me: an honest, hard-working optimist who has been earning money since age 8, has been responsible for all my personal financial needs since age 10, and started contributing to my family by age 12, but found myself broke and in debt at age 45. What do you do?

Suppose that you're like me: a fairly nice person with really good intentions who sometimes puts off contacting the people who make the biggest difference in my life. What do you do?

Suppose that you're like me: a reasonably healthy individual who tries to make good choices about food and exercise but who occasionally lets unwanted pounds slip back on. What do you do?

Suppose that you're like me: a person who sometimes isn't doing whatever it is that I've set out to do. What do you do?

Success is a process, and as such can be every bit as fleeting as failure. The saying "You win some, you lose some" survives because it's true. In this chapter, I take a look at some events that may impede your progress on the road to success and show you how to deal with those events so that they don't hold you back for long.

As F. Philip Everson said, "Mountain tops inspire leaders, but valleys mature them."

# Understanding That Failure Is an Event, Not a Person

Say that you opened a business and it failed — does that make you a failure? You got married and then divorced — does that make you a bad person? You got a demotion at work — does that make you a loser? You got hurt and you can't work — does that make you useless? No. No. No. No.

Failure is an event that happens to you. Failure isn't who you are. If an event like one of the preceding examples happens to you, pick yourself up and get ready for the next event in your life. When you know in your heart that you can survive whatever happens, you can relax and begin to extract from life what life has to offer.

# Adjusting Your Attitude

Oftentimes, an attitude of expectancy has more to do with success or failure than any other factor. If you expect to do well, more often than not you do. If you expect to do poorly, you do. People go out of their way to fulfill their expectations.

I know a man who had an especially bad case of "stinkin' thinkin'." He refused to get close to his wife because he was convinced that she was going to leave him one day, and he thought that her departure wouldn't hurt as much if he wasn't too attached to her. Well, you guessed it: She felt the urge to leave because he acted like she didn't exist. Fortunately, his wife had a better attitude than he did, and when he realized how wrong he had been and began to show her the attention she deserved, she took him back.

This man wasn't a failure, but his ideas about his marriage made it fail temporarily. He changed his ideas, and his marriage is now strong, fulfilling, and very good by anyone's standards.

An attitude of enthusiasm has much to do with success, too, as the next story illustrates.

Little Johnny, a second-grade student, was a "pistol." One Friday afternoon, his teacher told the class that if anything exciting happened to them over the weekend, they should come prepared to share the story with the class on Monday morning. When class started, the teacher saw that little Johnny was all worked up and eager to share, so she called on him.

With great enthusiasm, he said, "Teacher, it was wonderful! My dad took me fishin', and we caught 75 catfish, and each one of them weighed 75 pounds." Teacher said, "Now, Johnny, you know that could not possibly be true." He said, "Oh, yes, ma'am, it is! My daddy is a great fisherman, and I'm even better than he is! We caught 75 catfish, and each one weighed over 75 pounds." The teacher said, "Now, Johnny, you know that cannot be the truth! Why, what would you think of me if I said to you that on the way to school this morning I was confronted by a big ol' thousand-pound grizzly bear? He was just about to jump on me and eat me up when an eight-pound yellow dog suddenly appeared, jumped up and grabbed the grizzly bear by the nose, threw him down, bounced him back and forth, broke his neck, and killed him dead? Would you believe that, Johnny?" With even more enthusiasm, Johnny said, "Yes, ma'am, I sure would. As a matter of fact, that's my dog!"

The message? If you maintain your enthusiasm, little things don't inhibit your progress. Even big disappointments can't squelch true enthusiasm.

# Don't Compromise Your Integrity

A strong movement is on in the United States to teach ethical behavior. Actually, the emphasis is on the wrong concept. The focus should be on teaching *integrity,* because a person with integrity behaves in an ethical manner. Integrity is who you are; it encompasses your whole moral character and guarantees that you do the right thing because it is right and not because it is expedient.

In the March 17, 1995, issue of *Virtues,* Kevin Dolan tells a story about Norman Strauss, chairman of the J. Walter Thompson Advertising Agency. Strauss marched into the office of RCA's CEO and announced that the new reel-to-reel tape recorder they wanted to market chewed up tape and turned it into spaghetti. Strauss said, "The product doesn't work. We can't advertise it." The RCA CEO replied, "If that's your decision, we'll give some other agency the entire RCA account." Strauss turned to walk out the door. "Wait a minute!" shouted the RCA chief. "If you feel so strongly you're willing to sacrifice the whole account, it must be a bad product. We'll fix it." So J. Walter Thompson kept the account.

The experience made a lasting impression on Dolan. Later, he became deputy head of J. Walter Thompson's international accounts. A famed purveyor of kinky lingerie wanted to give him its international account. "It turned out they needed our good name," said Dolan. "I told them that's exactly the reason we wouldn't handle it. If we gave [this company] our name, it would no longer stand for a certain ethical standard."

Protect your integrity; it's your greatest asset. When you have integrity, you do the right thing, which eliminates guilt. When you have integrity, you have nothing to fear because you have nothing to hide. When you eliminate fear and guilt, you can focus on your goals and quickly get back on track if unexpected events temporarily derail you.

# Stay with It

Volume 11, Number 2, of the *Executive Speechwriter Newsletter* reports: "In the 1940s, another young inventor named Chester Carlson took his idea to 20 corporations, including some of the biggest in the country. They all turned him down. In 1947 — after seven long years of rejections — he finally got a tiny company in Rochester, New York, the Haloid Company, to purchase the right to his electrostatic paper-copying process. Haloid became Xerox Corporation."

Chester Carlson could have seen himself as a failure, but he got past each rejection. His enthusiasm carried him as far as he needed to go. Sure, he felt dejected at times, but he saw failure as an event, not a measure of himself, thus he was able to move on to the next opportunity. You can do the same if you will.

# Keep Looking for Opportunities

Opportunities are everywhere; you just need to be on the lookout for them. H. C. Booth certainly was on the lookout for opportunities one evening in 1901. As the story goes, Booth was enjoying the Midwestern sunset — and watching the dust blow — from his front porch. Surveying the scene, he thought, "What if we could reverse the wind and pull dust instead of blowing dust?" Within the year, Booth had invented the vacuum cleaner.

Maybe you have time to ponder things you never thought much about before because a downsizing at your company has put you out of work temporarily. You can look at your new free time as a blessing or a curse. Just having an opportunity to consider things that were previously out of your realm of interest can produce incentive to move in a new direction.

# Forget Those Who Say That You Can't

On occasion, you've probably been told that you can't do this, have no talent for that, and so on. If you overcame those negative comments and did what you were told you couldn't do, you smile at the memory of the satisfaction you gained by proving them wrong. You didn't listen to what they had to say, and you succeeded — in spite of, in some cases, and because of, in other cases, the negative comments of others. Perhaps you also overcame some problems you had early in life. However, just in case you're at the crossroads and are still struggling, look at some folks who got off to a slow start, had more than their share of detractors, and still did okay:

- ✔ Benjamin Franklin and psychologist Carl Jung were poor mathematicians.

- ✔ Albert Einstein didn't speak until he was nearly 5 years old and was considered "mentally slow."

- ✔ Inventor James Watt was declared "dull and inept."

- ✔ Cartoonist Walt Disney was fired from his first job because he "had no imagination."

- ✔ Inventor Thomas Edison was asked to leave school at age 9 because he was at the bottom of his class.

- ✔ Writer Edgar Allen Poe, poet Percy Bysshe Shelley, and painter James Whistler were all expelled from school.

- ✔ Grandma Moses wasn't exactly a "child prodigy," having developed her talent and achieved all her fame and success after age 80.

- ✔ Abraham Lincoln had the equivalent of three months of school, and people ridiculed him for his appearance.

Sometimes the "experts" (or other well-meaning people) are misguided in their efforts and just plain wrong in their thinking. You can measure IQ but not "want to." You can measure the size of your head but not the size of your heart.

Follow your heart as you use your head to develop your skills and talents. An inspired you can accomplish awesome tasks.

# Take from the Past and Leave Something for the Future

Every individual receives a great deal from preceding generations. Dr. Thomas Gibbs, Jr., says, "Every man has leaned upon the past. Every liberty we enjoy has been bought at incredible cost. There is not a privilege nor an opportunity that is not the product of other men's labors. We drink every day from wells we have not dug; we warm ourselves by fires we have not kindled; we live by liberties we have not won; we are protected by institutions we have not set up. No man lives unto himself alone. All the past is invested in him. A new day is a good time to say, 'I am under obligation to accept my share of the world's grief, my share of its opportunities.'"

Life is like tennis — he who serves best seldom loses. Responsibility demands that you pay your own way and leave something behind for those folks who follow. Leaving a heritage of having lived an ethical, moral, and productive life is something that everyone can do. Unfortunately, too many people labor under the illusion that unless they can do something monumental, they can do nothing. That's too bad, because pleasant smiles, words of encouragement, and examples of gentle kindness and thoughtful consideration for others are much needed in society today. Actions like these leave your impact on future generations.

I am fairly certain that most readers of this book have lost loved ones. Did your loved ones do something monumental in the eyes of the world? Probably not. Did they do something monumental in your eyes and make a difference in your world? Undoubtedly so! Would you say that what they did while they were here on this earth was enough? Of course! The message: Don't hold yourself to a standard that's any different from the one you hold for your lost loved ones.

Doing things for others brings you greater happiness and success, especially when you have been struggling to reach goals of your own. Sometimes people make the mistake of putting so much pressure on themselves to achieve that they lose their creative edge. Doing things for others frees your mind to think about things other than your problems. When you give your brain a break, solutions are more readily found.

# Understanding the Awesome Power of Forgiveness

Forgiveness is something that you do for yourself. Many people argue that their offender doesn't deserve to be forgiven, but what the offender deserves is entirely beside the point. *You* deserve to forgive that individual. How many people do you know who are bitter and consumed with hatred because, years ago, someone — a parent, sibling, cousin, aunt, friend, neighbor, teacher, lawyer — did something hurtful to them? The person who hurts you damages your past and controls your present, as long as you allow it. Surely you're not going to give him or her permission to control and negatively influence your future, are you?

You can't go as high as you're capable of going or reach the goals you're capable of reaching when you're carrying the burdens of anger and bitterness. Those are heavy loads to carry, and the chances of your realizing your full potential with those two burdens on your back are nonexistent. Even if you were successful in your profession, how happy would you be as an individual? How many friends have you seen angry or bitter people acquire? How many of them have good relationships with their families and are optimistic, upbeat, and enthusiastic about the future?

## Warning: Forgiveness is dangerous

Forgiveness can be dangerous, too, simply because when others use or abuse you and you forgive them for doing so, you no longer have a convenient excuse for not being, doing, and having more. When you forgive, you accept responsibility for your future, and that's dangerous, because you're now exposed to the world.

I know of a woman who was molested by her father. She has had years of counseling, and still she refuses to forgive her father and get on with her life. She blames him for the problems she has in her marriage, with her children, at work, and with depression. If it weren't for him, she claims, she would be a happy person with a good marriage, and her children would love her. But because of him, she is helpless to do anything at all. He has been dead for many years, but his daughter works hard at keeping memories of him and all his vile wickedness alive for everyone who listens.

Contrast the story of this woman with the story of another woman who was molested by more than one close family "friend." Read about Mamie McCullough in Chapter 21 and see how she moved forward in her life, reaching goal after goal. No one, including you, has to be a prisoner to the past.

Accepting responsibility for your future is one of the most important steps you can ever take. Martha Thorilius put it this way: "How much more grievous are the consequences of anger than the causes of it?"

When all the energy is gone, life ends. An unknown author said, "Imagine that every time you seek revenge and let anger control your life, a double portion of that energy is burned. . . . In short, what you're doing is shortening your own life." And that's exactly what doctors say. Yes, you need to forgive.

The good news is this: The load you carry in your climb to the top is dramatically lighter when you forgive those people who wrong you. You simply can't be and do your best when you're carrying the double load of anger and bitterness.

Forgiveness is essential for your own growth and success. If you're incapable of forgiving on your own — and many people are — I encourage you to seek counseling to guide you through the maze so that you eventually can forgive. The day you do, you'll become happier, healthier, more secure, and more prosperous.

# Forget Your Ego — Take Good Advice

As I mentioned earlier, my career — especially until I reached age 45 — has been a roller coaster. I had an extraordinarily difficult time getting started in the world of sales, but after P. C. Merrell inspired me, my career took off big-time. For the next four years, my success was unbelievable.

Then I stopped growing and started swelling. The results were catastrophic. In the following five years, I was in 17 different companies. Some of those companies were just slick new deals, but others represented real opportunities. However, my ego had reached the point where I actually believed that I had the answer to everything.

If the company I was working for didn't buy into my brilliant suggestions, I said, "I don't have to put up with this!" and off I went to a company that appreciated me. As I left, I predicted failure for that company, though it may have been in business for 50 years. Seventeen deals in five years. Many of them were "get-rich-quick" deals, but after five years, not only had I not gotten rich quickly, but I hadn't gotten rich at all. As a matter of fact, I was getting deeper and deeper into debt. Finally, I decided to do something that I had vowed that I never would do: get back into the cookware business, where I had earlier enjoyed remarkable success.

The president of the Saladmaster Corporation in Dallas made me a significant loan, bailing me out of a really tight spot, and I was back in the cookware business. I was a franchise dealer in Columbia, South Carolina. Soon after I joined the team, the division supervisor came to visit with me and offer some suggestions. He had been a preacher all his life and had gotten into the cookware business to pay his daughter's medical bills.

To be honest, I thought that I knew more about the cookware business than this man did and that *I* should be the supervisor. Consequently, I didn't like the fact that he was my boss, and my ego and attitude stopped me from being in much of a listening mood. However, as he talked, I realized that in the last five years I had jumped from pillar to post and had less than nothing to show for it.

One of the man's statements made a great deal of sense. He said, "Zig, you are an excellent salesman — one of the best I've seen. But your ego makes you vulnerable to being manipulated. People brag on you, feed your ego, and lead you to believe that you can do things that simply are not doable. You've tried virtually everything that's come down the pike, and your results have not been very good." Then he said, "Now, Zig, I'm going to give you some advice. It's free . . . and as you know, most free advice is worth about what it costs, but let me offer a suggestion.

"You've set some records in this business. You've gained some national respect as a result. But, Zig, the next time one of these 'good deals' comes your way, why don't you put the blinders on. Tell the person that regardless of how attractive the offer is, you've made a commitment. You're going to stay in this business until you stabilize yourself from a financial point of view and rebuild your reputation as solid and dependable, instead of just flashy and always looking for a 'deal.' Zig, if those deals are all that good, they'll still be good a year from now. And if they're not good a year from now, they're not good now."

Though I hated to admit that I had an ego problem, I recognized the wisdom of what my supervisor was telling me. Things were tight for a number of months, but thanks to much hard work and that commitment to stabilize myself, I managed to finish fifth in the nation out of over 3,000 franchises that year. The following year, I was number one in personal sales in the United States.

Regardless of what you may think of the messenger, listen to the message. My supervisor gave me some of the best advice I've ever gotten, and over the years, we developed a genuine friendship. I would have missed a great deal had I not swallowed my ego, put my nose to the grindstone, and gotten back on sound financial ground.

I sincerely hope that you haven't missed great opportunities because of a swollen ego, and I sincerely hope that if you have, you recognized your ego as the culprit of your demise. Nothing knocks you down a notch quicker than an inflated opinion of yourself. Don't get me wrong; being proud of your accomplishments is good, but when you start thinking that you know more than the next person, watch out!

# Know That Words Make the Difference

I'm amazed at the huge role that language plays in success. Words can be the determining factor in whether you feel encouraged or discouraged, inspired or dejected. And words speak volumes about you. The following sections talk about how words make the difference.

## Words can tear you down

As a child, I often heard the statement, "Sticks and stones may break my bones, but words can never hurt me!" As an adult, however, I quickly discovered that nothing is further from the truth. A thoughtless, cruel, condemning word, especially from a person you love or respect, can have a devastating, long-lasting effect.

On the other side of the coin, the proper words can inspire and encourage people to do marvelous things with their lives. Newspaper columnist Sidney Harris points out that when most people tell you that they're going to tell you something "for your own good," they generally proceed to tell you something bad. How much better it would be if parents told their children something good "for their children's own good."

Focus on telling your child the positive benefits of a particular course of action rather than threatening your child with stories of the negative possibilities of the opposite course of action. Instead of saying, "If you don't start studying, you won't get into a good college, and then you'll never find a decent job," you can say, "If you study your lessons diligently, you have an excellent chance of winning a college scholarship."

Here are some other sample statements that give positive rather than negative reinforcement:

- ✔ "If you continue to treat people that way, you'll have friends all over the world."

- ✔ "If you continue to work with the enthusiasm you now have, one of these days you'll be the president of your own company."

When children are encouraged, they get the idea that they can achieve their dreams. Children with dreams get on track to life's rewards much earlier than children who have to overcome negatives.

Mother Teresa put it this way: "Kind words can be short and easy to speak, but their echoes are truly endless."

## Words can improve your life

If you choose to accept them, words can have a solidifying impact on your life — just as my division supervisor's words had an impact on mine, as I explained earlier in this chapter (see "Forget Your Ego — Take Good Advice").

I often look to the Bible when I'm feeling frustrated or I feel that I've strayed a bit off-course. In the book of Proverbs, Solomon gives some significant thoughts with an amazing economy of words (and I added my own two cents' worth to the following list):

- ✔ "Well-spoken words bring satisfaction; well-done work has its own reward." Often, just taking the first step back toward your goal is all the momentum you need to get back on track.

- ✔ "Rash language cuts and maims, but there is healing in the words of the wise." Speak with your mentor about the problems you're having with staying focused on your goals, and ask him or her to help you reevaluate your plans.

- ✔ "Worry weighs us down; a cheerful word picks us up." When the prospect of reaching your goal looks bleak, call a friend who always has an encouraging word for you.

- ✔ "Irresponsible talk makes a real mess of things, but a reliable reporter is a healing presence." Listen to people you respect. Weigh what they have to say, and use what you can to keep yourself on the right track.

✔ "Congenial conversation — what a pleasure! The right word at the right time — beautiful." Take a break, call a friend, relax, and let your creative instincts flow.

✔ "Words satisfy the mind as much as fruit does the stomach. Good talk is as gratifying as a good harvest." This is the reason brainstorming sessions are so popular. Find a strong group of people to talk with and bounce your ideas off of, and you'll be more confident than ever about your direction.

This question from Bruce Barton is a good one for you to ask and answer: "For good or ill, your conversation is your advertisement. Every time you open your mouth, you let men look into your mind. Do they see it well-clothed, neat and business-like?" Words can and do make a difference.

## Clearing up your communication

The English language is truly fascinating and has many twists and turns, including oxymorons (phrases that combine contradictory words). For example, someone may say, "Same difference." Another person may talk about "jumbo shrimp." As you reflect on these and other word turns, you realize that some words and phrases are easily misunderstood. An old, negative expression says, "Those things which can be misunderstood will be misunderstood."

When you explore words, you realize that you're talking about *communication,* and when you talk about everything from winning relationships to good leadership, you're talking about the ability to clearly communicate a message. If you can't communicate effectively, few people understand what you expect of them. The individual who gets things done is an effective communicator.

Use kind, inspiring words with a helpful intent and a gentle tone of voice, and you build better relationships and move up the success ladder more quickly and surely.

Words differ in their importance. The most important words you can say to your child or mate are "I love you." The second most important words you can say are "I made a mistake. Please forgive me." Those words say, "I'm wiser now and have better judgment than I had an hour earlier or yesterday." Nothing pleases a child or your mate more than to know that you are willing and secure enough in your role to say "I made a mistake."

"I appreciate what you said or did" are very important words. So are "You are a big help," "That's a great idea," "What is your opinion?" and "Thank you." The most important word is *you.* The least important word is *me.*

# Mistakes Are the Springboards of Accomplishment

Wouldn't it be wonderful if you had as much foresight as hindsight and were able to avoid mistakes altogether? Not only is that hope unrealistic, but it's also unwise. Mistakes are often the springboard for major accomplishments. Here's an example:

> Thomas Edison was working with a lab assistant who was coming up dry after over 700 experiments. In discouragement, the assistant told Edison that after all these mistakes, errors, and false starts, he simply didn't believe that the project was valid. Edison quickly told him that he wasn't wasting his time and that the assistant now knew more about the project than anybody alive. Edison wisely observed that the assistant hadn't made mistakes but instead had acquired an education as to what didn't work. Needless to say, the assistant went back to his project with renewed vigor.

If you take Edison's approach to life, you end up accomplishing much, much more. You need to understand that, after every mistake, you can look back and grow from the experience so that you can move forward with confidence and avoid making the same mistake again.

Here are three tips for handling a mistake, either at home or at the office:

✔ **Don't let a mistake depress or discourage you.** See a mistake as a step on the road to a solution. Realize that depression and discouragement are negatives that limit the future.

✔ **Admit the mistake.** Yes, admitting your mistakes takes courage, but recognition of errors is a sign of maturity. Not to recognize them is to deny them, and denial limits your future.

✔ **Understand that when you confront your mistakes, you can take full advantage of them as the positive experiences they can be.** When you ignore mistakes or try to conceal them, they almost always have a negative impact.

# Part IV
# Your Goals in Life

The 5th Wave                    By Rich Tennant

"Of course we offer a generous vacation plan. If we didn't let employees have time off to have kids, who'd we sell toys to?"

## In this part . . .

*H*ave you thought recently about what your goals in life really are? Do you have a vague notion that you'd like to achieve success in your marriage or learn to have a great relationship with your boss? Are you just unsure about how to express your goals? This part of *Success For Dummies* can help you accomplish these things. Read on!

# Chapter 10

# Achieving and Maintaining Optimal Physical Health

· · · · · · · · · · · · · · · · · · · · · · · · · · · · · · · · · · · · · · · · · · · · · · · · · ·

## In This Chapter

▶ Finding the right direction for good health

▶ Understanding the mental side of physical well-being

▶ Exercising and eating sensibly

▶ Avoiding the poisons and getting plenty of sleep

▶ Taking other simple steps to maintain good health

· · · · · · · · · · · · · · · · · · · · · · · · · · · · · · · · · · · · · · · · · · · · · · · · · ·

*P*hysical health is often ignored as an essential part of success, yet everyone knows how difficult concentrating and performing even simple tasks can be when pain and discomfort push their way into your consciousness. When the body is neglected, fatigue or illness ensues. Poor health and substandard physical conditioning adversely affect being productive at work or at home, enjoying time with friends and family, and even your ability to relax. This chapter covers the big picture on how to take charge of your physical health and also covers the mental side of physical well-being.

Individually and collectively, health problems often have no clear-cut solutions. Despite the billions of dollars spent on weight-loss programs, the average person today is roughly ten pounds heavier than he or she was ten years ago. Experts regularly change their minds about what's good for you and what's bad for you, what causes cancer and what doesn't, when you should go to the doctor and when you should avoid the doctor, and a host of other things.

I could go into a litany of physical health problems — such as the incredible toll that lack of sleep and stress takes on millions of people, or how back pain, fatigue, headaches, and ulcers keep people from performing their jobs to the best of their ability. I could tell you that 100 different experts have 100 different ideas as to why people have all these problems, but what's the point? The problems are there, so I want to concentrate instead on what you can do to avoid, alleviate, or, better yet, eliminate them.

Giving anything approaching a complete health program in one chapter of a book is virtually impossible. However, an increasing amount of information is available on the subject, and I encourage you to frequent your bookstore and library. Many health-food stores offer free pamphlets that you can take home and read, too. For more detailed information about diet, exercise, and health, I suggest that you read *Nutrition For Dummies,* by Carol Ann Rinzler, and *Fitness For Dummies,* by Suzanne Schlosberg and Liz Neporent (both published by IDG Books Worldwide, Inc.). Educate yourself as though your life depends on it — because it does!

# Teaming Up with Your Physician

One of the most important components of the healing process is the physician and patient working together. You can't go to a doctor with a problem and expect him or her to heal you without making any efforts of your own. The treatment the physician gives you, combined with the words of encouragement you hear, is enormously helpful in the healing process. However, you must take steps to help ensure that you recover from your current ailment and then remain in good health. You go to a doctor in whom you have confidence, either from reputation or from experience. Carefully ask questions, listen attentively to what he or she has to say, assure him or her that the two of you are going to work together, and follow through on that promise.

# Understanding the Impact of Your Thinking on Your Health

Fortunately, many people are beginning to recognize that, to a large degree, their physical well-being is their own responsibility. Start thinking in terms of making decisions today that benefit you immediately and also impact your quality of life 20, 30, 40, and 50 years from now. Considering your future quality of life is critical because medical technology is keeping people alive longer and longer. Do you want to spend months and even years in hospitals or nursing homes, having all your needs met by someone else because you were unwilling or unmotivated to take a few simple steps to take care of your health earlier in your life? Obviously, there are some things you can't control, but you *can* make decisions and take actions now that dramatically increase your chances of a better quality of life in your later years.

The more optimistic you are that results are just around the corner, the more likely those results are to take place. The magic word is *expectation.* If you plan and prepare for good health (by thinking positively, eating right, exercising, and doing the other things that I recommend in this chapter), you can expect good health.

# *Positive thinking versus negative thinking*

These three stories clearly illustrate the positive or negative impact that your thinking can have on your health.

- A friend of mine who was under the care of a mental health professional said that he frequently told her that she would always need him. One day, she received a set of motivational tapes. Listening to those tapes reminded her that she had been quite successful earlier in her life, and slowly her hope started to build. The more she listened, the more optimistic she became. In a matter of weeks, after having been under the professional's care for over five years, she no longer needed him. She is now enjoying a successful life and a career in business.

- As I was writing this book, my wife and I had dinner with some friends who were thinking about getting married. Both had been through unpleasant divorces earlier in their lives. The woman revealed that after her divorce, she was so depressed that she didn't have the energy to get out of bed. (Depression can be a very serious illness.) However, she had family responsibilities, and those responsibilities made her recognize that she had to take control of the situation.

   Each evening before she went to sleep, she listened for a few minutes to inspirational tapes for words of hope and encouragement. The first thing she did in the morning when she awakened was to turn those tapes back on. As she put it, she wanted to make certain that she started her day optimistically, before a negative or depressing thought entered her mind. That approach was effective for her, and in a matter of weeks, she was able to go back to a fairly normal routine and later recovered completely.

- The most startling example I've ever participated in involved a young man from Rochester, New York, who was diagnosed with a rare form of cancer that has no known cure. He checked into the hospital for final tests but was expecting to die. The tests revealed that he had been misdiagnosed and that he didn't have that rare cancer. However, he had so conditioned himself to believe that he was going to die that his health continued to deteriorate.

   After a couple of days, an internist played some motivational tapes at the patient's bedside, and the young man was too weak and depressed to protest or turn them off. As he listened, he caught a glimpse of hope. As he continued to listen, he was genuinely encouraged. I had the privilege of meeting that young man while on a speaking engagement in Rochester. I was so moved by what happened to him that, although he gave me his name, I didn't even register it.

Because of the way I greet people, people frequently say to me, "Well, you sure do feel good today!" My response is always the same: "Yes, many years ago I planned to feel good today." Actually, I plan to feel good every day. I emphatically believe that attitude has a direct bearing on what happens to me in every area of life, including my health. If you take that approach, you'll stay healthier.

I tell you these stories to show you that, yes, your attitude and your mind play a tremendous part in the healing process. In addition to seeking the care of qualified physicians, you need to remember to "heal thyself."

## Feeling that you're in control

Perhaps the most significant part in healing and regaining good health is that you yourself are doing something about your health, which makes you feel that you have a certain amount of control. When that feeling is part of the healing process, the healing process has a substantially better chance of being successful. Among other things, feeling in control has a great impact on your attitude, which reduces your anxiety and definitely affects the efficiency of your immune system. And although your attitude may not attack an illness or disease directly, its impact on your immune system is significant.

## Attaining good health through motivation

When you recognize both a need and the advantages of meeting that need, you're motivated to take action. You're sold on the idea. However, you need to remain sold. For this reason, step number one in preparing for a healthy future is to understand that you need to deliberately, regularly go back to the "hows" and "whys" of maintaining good health: how you first got interested, why you were excited to begin with, and how you can remain that way.

When the brain is stimulated, it gets flooded with dopamine and norepinephrine, the two energizing neurotransmitters. Your brain is also flooded with endorphins, which are the endurance neurotransmitters, and serotonin, which is the feel-good-about-yourself neurotransmitter. Therefore, I suggest that you listen to something that motivates you on your way to work. It can be an upbeat song, an inspiring sermon, or an enthusiastic presentation by someone you trust and like to listen to. Doing those things activates the neurotransmitters in your brain, and your energy level goes up. When you're motivated, you follow through on your goals and are more confident that you can achieve the desired results.

With a higher energy level, you're also more inclined to walk up those two flights of stairs instead of taking the elevator and to park your car at the far end of the parking lot. In short, when you have more energy, you seek little steps to burn calories and regenerate your body.

Most people experience an energy slump in midafternoon. When that happens, you feel compelled to eat "just a little something" to give yourself energy. Unfortunately, your body wants a quick fix, so you crave foods that are rich in fat, heavy on carbohydrates, and inundated with sugar. Instead, try a snack of fruit, raw veggies, or low-fat cheese and crackers, which gives you an energy boost without all the calories and fat.

On your way home, listen again to a powerful inspirational message. Again, you flood your brain with dopamine and norepinephrine, which makes you more inclined to walk around the block when you go out to pick up the mail and gives you more energy. The difference these actions make in how you feel and look over a period of time can be dramatic.

# Engaging in Physical Activity for Better Health

When you're motivated enough to take the stairs instead of the elevator and you move from a sedentary lifestyle to a more physically active one, you discover incredible benefits. Look at some of them:

- Being physically active causes a substantial reduction in stress and a huge increase in energy.

- Exercise is a depression-breaker; it increases self-confidence and gives you a sense of well-being.

- Physical activity is good for weight management, gives greater stamina, and substantially decreases back, neck, and shoulder pain.

- Being physically active improves sleep, increases alertness, and helps you to maintain your independence as you add birthdays.

- Physical activity expands creativity and enhances sexual response.

- Exercise gives you a feeling of achievement and of being in control, makes your outlook more positive and optimistic, and improves your productivity.

- Being physically active enhances and encourages other healthy habits and may reduce your need for some medications.

For the first 19 years after I got physically active, I didn't miss a single day of work (except when I had emergency surgery for a ruptured gall bladder). The time I committed to daily exercise rewarded me with an improved energy level that resulted in a two-hour increase in higher-quality productivity. The combination of exercise and sensible eating boosts your ability to relax, improves your muscle tone, aids digestion, and clears your mind. It also helps you to avoid embarrassment. Gasping for breath after climbing two flights of stairs isn't one of life's brightest moments!

## Sometimes exercise has extra perks

I started my exercise program in 1972, and for the first 20 years, I jogged. Then Dr. Ken Cooper's research revealed that walking is better, so since then I've been walking at a pretty good clip of about 13 minutes to the mile. A big part of my walking enjoyment comes about because my home is on a golf course. Although the golf course has a fence around it, those golfers do hit balls over that fence, and when I find a ball, I feel happy! My quest for those errant golf balls increases my enjoyment of my walk and my determination to walk even farther. As a result, I'm able to supply most of my golf balls from lost balls that I pick up on my walks — but the fun of finding them is the important part of the picture.

## *Getting into a sensible exercise program*

You need to keep some basic fundamentals about exercise in mind:

- Experts agree that exercising three to five times a week is enormously beneficial.

- Experts also agree that you have to get a certain amount of enjoyment from your exercise program in order to maintain it for a long period of time. Some people enjoy exercising in groups.

  For example, Krish Dhanam, a member of our staff, says that his retired father is involved in a walking club of sorts with a group of senior citizens in his neighborhood. They set a rendezvous point where they meet halfway, exchange pleasantries, and visit for a few minutes; then they go into the second portion of their walk, ending it at another rendezvous point, where they visit again for a longer period of time. These men are so gung-ho about this approach that they consider having to miss a walk to be something of a crisis. In short, they have worked out a way to really enjoy aerobic exercise.

- Aerobics are important, but so are stretching and strength training programs. I stretch regularly, work out with light weights, and do what some call *dynamic tension,* working my muscles against each other. In addition, I do push-ups and rowing. Muscle toning and strength training are an important part of maintaining a good physical condition.

## Using common sense while exercising — even if you're already fit

I'm sure that you've read and heard stories about "weekend warriors" who decide to make up for a ten-year span of no exercise by trying to run five miles, doing aerobic exercises for an hour, or playing a fast-paced game of touch football or soccer — and then keel over with a heart attack. That's not smart. Instead, you need to build your level of fitness one workout at a time. Start by seeing your physician and letting his or her evaluation influence the direction you take.

I can't overemphasize the importance of listening to your body. For example, in 1993 I felt a tightness in my chest while jogging. To be candid, my first inclination was to ignore the tight feeling in my chest, but I quickly realized that I had too much to lose not to see my physician. So I called Dr. Cooper, who immediately gave me the treadmill test. Seven minutes into the test, I again felt tightness. Subsequent tests revealed that I had a 50 to 60 percent blockage in a major artery and nearly 90 percent blockage in a small artery leading into my heart. Yet I looked fit and healthy and had been eating sensibly and exercising regularly for 20 years. With careful dieting, medication, my ongoing exercise program, and plenty of prayer, just two years later the problem had actually reversed itself, and I haven't felt any tightening since. As my mother would say, "An ounce of prevention is worth a pound of cure."

Part of the common-sense approach is to understand that you need to find a good balance between doing your body good by exercising sensibly and doing it harm by going overboard. If you jog more than 15 miles a week, for example, you may not really be improving your health. In many cases, just the opposite happens, because jogging involves a greater risk of injury than walking. Dr. Cooper says that walking gives you the same health benefits as running without the risks, so walking is better than jogging for non-athletes. According to Dr. Cooper, if you run marathons regularly, you may have medical problems in front of you. To set a goal to run one marathon and then train and prepare for it is one thing; but to run several marathons each year for a number of years puts you on a fast-track to problems. The human body isn't designed for that kind of pounding.

# Digging Your Grave with Your Teeth

With all the studies you see in newspapers and magazines and hear about on television, you may be confused about what foods to eat and how and when to eat them. And no wonder! Each new theory about nutrition seems to contradict all the existing ones. But you really don't have to be an expert to eat properly.

First, a few ground rules for eating:

- **Eat only when you're hungry.**

- **Decide in advance how much you're going to eat.** Many people eat whatever is on their plate or whatever is available. If they're at a family-style dinner, they try to make sure that no food is left over. Sunday buffets are particularly disastrous. When you eat with a group, particularly when you're laughing, talking, and having a good time, you're inclined to get carried away and eat more than you normally do. With that in mind, decide in advance what you're going to order and make sure that you eat according to your predetermined plan.

- **Choose a plate that's smaller than the one you normally use.** A small plate makes the amount of food on it appear larger, whereas on a large plate even a reasonable amount of food looks small.

- **Never eat while standing up.** Instead, always eat while seated in the same place at home.

- **Don't eat in front of the television.** You can consume an unusually large amount of food simply because it is available and because you're not paying attention.

- **Stop eating when you're full and long before you're stuffed.** Your stomach becomes full long before your brain gets the message. Eat slowly and chew your food thoroughly. Lay your fork down after each bite. You may even want to place your fork at an odd angle requiring a slight reach to pick it up again to remind yourself to slow down. Beware of eating huge meals where, as we say down home, "You don't eat until you get full; you eat until you get tired."

- **Be careful about the music you listen to while you're eating.** With soft, soothing music, you eat less and more slowly. When you listen to loud music with a fast beat, you eat more and faster — and frequently whatever is in sight.

- **Eat healthy snacks between meals and then eat smaller meals.**

- **Eat something healthy, such as half a grapefruit, 30 minutes to an hour before a meal.** Filling up on a low-calorie, low-fat, highly nutritious food before sitting down to a meal has a definite impact on your appetite.

- **Develop an appetite for many different foods.** The more foods you enjoy, the easier it is to satisfy your hunger cravings.

- **Make your last meal of the day a light one.** And finish eating your last meal of the day before 7:00 p.m.

# Choosing the right foods

Forest Tennant, M.D., P.H., says that a dependence on carbohydrates is the number-one eating problem today. If you find that you're constantly fatigued or that you get tired or sleepy after meals, you may be eating excess carbohydrates. The question is, what *should* you look for in a diet? Dr. Tennant believes that you should eat a balanced diet, but also that you should consume much more protein than the average person does today.

Foods that are rich in protein and low in carbohydrates include lean meat, poultry, and fish; eggs; cheese; and dry beans. Other good low-carbohydrate foods are almonds, apricots, artichokes, asparagus, beets, broccoli, brussels sprouts, cabbage, cauliflower, celery, collard greens, cucumbers, green beans, lettuce, mushrooms, olives, peanuts, pecans, soybeans, spinach, summer squash, sunflower seeds, tomatoes, turnip greens, turnips, and walnuts. (But be careful: Nuts are generally high in fat.)

You don't have to go looking for fat and sugar; they show up in unlikely places in large enough quantities to take care of your body's needs. A certain amount of fat (about 30 to 50 grams a day) is fine, but all fat isn't the same. Some fatty acids, particularly those found in fish and nuts, are necessary building blocks for some biochemicals. Certain fatty acids are believed to provide protective effects against heart attacks and strokes.

The things that taste best are often the things that can wreck your health. Don't misunderstand: Unless a food tastes reasonably good, your inclination to eat it is small. Unfortunately, foods with a high fat and/or sugar content taste so good that most people are inclined to choose them over other, more healthful foods. You need some of each food group, but you need to keep in mind which foods have the most fat and calories and eat those foods sparingly. Fat from food is stored as fat in the body, and a calorie is a calorie is a calorie. If you don't count calories and fat grams, they add up much more quickly than you think.

Go shopping for your groceries right after you've had a satisfying meal. Never shop when you're hungry. The subconscious thought pattern runs to indulging yourself, and when you're hungry, you're far more inclined to buy sweets and foods that are loaded with fat, which can create serious eating problems and subsequent health problems.

# Maintaining your common sense while dieting

Use common sense. Don't rush blindly into every fad diet that comes down the pike. Some of the hundreds of diets out there are effective, but many others are simply fads to grab the public's attention or get you to buy a book. Oftentimes, "quick-fix" diets distract you from long-range health goals.

---

## The benefits of alternative medicine

More and more physicians are recognizing that you can take more than one approach to healing, so look into alternative medicines. For example, I've been going to chiropractors for years, and my entire family has received substantial benefits from chiropractic treatment. Osteopathic medicine is another alternative that offers advantages not normally found in regular medical treatment.

Many experts now recognize various herbs — St. John's Wort, for example — as alternatives to Prozac and other tranquilizing drugs. Ginseng has fascinating benefits, and Ginkgo Baloba is an herb that's apparently accomplishing remarkable health results — just two of many examples. Be open-minded and at least get additional information about herbs.

---

Using good, solid documentation from recognized authorities in the field is always a sound approach. Getting expert instruction before embarking on a weight-loss program is important, because if you don't lose weight properly, you can do serious damage. Temporary — and on occasion, permanent — setback is the result.

I have talked with countless overweight people and have seen startling results when they recognize the mental aspect of their weight problem. I experienced those results firsthand when I lost 37 pounds back in 1973, and I'm happy to report that I have maintained that loss. I was able to lose the weight because I thought slender, ate slender, and asked myself at every meal, "Would a slender person eat this food?" I changed my eating habits and started a sensible but disciplined exercise program.

As one who has a passion for sweets (I've never met one I didn't like), I knew that I wouldn't be able to permanently stick to a diet that was too restrictive and eliminated sweets all together. So I decided that the only time I would eat sweets would be on Sunday after church. For the ten months I took to lose the weight, I got a double dip of my all-time favorite, Braum's French Chocolate Almond ice cream, each Sunday. I enjoyed every bite of it and set my sweet clock to go off on the next Sunday at the same time. By following this procedure, I was able to indulge — and control — my sweet tooth rather than allowing it to control me.

## *Avoiding the Poisons*

Common sense tells you to avoid the poisons. You know that when you overload on sugar or have too much caffeine in your system, the negative impacts are substantial. The Surgeon General's warning on every pack of cigarettes should be enough to convince you that tobacco is something to avoid. Alcohol is a poison that wreaks havoc in many cases, despite the fact that some studies indicate that a minimal amount each day helps to reduce heart problems. (Some research indicates that grape juice carries the same benefits as wine without any of the side effects and possibilities of alcoholism.) France and Italy have the two highest rates of wine consumption in the world and, not by coincidence, the two highest rates of cirrhosis of the liver.

Obviously, illegal drugs (for more reasons than I need to go into) are an absolute no-no. No one smokes that first joint with the objective of becoming a drug addict, but people become addicted every day.

Research from countless sources validates that alcohol, tobacco, and illegal drugs are health-killers, relationship-destroyers, and career-albatrosses. Needless to say, realizing your potential is difficult when you're boozing, puffing, or snorting.

# Getting an Adequate Amount of Sleep

You require a certain amount of sleep, preferably at regular times (meaning that you go to bed and arise at the same times each day to establish a rhythm). The only time the brain produces certain chemicals that the body needs to stay in balance is when you're sleeping. The required amount of sleep varies from person to person, but you can use this test: If you enjoy good health but have to force yourself to get out of bed each morning, you probably aren't getting enough sleep.

Long hours are acceptable to a point, but burning the candle at both ends at the expense of a good night's rest becomes counterproductive:

- ✔ **Too little sleep results in a substantial energy loss.**
- ✔ **Not getting enough sleep causes you to lose mental sharpness and creativity and become more likely to make mistakes in judgment.** Those mistakes can negatively impact your career. You're just not as effective overall when you haven't gotten enough sleep.

# Taking Quick, Simple Measures That Cost Almost Nothing

Take a good look at some of the most neglected aspects of maintaining good physical condition — and the measures that cost the least amount of money.

## Breathing deeply

Stop for 90 seconds and take a huge, deep breath. Expand your chest and raise your arms, holding them out to the side, to get every possible molecule of air into your system. Hold your breath as long as you can and then exhale. One deep breath — or far better, two or three — taken at opportune times during the day energizes you. Before your workday starts, during your breaks, at lunch, and after work, take deep breaths. On occasion throughout the day, stop what you're doing and, whether you're at your desk and need to stand up to keep your circulation flowing or you're on your way to another department, take one long, deep breath to help you to relax and relieve tension and stress. Deep breathing has a positive, long-range impact on your health.

## Drinking plenty of water

Very few people drink even close to the amount of water that they should. Most experts agree that eight to ten 8-ounce glasses of water a day are mandatory for optimum health. By the time you realize that you're thirsty, the dehydration process has already started.

As more and more people become aware of the body's constant need for water, you see more and more folks carrying around water bottles. They already know that plenty of good, clean water every day keeps your skin supple, improves digestion, and helps to flush toxins out of the body. Getting rid of poisons in an expeditious manner is definitely a contributing factor to good health.

## Varying your activities

From a common-sense point of view, you need to alternate your activities. If you routinely stay seated for long periods of time, for example, your risk of blood clots goes up substantially. At least once every 90 minutes, stand up, stretch, breathe deeply, shift gears, walk to the water cooler and get a drink of water, or even do a couple of aerobic exercises if space permits. (Be sure not to interfere with or distract others!) Doing so helps to reduce stress — whether mental or physical — and when you reduce stress, you increase your energy level.

## Laughing your way to good health

For years, a good belly laugh has been described as "internal jogging." Physicians agree that a sense of humor is an enormous asset to maintaining good physical health. It gives you a better outlook on life, and it's good for you. In his forthcoming book, *Biological Unhappiness,* Leland Heller, M.D., gives some exciting information about the effects of worry and laughter on the immune system:

> "If worry worked, there would be no more poverty, war, famine, or tragedy in the world, because people have worried about these things for centuries. The reality is that worry doesn't work at all. What's more, it kills. Worrying impairs the immune system, which normally protects against infection and cancer. As bacteria become progressively untreatable (as has already happened with staphylococcus), you need a healthy immune system to prevent disaster. Having a healthy immune system is no longer just a good idea; it's medically necessary.

> "Laughter improves many aspects of the immune system, and it can make you a healthier person overall. Scientific studies show that 'natural killer cells,' cytokinins, and interferon levels double after a good laugh, and the effects last for a week. (Doing positive affirmations and listening to peaceful music have the same effects.) Norman Cousins was a pioneer in laughter treatment. He had a horrible arthritic condition and discovered that 20 minutes of laughter gave him two hours of pain relief.

> "Laughter also helps to reduce stress, which can have a huge impact on your health. Studies prove that stress increases the number of colds you get, and recent data shows that stress, depression, and anxiety are major causes of cancer and heart disease. AIDS is a disease that damages only one portion of the immune system, but stress damages the entire immune system. However, laughter directly affects your immune system. Your immune proteins, called globulins, go up by 33 percent with a good laugh, and the effects last for a full week.

> "Cortisol is a stress hormone that's designed for short-term use. Today's stressful society causes higher-than-necessary cortisol levels to persist. The high cortisol causes enormous physical damage — particularly to the immune system. A good, intense laugh drops the blood cortisol level by 50 percent, and the drop lasts for 24 hours. 'An apple a day keeps the doctor away' hasn't been proven, but a good belly laugh every day indeed keeps you healthier.

> "We're supposed to laugh — humans are made that way. Now we know that you can literally laugh your way to good health — as long as that laughter is the result of kind, mirthful humor. Hurtful, insulting, and demeaning humor doesn't work to build you up in the same way. If you're always kind and happy, you have an excellent chance of being healthy."

## Self-talking for good health

Scientific evidence validates that saying positive, encouraging things to yourself can have significant influence. Wrong things said to yourself are as significant as right things. Looking yourself in the eye and saying, "I feel miserable, " or "My head hurts," or "I just know that I'm coming down with something" brings about negative results. I encourage you to talk to yourself positively about your health. Following this chapter's suggestions about preventing illness and maintaining good health, and combining those suggestions with self-talk procedures, can definitely have long-range bearing on your health. Self-talking takes only a couple of minutes each evening and a couple of minutes at the start of your day.

Now get started. Square those shoulders, look yourself in the eye, and quietly but firmly say aloud:

> I, [say your own name], am a highly motivated, health-conscious individual who is committed to taking care of my health now so that I will enjoy a high quality of life all my life. I am committed to a physical activity program that will increase my energy level and keep my weight under control. I will talk positively about my health and think positive health thoughts. I will eat sensibly and ask myself this question every day: "Would a slender, healthy person eat this food or drink this drink?" I will regularly get physical exams as a step to preventing serious problems, and I understand that my physical health has a direct bearing on my happiness, my attitude, my family, my job success, my peace of mind, my finances, and my corporate or business success.

The eyes are the windows to the soul. You can't look yourself in the eye, make the preceding statements with sincerity and conviction, and not have them impact your life in a positive way.

# You Can Always Do Something

Regardless of your age, you can always do something to improve your present and future health. For example, people in wheelchairs — even folks who are 90-plus years old — who start doing simple weight-lifting exercises are frequently able to get out of those chairs and live far more active lives after beginning such an exercise program. Obviously, you need to check with your physician before taking steps that represent such a dramatic change, but I remind you that the choice to do so is yours.

# Chapter 11

# Finding the Right Mental Attitude

. . . . . . . . . . . . . . . . . . . . . . . . . . . . . . . . . . . . . . . . . . .

## In This Chapter

▶ Understanding that a positive attitude alone doesn't make you successful

▶ Looking upward, not downward

▶ Avoiding cynicism

▶ Using what's left

▶ Surviving the traffic jams of life

▶ Understanding the impact of words on your attitude

▶ Improving your attitude through positive affirmations

▶ Being persistent

▶ Finding your happiness

▶ Remembering that every day is a great day

. . . . . . . . . . . . . . . . . . . . . . . . . . . . . . . . . . . . . . . . . . .

*M*any people contend that attitude is everything when it comes to being successful. They believe that a positive attitude is the answer to all their challenges and problems. In my opinion, attitude is extremely important, but it certainly isn't everything.

Attitude plays a part in virtually every phase of your life. For example, I believe that a poor attitude gets more people fired than any other single factor — and that a good attitude gets people jobs and helps them keep those jobs more than any other factor.

Losing a job, mate, or friend because of a lousy attitude is unfortunate — especially because a bad attitude can be fixed. I believe that this chapter, particularly when combined with the information in the rest of this book, can help you to adjust your attitude so that it serves you well in your profession, your family, and all your other relationships. I approach the subject with a series of thoughts, examples, and vignettes.

## What is attitude?

In his book *The Winning Attitude,* author and speaker John C. Maxwell says that attitude . . .

✔ Is the "advance man" of our true selves.

✔ Has inward roots but outward fruits.

✔ Is our best friend or our worst enemy.

✔ Is more honest and more consistent than our words.

✔ Is an outward look based on past experiences.

✔ Is a thing which draws people to us or repels them.

✔ Is never content until it is expressed.

✔ Is the librarian of our past.

✔ Is the speaker of our present.

✔ Is the prophet of our future.

Attitude is many, many things. Consider for a moment what you can add to the list from personal experience. A thoughtful glance over the list shows you that although attitude isn't the only thing that contributes to success, it is one of the most important components of successful living.

# *The Importance of Attitude*

Your attitude affects many people, from your family to the stranger you smile at on the street corner. Your attitude is particularly important when you face seemingly hopeless situations. That's where Rochelle Johnson found herself. If you ever develop even a mild case of "stinkin' thinkin'," I encourage you to turn back to this chapter and reread Rochelle Johnson's story (which comes from Volume 9, Number 4, of the *Executive Speechwriter Newsletter*).

Rochelle was a divorced mother of four children, all under eight years old, living in a public housing project in Paducah, Kentucky. She was a high-school dropout, and she was African-American, which limited her opportunities and subjected her to considerable racial prejudice. Her situation seemed hopeless, but, as the saying goes, there are no hopeless situations, only people who lose hope in their situations. Fortunately, Rochelle didn't lose hope; she went to bat for herself and her children and changed the odds.

Rochelle determined that her children weren't going to start school with the same disadvantages that she had started school with, so she enrolled her children in a readiness class to prepare them for first grade. Was it tough? Absolutely! Rochelle also realized that she needed a dependable income and that the kind of jobs available to someone with her limited education didn't provide enough income by themselves, so she worked during the day as a teacher's aide and a street-crossing guard and at night as a cleaning lady. Her workday started at seven in the morning and lasted until midnight. Despite this schedule, she still managed to provide her children with a stable home life. Many times, she was tired and discouraged, but her children's continued success at school always revitalized her.

The results of Rochelle's efforts were spectacular. Barbara, the eldest child, and Earl went to the University of Kentucky. Younger brother Greg earned a straight-A average in high school and was a Presidential Scholar. President Ronald Reagan entertained him and his mom at the White House. Greg was also a National Merit Scholar and was his high school's first ever African-American valedictorian. He won a scholarship to Brown University to study medicine. Rochelle's youngest child, Brad, duplicated Greg's performance in high school and accepted an appointment to West Point. Greg summed it up best when he said that his mom had set a great example and "inspired us with her stamina."

Rochelle's story proves that an unbreakable will, a vision, and hard work are an unbeatable attitude combination, especially when you add a mother's love and determination to make her children's start in life better than hers had been.

# Looking for the Stars

You can find at least two ways to look at virtually everything. A pessimist looks for difficulty in the opportunity, whereas an optimist looks for opportunity in the difficulty. A poet of long ago put the difference between optimism and pessimism this way: "Two men looked out from prison bars — one saw mud, the other saw stars."

Unfortunately, many people look only at the problem and not at the opportunity that lies *within* the problem. Many employees complain about the difficulty of their jobs, for example, not realizing that if the job were simple, the employer would hire someone with less ability at a lower wage. A small coin can hide even the sun if you hold the coin close enough to your eye. So when you get too close to your problems to think objectively about them, try to keep in mind how your vision can be obstructed, take a step back, and look at the situation from a new angle. Look up instead of down.

Pessimism muddies the water of opportunity. Think about this example: Anytime a new innovation comes along promising to make life easier and people more productive, someone always complains that it will put people out of work. When Eli Whitney invented the cotton gin, protesters said that it would put thousands of people out of work. Instead, the invention made the production of cloth much cheaper, and millions of people could afford more clothing, which created countless jobs.

## Optimism leads to great things

Most people consider me an optimist, but I don't hold a candle to the ultimate lady optimist, who lived in a retirement home. One day, a distinguished-looking gentleman also became a resident. As luck would have it, he and the lady optimist sat across the table from each other at lunch the first day. After a few minutes, he grew uncomfortable because she was staring intently at him. He finally expressed his discomfort and asked why she was staring. She responded that she couldn't help but stare because he reminded her so much of her third husband — same demeanor, same smile, same height and weight, everything. The gentleman replied in some shock, "Third husband! How many times have you been married?" The lady smiled and said, "Twice." That's optimism!

In my lifetime, I have seen the advent of the computer. Initially, folks believed that many people would lose their jobs because computers can do certain tasks much faster than humans can. Some people have had to retrain themselves to stay marketable, but almost everyone agrees that computers have created — not deleted — jobs and have improved our capabilities immeasurably.

You can't do anything to change the fact that a problem exists, but you can do a great deal to find the opportunity within that problem. You're guaranteed a better tomorrow by doing your best today and developing a plan of action for the tomorrows that lie ahead. Just remember to maintain a positive mental attitude so that, as you plan for tomorrow, you're doing so with the sense of expectancy that produces substantially better results.

# Cynicism versus Optimism

My favorite description of a cynic is "someone who would demand a bacteria count on the milk of human kindness." Cynics still believe that somebody pushed Humpty Dumpty, and they'd vote against starting a Pessimist's Club because they don't believe that such a club can work.

I've read that almost half of American workers fall into the cynic category. They mistrust just about everything — government, big business, the products they purchase, their employer, supervisors, and colleagues. An additional portion of workers is classified as *wary*, with strong cynical leanings.

On the brighter side of life are the idealists — individuals who have the capacity or tendency to see the best solution or possibility in any situation. Sow those optimistic seeds, and you raise the optimist hidden inside you.

How many friends and how much peace of mind do cynics have? How well do they get along with their mates, children, and neighbors? Not many, not much, and not very well. Unfortunately, the book *The Cynical Americans,* by Donald L. Kantner and Philip H. Mirvis, points out that cynicism is rising fastest among poor people and young people under age 21. I believe that this rise in cynicism is due in part to the many politicians and media outlets that constantly harp on the idea that the rich are getting richer and the poor are getting poorer.

I am convinced that much cynicism is caused by unrealistic expectations — expecting great things to happen to you with no effort on your part. Having high expectations for yourself is an important part of success, but you must also develop a solid goals program (which I thoroughly cover in Chapter 6) to make those expectaions a reality. People too often view the world through rose-colored glasses, and when their unrealistic expectations fall short, they become cynical and put on woes-colored glasses.

A positive attitude doesn't guarantee success, but a cynical attitude guarantees failure.

# A Winning Attitude Is Using What's Left

This story from the September 12, 1995, issue of the *Detroit News* conveys a wonderful message about using what you have instead of dwelling on what you've lost:

In 1983, 19-year-old Dwayne Pingston's bright future was altered when he swerved his car sharply to his right to avoid a head-on collision and hit the shoulder of the road. Dwayne was thrown from his car, and his neck snapped, rendering his legs useless. For many people, that accident would have meant the end of their dreams. Fortunately, Dwayne has an incredible attitude, and as a result, he considered the accident a challenge to take what he had left and use it to his maximum ability.

Today, Dwayne is good-natured, unassuming, and more active than most people with two strong legs. He's an enthusiastic fisherman and deer hunter. He plays wheelchair basketball for the Easter Seals All-American Team and helped start a basketball camp for inner-city kids with disabilities, from cerebral palsy to spina bifida. He races cars at the Milan Dragway near Ann Arbor, Michigan, swims exuberantly, and helped crew a 38-foot sailboat in the Port Huron-to-Mackinac race.

He holds down two jobs and restores old cars in his spare time. His sense of humor is incredible, and he even points out advantages in having no feeling in his legs — like when he broke both ankles playing wheelchair rugby.

## Negativity on the job is like a virus

Marvin Walberg said, "A negative attitude is as deadly to your job search or career as the most potent virus. Build up your immune system by focusing on your daily objectives. When someone else's negative attitude 'coughs in your face,' walk away. Don't get infected."

When you associate with gloom-and-doom chronic complainers at work, you can't help but become more and more like them. Your reputation is affected by the people you keep company with as well. If management continually sees you associating with problem-makers, they'll assume that you're a part of the problem, too, even if you never add fuel to negative fires.

Avoid being labeled by association; spend time with people who look for and find the good in every situation.

Is Dwayne in denial? No. He recognizes that he is paralyzed from the waist down and will be that way for life. He can either bemoan his fate or recognize all the things that he still can do and then do them.

REMEMBER

Dwayne's attitude toward life teaches a tremendous lesson: Don't moan about what you have lost; rejoice about what you still have.

With the right attitude, you may be able to do even more with your life after a tragedy than you would have if the tragedy had never occurred. I'm thinking specifically about Christopher Reeve. Since his paralyzing accident — and he is in infinitely worse shape than Dwayne Pingston — he has given hope and encouragement to literally millions of people, disabled or not. His optimistic, upbeat approach to life, his hope and belief that he will continue to get better, inspire people around the world.

REMEMBER

Regardless of what happens to you, something good can come out of it. Yes, attitude is important.

## *Making Your Way through the Traffic Jams of Life*

Have you ever been stuck in a traffic jam at the worst possible time? I bet you nodded yes and thought, "It's *always* at the worst possible time!" Are you honest enough to admit that, on more than one occasion, you stomped your foot, pounded the steering wheel, shook your fist, leaned on the horn, and exclaimed in a demanding tone, "When are they going to do something about this?" I bet you said yes. I'm sure you found that the louder you blew your horn and the nastier you got when you shook your fist, the more quickly the traffic in front of you miraculously opened up and permitted you to go through.

Seriously, though, if you knew a better way to handle the situation, you would do it, wouldn't you? If you follow that foot-stomping, horn-blowing routine often enough, you raise your blood pressure, increase your chances of having a heart attack or developing ulcers, and generally ruin your disposition and shorten your life span.

A better alternative: Look at that traffic jam, smile, and say, "Oh, boy! I'll bet it's going to take at least 30 minutes to get through this mess! In 30 minutes, if I listen to motivational or informational tapes, I can add to my vocabulary, discover new leadership principles, or increase my knowledge!" Or if you have someone in the car with you, view a traffic jam as an opportunity for an uninterrupted visit. Pick up your cell phone and call someone you love — your parents, mate, or children. Use the time to make out a grocery list or plan a surprise for your mate's next birthday. Your options may not be plentiful, but using your time to accomplish meaningful results sure beats "stewing without doing."

You do have a choice — either you can gain or accomplish something while you wait, or you can get upset and bring on strokes, heart attacks, and high blood pressure. "People jams" in the office, home, neighborhood, school, playground, and ballpark can be handled in a similar manner. Although you may not be able to pop in a tape or read a book when other people's schedules don't conform to yours, you can still relax and people-watch or use the extra time to work on ideas. You'll be healthier and happier at the end of your day if you take that approach.

# Harnessing the Power of Words

Words influence your perception of the world. The right words can do wonders for your attitude; the wrong words also can have a great impact on your attitude. The right words make you feel positive; the wrong words make you feel negative. The following little vignette demonstrates what an overheard negative statement can do to an individual.

One day last summer, my son Tom and I played a round of golf with a friend and a client. It was a beautiful day with a slight breeze, a great temperature, wonderful companions — ideal circumstances for golf.

Three of us were having a fair-to-good day. Tom, who at one time had played sub-par golf, was having a phenomenal round. He had eight birdies going into the 17th hole. As we climbed the steps to the 16th green, I commented to one of our guests that unless a disaster occurred, Tom would shoot in the 60s that day. I didn't realize that Tom could hear my comment.

When we got to the 17th hole, a difficult par 3, Tom earned his second bogie of the day. Unfortunately, the 18th turned into the disaster that I had mentioned. He missed his approach shot to the green and hit the ball into the water. His next shot landed in the bunker next to the green. He finished with a 7 and ended up shooting a 70 — still a great round of golf, but not what he had hoped for.

I'm convinced that had I not made that unfortunate remark, the disaster on the 18th wouldn't have taken place. Tom assured me that my statement wasn't the problem, but I know that a negative seed can, and often does, have a negative impact.

Here's why: After a disaster thought gets planted in the mind, the imagination goes to work — with disastrous results. When I used the word *disaster,* Tom's imagination went to work, and the disaster took place. I'll always wonder what would have happened if I had said, "The next two holes are both birdie holes for Tom, and I'll bet he gets at least one."

Another story that demonstrates how words can affect your attitude, and thus your performance, involves Jaime Escalante, who taught at Garfield High School in inner-city Los Angeles. (The movie *Stand and Deliver* depicts Escalante and some of his former students.) He achieved remarkable results with his students, teaching advanced calculus and inspiring many of them to earn college scholarships. Until then, the school had not established a reputation for academic excellence.

Not depicted in the movie was the story I read about "the other Johnny." Escalante had two students named Johnny in his class: One was a straight A+ student, and the other was a D- student. The A+ student was easy to get along with, cooperated with teachers, worked hard, was popular with his peers, and so on. The D- Johnny was sullen, angry, uncooperative, disruptive, and in general not very popular.

One evening at a PTA meeting, an excited mother approached Escalante and asked, "How is my Johnny doing?" Escalante figured that the D- Johnny's mother wouldn't be asking such a question, so he described in glowing terms the A+ Johnny. He said Johnny was a wonderful student, popular with his classmates, cooperative, a hard worker, and would undoubtedly go far in life. The next morning, Johnny — the D- one — approached Escalante and said, "I really appreciate what you said to my mother about me, and I want you to know that I'm going to work real hard to make what you said the truth." By the end of that grading period, he was a C student, and by the end of the school year, he was on the honor roll.

Yes, words affect your attitude, and your attitude affects your performance. So make sure that your words are positive, because input influences outlook, outlook influences output, and output determines the outcome.

# Using Positive Affirmations

Just as other people's words affect you, the words that you say to yourself also affect your attitude. Whether you feel negative or positive depends on the input that you get, including the input you get from yourself. "You can't change from a negative mindset to a positive mindset without changing from negative talking to positive talking. To do that, you must change the input from negative to positive," says Shad Helmstetter, PhD.

Using positive affirmations is a proven technique that works miracles in many lives. Ideally, you should look yourself in the eye as you make these positive affirmations. Don't be shy; go ahead and get started! Repeat the following statements to yourself every Monday morning to get your day and week off to a great start:

- ✔ I clearly understand that failure is an event, not a person; that yesterday really did end last night; and that success isn't final and failure isn't fatal because I only fail if I quit.

- ✔ I have the courage to admit a mistake and to say that I was wrong. I have the courage to ask for help and the courage to say "I don't know." I have the courage to continually strive to be the person that I am capable of becoming. Sometimes that's tough, but it's the right thing to do, and it gives me marvelous preparation for tomorrow.

- ✔ I have vision in my life, which means that I see not only with my eyes but also with my heart.

- ✔ I have 525,600 minutes in every year of my life, and I utilize them well to maximize my ability.

- ✔ I am successful because I believe that to be truly educated, I must be mentored — either in business or in my personal life, by reading or by association — by superior minds with greater skills and mature spirits.

- ✔ I discipline myself to do the things that I need to do when I need to do them, because I know that doing them will enable me someday to do the things I want to do when I want to do them.

- ✔ I clearly understand that if I develop yearning power and apply learning power, I will increase my earning power.

- ✔ I am successful because I don't confuse activity with accomplishment. I know that I can't make it in life as a *wandering generality,* so I am a *meaningful specific.*

- ✔ I am successful in all areas of my life because I have a great sense of humor and the ability to laugh at myself.

- ✔ I am like an eraser. I recognize my mistakes, I learn from my mistakes, and then I erase those mistakes from my memory.

- ✔ I am not bothered by someone else bragging and accepting undeserved credit. I fully understand that it's not the whistle that pulls the train.

- ✔ I move forward in my life every day, even if it's only a tiny step, because I know that great things are accomplished with tiny moves, but nothing is accomplished by standing still.

- ✔ I'm a hard worker, but I don't overdo it, because I know that the person who is always as busy as a bee may awaken to discover that someone has swiped his or her honey.

- ✔ Today I will seriously look for the good in every situation and find something about which to praise every person who works with me. Today I will be friendly to the people I work with and will treat them as though they were completely responsible for my career. Today I will express gratitude for the career that I have and the society of which I am a part, and specifically for my family and friends. I will also express gratitude for the fact that my career is rewarding in ways that go far beyond financial remuneration.

# Understanding the Benefits of Persistency

For nine long years before George Bernard Shaw got anything published, editors turned down everything he sent in. But Shaw was particularly persistent and kept working, kept submitting, kept believing, and kept hoping. In the process of all that writing, he got better and better until, ultimately, nine years after he submitted his first manuscript, he got something published.

Several factors are important in this story. Shaw believed that he had ability. He patiently persisted in honing his skills and pursuing publishers until finally somebody said yes. That's a good procedure to follow. If you really believe in what you're doing and have confidence that it is significant, you persist until something positive happens, knowing that it's always darkest just before the dawn.

Based on my personal experiences and research, I'm convinced that many roads lead to success, but that sheer, dogged persistence is one attitude that everyone can use. As Goethe said, "Austere perseverance, harsh and continuous, may be employed by the smallest of us and rarely fails of its purpose, for its solid power grows irresistibly greater with time."

TIP

## Using your spare time

Virtually everyone carries a spare tire in the trunk of the car. Just yesterday, we had occasion to use ours. As you may suspect, it was an emergency — emergencies are why you carry spare tires. You carry a spare tire in your car for tens of thousands of miles and seldom use it, yet most people are hesitant to leave on a trip without one.

What you do with another spare, one that everyone has, has a daily impact, as well as a long-range impact, on your life. I'm talking about "spare time."

People seem to be busier than ever — but studies have reported that the average employed woman today puts in just over 30 hours per week; the average man works 40 hours. So where does the time go? Research reveals that people are using it to relax in front of the television set. Every additional hour that people don't spend at work they spend as

"couch potatoes," often watching mindless programs.

Imagine what would happen if you invested a few more minutes every day studying and increasing your knowledge in your chosen profession. How many more friends would you have if you took the time to be a little more thoughtful and considerate? Suppose you took more time to call or visit friends in their homes or at the hospital. How much more energy and vitality would you have if you spent that time developing better eating habits, exercising, and getting the right amount of sleep? How much happier would you be if you spent more time with your mate, your children, your parents, and so on?

As you think about these things, remember that you still have time to do them. Why not get started right now?

# Having the Happiness Attitude

Everyone wants to be happy, yet many people base their happiness on whether they have what they want or whether they want what they have. Doing so puts their emotions on a roller coaster that's controlled by what happens in their lives. Many people equate wealth with happiness and actually believe that if they win the lottery, they will be happy. Thousands of years ago, the wisest, richest, most powerful man in the world, Solomon, accumulated more things than anyone in history and experienced more pleasure than most people can imagine. Despite his wealth and power, however, Solomon felt empty.

One key to happiness is humility. The reason is simple: Humility reduces stress. Humble people don't believe that they have to have all the answers; consequently, they don't have to fake having those answers, which reduces anxiety. When anxiety goes down, happiness goes up. Humility certainly improves your relationships — nobody likes a know-it-all. A humble approach enables you to be genuinely interested in and to respect other people. And they, in turn, become genuinely interested in you. The number of your friends and positive acquaintances (those people who encourage you and build you up) grows, and your happiness increases.

Another key to happiness is your willingness to accept that happiness is a "here" and a "now" — you can't wait for it to come to you. Will Rogers said it well: "Most people are about as happy as they make up their minds to be."

Of course, certain activities increase your chances of being happy — for example, when you do something for someone else for purely altruistic reasons and have nothing to gain except delight in rendering a favor or doing a good turn. Committing selfless acts is a major step toward real happiness.

People who are only out for themselves miss out on the joy that comes from giving. People who do things for others with no personal gain in mind reap great benefits. For example, look at the glow on the faces of the volunteers who serve holiday meals to the homeless. The smiling faces of the recipients of the meals are a beautiful sight, but infinitely more beautiful are the even broader smiles of those volunteers.

# Every Day Is a Great Day

Ralph Waldo Emerson said, "Write it on your heart that every day is the best day in the year. He or she is rich who owns the day and no one owns the day who allows it to be invaded with threat and anxiety. Finish every day and be done with it. You have done what you could. Some blunders and absurdities no doubt crept in. Forget them as soon as you can. Tomorrow is a new day. Begin it well and serenely with too high a spirit to be encumbered with your old nonsense. This new day is too dear, with its hopes and invitations, to waste a moment on the yesterdays."

Each day is a miniature lifetime, and your attitude concerning each day makes a difference. If you make today a good day and repeat that process daily, you'll live a lifetime of good days. I confess that this approach to life is simple, but it isn't simplistic.

Occasionally, someone accuses me of saying that today is a good day regardless of how it's going. A degree of truth lies in that observation, but years ago I decided that every day was going to be a good day. This expectation has had a direct influence on what has happened in my life — and it can do the same for your life.

Expect today to be a good day, and then do what's necessary to make your expectations come true.

# Chapter 12

# Growing Spiritually

● ● ● ● ● ● ● ● ● ● ● ● ● ● ● ● ● ● ● ● ● ● ● ● ● ● ● ● ● ● ● ● ● ● ● ● ● ● ● ● ● ● ● ● ●

### In This Chapter

▶ Understanding the benefits of spirituality

▶ Recognizing the signs of spiritual health

▶ Knowing how and where to grow

● ● ● ● ● ● ● ● ● ● ● ● ● ● ● ● ● ● ● ● ● ● ● ● ● ● ● ● ● ● ● ● ● ● ● ● ● ● ● ● ● ● ● ● ●

*V*irtually everyone recognizes that life has three aspects:

✔ The physical

✔ The mental

✔ The spiritual

Unfortunately, many people either ignore or deny that third aspect, the spiritual. Perhaps they've never been exposed to the spiritual aspect. Maybe they were exposed to spirituality but didn't understand it and were intimidated by the terminology that often goes with things of a spiritual nature. Perhaps people ignore spirituality because it isn't a cut-and-dried issue; spirituality requires believers to have faith — to believe that something they can't physically put their hands on or see with their eyes does exist.

Another factor in the lack of attention to the spiritual may be the media, which is often inclined to ridicule anyone who professes faith of any kind. For example, in an episode of *The Simpsons,* Bart Simpson's prayer was "Dear God, we pay for all this stuff ourselves, so thanks for nothing."

Many times, individuals blame their aversion to the spiritual on far-out TV evangelists or pious Christians suffering from crushing legalism — rigid adherence to Old Testament religious law. These unfortunates believe that their relationship with God is based on what they *do,* and they can get pretty righteous when they start telling you what you should and shouldn't do. I love what Max Lucado has to say about these folks in his book, *He Still Moves Stones:*

"Legalism . . .

"Turns my opinion into your burden. There is only room for one opinion in this boat. And guess who is wrong!

"Turns my opinion into your boundary. Your opposing opinion makes me question not only your right to have fellowship with me, but also your salvation.

"Turns my opinion into your obligation. Your job isn't to think, it's to march."

It's no wonder that people who are exposed to this condescending attitude don't want any part of organized religion. But spirituality isn't a burden, and it isn't something that requires you to wear blinders. Rather, getting in touch with your spiritual side opens up countless doors. In this chapter, you can discover the benefits of living life with spirituality as your foundation and, I hope, find the purpose for your life as I have found mine. My challenge to you is this: Ask your own questions and form your own opinions based on what you discover yourself, not based on stereotypes, TV programs, or preconceived notions. The most important thing is to start your search for, or step up your growth in, spiritual wisdom.

*Note:* Many different belief systems exist throughout the world, and I respect each person's right to his or her own personal beliefs. However, as a Christian, I am going to speak in the language of my own faith and use the Bible as my source in this chapter and this book. Please feel free to substitute the terminology that you feel comfortable with.

# Getting Started Down the Road to Spirituality

Often, the search for the spiritual doesn't occur until a crisis strikes or you achieve everything that you thought would make you happy only to discover that something is still missing from your life and that happiness is as elusive as ever. For example, take the alcoholic who has lost his or her job, home, family, and the respect of friends and has reached what Alcoholics Anonymous members call "the bottom." The program of AA teaches members to find "a God of their understanding" and to pray to whomever or whatever that is, even if they don't believe in it.

This approach, called "fake it 'til you make it," may work for you, even if your only crisis is a nagging feeling that there must be more to life. "Faking it" is a logical first step in the process of discovering spirituality. You may want to pray this prayer:

"God [or, if that word goes against your grain, say "Whoever you are . . ."],
I don't know whether you exist, but I pray that, if you do, you will reveal
yourself to me."

This first step is so simple that many people miss its significance. The
beauty of the AA approach to discovering spirituality is that it doesn't
require commitment or belief or faith from the person praying. It only
requires that the individual be open to the possibility that a God of their
understanding, whom they may or may not have previously acknowledged,
may exist.

# Expressing Your Faith

After you use the "fake it 'til you make it" approach for a while, you may find
yourself starting to believe that the God of your understanding does exist
and that you're developing a faith in that God. The *1828 Noah Webster
Dictionary* defines faith as "belief; the assent of the mind to the truth of what
is declared by another, resting on his authority and veracity, without other
evidence; the judgment that what another states or testifies is the truth." In
other words, faith is the belief that what's being said is true. Faith is required
in order to adhere to any religion — Judaism, Hinduism, Islam, and so on.

The central theme of *Success For Dummies* is relationships, and success
includes having a good relationship with the God of your understanding.
The depth of your spirituality is, in my opinion, the degree to which you
have a personal relationship with the one whose governing power you
honor and obey through your faith. For example, I believe that Christianity
is a relationship, not a religion, because it is based on a personal faith in
Jesus Christ rather than on ritual, church membership, and good works.
Christianity isn't a list of do's and don'ts that get you into heaven; it is a
peaceful and joyful relationship with your Creator.

Every individual is free to express his or her faith through organized religion, where people with common beliefs come together to worship, or
unorganized religion, where individuals practice their faith and prayer life
without a structured doctrine. You don't have to join any group or denomi-
nation to have and practice your faith and what you believe about the God
of your understanding, but many people do choose to join others in their
search to satisfy their spiritual hunger.

For example, in June 1997, an Assembly of God church just outside
Pensacola, Florida, celebrated the fourth anniversary of a revival that has
attracted 1,800,000 people since its inception. That's a lot of attendees!
According to church officials, people from over 100 different countries and
all 50 of the United States have attended the revival. Sessions are held every
night from Wednesday through Sunday and often last until 1:00 a.m.

## What "spiritual wealth" means to me

Sir John Templeton, one of the wealthiest people in the United States, said:

"If we have not developed a reservoir of spiritual wealth, no amount of money is likely to make us happy. Spiritual wealth provides faith. It gives us love. It brings and expands wisdom. Spiritual wealth leads to happiness because it guides us into useful or loving relationships. With spiritual wealth as the foundation and security for our lives, we gain a deep and abiding peace that can't be obtained with material wealth alone."

To me, spiritual wealth is the assurance that there is a just and loving God who has a vested interest in me because He created me, that He loves me no matter what, and that He hears and answers my prayers. My spiritual wealth gives me great peace of mind because my past has been forgiven, God's presence as my Heavenly Father is assured on a daily basis, and my eternity is guaranteed. It increases my happiness substantially because I believe that one day I will again see my parents, daughter, brothers, sisters, and friends who have passed away.

My spiritual wealth includes a road map for life in my Bible, which provides me with specific directions on how to live life to its fullest and reap considerable benefits in the present and even more benefits (joy, peace, love, and so on) in the future.

People who lack faith often carry hurt, resentment, anger, and bitterness toward others. They are seldom, if ever, happy people who have peace of mind. The solution to this situation is forgiveness — a big part of being a spiritual human being.

It's important to understand that when you refuse to forgive someone who has wronged you, you retain the hurt, anger, and bitterness within yourself. When you forgive that person, your faith in a higher power and your belief that there is a grand design for the universe enable you to release those hurt feelings and focus on the truly important things. Ask your doctor which state of mind is healthier!

# How Spiritual Growth Can Improve Your Life

If you have operated your life to this point without a foundation of faith, let me tell you what you can look forward to after you add spirituality to your everyday life. Because of my Christian faith and to simplify wording, I am going to use the word *God* to describe "the higher power of your understanding" throughout these sections. Again, please feel free to substitute your own terms.

## Faith gives you security and comfort

You feel an incredible sense of security when you know in your heart that God is in control and that life's ultimate answer doesn't begin and end with you. Believing that your Creator will provide you with strength and knowledge when your resources are exhausted lifts the weight of the world from your shoulders.

Knowing that you have a never-ending source of strength, love, and wisdom that you can rely on is wonderfully comforting. Understanding that all things work together for good is powerful and reassuring. (This doesn't mean that each thing that happens is good, but that all events combined work for good.)

## Faith reinforces your stand for what's right

The college football season was over, the All-American selections had been made, the Heisman Trophy had been awarded, and the national champion had been crowned. The All-American kicker, Phil Dawson, was from the University of Texas. The Heisman Trophy winner was Danny Wuerfel from the University of Florida.

Interestingly enough, these two young men were preseason All-American choices by *Playboy Magazine.* They were invited to appear on national television with the other preseason All-American selections. They would have been treated royally, been given national publicity, and gotten a head start on postseason recognition. However, I understand that both of these outstanding young men declined that offer because of their faith and the conviction that the values advocated by *Playboy* and their own values were worlds apart.

I'm confident that Dawson and Wuerfel took a certain amount of good-natured ribbing from their teammates and some not-so-good-natured criticism from scores of other people who may have labeled them "narrow-minded" and "uptight." But Dawson and Wuerfel understand that character is important and that everyone must take a stand from time to time. These two young men stood their ground and, from my perspective, are better off because they did so. Not only that, but thousands of impressionable youngsters found worthy role models in them.

In this world where so few people believe in absolutes, knowing that some people do believe that absolutes exist and that not everything is "relative" is refreshing. That number includes my wife of over 50 years, who has never asked me after one of my trips whether I have been "relatively" faithful to her while I was away.

## Faith helps you to laugh instead of cry

In the summer of 1996, I had health problems that resulted in two days of hospitalization. A few days after my hospital stay, I had an early-morning dental appointment. As I walked into the reception area, where the staff members had assembled temporarily, one of them asked, "How are you doing?" I responded, "Actually, I'm not doing well at all. I've had a bad case of the shingles combined with diverticulitis, which resulted in the loss of over three pints of blood, and my energy level is low." Then I smiled and said, "As a matter of fact, as I reflect on my miserable condition, I realize that if I were to give you all the details, all of you would be reduced to tears. Mass depression would saturate this office. Frankly, my condition is so unique and awful that I'm seriously contemplating a full-length book on it, and maybe even a television special!"

Needless to say, by then everyone was smiling and laughing. I've been their patient for years, so they know me pretty well. My conditions really did exist, but a lifetime of experience told me that when people ask you how you're doing, they aren't really asking for a medical report.

If I laugh about my health problems, my survival chances are much better than if I detail all the pains and aches and handicaps under which I'm laboring (see Chapter 10). Don't misunderstand: I'm not into denial. Shingles are painful, and diverticulitis is a serious condition. But thanks to good medical care, prayer, and an abiding faith that God is in control, I can laugh about my condition, whatever it may be.

If you take the optimistic, humorous approach to your difficulties, you improve your future, win more friends, and influence more people.

## Faith keeps things in perspective

This little gem from "Words to Live By," a mini-magazine published by *Farming Magazine, Inc.*, gives you something to think about:

"If you want to feel rich, just count all the things money can't buy. If you removed the rocks, the brook would lose its song. There are hundreds of languages in the world, but a smile speaks all of them. One thing you can give and still keep is your word. We're all faced with a series of great opportunities, brilliantly disguised as 'impossible situations.' If we fill our hours with regrets over the failures of yesterday, and worries over the problems of tomorrow, we have no time in which to be thankful for the laughter and the sunshine, the love and the joy of today. If I cannot do great things, I can do small things in a great way. There are two ways to get to the top of an oak tree: Catch that first limb and climb, or find a good, healthy acorn and sit on it."

The message so beautifully expressed in this paragraph is that you need to start from where you are with what faith you have in order to get full measure of what life has to offer. The problem is that many people want to wait until everything is "just right" before they start anything. But you don't have to see the end of the road in order to take the first step; taking that first step without seeing the end is what faith is all about. The rule is simple: Go as far as you can see. When you get there, you're able to see farther, so again go as far as you can see.

Don't wait for all circumstances to be just right. Start and take control of the circumstances. That way, you don't have to wait for the acorn to grow — you'll be climbing the tree, with faith providing a substantial boost.

## Faith brings you love

One of my favorite hymns is "Love Lifted Me." That's doubly true when that love is strengthened with faith. This poignant story gives love strengthened with faith a special meaning:

An 8-year-old girl in a Pennsylvania orphanage was shy, unattractive, and regarded as a problem. Two other homes had transferred her, and now the director of the girl's current home was seeking some pretext for getting rid of her. One day, someone noticed the little girl writing a letter. An ironclad rule of the institution was that any communication from a child had to be approved before it was mailed. The next day, the director and her assistant watched the child steal out of the dormitory and slip down to the main gate. Just inside the gate was an old tree with roots showing above the ground. They followed and watched as the child hid the letter in one of the crevices of the root. Carefully looking around, the little girl scurried back to the dormitory.

The director took the note and tore it open. Then, without speaking, she passed the note to her assistant. The note read, "To anybody who finds this: I love you."

You can't experience life to the fullest until you experience love. Faith helps you give others the benefit of the doubt, which is another way you demonstrate your love and help others to feel loved. Marriage is a good example of how that works. When you get married, you're saying, "I am with you, I cast my vote for you, I trust you, and because I believe in you, I can experience life and love to a larger degree." Faith in God delivers the same thing, only on a much, much larger scale.

## Everyone believes in something

I'm convinced that, deep down, everyone — even agnostics and atheists — believes that there is a God. For example, one night, Mordecai Ham, the hellfire and brimstone preacher who was preaching when Billy Graham made his commitment to Christ, was confronted just before he was to preach. The man who confronted him said, "I'm here, Mr. Ham, because I'm curious. But I just want you to know that I don't believe in heaven, I don't believe in hell, I don't believe in God, and I certainly don't believe in prayer."

When Ham stood up to preach, he told the congregation, "Folks, we've got an unusual man here. He doesn't believe in heaven, doesn't believe in hell, doesn't believe in God, and certainly doesn't believe in prayer. I want all of us, the entire time I'm preaching, to pray that God will kill this man before I'm through."

With that, the man jumped out of his seat and ran out of the building, screaming, "Don't you do it! Don't you do it!" Like I said, I believe that, deep down, everyone believes that a God exists.

Two thoughts on this story: First, neither Ham nor any Christian in the group would have prayed that prayer. Second, I believe, based on this incident, that anyone facing what he or she believes to be his or her imminent death would at least pray the prayer that renowned atheist Ralph Ingersol prayed as he lay dying: "Oh God, if there be a God, have mercy on my poor soul."

# The Signs of Spiritual Health

I find that the promises in the Big Book of Alcoholics Anonymous are a good description of spiritual health, and I would be remiss if I didn't call them to your attention. I paraphrase by replacing the words *we, us,* and *our* as they pertain to the alcoholic with *you* and *your* as they pertain to you and what you will experience as you grow in your spiritual health and maturity.

> "You are going to know a new freedom and a new happiness. You will not regret the past nor wish to shut the door on it. You will comprehend the word serenity, and you will know peace. No matter how far down the scale you have gone, you will see how your experience can benefit others. That feeling of uselessness and self-pity will disappear. You will lose interest in selfish things and gain interest in your fellows. Self-seeking will slip away. Your whole attitude and outlook upon life will change. Fear of people and of economic insecurity will leave you. You will intuitively know how to handle situations which used to baffle you. You will suddenly realize that God is doing for you what you could not do for yourself."

All the benefits described in this passage can and will happen to you as you learn to "Let go and let God."

# You feel and express gratitude

In his forthcoming book, psychiatrist Louis Cady makes this observation:

"Whether or not one believes in a Supreme Being, the notion that there is nothing to be grateful for outside of the self is, in my professional opinion, the first step down a very slippery slope to nihilism, despair, self-pity, isolation of the self, depression and death. If we have 'nothing to be thankful for' we must by definition not feel grateful for the beauties of nature, marvelous sunsets, snow-capped peaks, peaceful sandy beaches, green and peaceful forests, and the melody of the wind.

"If we have nothing to feel grateful for, let us abandon gratitude for the miracle of new life which emerges every season as the trees and flowers bloom, and the cries of every newborn baby. If we have nothing to be grateful for, let us forget about looking into our sweetheart's eyes, walks on the beach together, and the experience of campfires. If we have nothing to feel grateful for, let us abandon all love, respect, admiration and devotion to our parents who did the very best they could for us.

"If we have nothing to feel grateful for, let us state unequivocally that we care nothing for our marvelous bodies which, for most of us, carry us wherever we want to go and are capable of athletic mastery. Let us forget that with a moderate amount of exercise we can stay in finely tuned shape and live a minimum of our three-score and ten years on this planet, enjoying our 'holiday on earth.'"

Cady reminds us that we have much to be thankful for. The truth is, if you express gratitude for what you have, you have more to express gratitude for. I believe that gratitude is a spiritual aspect. When you fully understand that a creator — your Creator — made all that is wonderful and beautiful for your pleasure and enjoyment, the concept can be overwhelming at times. God went to such great lengths for you and for me. The gratitude that you feel at that realization truly takes on a spiritual aspect that is so large that many an author has been hard-pressed to find just the right words to describe it — including me.

Dr. Jack Graham of Prestonwood Baptist Church in Dallas suggests that if you can't think of something to be grateful for each morning, then think of some of the things you don't have that you can be grateful for not having. For example, you can be grateful that you don't have a fatal disease, a sick loved one, or unemployment staring you in the face. Of all the attitudes you can acquire, surely the attitude of gratitude is the most important and by far the most life-changing.

## *You believe in the Golden Rule: A universal religious principle*

The Golden Rule is a principle that is universally accepted. Consider the following list of tenets from various faiths and philosophies and note the similarities:

- **Brahmanism:** "This is the sum of duty: Do naught unto others which would cause you pain if done unto you."

- **Buddhism:** "Hurt not others in ways that you yourself would find hurtful."

- **Confucianism:** "Do not unto others what you would not have them do unto you."

- **Hinduism:** "The true role of life is to guard and do by the things of others as they do on their own."

- **Islam:** "No one of you is a believer until he desires for his brother that which he desires for himself."

- **Taoism:** "Regard your neighbor's gain as your own gain and your neighbor's loss as your own loss."

- **Judaism:** "Whatever is hurtful to yourself do not to your fellow man. That is the whole of the law, the rest is merely a commentary."

- **Christianity:** "Do unto others as you would have others do unto you."

The Golden Rule is the same — on any continent, in any country, in any home, and in any religion. The world would simply be a much better place if everyone adhered to serving others in the way that they would like to be served. Living life based on that principle enhances personal spirituality.

# Growing Up Spiritually

You can take a wide variety of steps to enhance your spiritual growth. The following sections discuss some of the steps that I have found to be helpful.

## Associate with like-minded people

I believe that the most important factor in spiritual growth is associating with other people who are pursuing spiritual growth. Fellowship is the greatest secret of people who are on a quest for spiritual knowledge. By associating with others of similar faith, you expose yourself to individuals who can share their years of study and of living their faith with you. Good teachers are important to continued growth and interest in any area of life, but especially in the area of spiritual growth.

## Memorize one new spiritual passage each day

Another way to grow spiritually is to memorize one new spiritual passage each day. As you memorize passages, record them on a hand-held tape recorder. Listening to those recordings reinforces your memorization, and when difficult situations arise in your life, you're better able to recall spiritual passages that can help you decide how you want to handle your circumstance. An added benefit is that this process not only improves your memory for the spiritual teachings but also improves your memory of everything else.

## Mark favorite spiritual passages for rereading

Another method of growing spiritually is to mark those passages in your favorite work on spirituality, and then do a little cherry-picking. Sometimes, when my time is limited, I get into the Proverbs or the Psalms or the writings of Paul and read over the promises that my God has made. Not only does reading these passages help me grow spiritually, but it also gets me excited for the day's opportunities.

When you hear inspiring sermons, get tapes of those sermons so that you can listen to them again and again. An inspiring sermon lifts you up. When you listen to it a second time, you're listening from a higher level, and you hear things that you didn't hear before. When you're emotionally down or discouraged and listen again to a sermon, you hear the sermon from a different perspective, and it takes on new meaning. When you're on a spiritual, emotional high, you listen from an entirely different point of view and get even more from the message.

As you listen repeatedly to the same message, I encourage you to take notes. Keep a record of favorite verses or stories that have special meaning to you. Perhaps my greatest benefit from this exercise is that I often get ideas.

That's really what motivation is all about: pulling out of you what's already inside you. The new knowledge that I acquire in listening, combined with the knowledge I already have, creates new ideas. That's a major contributor to spiritual growth.

## Enroll in religious or spiritual study

An obvious spiritual growth opportunity is to enroll in religious or spiritual study, where you get more in-depth explanations of some of the writings that you may regularly hear but have not really explored.

## Pray

In the spiritual world, prayer leads to one of the greatest growth possibilities of all: the ability to see yourself and the changes you need to make in your life clearly so that you can live more fully and abundantly. Virtually every religion espouses this principle of growth through prayer or meditation. In Christianity, which I believe is a relationship and not a "religion," the Bible says that Christians literally have the "mind of Christ," and because He is the creator of the universe, Christians have access to incredible amounts of knowledge. So prayer and study are wonderful tools that you can use to grow, which is probably why hieroglyphics from around the world and across the centuries depict people praying to their gods as I pray to Christ.

The problem that most people have when they pray is that they too frequently expect a positive answer. Sometimes God says yes, sometimes no, and sometimes He says to wait. Many times when God says no, the no turns out to be the best answer for you. I vividly remember two occasions when I prayed long and hard for a specific thing. I even carefully explained to God that a yes would be in both His and my best interests. In both cases, nothing happened, which means that God either said no or said not yet. Within a year, I found out that if God had said yes to the first prayer, the result would have been a disaster for me. Five years later, I understood that a yes to the second prayer would have resulted in disaster, too.

## Sleep well and profitably

The last thing you put into your mind before you go to sleep gets firmly lodged into your subconscious mind and affects your thinking and your sleep. It also affects your creativity and your outlook on life. Despite this fact, millions of people watch the evening news, much of which is negative, and then go to bed hoping for a good night's sleep. Doesn't make sense, does it?

## Does prayer really work?

Does prayer have an impact? Is it effective? A study by Dr. Randolph Bird, a cardiologist at the University of California at San Francisco School of Medicine, emphatically says yes. In 1988, Bird tested the impact of distant prayer, much like a new medication. He recorded its effects on nearly 400 patients who had severe chest pains and/or had had heart attacks. Half these patients were prayed for, and the other half were not.

Only 3 of the patients who were prayed for required antibiotics, compared to 17 in the group who were not prayed for. The prayed-for group had no need for mechanical respirators, compared to the 12 people who were not prayed for who needed mechanical respirators.

Only 5 of the prayed-for patients needed diuretics, compared to 15 of the non-prayed-for patients. The prayed-for group suffered only 8 cases of congestive heart failure, compared to 20 cases in the group that was not prayed for. The prayed-for group experienced 3 cardiopulmonary arrests, compared to 14 in the unprayed-for group. Three people who were prayed for fell ill with pneumonia, compared to 13 who were not prayed for and got pneumonia.

Factual results like these ought to make a pray-er out of you, even if you have no idea who you're praying to! When you feel helpless to do anything for someone with big problems, pray. Prayer changes lives positively.

What is the proper procedure, then? The answer, I believe, is to read or listen to something of an encouraging, uplifting, positive nature before going to bed. The Bible is certainly a marvelous source, as is beautiful, encouraging poetry; short stories out of uplifting magazines; and inspirational writings that give you encouragement by people you admire.

That procedure ensures that the last input into your mind is informative and encouraging. Over a period of time, you not only acquire significant information but also are able to get a good night's sleep every night. Additionally, this procedure increases your potential for creativity because the new information and ideas, combined with the peace that the message gives you, gets your creative juices flowing and enables you to more completely utilize all the information that you've accumulated over a lifetime.

For maximum results, follow the go-to-bed procedure with a similar get-up procedure. Start your day by listening to inspiring, upbeat music; doing some spiritually uplifting reading; or praying. When you start and end your day properly, the time in between goes far better.

## Where to Go from Here

If you're new to the idea of spiritual growth and are wondering how to start your journey, let me suggest the following:

✔ Question the people in your life who already seem to have spiritual direction and whose lives and lifestyles attract you. What are their foundational beliefs? Where do they worship? Ask to attend worship services or study group sessions with them.

✔ Go to the library or bookstore and pick up books that detail various religious beliefs. Josh McDowell's *Evidence that Demands a Verdict* and *A Handbook on Today's Religions,* which covers all the major religions, are excellent resource books. Read and research just as seriously as you would if you were investing your life savings — after all, you're investing your mind, your heart, and your soul. That's just about everything, in my book!

✔ Understand that finding out what you believe takes time. Few people come to know what they believe without undergoing something of an internal struggle. Keep a positive attitude about your quest, and remember that few things are more confusing — or more rewarding — than spirituality.

# Chapter 13

# Developing Fantastic Friendships

● ● ● ● ● ● ● ● ● ● ● ● ● ● ● ● ● ● ● ● ● ● ● ● ● ● ● ● ● ● ● ● ● ● ● ●

## *In This Chapter*

▶ Using the Golden Rule philosophy

▶ Finding good rather than faults

▶ Giving more to get more

▶ Building friendship "teams"

▶ Turning foes into friends

▶ Maintaining your optimism

▶ Developing a pleasant personality

● ● ● ● ● ● ● ● ● ● ● ● ● ● ● ● ● ● ● ● ● ● ● ● ● ● ● ● ● ● ● ● ● ● ● ●

*E*veryone speaks of the need for friends and the roles that friends play in your life. An anonymous writer put it this way: "Friends in your life are like pillars on your porch. Sometimes they hold you up and sometimes they lean on you. Sometimes it's just enough to know they're standing by." Writer Elisabeth Foley points out that friendship doubles your joy and divides your grief, and that the most beautiful discovery that true friends make is that they can grow separately without growing apart.

Easily the most important place to have a friend is in marriage (see Chapter 14). For that reason, marriage counselors continually advise husbands and wives to be friends, pointing out that you may divorce your spouse, but you don't divorce your friend.

I'm especially pleased and grateful that my best friend is my wife. When I enjoy a unique experience in my travels, I invariably think to myself, "If she were here, it would be even nicer!" On the other hand, when I've had a tough day or I'm not feeling well, having her near is comforting and increases my enjoyment of living.

Friendship stabilizes plenty of relationships, not only in marriage but in the business and social worlds as well. A friendship is priceless and should be cherished, cultivated, and nurtured. But how do you develop and maintain solid friendships? This chapter outlines some principles of friendship that can help you improve the friendships you already have and build even more friendships in the future.

# Remembering the Golden Rule

Without a doubt, the greatest friend-maker and human-relations principle going is to *treat other people like you want to be treated.* Friendship requires many qualities — unselfishness, genuine care for the other person, and the ability to listen when the other person needs to talk, to name a few. When you show respect for your friends and gratitude for their friendship, you'll be blessed in untold ways.

Sometimes just being there — particularly in times of grief, when nobody knows what to say — can make a difference. The fact that you're there to share the pain is what counts. Not knowing what to say doesn't matter; your presence speaks volumes and says everything that needs to be said. People need to share their grief and love to share their joy. If friends were there only for those two occasions, they would still be invaluable.

## Apply the Golden Rule to everyday living

In one form or another, the Golden Rule has been embraced by every major religion in the world (see Chapter 12). I recently came across a list of golden rules for living by an unknown author. These rules, if followed, can increase your enjoyment of life and improve your relationships with your friends, as well as with your family and your associates:

- ✔ If you open it, close it.
- ✔ If you turn it on, turn it off.
- ✔ If you unlock it, lock it up.
- ✔ If you break it, admit it.
- ✔ If you can't fix it, call in someone who can.
- ✔ If you borrow it, return it.
- ✔ If you value it, take care of it.
- ✔ If you make a mess, clean it up.
- ✔ If you move it, put it back.
- ✔ If it belongs to someone else, get permission to use it.
- ✔ If you don't know how to operate it, leave it alone.
- ✔ If it's none of your business, don't ask questions.

## Love them anyhow

Although the way you treat others affects the way they treat you, the way another person treats you shouldn't determine the way you treat that person. I've often explained to my children that they should respond to rude behavior with the utmost kindness. You can't know what has gone on in the rude person's life that day, but you can assume that his or her day hasn't gone well. Maybe a loved one lost his job, her boss reprimanded her unjustly, he's coming down with the flu, or she just found out that her teenager is doing drugs. Whatever the cause of the rudeness, you don't have to join in and accentuate the problem. A kind word or a gentle, understanding smile is sure to help the person more than returned rudeness would. When people are rude and ugly to you, they're probably behaving that way because they're hurting, not because they want to hurt you.

Chances are good that you know the story of Helen Keller. Helen was born a normal, healthy little girl. As a child, a terrible disease took away her sight and hearing. To compensate for her loss, her family petted, pampered, and spoiled her, and she became absolutely incorrigible, a little girl whom nobody could get along with. Feeling sorry for her because she was so afflicted was easy, but face it: She was a spoiled kid.

The first day that Anne Sullivan came into the Keller household to work with Helen, Helen threw food at her, trying to scream. Anne simply looked at her and said, "Little girl, you can act like you want to, you can be as mean and as obnoxious as you choose to be, but I don't see you in the same way you see yourself. I believe that you were put here for a purpose. I believe that there is enormous potential inside of you. I'm going to love you so much, and treat you in such a way, that the potential inside you is going to come out."

Who was the big winner in this exchange? Helen Keller positively influenced millions of people through her books and the movies based on her life, as well as her personal appearances as she toured the world telling her story of overcoming adversity, but Anne Sullivan was the individual who made that story possible. In the process, Anne, too, became a winner.

# Don't Criticize Your Friends Unjustly

Human nature being what it is, most people tend to see problems and faults more easily in other people than in themselves. Lucy (of *Peanuts* fame), the sage of humor and wisdom and certainly one of the great philosophers of all time, puts this observation into perspective.

Linus, obviously troubled, appeared with his security blanket in tow and his thumb safely in his mouth and asked Lucy, "Why are you always so anxious to criticize me?" Lucy's response was classic: "I just think I have a knack for seeing other people's faults." Exasperated with that answer, Linus threw up his hands and asked, "What about your own faults?" Lucy never hesitated: "I have a knack for overlooking them."

This story may make you laugh, but it isn't completely humorous. Lucy's approach to life brings discomfort and misery, particularly to the one who dishes out that kind of criticism. The recipient of cynical put-downs is hurt, but the one who gives them is ultimately hurt much more. Acid destroys the container in which it's stored, and Lucy's approach — which is one that many people take — breaks down the person who holds that attitude in a similar manner.

Instead of being eager to dish out criticism all the time, take the humane, sensible approach. Look for the good in other people. Encourage them. Build them up. That method may not be as much fun as Lucy's approach, but it's satisfying, beneficial, and a great friendship-builder.

The secret is simple: Be a good-finder, not a fault-finder.

# Giving More, Getting More

I love this story because it communicates one of the great messages about friendships.

A city man bought a farm. When he went out to look at the line fence, which had been the source of much quarreling for the previous owner, the neighboring farmer said, "That fence is a full foot over on my side." "Very well," said the new owner, "we will set the fence two feet over on my side." "Oh, but that's more than I claim," stammered the surprised farmer. "Never mind about that. I would much rather have peace with my neighbor than two feet of earth," said the man. "That's surely fine of you, sir," replied the farmer, "but I couldn't let you do a thing like that. That fence just won't be moved at all."

This story says a great deal about being reasonable and fair, but it goes beyond that. It also talks about being generous and how generosity can produce surprising benefits. You must weigh what you lose against what you gain.

When evaluating the city man's approach in retrospect, most folks say, "That was a smart thing to do!" But most people are so concerned about looking out for number one that they seldom think through each situation completely and consider the other person's rights and point of view. If you take the time and effort to do those things, I bet you'll end up with more friends.

# Love, Loyalty, and Friendship for Sale

The heading of this section may seem a little strange. You may be thinking to yourself, "That simply isn't true. Those things are extremely valuable and can't be bought at any price." I beg to differ.

As newspaper columnist George Matthew Adams said, "We always buy our friends. Not in any material sense, but we pay in pleasantness, sincerity, warmth of heart, or an inspiring personality. These are things which are not matched in mere money measure. They're the quality of people, something of finer design and workmanship than the most exquisite spun wool or even threads of gold."

To this statement, I add that *you buy love by giving love*. What you send out truly is what you get back. Surely you've noticed that when you greet people with a pleasant smile and a cheery "Good morning!" you're far more likely to get a friendly greeting in return. When you ignore people, you're likely to be ignored. And when you treat people in a grouchy, discourteous way, you're far more likely to be treated similarly.

You "buy" loyalty by being loyal; you "buy" friendship by being a friend; you "buy" hope by giving hope; and so on. No person is happy or has friends or love who is not truly a giver or "seller" of the qualities I mention.

The bottom line is that you really can buy friends, happiness, and love, so buy plenty. The purchase price is the best investment you can make.

# Friendship Is Really Team-Building

I've heard it said that a group becomes a team when all the members are sure enough of themselves and their contributions that they can praise the skill, abilities, and contributions of the others. A friendship is simply a mini-team. When you're comfortable with yourself, fear and prejudice go right out the window, and you build friendships.

I think that one of the most moving photos I've seen in a newspaper was taken at the end of the 1992 Army-Navy game, which Army won. Brian Ellis, the Navy quarterback, had just thrown a last desperation pass, and it had been intercepted. The photo shows Brian on his knees, head bowed, as Army defensive back Cadet Gaylord Green stands by with his helmet in his hands, his face against the helmet of his defeated adversary. The picture said it all: "We just played a tough game, but underneath we're on the same team. We're brothers."

# Converting Foes to Friends

I know that you recognize the substantial difference between friends and foes. A friend looks after your own good, is attached to you by affection, and entertains other sentiments of esteem. A friend is really interested in serving your best interests. On the other hand, an enemy or foe is someone who really isn't interested in your well-being. Who knows — he or she may even wish you harm.

I believe that a friend is someone who, knowingly or unknowingly, intentionally or unintentionally, takes action that brings you joy or other benefits. For example, many salespeople consider a competitor who takes away one of their customers to be anything but a friend. The salesperson may have been hurt temporarily, but if that salesperson finds out why the competitor was able to lure the customer away, he or she can make the changes that are needed to get the customer back. If the salesperson takes that approach, the foe becomes a friend by rendering a real service and helping business to increase over the long haul.

Similarly, some students don't want to go to school and may even view their teachers as enemies. However, a moment's thought helps you realize that a student's success in school partly depends on the teacher's effectiveness in the classroom. Instead of being an enemy, a teacher who corrects you and helps you to achieve can be the best friend you ever had.

Most people prefer to be around folks who are friendly and who say nice things to and about them. I confess that when I receive criticism, I may not appreciate it at the moment, but in many cases, the critic turns out to be more of a friend than a person who praises, because the criticism prompts me to improve. If you properly evaluate each piece of criticism you receive, I'll lay odds that you realize that those people really are friends. This kind of thinking, along with a little attitude adjustment, helps you to convert foes to friends, and both of you are better off.

Ralph Waldo Emerson said, "He who has a thousand friends has not a friend to spare, while he who has one enemy shall meet him everywhere."

# Making Friends by Being an Optimist

Do you enjoy being around a pessimist, someone who is generally described as being able to brighten up a room just by leaving it? The answer is obvious. Most people, when given a choice, prefer to be around people who believe that tomorrow is going to be better than today, rather than being with people who believe that today is even worse than yesterday.

I love what Lawrence Fargher has to say about optimists:

"Our American way of life is so full of blessings that no man can count them all, but the greatest of them all is the optimist; he exudes cheerfulness like an atomic bomb diffuses radiation.

"There is a mellow radiance about the optimist that sheds its light on social and business ventures and which pervades our souls to a depth that brilliant intellect can never reach.

"The optimist is a double blessing — a blessing to himself and the world around him; he carries an atmosphere of hope and encouragement which becomes infectious and his associates lose their gloom in the light of his benevolence.

"No matter what his personal trials and troubles are, the true optimist never pours them into public circulation; nor does he solicit sympathy with which to lull his grief but which never cures his ills.

"Fortunately this nation is populated with millions of optimists whose vision and foresight built mills and railroads, raised wheat, drilled oil wells, and invented telephones and television."

Optimists spread cheer wherever they go and make others feel good about themselves. That's a guaranteed way to make friends.

# Capturing the Personality Attitude

In the 1700s and 1800s, character was the foundation of American education and life. Then, at the turn of the 20th century, personality entered the picture. By the middle of this century, personality was the "in" thing. Today, the pendulum is swinging again, and people are going back to esteeming character and belittling personality. That's too bad, because personality is the sum total of all your personal qualities, and it's very important.

Virtually every time you say that so-and-so has "charisma," you're really talking about what a great personality he or she has. You mean that when he walks into a room, he has a presence — not just looks — that attracts attention from the people around him. Or you mean that when she walks into a crowded room, you soon hear a soft buzz coming from the area where she is.

Yes, having a great personality comes with certain innate advantages. One advantage is that people relate to you from the beginning of a relationship — an important advantage because making a permanent friend is impossible until you've made a temporary one. Making the sale before you get into the good graces of the person you're dealing with is difficult, too.

Another advantage to a pleasing personality is that when people like you, they're more likely to trust you. They're also less likely to lie to you or deceive you. When people genuinely like you, they're more than fair with you and may even help you to expand your business.

Naturally, you like to help your friends and want to do things with and for them. Who knows — some of them may even invite you to play a round of golf or go to dinner or to a ball game. Over the long haul, being a trustworthy person with a pleasing personality leads to good, long-term relationships.

The question is, how do you develop that pleasing personality? Here are some steps you can take:

- **Smile when you see someone.** You don't have to give a wide grin — just a pleasant, friendly smile.

- **Speak in a pleasant, upbeat tone of voice.** Talk to people as if they are really good friends of yours, even if they don't really fall into that category yet.

- **Take a course in public speaking.** Courses are offered in many schools and commercial ventures, such as my own company, Ziglar Training Systems, and Dale Carnegie. The ability to express yourself is of paramount importance and attracts favorable attention from many sources.

- **Become a better-informed person and develop a sense of humor.** I particularly encourage you to pick up a couple of good joke books. The *Anguished English* books, which take examples from schoolrooms, bloopers from churches, misprints from newspapers, and so on, are the funniest joke books I've read. As I read them, I can't help but laugh. You can share the one-liners that you read with others, and you don't have to be a comedian to get a smile from them.

  This process makes you a little more outgoing and friendly. When you combine that quality with the ability to express yourself before a group, your confidence grows and your competence increases. When you add the right attitude to confidence and competence, you've got a winning combination.

Personality opens the door and helps you to win friends and influence people at least temporarily, but *character* keeps those friends and maintains that influence. (You can read more about character in Chapter 3.)

# Chapter 14

# Developing a Lifetime Romance: Marriage Goals

*Y*ou can identify happy, successful marriages by watching couples in action. The way a couple interacts when walking, having a meal, or just sitting together tells a great deal. Frequent smiles and occasional laughs, touching, hugging, and hand-holding are all outward signs of inward contentment and affection. But a couple doesn't show such affection and achieve such contentment by accident; their outward interactions reflect the commitment and effort that they bring to their marriage.

The happy, successful marriage that I just described can be yours — if you're willing to work at it. In this chapter, I tell you how to go about building that marriage. I won't tell you that doing so is easy, but I can tell you that much of the effort is fun, and I can personally attest to the fact that the end result is well worth it.

Divorce, from a statistical point of view and from personal observation, often devastates both husband and wife, and it devastates the children in an even higher percentage of cases. Staying married is the goal of every marriage. Practicing the procedures that I talk about in this chapter can help you strengthen that foundation and bring love and romance back into your marriage.

You want to keep the romance alive because every marriage — including yours — has the potential for fun. And when you're having fun, chances are good that divorce is never going to happen. Yes, the evidence is in . . . and it's solid. You need to work at improving your marriage and have fun in the process. Having fun in your marriage doesn't mean a comedy every day, but it does mean establishing respect for each other and continuing the court-ship throughout your lifetime.

### Before you say "I don't"

At times, difficulties seem to get out of control, and husbands and wives think that calling it quits would be a relief. To put an end to that destructive thinking, many marriage counselors suggest that in addition to counseling, couples should attend a half-dozen sessions of Parents Without Partners. At these sessions, they get a reality check on what is involved, as a single parent, in juggling appointments with beauty shops, barber shops, doctors, and dentists, as well as arranging for car repair, lawn care, bill-paying, laundry, house cleaning, and so on — and then add early-morning meetings, late-night meetings, lunches with clients, deadlines requiring overtime, and a host of other things.

Now consider the children: Add more trips to doctors and dentists, getting them up and putting them to bed, dropping them off and picking them up from the day-care center and/or school, shopping, meals, school plays and other activities, conferences with teachers, recitals, athletic events, sickness, vacation, and so on.

Now throw in the loneliness factor (assuming that no third party is involved) and having to make all or most of the countless decisions that were normally made together, and many couples see that as difficult as the marriage may be, doing all those things all the time on their own would be even more difficult. At any rate, the Parents Without Partners sessions highlight a multitude of reasons why saving the marriage is certainly worth the "good ol' college try."

Obviously, this rule has exceptions. If you've done everything you know to do to salvage your marriage and your mate is still not responsive, a separation may be the catalyst necessary to move your mate to do what it takes to mend the relationship. If your mate is physically or emotionally abusing you and is unwilling to go into counseling, you have no obligation to remain with that person and be abused in the process. Repeated adultery or child abuse are other reasons why you aren't obligated to stay with your mate. Again, however, many times counseling can help a person to understand the importance of and need for a change in his or her behavior.

# Ordinary People, Extraordinary Marriage

Perfect marriage doesn't require perfect partners. "Ordinary" partners can have an extraordinary marriage. My friend and mentor Fred Smith says, "I know it sounds radical, but I am persuaded that almost any man and woman of good will desiring to build a good marriage have an excellent chance at doing it."

Your attitude and approach to your marriage are keys to attaining happiness and harmony — which sound like great goals! Take note of these two basic ideas:

> ✔ Start with the optimistic attitude that regardless of where your marriage is at the moment, you can take actions to make it better.
>
> ✔ Keep in mind that harmony and happiness in marriage come through constant compromise — not occasionally, but every day.

Hope is what you base your commitment on — hope for a life enhanced by the presence of your mate and hope for the future you will share with that mate. An optimistic attitude coupled with the willingness to take action, even when it would be more comfortable to retain the status quo, goes a long way toward building a satisfying, happy relationship with the one you love.

# Goal: Building the Marriage Foundation

For years, I labored under the illusion that if my wife and I needed to be across town in ten minutes, we had to leave immediately. On many occasions, that beautiful redheaded wife of mine wanted to tell me something before we left. I felt that she could tell me on the way, but I was wrong. I don't know why it took me so long to realize that she wanted to share what she had to say while she was looking me in the eye and had my undivided attention. I finally realized that another 60 to 90 seconds were not going to make any real difference in what happened when we arrived at our destination. However, giving her that attention and respect made a great deal of difference to her and to our relationship. When I developed the patience to stop and listen, I eliminated one of those stress points that ultimately has a negative impact on any marriage.

Understanding your mate in all of life's situations is an important foundation for a successful marriage. The way you amuse and please each other, as well as the way you respond to and support your mate in difficult times, indicates the degree of success of your marriage. The following questions can help you see whether you are on target for having a strong marital foundation:

> ✔ **What activities do you enjoy together?** Enjoying *everything* together isn't necessary, but you should enjoy *some* things as a couple — attending worship services; going to an occasional ball game, play, or movie; visiting with other couples; or cooking out with people whose company you both enjoy. Do you have some of the same friends? Do you enjoy trips together? If you share leisure time, you will share some of the best times, which always makes feelings of intimacy grow.
>
> ✔ **How do you treat each other's families?** (You marry the entire family, you know.) Do you put down your mate's family, or are you willing to go at least for short visits, even though you don't necessarily enjoy that time? In a successful marriage, neither partner always has his or her way, and one of the genuine manifestations of love is being willing to understand that your mate needs his or her way as often as you need yours.

> ✔ **Can you criticize your mate's actions without being critical of your mate?** In happy marriages, each partner is able to express displeasure over certain actions without belittling the other person in any way. *Never* make disparaging comments such as "That was a stupid thing to do!" or "How on earth could you possibly believe that?" Rather than putting each other down, successful marriage partners seek to correct actions that displease them but remain kind to one another and forgiving of one another.

## Decide on commitment

Genuine commitment is never tentative, half-hearted, or casual. Marriage is an ongoing decision. Making that commitment enables you to grow together through the hard times. It makes it possible to overcome, persevere, and press on when relationships of lesser stature would have disintegrated long before.

In the later years of her life, the wife of the fabled Frank Gabelein — Princeton scholar, mountain climber, concert pianist, and founder of Stony Brook School — became an invalid. Frank stopped his work to take care of her. In taking care of her, he discovered that his love for her grew. For him, commitment was a reward greater than the penalty of her disability. You need this kind of total commitment for love between two people to be healthy and deep-rooted. Keep in mind that where you have tentativeness, you can never have deep-rootedness.

Fred Smith shares an experience that he had in a donut shop in Grand Saline, Texas: "While there, we noticed a young farm couple sitting at the next table. He was wearing overalls and she a gingham dress. After finishing their donuts, he got up to pay the bill, and I was surprised that she didn't get up to follow him. But then he came back and stood in front of her. She put her arms around his neck and he lifted her up, revealing that she was wearing a full body brace. He lifted her out of her chair and backed out the front door to the pickup truck with her hanging from his neck. As he gently put her into the truck, we all watched but no one had said anything until the waitress remarked, almost reverently, 'He took his vows seriously.'"

Anyone who has taken his or her vows seriously finds out firsthand over time what J. Allan Petersen said so well in the October 1995 issue of *Better Families*, "Love is something you do — not something you feel — an activity directed toward another person. Love is not a victim of our emotions, it's a servant of our will. It's time for us to stop just saying we love others. It's time for us to really love them and show it by our actions. Love is a practice we initiate; an action we choose."

## Compromise for harmony

Compromise isn't denying right and wrong; it's simply admitting that both sides can have some right and some wrong. For one person to profess to represent all the right and the other person all the wrong is generally self-righteous and creates an insoluble conflict. If harmony is your end, then compromise is your means.

Most people are willing to go 50-50, but in compromise, both parties are willing to go 60-40, and that 10 percent overlap in the relationship forms the bond of harmony. When each person struggles for a 50-50 partnership without being able to define what 50-50 means, the two sides keep clashing without an overlap that bonds them.

Folks with a magnanimous spirit see compromise as a useful tool, not a score-keeping device. They say, "I want you to see my point, but I also want to respect yours." Each compromise must be a completed deal, not bleeding over into the next — keeping score builds a reservoir of conflict. A harmonious compromise is more than a victory for one and a defeat for the other; each person must get a fair share from the compromise.

Compromise is the only constructive alternative to fighting. Because fighting usually ends in "negotiated peace," or compromise, the wise thing to do is to compromise *before* the fight so that you avoid all the pain and anger that come with fighting.

Good compromise requires both skill and spirit. When a difference begins to arise in a happy, successful marriage, you can generally avoid a fight if you or your partner remembers to say, "Please, let's talk quietly to each other." If you approach compromise with an honest spirit, you'll feel glad that you reached a compromise because the solution was mutual. A successful compromise usually ends with a hug or a laugh.

## Communicate clearly and kindly

Communication is extremely important. I love the message about communication that's delivered by the story of the village blacksmith who hired a new apprentice. On the apprentice's first day on the job, the blacksmith explained that when he took the red-hot horseshoe out of the fire, placed it on the anvil, and shook his head, the apprentice was to hit it. The next day, the village had a new blacksmith.

Happy marriages are comprised of people who are able to communicate their feelings through word and deed. Most communication isn't a matter of life and death, but the death of a marriage can occur because of a lack of effective communication. The following sections cover several different kinds of communication and explain how to use them to better your marriage.

### Don't confuse understanding with persuasion

Many husbands and wives misunderstand communication because they confuse *understanding* with *persuasion*. Communication is designed to bring understanding, but not necessarily persuasion. If you understand what I say, then I have communicated, whether or not you are persuaded.

Understanding your partner's message doesn't mean that you agree or disagree — some people, if they truly understood each other, would fight all the time. You must understand and communicate with each other that you're seeking to discover what is loving and fair and not necessarily who is right. Marriages can't be saved by communication alone because communication is a means of expressing attitude and desire, and attitude and desire can either make or break a marriage. Having said that, I hurry on to say that communication is important in a good relationship, and keeping an open mind in communication is essential.

The spirit of communication is the genuine desire to hear and understand — and the patience to be heard. So often, I hear a wife say, "My husband doesn't listen to me." But actually he does listen to her; he simply doesn't want to agree with her or argue with her. Sometimes when a man says, "My wife doesn't understand me," he's really saying, "She doesn't understand that my sagging self-image needs propping up." The important thing is to listen for the need behind the words and encourage your mate to share those needs by doing what you can to meet them.

### Appreciate silence and other forms of nonverbal communication

Silence is a big part of marital communication. The longer people live together, the less they really have to say, and sometimes silence dominates their time together. I'm not speaking of icy silence that hangs in the air when differences are left unresolved; I'm talking about the kind of companionable silence that can be a great gift that you give to each other when you sit quietly and comfortably in close proximity. Unless a couple can enjoy quiet time together, they haven't come along as far as they should have in communicating.

Outward appearance also communicates internal feelings. When a husband comes home and his wife is dressed up, even though they're not going out, it says something to him about the importance of their relationship to her and tells him that she still thinks of him as special. If he sits around the house all the time in his undershirt, he communicates that he isn't thinking of her comfort or how he appeals to her. (Appeal and attractiveness are part of nonverbal communication.)

Fred Smith says, "Sometimes our best communications are demonstrations." Fred tells the story of his friend, Ron, whose two rambunctious sons, ages 10 and 12, were in the kitchen with their mother, giving her a hard time. They were verbally harassing her when Ron walked in, appraised the situation, took both boys by the back of the neck, and uttered these profound words: "Listen, kids. Fortunately for you, your mother and I were married before you got here, and fortunately for us, we're going to be married after you're gone. Now quit hassling my woman."

### Don't overreact

In marriage and in life, you should never make mountains out of molehills. Treating events according to their place in the overall context of life is important.

Dr. David Rubin points out, "Marriage is like a long trip in a tiny rowboat. If one passenger starts to rock the boat, the other passenger has to steady it. Otherwise, they'll go to the bottom together." It takes two to tango, and it also takes two to fight. Most big fights start over little incidents that escalate over a period of time. But life is too short to engage in ongoing conflict. Husbands and wives need to understand that they're in a partnership together, that it really isn't "my chair," "my bank account," "his responsibility," "her obligation," and so on. When you realize that you can't sink only part of the boat, you've laid an important stone in the foundation of your marriage.

### Don't say it — you'll be glad you didn't

More wise advice comes from another anonymous individual, who said, "The difference between a successful marriage and a mediocre one consists of leaving about three or four things a day unsaid."

An offhand remark, a careless statement, or a comment made in anger can be devastating to your mate. (That's why the comments on temper control later in this chapter are so important.) Sometimes things said in jest are taken seriously. So what's the solution?

- ✔ Communicate regularly your love for your mate.

- ✔ If you say things that are upsetting, say that you're sorry and ask for forgiveness. After you receive forgiveness, remember that the behavior for which you were forgiven is a no-no and is not to be repeated.

If you're wise and sensitive, you let your mate know about the little sayings or attempts at humor that upset you. I tell quite a few jokes, and many of them involve my wife. However, if I ever say something that displeases her, she makes a point of letting me know (fortunately for me, in the privacy of our home), and I don't repeat my mistake. Upsetting or offending my wife in order to get a laugh from an audience is a price that I'm unwilling to pay. Be careful about what you say to anyone, of course, but especially to or about your mate.

Things that are left unsaid can save your marriage, and things said in love and kindness can energize your marriage.

## Give and forgive

Giving is important in any relationship. You need to give the extra effort, go the extra mile, and do the little things without being asked — such as putting your things away, not cluttering up the house, and putting the cap back on the toothpaste. Call home when you're running late, and include your mate in any change of plans to make sure that the new plans fit his or her schedule.

Perhaps the single most important thing that you can do is to forgive your mate for intended or unintended slights and past hurts. To "forgive and forget" is virtually impossible, but you can forgive and remember that you're giving up any rights for retribution. In other words, don't try to get even.

## Be courteous and respectful

Treating your mate with courtesy and respect is a great stabilizer in a relationship; doing so builds a lasting friendship and keeps the hope and love light burning. Joanne Woodward said, "Sexiness wears thin after awhile and beauty fades, but to be married to someone who makes you laugh every day — aah, that's a real treat!" Woodward is on the right track, but I believe that building that lasting friendship not only keeps the hope and love light burning but also increases substantially your attraction to each other.

For example, I find my wife to be more beautiful today than she was on our wedding day. That statement covers quite a bit of territory, but she still "rings my bell" — and we've celebrated our 50th honeymoon. I know her thoroughly, and her external beauty is enhanced by the beauty that lies within.

Unfortunately, at the first sign of trouble, many people start thinking that their spouse is "stepping on my toes," "denying my personhood," "invading my rights," "taking advantage of my good nature," or "not acting as he or she did before we got married." The nitpicking continues to escalate until you talk yourselves into believing that your differences are irreconcilable.

Instead, if you have one, listen to the audio tape or watch the video of your wedding. Pay special attention to the vows you made, listen to the tone in your voices, and — if it's a video you're watching — see the love and adoration on your faces. Know that you can recapture the good times, the respect, and the adoration because just as you chose to marry your mate, you can choose to love your mate into loving you again.

# *Recognize your partner's differences*

A happy, successful, loving marriage begins with the clear understanding that men and women are different. They have different needs, different interests, different emotions — yet both men and women want many of the same things. Each wants to be treated with love, courtesy, and respect; each wants to be happy; each wants to feel important; and each wants to be listened to and cared for. So while the differences are there, the similarities are also there. Enjoy the similarities and work to understand the differences.

**ZIG SAYS**

In most cases, men are more goal-oriented than women, and women are more relationship-oriented than men. This example might be a little simplistic, but I think you'll get my point. Sometimes the Redhead and I stop by the grocery store to pick up a few things. I'm on a mission to get the goods and go; the Redhead is saying hello to and visiting with the people she has gotten to know over the years. She knows how many children they have, how long they have worked at the store, whether they have had any health problems, and the list goes on. Even if I did the majority of our grocery shopping, I would never get to know the details of the lives of the people I came in contact with. I would be too busy getting the goods and going on to the next thing. When both husband and wife understand this difference in temperament, they establish the foundation for a permanent relationship.

Ladies, a good place to start is with the understanding that your husband doesn't give a hoot about what's on television. All he wants to know is what *else* is on television. So what's the solution? On Sunday, take the television programming guide and choose the programs that each of you wants to watch in the coming week. A simple step like compromising about watching television can have amazing effects on unity. This practice at compromising can help to make you more considerate of each other on issues such as where to eat, where to shop, who's going to take the kids to the dentist this time, and who's going to attend this play/concert/recital/ball game. When you work out those "little things" together, the whole family benefits.

In all my years of travel, I've gone out to eat several hundred times with groups of people. Not once have I seen a man stand up at one of these dinners and say, "Charlie, would you, Paul, and Billy like to go to the rest room with me?" (If it ever does happen, I don't plan to go.) However, I have seen a woman stand up and nod to the ladies at the table without saying a word on numerous occasions. Miraculously, a crowd assembles, and off they go to the powder room. Yes, men and women are different, and do I ever love that difference!

## Lighten her physical burdens

One step that a husband can take to make his wife feel loved and boost her spirits is to offer to do some of the things that she normally does. Doing so makes her feel that he understands why she feels the way she does and that a little TLC is in order. It also lets her know that he is tuned in to the problem, that he wants to make it as easy as possible for her, understanding that he cannot solve the problem but feeling compassion for her and wanting to do what he can. He can have a tremendous impact by, say, grabbing the vacuum cleaner or volunteering to cook dinner.

### *Adjust your approach — "I'm proud of you" versus "I love you"*

Another major difference between men and women is that most men respond more favorably to the words "I'm proud of you for taking that stand" or "I'm proud of the way you solved that problem," and most women respond more favorably to the words "I love you for being so gracious under those difficult circumstances" or "I love you for handling that situation with the kids so fairly." Most of all, women love to hear "I love you," period.

✔ Ladies, I can tell you that feeling discouraged (when he loses his job, is denied a promotion, or is unfairly criticized at his job, for example) takes something out of your husband. A series of little incidents can deflate him bit by bit until he is genuinely down and needs encouragement. At times like these, a sensitive, loving wife can play a major role in boosting his ego and escalating his feelings of self-worth, which builds his confidence and enables him to climb back to even greater heights.

As a wife, you can help to rebuild his self-esteem by listening without asking many questions and by becoming the aggressor in the sexual relationship. Nothing boosts a man's ego and builds his confidence more than to know that even when he's at his lowest and is hurting all over, you still find him attractive. If your husband knows that you respect and desire him, that ego of his will soon have him on his way back to being the loving, productive man that you fell in love with.

✔ Fellas, you want to take exactly the opposite approach with your wife. When she's down in the dumps as a result of rejection, disappointment, a setback, the loss of a job, unfair criticism, public embarrassment, or any number of things, you *can* do something.

As a husband, you can listen and be kind, thoughtful, gentle, understanding, and, most of all, non-aggressive sexually. If you mistake her need for holding as sexual desire, in virtually every case you will have sadly misread your wife. If, at that point, you think in terms of passion, your wife is probably going to be hurt to the core, thinking, "On top of all my other problems, now my husband is showing his lack of sensitivity by thinking only of himself." Whether or not your motive is selfish, your wife will most likely feel that it is. You just need to be affectionate, be attentive, and listen carefully to what she has to say. Hold her. At times like these, she wants you to be her confidante and comforter, not her lover.

### Remember that marriage is a joint venture

Although I've been speaking in generalities about men's and women's tendencies, I want to emphasize that a successful marriage is a joint venture. Each partner has a part to play, and I don't believe that these parts can always be played successfully by the common male and female stereotypes. For a marriage to operate smoothly, the two partners have to accept their own responsibilities to the partnership, not as they relate to stereotypes. Two people with a mix of needs and desires shouldn't be forced into a predetermined formula; working out a formula of your own will make you more successful. Traditional roles may be helpful as a basis for thinking, but not as a concrete formula. Both flexibility and compromise are in order.

To start, list the natural gifts that each person has, and determine how each gift can be used to promote the marriage. In our marriage, my wife and I learned that I was better at earning money and that she was better at organizing and handling it, so for many years she has kept the records and paid the bills with the money I earn.

## Cooperate — don't compete

Competitiveness is probably the most dangerous element that a husband and wife face in a cooperative marriage. Cooperative living is complementary, not competitive. Too often in competition, you accent your rights, which are often competitive, rather than your responsibilities, which are complementary. Couples must complement each other by capitalizing on their individual strengths, not by competing with each other.

One of the most unfortunate occurrences in life happens when husband and wife compete for their child's favor and use every subtle trick of the trade, including buying frivolous gifts and indulging him or her in socially unacceptable behavior, to induce the child to love him or her more than the other parent. Much of the time, the guilty party is either unaware that he or she is competing or denies it completely. In this competitive situation, all parties lose, especially the child.

A far better approach is for husband and wife to remember that the child is "theirs," not "his" or "hers," and that their number-one responsibility is to look after the best interests of the life that they created together. They must make certain that the child sees them as a team. They do this best by loving and caring for each other and agreeing in advance on major decisions, such as meal times, bedtime, household responsibilities, dating age, and so on, and supporting the decision of the mate who has to make a decision alone when both parents are not available.

## Build a genuinely happy marriage

Understand that mountaintop experiences in a marriage — those times when things couldn't be better, and you and your spouse couldn't be happier with each other — don't happen every day. But dependability, loyalty, commitment, affection, kindness, respect, consideration, and a host of other character qualities are the foundation stones upon which you build a lifelong romance that's even more enjoyable at the end than it was at the beginning. You may not find intense pleasure as frequently after many years of marriage, but steady, genuine happiness is a more-than-adequate replacement.

Keep in mind that the mountaintop experiences in a marriage are made possible by a couple first having gone through a series of valleys in which their love and commitment are put to severe tests. During these "valley" experiences, you find out much about your own character and about the character of your mate. You discover how serious you were when you exchanged those wedding vows.

# Goal: Rekindling the Flame

A woman stood in front of a judge with her petition for divorce. The judge expressed astonishment, pointing out that she had been married to her husband for only three months, that they met as a result of a computer match-up, and that everything indicated that they would be an ideal couple. Their ages, interests, backgrounds, personalities, educations, religion, and everything else said, "Here is the perfect match." The judge said, "The computer says that your husband is the ideal man for you." The woman responded, "Well, Judge, to be honest, I just don't understand what the computer saw in him."

Sometimes, after only a short time of being married and actually living together, you wonder what you saw in another person that attracted you so strongly. One of the advantages of the two-year courtship period that most marriage counselors encourage before saying "I do" is that couples can really get to know each other — their quirks, personality differences, and true interests, as well as the "dark sides" of their lives that are so carefully hidden in short-term courtships.

You may be thinking, "Okay, Zig, I agree with you, but the reality is that at this point in our marriage, we both feel that we have made a mistake. What can we do?" If your goal is to rekindle a smoldering flame, these next sections tell you how to go about it.

# Remember how you got started

Rewind the tape in your mind and think of all the things that attracted you to each other. Write those qualities on a sheet of paper, and for the next 30 days, concentrate on each of them. This works best if both partners partici- pate, but it is far better for one to do the exercise than it is for none to participate.

> ✔ If you were attracted by your wife's personality, for example, say to yourself, "I was attracted to my wife because she has such a great personality, and she still has that great personality. I have to confess that even though we're having difficulty at the moment, I still like that quality in her."

> ✔ If you were attracted to your husband because of his integrity, say to yourself, "I was attracted to my husband because of the way he lives with complete integrity. As a matter of fact, I still greatly admire that quality in him. For the next 30 days, I'm going to focus on that quality that initially attracted me to him."

Go right down the list. You may be surprised at the number of good qualities that you genuinely love about your mate. Maybe you fell in love because of your mate's grooming habits, her promptness in taking care of her promises, or his commitment to providing a good home and income. The items on the list that you create can number in the dozens.

The simple act of recalling the virtues of your mate will help you see him or her in a softer light and be less critical and more open to accepting the good when it is apparent. If you can remember the good times, you can recreate them and oftentimes surpass them after your relationship is restored.

# Start over and date your mate

Whether you've been married for 30 days or 30 years, the best approach is to restart the courtship process that you followed before you were married. I believe that the following simple suggestions can make a substantial difference in your marriage — not just in the beginning stages, but through- out your lifetime:

> ✔ **Do something for each other every day that the other person could do for himself or herself.** In the 50-plus years that my wife and I have been married, I don't believe that she has opened her car door a dozen times when with me. My wife is quite capable of opening her own door, but each time I walk around the car, I'm reminded that here is the most important person on earth to me. I open her door whether we're changing drivers on the highway or we're in our garage with not another human being in sight. I do it at shopping centers, at the grocery store, at church — in short, everywhere we go.

Here's one thing my Redhead does for me that I'm very capable of doing for myself. Many years ago, I stopped carrying my money in a wallet and started folding it and carrying it in my pocket. At night, I place it on the bathroom counter. Several years ago, she started counting my money. If she thinks that I don't have enough cash to cover emergencies when I'm packing to leave town, she goes to the ATM machine or grocery store and picks up additional cash. Not a big deal, but what this says is, "Honey, I really do love you, and I'll be more comfortable knowing that in the event the unexpected happens and you need cash, you won't be embarrassed by not having it." That kind of thoughtfulness is what keeps the love light burning.

Keep in mind that these little acts of love have to be things that your mate is capable of doing for himself or herself. If he or she can't do it, you have an obligation or a responsibility to do it. But obligations and responsibilities don't generate *romantic love,* and that's what I'm talking about. Romantic love can and should extend for the entire life of the marriage.

✔ **Do a lot of hugging.** For your information, gentlemen, your wife resents it when you ignore her all day and then give her your undivided attention when the lights go out at night. She wants a hug when all you've got on your mind is a hug.

My wife and I take the opportunity to hug hello and goodbye, and we even hug when we pass in the hallway. The hugs are neither long nor suggestive; they simply say "It's nice to have you around" and "You're very important to me." I'm convinced that our hugging habit has much to do with our marital happiness. Staying upset with someone who has his or her arms wrapped lovingly around you is virtually impossible, and making a good situation even better in the same way is really easy.

✔ **Play games with each other.** Husbands and wives need to have fun. For example, that beautiful redheaded wife of mine has a passion for chocolate-covered marshmallows. She comes close to running a fever when she enters a store that sells them. Because I know about her cravings, I go into a store periodically — such as on Valentine's Day, birthdays, Thanksgiving, or any other day — and buy a card and about a dozen foil-wrapped, chocolate-covered marshmallows. I lay one candy on the kitchen counter with the card. When she sees the card and candy, she laughs aloud or gives a delighted squeal because she knows that the search is on. I hide the other chocolate-covered marshmallows around the house, and history tells her that they may turn up in the rice canister, in the freezer, among her clothing, in her desk drawer, atop the chandelier, and so on. Every time she finds one, she laughs, and if I'm in the house when it happens, we again exchange hugs.

✔ **Keep boredom at bay.** Statistics show that the biggest problem in marriage, particularly after about 15 years, is boredom. Married life settles into a rut because each partner tends to depend on the other to keep it out of a rut. Each wants to be married to an exciting spouse but doesn't want to or can't generate excitement. In our years together, my wife and I have had exciting times and boring times. We've found that in order to avoid boredom, we have to plan excitement.

✔ **Continue your courtship after marriage.** Courtship before marriage is planned and expected. You make a date, one of you makes plans on where to go and what to do, you decide what to wear, and you make a big production of getting ready for your date. It is also true that before marriage, you would on the spur of the moment drive 50 miles to a special spot for dinner, decide at the last minute to go to a late movie, and so on. Those were major reasons that you got married, and if you keep on doing them, they will help keep you together.

If courtship after marriage is important, then whose responsibility is it? Here's where stereotypes often cause a breakdown. Some women feel that they shouldn't initiate any part of courtship, and some men are too embarrassed or stubborn to do so, so the couple continues in the rut of boredom. Courtship is a mutual responsibility, not a tug of war. Keeping a count of who did what and when and whose turn it is to make a move is death to a marriage.

✔ **Develop a sense of humor and laugh together.** Laughing together is a marvelous way to keep romance blooming. Virtually every morning that I'm home, I read the funnies to my wife. Several comic strips typically elicit laughter from us. Any time a couple starts the day laughing together, you can rest assured that it's going to be a good day. When you share a laugh with your mate, you create a romantic bond, which forms a special closeness between you.

## Whose day is it, anyway?

That special bond that a sense of humor creates was demonstrated this past Mother's Day when I received a beautiful necktie from the Redhead. At first I was puzzled because I, like most men, had always felt that the mother should be recognized and rewarded on Mother's Day. But that redheaded wife of mine carefully explained that I was responsible for her being a mother, and recognizing that she had needed help in the production, she felt that I should be remembered with a gift. I thought her idea was hilarious and really neat. In addition, the tie is beautiful!

Of course, she received a special remembrance from me for Father's Day, because without her, I wouldn't be a father. As usual, however, she outdid me on Father's Day when she gave me another card with this message: "For my husband. Of course, I know it's Father's Day, but why the fuss and bother? If it hadn't been for me, you know, you wouldn't be a father. Happy Father's Day."

The idea behind this story is simple: Have a little fun in your marriage. On occasion, put your creativity to work and delight your mate with a special gift at an unexpected time. This kind of act is no big deal, but doing these things on a consistent basis amounts to a great deal — and a romantic involvement that draws you closer as friends, companions, confidants, supporters, lovers, and lifetime journey-mates.

✔ **Welcome each other home.** Former U.S. President Ronald Reagan once said, "There's nothing more important than approaching your own doorstep and knowing that someone on the other side is listening for the sound of your footsteps." One of the most significant steps in building and maintaining romance in a marriage is the welcome home that you give each other. After 50-plus years of marriage, I don't recall ever not being welcomed home by the Redhead. I've come home from a business trip many times well past midnight when she's sound asleep. Yet 100 percent of the time, she turns to me, gives me a welcome-home hug, and tells me that she's glad I'm home.

Just as you should part for the day with a hug and a kiss, you should greet each other at the end of the day in the same way. Your initial conversation should be about something good that happened during the day — something funny, exciting, or rewarding. After you settle in, you can sit down and talk about the other events of the day. I can't overstate how important it is to keep the beginning conversation light and pleasant.

Unfortunately, too many couples walk in complaining about the difficulties of the day, the impossible people they've had to deal with, and the headaches they have as a result. Over a period of time, couples subconsciously associate going home with unpleasant news — a feeling that doesn't build romance or a stable marriage.

## Concentrate on changing yourself

Your current marriage probably has a better chance of working than a future one does. Psychiatrist and theologian Paul Meier says that a first marriage has only a 50 percent chance of succeeding, a second marriage has only a 40 percent chance of succeeding, a third marriage has only a 30 percent chance of succeeding, and a fourth marriage has virtually no chance of succeeding. The reason is simple: Many divorces are caused by one person's own problems. If that person marries again, he or she takes those problems into the next marriage.

Don't misunderstand; I'm not saying that a failed marriage is always one person's fault. I'm saying that when you change yourself, the odds are much greater that the other person is going to change also — or your *perception* of the other person is going to change. The relationship difficulties may not be your fault, but working — and working hard — at mending the relationship is your responsibility and opportunity. You are the logical place to start.

# Goal: Dealing with the Problems in Your Marriage

Every couple should have the goal of making their marriage better. One of the easiest ways to achieve this goal is to deal with problems effectively. Even the best marriages have plenty of room for growth and improvement. That's why marriages that have lasted for decades are by far the happiest and most fulfilled ones around — those folks have had the time that it takes to grow their relationship. Though the passage of time often makes rekindling the flame necessary, improving your marriage is something that you must do on a daily basis.

## Recognize the problem

Many marriage problems are caused by unpleasant characteristics that surface after the marriage vows are exchanged. The problem may be your spouse's sloppiness around the house, lack of punctuality, neglect to show affection toward you, or tendency to gossip. It may be the way your mate criticizes your parents or other members of your family or wants you to drop all your friends and concentrate only on his or her friends. Or the problem may be more serious, such as an explosive temper, violent or filthy language, or a tendency to drink too much or do drugs. Regardless of the problem, you can't deal with it until you acknowledge it.

## Find a solution

One of the solutions to handling problems, whether they're minor or major, is to make the solutions fun if at all possible. In many cases, it *is* possible.

Before minor problems become major and a wall is built between husband and wife, I encourage you to confront the problem head-on. But do so properly and at the right time, when neither of you is coming off a disagreeable experience outside the marriage. The right time may be after a pleasant meal, a quiet walk, or a pleasing conversation, or after watching a television program that you both enjoyed.

At that time, say kindly to your mate, "Honey, it's time we had a fight — but let's do it in the proper way." Then reach over and hold both your mate's hands and say, "Sweetheart, it really bothers me when you fail to put your coffee cup in the dishwasher" or " . . . say mean things about my mother" or " . . . work so late that you don't get to spend time with the kids before they go to bed." Or say, "It deeply concerns me when you pay excessive attention to another man/woman when we go out." Whatever the problem, speak about it softly while holding hands. The sooner you bring your concerns out into the open, the more quickly the problem is solved and the less likely the problem will escalate. And when you air your concerns while demonstrating your love for your mate (by holding hands rather than standing across the room and shouting defensively), you resolve the problem in a way that deepens your commitment to each other.

When you walk through the valley of frustration and disappointment by solving those nagging problems, the sense of relief and security that comes to both of you will take you to a romantic mountaintop and restore joy to the marriage.

## Think like a child

I love the story of the 7-year-old whose teacher asked him about his brother. The teacher said, "I'm a little confused. There's only four months' difference in your birthdays and you're not twins, so what's the story?" The little boy smiled brightly and said, "Well, one of us is adopted, but we keep forgetting which one."

In your marriage, take a childlike attitude and approach to each problem you face. If you recognize that one of you is the problem but you "keep forgetting which one," you can both work more effectively toward solving whatever problems exist.

---

### Boost your EQ

Research proves that the way a couple handles irritations, disagreements, hurts, frustrations, and difficulties determines their enjoyment of the marriage — and the length of their marriage as well. In his book *Emotional Intelligence*, psychologist Daniel Goleman says that if you want a happy, enduring marriage, your EQ (emotional quotient) can make the difference. People with a high EQ are sensitive, caring, outgoing, optimistic, and sympathetic — qualities that enable them to handle the emotional difficulties that we all encounter. Goleman says, "The most stable unions are among couples who have found ways to air differences without escalating into personal attacks or retreating into stony silence."

Get out a pen and paper and, keeping in mind the EQ qualities (be kind, sympathetic, and so on), air your differences by listing the things that you know irritate each other and cause a rift between you. After each item, come up with a solution together. When you make a commitment to follow through on your solutions, you have taken a giant step toward resolving many difficulties and making your marriage more secure.

(**Warning:** If you and your mate can't follow the EQ qualities and you insist on placing blame, don't do this exercise.)

# Recognize positive behavior

Each time your mate reverses behavior and, for example, says something nice about your parents or makes an effort to eliminate a bone of contention, say something complimentary. Statements such as "You know, honey, I really like it when you keep your composure under difficult circumstances" or "It really pleases me when you go out of your way to be pleasant to my parents" or "It delights me when you give me your undivided attention when we go out to dinner" or "I appreciate it when you offer to pick up the dry cleaning on your way home" can make a real difference in getting even more positive behavior from your mate. Behavior that is recognized and rewarded will be repeated.

# Control the temperature

To maintain a long-term, romantic relationship with your mate, you need to create the right "atmosphere" or "temperature" in which the relationship can thrive. You control the temperature of your relationship by controlling your temper. If the atmosphere is wrong, the least little thing can set off an act of hostility or a temper explosion. However, the good news is that you have probably already demonstrated that even under difficult circumstances, you can immediately bring your temperature — or your temper — under control if you have that as an objective.

✔ For example, say that you and your mate are having a heated argument when the telephone rings. You pick it up and in a pleasant, cheerful, and even enthusiastic tone of voice say, "Hello." Chances are pretty good that you just smiled and remembered such an occasion. Here's the key to future control: The next time things begin to heat up, just think "telephone," and you'll remember to cool off. You may have to sit down, get a drink of water, or go for a short walk, remembering to close the door gently as you leave. As you exit, say, "Excuse me. I need to take a short walk." The short walk may involve just going into the next room, where you can sit quietly and think for a moment.

When you need to discuss difficult subjects, make it a point to sit down for the discussion. Being seated is comforting and far less threatening than standing toe to toe, and it carries substantially less danger that a disagreement will turn violent.

✔ On the positive side, the way to control the atmosphere and breed ongoing romance is to pay sincere compliments or give special recognition to your mate. For example, for many years, I have answered the telephone by saying, "Good morning! This is Jean Ziglar's happy husband." I say it first of all because it's true; second, it's amazing how many points I score with that Redhead by that simple little act. I also have a much more profound reason for answering the phone this way: You can't repeatedly profess to be a happy mate and then act in an unhappy or even antagonistic way. Give it a try.

# Build your relationship skills

Conflict that arises in a marriage may not stem from not loving and respecting your mate. Perhaps you just don't have the skills necessary to build that relationship and handle that conflict appropriately. My wife and I had more minor conflicts in the first two years of our marriage than we've had in all the years since. Fortunately, two things worked to our advantage:

- ✔ We were totally committed to the marriage. We never discussed separation or questioned whether we had made a mistake.

- ✔ We were told (and we listened) that having those conflicts was normal for newlyweds. Over the years, we acquired the necessary skills not only to make the marriage work but also to have fun in the process.

Thanks in large part to Hollywood and the entertainment industry, you hear much more about the romantic (read *sexual*) side of marriage than about developing real love in a marriage. Actor Ricardo Montalban summed up the definition of a great lover when he said, "A great lover is someone who can satisfy one woman her entire lifetime and be satisfied with one woman his entire lifetime. It is not someone who goes from woman to woman." To that, I would add that great sex is the result of great love — seldom, if ever, is great love the result of great sex.

So what skills do you need to build a loving relationship? Here are some of the most important ones:

- ✔ **Start with the commitment to make the marriage work.** (See the section "Decide on commitment" earlier in this chapter.)

- ✔ **Understand that you deceived each other in the courtship process and practice the skill of forgiving.** While you were courting, you always put your best foot forward in order to accomplish your objective: marriage to the one you were courting. For this reason, you probably agreed to almost everything. Fortunately, you can overcome the problems that arise when you reveal those deceptions with a strong commitment and by recognizing that you not only want the marriage to work but also want to make it *thrive*.

- ✔ **Work at verbalizing your true feelings without taking punitive action against your mate.** Say that you and your spouse swap cars, and when you switch back, you find that your mate has returned your car with the gas tank almost empty. Punitive action would be returning your mate's car with an empty tank the next time in order to get even. Instead, pleasantly say to your mate, "Honey, you may have noticed that when I use your car, I return it at least half full of gasoline. I would really appreciate it if you would show me the same courtesy." Chances are superb that if you handle the situation gently, lovingly, and with a big hug and smile, your mate will respond appropriately.

The second example is tragic. A couple I know were having serious troubles. In anger one night, the husband cheated on his wife. When she found out what he had done, she did the same thing. The result was that neither trusts the other anymore, and the marriage is now in divorce court. The husband was obviously wrong to commit adultery as punitive action against his wife. He asked for forgiveness, but his wife was unable to forgive and proceeded to take punitive action herself. The marriage was destroyed. Who knows — maybe forgiveness could have saved it. I've seen a number of marriages saved and even strengthened because the couples had the capacity to forgive without taking punitive action.

✔ **Take time to build the skill of courteousness.** When I was a child, my mother taught me that we may not all be smart, but we can all be courteous. Building the skill of courteousness is good advice for husbands and wives to follow. Discourtesy is really disrespect; you're seldom discourteous to anyone you truly respect. Marriage counselors say that one thing lacking in many poor marriages is genuine respect for each other. In marriage, we are often more discourteous than we are in friendships or in business relationships. Venting your anger in marriage and thinking that doing so costs nothing is irresponsible. Hurt relations always cost, especially in marriage.

When you "lose it" and blow your cool, acknowledge your mistake and apologize immediately so that you can stop the anger and resentment from festering. Admittedly, you can't always be loving during a heated exchange, but you can be courteous. If you are courteous in those tense situations, you won't have nearly as much repair work to do afterwards. Courtesy certainly has power, and it's a good starting place for deeper love.

✔ **Eliminate the words *always* and *never* from your vocabulary — as in "you always do this" or "you never do that."** Those statements aren't true, and they can elicit nothing but a defensive retort from your mate.

✔ **Practice looking for the good in your mate and work on finding the humor in problems.** Many couples report that, in the midst of a heated argument, something hilarious happens or is said, perhaps an interruption by a child or an innocent but appropriate remark that hits the funny bone. At any rate, the anger immediately dissipates and laughter sets in — not *at* each other but *with* each other.

✔ **Remember that your mate is not a mind-reader.** Many couples expect each other to know that they really don't enjoy being kidded about their expanding waistline, their receding hairline, their inability to wake up instantly, their dislike of sloppiness, or their need for support and encouragement about a specific thing. But you need to gently tell your mate what your needs are. He or she can't read your mind. Resentment builds within you if your mate doesn't meet a need or conducts himself or herself in a way that displeases you, but he or she may not have a clue as to the nature of the problem.

✔ **Don't labor under the illusion that you are communicating just because you take turns talking.** You need to listen — really listen — to what your mate is saying, not mentally prepare a retort to his or her comments. Planning what to say on your next "turn" causes you to miss the major point of your mate's message. Even more important, the feeling you generate as you ready your response is not one of love and empathetic understanding, but rather one of "I'll teach him!" or "I'll show her!" That not only creates problems but also kills any chances for a long-term loving relationship.

✔ **Choose carefully the time when you state your case.** If your mate is under intense pressure or is angry or disappointed about an outside event, that's not the time to register your needs. Wait patiently for a time when things are going well and you're communicating under appropriate circumstances. You always need to remember that *telling is sharing, but listening is caring.* I've never yet heard of a couple listening themselves out of a marriage.

Psychologist Howard Markham says, "To be heard is a powerful tool by itself. It's at the core of all intimate relationships. You don't even need to solve the problem. In fact, it's critical not to resolve things and just be heard by your partner. People want understanding from each other, not resolution. Couples are really arguing over things from the past. Once they clear the air, things get resolved by means of acceptance."

✔ **Never punish your mate.** When you're disappointed by something your mate has said, done, or failed to do, your natural tendency may be to get even. The danger of doing so is obvious: You soon get involved in "one-upmanship." Your mate may not have a clue that he or she has done anything wrong, so your punitive behavior can only confuse and anger your mate.

✔ **Don't store hurts and develop a laundry list of your mate's wrongdoings.** Instead, gently confront your mate and say, "I feel bad when you say things like this or do things like that." Note that you're not saying "You did such-and-such." What you're doing is expressing your feelings and letting your mate know that his or her behavior is having a negative impact on the relationship.

# A Real Love Story

I conclude this chapter with an uplifting story about love and commitment. Hopefully, this story (published in the January 13, 1997 issue of the *Daily Oklahoman/Oklahoma City Times*), along with the rest of this chapter, will inspire you to remember what your marriage means to you and take steps right now to make your marriage better.

Robertson McQuilkin's wife was sinking deeper and deeper into the grasp of a living kind of death. She suffered from Alzheimer's disease, knew nothing about those around her, and could not respond to their presence or their gestures of love and concern. Caring for her had become increasingly burdensome for her husband, who was trying to juggle a demanding job as president of a major institution while giving his beloved wife time, love, and tenderness.

The day came when, according to Jim Priest in his column "Family Talk," Robertson had to make a choice. He chose to resign his position and so notified the Board of Trustees at a monthly meeting. Later, a well-meaning trustee approached him during a break in the meeting and said, "There are two things I want to tell you about this situation. First, there are others who can care for your wife besides you. And second, she doesn't even know who you are, anyway." Robertson responded, "I know, but I know who she is."

Priest went ahead to say that the ancient Hebrew language includes a word for love called *hisson,* which literally means "steadfast commitment." That kind of commitment to one who doesn't even know who she is stands in stark contrast to the on-again, off-again commitments of convenience that too often permeate relationships today.

Priest says that love is not a feeling — it's a decision that you make every day. Sometimes the feelings of love are strong: The music is right, you have a little money in your pocket, the sun is shining outside, and all's right with the world. But sometimes the feelings of love are faint and the music is off-key. Your last quarter just slipped through the hole in your pocket, and the sky is leaden gray. At those times in your relationship, love hasn't died; it's just calling for a decision. It's calling for a deeper commitment, calling for you to dig into your heart and pull out that *hisson.*

Priest eloquently points out that we don't always feel like doing what we should do. He said, "There are days I don't especially feel like being loving. It's on those days that we have to act better than we feel. We have to decide to choose commitment over feelings. Feelings are fickle. They rise and fall on a whim. Our lives and our relationships have to be based on something stronger than that. Relationships need to be based on steadfast commitment. They need to be rooted in love and built on the kind of thing that makes a man like Robertson McQuilkin resign his post because he knows who his wife is and he knows she needs him."

How do you love your mate like Robertson McQuilkin loved his? You begin by reaffirming your steadfast commitment to the one you love. Say it out loud: "I love you. Whatever happens, I'll be here for you." The next part is both simple and difficult. In Priest's words, "If you've made a promise, just keep it. If your moral conscience tells you to do something, just listen. There's nothing glamorous or exciting about consistency, but it does pay long-term dividends."

## Stabilizing your marriage

What can you do to stabilize a marriage that has experienced some difficulties and bring it back to a happy, romantic relationship?

Many people have told me (in the marriage seminars that I have conducted over the years and in the reports that we get back from couples) that their marriages were in serious trouble when they started making a few changes. You can follow their example and use these steps to start the changes:

1. **Understand that at one time, in all probability, you deeply loved your mate.**

Like a leaking tire, the love — because of unrealistic expectations, broken promises, and little incidents that destroyed trust — may have gone out of your marriage.

2. **Reexamine your commitment and recommit yourself to it.**

Commitment is important because without it, you look for an escape when problems arise. With a commitment, you look for solutions when problems arise (as they inevitably do).

Keeping your marriage commitment is not easy, but doing so is very much worthwhile. If you follow Priest's advice, your world will be an infinitely better place and, over the long haul, much more happiness will be the result.

# Chapter 15

# Being a Successful Parent

. . . . . . . . . . . . . . . . . . . . . . . . . . . . . . . . . . . . . . . . . . . . . . . . .

## In This Chapter

▶ Approaching your role as a parent with the right attitude

▶ Teaching your child the big stuff: responsibility, respect for authority, and so on

▶ Doing the little things that make a tremendous difference

▶ Avoiding the "if only . . ." regrets

▶ Reconciling with your own parents or your adult children

. . . . . . . . . . . . . . . . . . . . . . . . . . . . . . . . . . . . . . . . . . . . . . . . .

*I*t really is true that after you become a parent, you remain a parent for life. With years and years of parenting ahead of you, why not make the effort to make your relationships with your kids as good as they possibly can be? The benefits that both you and your children gain from those efforts are tremendous, as the following story demonstrates.

Several years ago, a newscaster on a Dallas radio station announced promotions to president and chairman of the board of a large local company. The president had been made chairman, and the vice president was promoted to president. Because the men named were friends of mine, I pulled into their company parking lot and headed inside to congratulate them.

When I walked into the new chairman's office, he greeted me warmly. After we exchanged pleasantries, I told him that I was pleased to hear about his promotion, that I believed it was well-deserved, and that I knew he would do a super job in his new role. He invited me to sit down and said to me that I was partially responsible for his promotion.

He explained that he had heard my "Raising Positive Kids in a Negative World" lecture and decided to make some changes. He said, "Zig, do you see this telephone on the back of my desk? Only a very few people know about this phone. Ninety-nine percent of the calls I get on this phone are from my family, and on occasion, I've been tempted to pick up that phone when it rings and say, 'What have they done now?' Things simply were not good with us in any way.

"My 16-year-old son played his music so loudly that the neighbors could clearly hear it, and we couldn't hear anything else going on in the house. His room looked like a pigpen; his hair was not only long, but it was unkempt as well. Truthfully, Zig," he said, "when combined with the conduct of my 12-year-old daughter, who was rude, rebellious, and extremely difficult to get along with, I was not very happy in my home life. As a matter of fact, I'm embarrassed to admit it, but I frequently got up and came down to the company before breakfast so that I would not have to deal with my own children that early in the morning. Also, I frequently made dinner engagements with clients so that I could miss the evening meal with the family. Lunch would have served equally well, but I was in an 'escape' mode.

"After your lecture, I decided something very important — namely, that I deeply loved my children despite their conduct and the way I was handling their behavior. As I reflected on it one morning at my desk, I picked up the phone, called my son, and asked if he would like to go see the Rangers play that evening. After a moment of stunned silence, he recovered and said, 'Sure, Dad, I'd love to do that.'"

He then explained that he had left the office early so that they would have plenty of time to get to the ballpark and claim the good seats that he had reserved. He said, "The seats were right behind first base, which is my favorite position. During the game, we did all the things that baseball fans do: We cheered for the home team, booed the umpires when they made idiotic decisions (meaning that they went against the Rangers), ate hot dogs and had cold drinks, took the seventh-inning stretch, and bantered with other fans as we identified the obvious mistakes the Rangers were making and how we would have handled them.

"Zig, it was an absolutely wonderful experience. I spent more time with my son that night than I had in the previous six weeks. We stopped on the way home for a snack and continued our conversations. I realized some significant things that evening. My son is of high moral character. He has dreams and ambitions for his life, and without either one of us discussing it, I realized that his behavior was his method of trying to get my attention.

"Two days later, I made a 'date' with my 12-year-old daughter to go out to one of the fancy restaurants I'd been taking my clients to. I went the extra mile and bought her a nice little corsage, and we spent well over two hours that evening talking. I discovered, in essence, the same thing about my daughter that I had discovered about my son: She's a delightful young woman. She has real hopes and dreams and ambitions. Her character came shining through. It's amazing how much I'd overlooked in both my kids because they were so busy trying to get my attention when all I could focus on were the things they were doing 'wrong,' which they must have known I disapproved of. It was a wonderful evening.

## Dad: Are you their second choice?

That relationship with your kids is important, particularly when you understand the impact that parents can have versus the impact that television is having. Several years ago, a study revealed that one-third of kids between ages 4 and 5 in the United States said that if they were given a choice, they would choose the television set over their dads. It's a sobering thought to realize that nearly one-third of our kids would rather sit in front of the TV than spend time with their fathers. Dad, if you put paying attention to your child in the top one-third of your priorities, you won't have a child who prefers watching TV to spending time with you.

"I've got to confess, Zig, that the radical changes in my son and daughter did not take place the next day or even the next week. But the communication doors were opened, and love started to walk through in obvious little behaviors and gestures over the following weeks. I never said another word about my son's hair, the loud music, or the pigpen called his room. But, Zig, without my saying anything, the volume of the music came down dramatically. Not only did he cut his hair to a more reasonable length, but he started taking care of it as well. Although his room still would not qualify for a grade-A rating if it were a restaurant, it's certainly no worse than my room was when I was a teenager. I can repeat the story with my daughter. Her rebellion, rudeness, and anger melted under the attention which she had so badly needed and I was refusing to give her. She had a substantial improvement in her grades. All in all, the experience was exceptional.

"Instead of getting up early to avoid breakfast with my kids, I started looking forward to our time together. The people on the job noticed the difference in my attitude, and to be candid, Zig, I now get more done working a fairly standard work schedule. I'm still here 30 minutes before anybody else, and I am still here an hour longer than anybody else, but an evening away from my family is a rare thing. I believe, without a doubt, that the changes I decided to make as a result of the suggestions you made were a factor in my promotion."

# Successful Parenting Begins with You

As the man in the preceding story discovered, parenting can be a delight if you approach it with an open heart and an open mind. The following points may seem like basic common sense to you, but many people are so rushed by the pressures of making a living that they don't give much thought to these issues. They wrongly assume that rearing children just happens — they are born, they go to school, they leave home. If only life were so simple!

If you do these things, you'll realize what a joy parenting can be:

- ✔ **Show unconditional love.** The most important step in successful parenting is to love your children unconditionally. You do not love your children because they are handsome or beautiful, are pleasant and courteous, make As, pick up after themselves, or for anything else that they do. If you put a condition on your love for them, they will always wonder whether they have earned or deserve your love. This wonder breeds insecurity within children, and it ensures difficult times ahead, including possible gang involvement, where acceptance is assured.

- ✔ **Accept that you are a role model.** Like it or not, as a parent you are a role model. A role model, in simple terms, is an individual whose behavior in a particular role is imitated by others. It is a parent's responsibility to demonstrate such noble qualities as courage, compassion, and genuine concern for others.

- ✔ **Remember that your kids are not a responsibility that you handle at your convenience.** They are part of your schedule and can bring infinite joy or considerable misery. Much of that is determined by the time and effort that you put into raising your kids. An hour at the end of a hectic day is not quite enough to get the job done, especially if both parents have been working outside the home. Your children need your time and attention.

- ✔ **If possible, stay together to raise your kids.** Two-parent families are the ideal arrangement for raising successful kids. It's more than just a cliché to say that the most important thing a father can do for his children is to love their mother, and the most important thing a mother can do for her children is to love their father.

In her book *The Divorce Culture,* Barbara DaFoe Whitehead points out that single-parent families are six times as likely to be poor, and children of divorce are two to three times as likely as those raised in two-parent homes to have emotional and behavioral problems. The evidence is overwhelming: Divorce causes immediate pain and problems and also has long-range consequences, as explained in the following sidebar, "The devastating impact of divorce on kids." *Los Angeles Times Syndicate* columnist Cal Thomas observed in a column published in the June 7, 1997 issue of the *Dallas Morning News,* "If the report by Ms. Wallerstein and Ms. Lewis had been about business rather than family, the children of divorce would have the right to file a class-action suit, citing breach of contract by their parents."

The message: Work at it. Work it out, parents. You and your kids will be glad that you did. (But if you're already divorced, please see the sidebar "The devasting impact of divorce on kids" for information about how to handle the situation.)

# The devastating impact of divorce on kids

Judith Wallerstein, a psychologist and divorce research expert, and Julia Lewis, a psychology professor at San Francisco State University, conducted a study involving 60 middle- and upper-class families from Marin County, California. The study covered a 25-year period, and the people involved had everything going for them. The studies show that far from having just an initial impact on small children, divorce is a cumulative experience that produces serious emotional scars that, in turn, shape the attitudes, behaviors, and relationships of the children of divorce well into adulthood.

According to this study, 50 percent of the children from divorced families became seriously involved with drugs and alcohol, and many of the children, especially the girls, became sexually active early in adolescence. Despite the fact that many of the fathers held degrees in professions that allowed them to make a good living, not one of the fathers provided full financial support for his child's college education, and 25 percent of them stopped sending financial help at all after the children turned 18. The inevitable result was that more than half the kids studied ended up with less education than their parents. (This occurred at a time when more education was desperately needed.) Professor Lewis noted that the long-lasting effects of their parents' divorce caused adult children to become "very, very anxious about marriage [and] fidelity."

Student achievement is significant when both parents stay together in the process of raising their kids. The May 8, 1997, edition of *USA Today* listed the 20 best and brightest kids in the United States. One hundred percent of these 20 "best and brightest" came from two-parent families. I hope that you carefully read and reread Chapter 14, which deals with the husband/wife relationship, because many times differences can be resolved and the family can be maintained.

Remember, too, that kids follow examples far more than they follow instructions. According to a study reported in *USA Today,* the more divorces and remarriages a child lives through, the more likely he or she is to divorce. Among adults whose parents had two or more failed marriages, 68 percent divorced, 26 percent two or more times.

Yes, the evidence is in . . . and it's solid. Successful parenting requires you to work at saving your marriage.

**Special note:** If you and your children have already suffered the devastation of divorce, take heart. Your kids don't have to be the ones on the downside of the statistics I just quoted. Even if you are financially strapped, remember this: Love and attention are by far the most important things any parent can give to a child. You don't need a marriage certificate or money to give those two things.

I also strongly recommend that you never say derogatory things about your ex-spouse in front of or to your children. That simply undermines their self-image — children believe that they are what their parents are. If their father or mother isn't everything he or she can or should be, the children will come to that conclusion on their own. If possible, do everything that you can to foster a good relationship with your ex. When children see adults acting like adults, they learn how to be civil, they learn what respect is, and they know that it's okay to love and show love for both parents. Don't burden your children with your grievances; give them the emotional freedom to love both parents as if the marriage were still intact. They will grow up healthier and happier because of your efforts.

# Building Character in Your Child

The most important things that you can teach your children are the ones that give them character, integrity, and values. In this section, I include what I consider to be mandatory, foundational issues that you must teach thoroughly and completely to give your child the best opportunity for a happy, balanced life.

## Teaching values and authority

ZIG SAYS

A number of years ago, I spoke at the largest high school in Rochester, New York, where I addressed the student body and later had a chance to talk with about 15 student leaders in a question-and-answer session. After we had been going back and forth for about 20 minutes, one of the young leaders said to me, "I notice that you put a lot of emphasis on your faith in God. Why is that?" I responded that one of the major reasons was that it helped to establish my authority at home, which brought forth more positive responses from my children.

He asked how that could be. I explained that when my children saw me bow my head in prayer to God, they recognized my action as a symbol of my respect for authority. Consequently, when I exercised my position of authority over them, they were far more likely to respond in a positive and cooperative way (for young children, even an obedient way). The young man responded, "Well, I don't believe in God, but what you're saying makes sense."

Children may ignore and disbelieve what parents say, but they always believe what we do. For that reason, one of the things my wife and I did as parents to establish our children's respect for authority was to show respect and appreciation for police officers. For example, on a number of occasions, I made it a point to stop and thank a police officer (who was not actively pursuing a law-breaker, of course!) for the role that he or she was playing, and to let the officer know that I appreciated that he or she was partly responsible for our safety. As a result, our children never felt afraid or intimidated by any authority in uniform, and all our children have a great deal of respect and admiration for police officers.

I believe that if every parent took that approach, boys and girls would again grow up wanting to be police officers, firefighters, and other law-enforcers. This would enable law enforcement to get the "cream of the crop," which would further reduce crime.

# Teaching the fundamentals of personality

Because your major responsibility as a parent is to work yourself out of a job, it's important that you teach your kids some fundamentals of personality. When your children know how to properly shake hands with an adult, they've taken an important step toward landing their first job. Teach your children how to do so. At the same time, emphasize that your children need to look the person they're greeting in the eye when they speak to him or her. The ages of 5 and 6 are good times to begin this procedure, and as your child grows comfortable with it, shaking hands will become automatic. And shaking hands is a great friend-maker. Also emphasize to the children the importance of a smile when they meet and greet people — remind them that cheerful, pleasant people are more readily accepted wherever they go.

Being cheerful and friendly involves yet another advantage: When people like you, they have a greater tendency to trust you. This is true in childhood as well as in adulthood. Because it's critically important for youngsters to be accepted by their peer groups, their attitudes can help them to win friends and be welcomed into various social circles. Teaching your children the elementary principles of friendship-building helps them to overcome shyness, which is present in an ever-increasing percentage of youngsters.

If you have a youngster who tends to be shy and withdrawn, I encourage you never to emphasize the problem. I cringe when I hear a parent say, "He's shy," to an adult as she attempts to introduce the child and the child hides behind her. The parent who makes this statement is only reinforcing that shy behavior. Instead, she should say something like, "He loves to play games, and hiding is the game of the moment. When he comes out of hiding, he's always pleasant and cheerful."

The next story spells out the importance of friends for kids — and, for that matter, everyone:

A busy executive was being pressured by his 7-year-old son to talk with him, play with him, do something with him. The father kept putting him off, saying that he had things to do. In one last effort for attention, the youngster said, "Dad, who do you like best — Batman or Superman?" The father, in a less-than-kind tone of voice said, "Oh, I don't know. I suppose Superman." And then he put his head back into his work. His son then asked, "Dad, aren't you going to ask me who I like best?" The father, somewhat irritated, said, "Oh, all right, Son, who do you like best?" The boy said, "I like Batman best." The father commented, "Well, that's nice," and went back to his work.

Then with a pleading tone in his voice, his son said, "Dad, aren't you going to ask me why I like Batman best?" And the father responded, "Okay, Son, why do you like Batman best?" The youngster replied, "Because Batman has a friend." With that, the father put aside his work, looked at his son and said, "Having a friend is really important, isn't it, Son?" The youngster responded, "Yes, it is, Dad."

That little story says something, doesn't it? I've never met anyone who would not, when pressed, admit that he or she really treasures friendships — even those who have managed to alienate almost everyone and who loudly protest that friendship doesn't matter. Deep down, we all know that these folks are not being real or honest, because the need for human companionship and friendship is present in all of us. We want someone we can call "friend" — someone who's always there in times of emergency or is there when we simply need to talk or just be around somebody. Friends are vitally important.

In my own life, outside my immediate family, I can say that all my closest friends go back more than 30 years, and several of them more than 50 years. I'm delighted that, besides my wife, my best friends are my children. I'm also pleased to say that when you raise your kids in the manner I'm describing, they learn the principles that enable them to build friendships for life.

## *Taking the eagle approach*

It's often said that you don't develop leaders or champions on feather beds. The "eagle approach" works best. Eagles build their nests high on mountains, exposed to the first rain, the first snow, and the strongest winds. When Mother Eagle builds the huge nest, she starts with limbs and rough pieces of bark. Inside that, she puts glass, stones, branches, and so on. Next, she picks up leaves, cloth, and similar objects. On top, she puts feathers — some from her own body — and in this nest she lays her eggs.

---

## Mothering is critical to a child's development

Dr. Selma Fraiberg clearly states the importance of mothering: "Children who have been deprived of mothering and who have formed no personal human bonds during the first two years of life show permanent impairment of the capacity to make human attachments in later childhood. The 'unattached' child's intellectual functions are also impaired during the first 18 months of life."

## Loving your child is extremely important

Dr. Hazen Werner said, "Twenty-one American GIs defected to communism after the Korean War. Nineteen of these 21 felt unloved or unwanted by their fathers or stepfathers, 16 had withdrawn within themselves, 18 took no part in school activities or sports, and only one was ever chosen by his class-mates for anything. It's quite obvious that we have here more than a lack of patriotism. The roots of the weakness of these boys run deeply into early life."

Communism was the "evil" to be avoided in the 1950s and 1960s, but our children face more and even greater evils today. Gangs and cults claim many unloved children every day. That's why it's so important that you express your love for your children and maintain good relationships with them.

Love, real love, is the prime ingredient in the recipe for successful child-rearing. Love demands that you do for the child what is best for the child — not necessarily what the child wants at the moment. Periodically, you must say no to the tears of today so that you can help ensure the laughter of a happy, healthy child of tomorrow and the stable, well-adjusted adult of the future.

When the little eaglets make their appearance, the eagle parents nurture the babies with food that they have eaten and regurgitated. As the eaglets grow, Mother Eagle removes the soft down from the nest, reducing the eaglets' comfort level. Later, she removes the leaves, soft branches, and cloth, further discomforting the eaglets.

By this time, the young birds begin to climb up the sides of the huge nest to escape the discomfort. Finally, Mother Eagle removes the smaller sticks and everything else so that the eaglets are exposed to the glass, cans, rocks, and other uncomfortable bedding. Now the eaglets stay on the sides of the nest. And here's where tough love really begins. When the eaglets reach the top of the nest, Mother Eagle nudges one of them over the side, and it goes hurtling toward what seems like certain death on the rocks below. At the last instant, Mother Eagle swoops underneath and catches the eaglet on her own back. She repeats the process until the eaglets are flying on their own.

Mother Eagle's job is done — she has worked herself out of a job. That's what successful parenting is about — working yourself out of a job and, in the process, developing individuals who are competent and ready to make their mark in the world.

Parents must behave like eagles if they want their children to soar.

## You can't do it for them

Many times, when children are hurt or ill, particularly if they are still too young to talk and explain how they feel, their parents silently wish that they could have that hurt and experience it in their children's place. But that's not the way it works. Children must learn and experience certain things for themselves. To attempt to do everything for a child denies the child not only the opportunity but also the privilege of growing.

One thing to remember, particularly with toddlers, is that many times, if a parent doesn't acknowledge having seen the misstep, the child will pick himself or herself up off the floor and go along his or her merry way. If the child falls hard and immediately cries loudly and strongly, that's a different matter that requires comforting and attention from the parent. When our children were small, I would keep a careful watch out of the corner of my eye, and if there was some doubt as to whether they were really hurt, I would ask, "Does that hurt?" They would acknowledge either yes or no, and

then I would ask if they wanted me to pick them up. Most of the time, they would say yes. Then I would say, "Well, come here and I'll pick you up." They would usually hop up and come running to me. I'd pick them up and hug and kiss them, but I would not ask whether they were still hurting.

Of course, every parent is naturally concerned when his or her child is sick or hurt. You need to give that child the necessary love, care, and attention to assure your child that you are there and that everything is under control. However, an undue or excessive amount of attention when a child is sick or hurt may lead the child to get sick or hurt more often in an effort to attract attention. Remember that behavior that is recognized and rewarded will be repeated, and one of the things excessive attention develops is a child's tendency to "cry wolf" or to pretend to be more hurt or sick than he or she really is. That kind of behavior can be destructive to the child if it is repeated often.

## *Teaching children responsibility by making them accountable*

There's a great need in society today for people to act responsibly. Responsibility must be taught early on. For example, children often forget their homework or neglect to get a permission slip signed. After realizing what has happened, the panic-stricken child calls home and says, "Mom, I've got to have this!" In today's climate, where frequently both parents work, delivering the forgotten item involves a real disruption in the parents' day, sometimes taking a couple of hours from their schedule when that disruption really isn't necessary.

The solution to this problem is to respond to your child's first request, but take the opportunity to explain that in the future he or she will have to accept responsibility for taking to school what he or she needs to have for that day. You may want to get your child up a little earlier each day so that the "we were in such a hurry" excuse will not exist.

Suppose your child calls home a little later and says, "I've forgotten my homework. If I don't have it, I will fail this grading period!" What do you do then? You say to the child, "I'm sorry. That's your responsibility." As serious as failing the course may be, if you do not hold your child accountable, you're setting up a situation that will lead to nothing but continued irresponsibility and disappointment and failing more than a report card grading period. The earlier you teach your child responsibility, the less likely you are to have serious problems later on.

## Helping kids set goals

Kids who have plans and goals, particularly kids in their early teens, are far less likely to behave in a destructive manner than are those who do not understand the importance of goals. The kids with goals are not likely to get involved in petty thievery, shoplifting, drugs, alcohol, or other rebellious behaviors, because the goal-setting process involves a plan of action that limits negative behavior.

One of the benefits of talking with your kids a lot, reading to them when they are small, and sharing your dreams and goals with them is that you can simultaneously talk with them about their goals for this year in school. Ask them questions, such as "What will you be doing next year and ten years from today?" If they are old enough, you can even show them the goal-setting chapters of this book (Chapters 6 through 9) and help them put their goals in writing. When they are focused on performing at their best today and have specific plans for the future, they are far less likely to get involved in destructive behavior.

## Helping children avoid drugs and alcohol

Former drug "czar" William Bennett says that we can do things to prevent kids from experimenting with drugs. According to him, children who have good lines of communication with their parents, attend worship services regularly, and engage in extracurricular activities (sports, band, debate team, drama club, and so on) seldom try drugs. He encourages parents to keep their kids busy and to remind them that they are moral and spiritual beings. He says to tell them that drug abuse is a degradation of character and spirit, something not worthy of them.

To this, I'll add a couple of significant thoughts:

- ✔ Children need order in their lives, including a schedule that's centered on positive activities. Eating meals with the family, going to bed and getting up at regular times, and setting aside a definite time to study are very helpful to young people.

- ✔ It's still true that you can teach kids what you know, but you reproduce what you are. If you experiment with drugs (including alcohol and nicotine), chances are much higher that your children will experiment with drugs and perhaps become addicts.

   If your children see you drinking beer or cocktails, they believe that you're taking something to reframe your thinking. They view that as desirable, and the concept of drug use becomes acceptable to them. It's well documented that tobacco and alcohol are invariably the entrance drugs to illegal drugs.

   When individuals take their first drink or smoke their first cigarette, their intention is not to abuse them or to take the first step toward illegal drug use. If people could tell in advance of the using who was going to end up abusing, this world would be a different place indeed. Maybe you have a drink or smoke cigarettes occasionally and have never used any drug illegally — I am happy that it has worked out that way for you. But can you be sure that those chemicals will have the same influence on your children? I'm not a gambling man, but. . . .

Bennett's suggestions, combined with these other thoughts, are marvelous guidelines that every parent should consider.

# Recognizing That the "Little" Stuff Counts, Too

My wife and I successfully raised four children, so we clearly understand something about kids. In addition, our I CAN course has been taught to more than 3 million kids in every section of the United States, giving us a large "living laboratory" to learn from in the form of parents, teachers, and kids.

I can honestly tell you that the seemingly small things that you do to involve yourself in your child's life often make the biggest difference. This section is full of information that I have had lots of hands-on experience with. I hope that it benefits you greatly; I can assure you that the knowledge gleaned was largely by trial and error when my children were small. I am happy to report that all my children have forgiven me for the things I got wrong and have thanked me for what I got right. One day, yours will do the same if you make it obvious that you always have their best interests at heart.

## Starting and ending the day properly

When my granddaughter Elizabeth was 4 weeks old, her parents brought her to my home for a visit. She was taking a nap in the back bedroom while the adults visited in the den. When she awakened with a little cry, roughly 600 pounds — comprised of four adults — sprang into action and made a dash for the back bedroom. Because Mom was the most in-tune with that little girl, she won the race. The first thing she did was to talk to her baby as she quickly and quietly lowered the side of the baby bed. She gently reached down, picked Elizabeth up, and held her close, talking all the while. She softly placed her back on the bed and continued talking as she removed the baby's wet clothing. She put on that stuff that you put on babies and started re-dressing her, all the while talking to and "making over" her. When Elizabeth was completely dressed, Mom picked her up and again held her close.

As I watched this scene between mother and child, I thought that this gentle, communicative style would be the proper way to get any child out of bed, regardless of age. Unfortunately, not all parents take this approach. Too often, parents are guilty of sleeping late and then awakening in a dead run. From that point on, getting things together in time to leave so that no one is late to their destination is a madhouse. Typically, we dash by the kids' door, banging on it and demanding in a loud voice that they get up right now, admonishing that we won't be back, and reminding them that they were almost late yesterday.

The question is, how would you feel if someone summoned you from a deep sleep with that kind of command in that tone of voice?

Get up five minutes earlier — that's all it takes. As you pass your children's doors, knock and say, "Okay, sweethearts, it's time to get up." I don't expect this to arouse the children from a deep sleep and have them instantly jump up and appear, completely dressed, two and a half minutes later. However, you have interrupted a deep sleep and set the stage. Go on into the kitchen, plug in the coffee maker and the toaster, come back, and gently knock again. Ask if you can come in before you crack the doors to make sure that your children are not in a state of undress. You may sit on the side of each bed and stroke each child's hair. If your children are beyond 10 years of age and you have always used the demand approach to get them up, don't be too surprised if they half-angrily turn away from you. Don't expect to touch them, but continue to talk.

Say positive things, such as "I can't begin to tell you how much I love you. I'm so grateful that you're mine and that you're going to have fun today. I know you're going to learn some things today, and I can't wait until this evening when we get home and can talk about them." If you begin this procedure early enough in your children's lives, you will make a substantial difference in each child's day.

In the evening, if 9:00 is bedtime, at 8:30 say to your children, "Okay, at 9:00 you go to bed. So if you need to put the cat out and bring your bicycle in, talk to Charlie about your homework, get two drinks of water, and take three trips to the bathroom, you should start doing those things right now because at 9:00 you're going to bed."

At 9:00, exercise your parental authority by taking control of the TV remote and hitting the most important button on it — the one marked "Power." Turn it off. *Never* put your children to bed during a commercial. The message that they will receive is clear: "We know you love us, Mom or Dad, but we can see that watching this program is more important than spending the next few minutes with us. We understand because we've grown accustomed to it." If you can understand that, for a child, love is spelled t-i-m-e, you've made a giant step toward successful parenting.

I clearly understand that the greatest con artists walking the earth are somewhere between the ages of 5 and 13, and that they will try to con you into letting them stay awake as long as possible. As you take your children by the hand at the appointed time and lead them back to their rooms, don't be surprised if they ask you some of the most preposterous questions you've ever heard — questions that they have absolutely no interest in having answered. Children love to con you, folks. They just want to keep you in there so they don't have to go to bed, and they think they're outsmarting you. No problem. After a few minutes of this inane little game, they begin to ask questions that count. They reveal their hearts to you. You can bond more in the few minutes that you spend with them at bedtime than you're able to bond with them all day long. The message you deliver by listening patiently is extremely important: "You're very special to me. I love you very much. I'm glad that you're mine."

During this time, you can read bedtime stories, talk with the children about their day, and tell them about yours. Share things with them that indicate your deep love for and interest in them. This time is also marvelous for teaching. My wife and I prefer to read Bible stories when the children are small, and the Bible later on. You can pray with your children, too. Simply being there with them is a marvelous way to end the day. Start the day properly, end the day properly, and the time in between will go much more smoothly.

## Do lots of hugging

Hug your kids — particularly little boys — often. Research indicates that by age 6, little boys have received only one-sixth as much genuine affection as have little girls. This lack of affection shows up in the first grade, where little boys get into six times as much trouble as little girls do.

## Eat meals with your children

Families who eat together bond more readily and completely than those who do not. This is particularly true if the parents refrain from discussing difficulties and disagreements at the table. A casual mention is one thing; expressing anger and frustration is altogether different. A peaceful, conversational meal, where you talk about the day, discuss what's been learned, and express feelings about specific incidents, can add enormously to the maturing of the child.

The Reverend Gerald Britt, Jr., co-chairman of Dallas Area Interfaith, told this story about family bonding: A little boy was asked by a real estate agent whether he was excited about the prospect of his family owning a home. The child replied, "We already have a home. We just need a house to put it in."

## Watch your language

I cannot overemphasize the importance of the input into your child's mind. Bill Glass, who has conducted thousands of one-on-one interviews in prisons over the past 30 years, says that 90 percent of those who are incarcerated point out that they were repeatedly told by their parents, "One of these days you will end up in jail." The results speak for themselves.

Suppose every parent looked instead for encouraging things to say when a child does something creative or positive? Suppose parents worded their criticism in a more positive frame, such as "I love you, and I know that you're a good person who knows better than to do something like that." Statements such as the following really make a difference:

- ✔ "If you keep treating people that way, one of these days you will have friends everywhere you go."

- ✔ "If you keep studying like that, you could earn a college scholarship and later get a good job in the business world."

- ✔ "If you keep working that hard at everything you do, one day you may even be president of your own company."

## *Praise in the proper way*

As a parent, it's important that you understand some basics about raising your children. They're all different and special. Some are more personable, and others are more athletically gifted. Some have unusual talents or interests. Some children are simply smarter than others; they have higher IQs, grasp complex concepts more quickly, learn more readily, solve problems more easily, and so on. Not everybody can be the smartest in the class. However, if you praise your children for effort instead of bragging on them for being smart, they are far more likely to perform better in school.

According to a psychologist at a leading American university, youngsters who are told that their good work reflects high intelligence begin using their performance to measure their intelligence. When they encounter setbacks, they falter in discouragement because they think that they lack the skills that they need to succeed. However, the psychologist claims that children who learn that success comes from perseverance do not suffer from this crippling discouragement and are more apt to keep trying.

## Be a good-finder

A teacher sensitively used the "good-finder" approach when one of her students made this statement: "I'm not the best at anything." The teacher didn't know what to say. She knew that the girl was an average student from a large family and that she was a hard worker who gave each subject a good effort. So the teacher asked her what she meant. One by one, the girl ticked off the subjects and who was best at each one.

Then the teacher started thinking about the girl's good qualities. She remembered how she quietly helped the children who struggled with their work, her friendly smile, how she spent time with the unpopular or "slow" students, and that she never ridiculed the mentally handicapped child in the class. Carefully choosing her words, the teacher said, "You are not a bad student. You're very good at reading and music, and you do pretty well in other subjects, as well as in sports. But there is one thing you're absolutely best at." The child looked up in disbelief and asked what that one thing was. The teacher responded, "You're kind. That may sound crazy to you, but it's very important. This classroom is a much nicer place because you're here."

The girl's benefits were real and immediate, but the teacher's sensitivity made her a winner, too. She thanks her student for that. After all, the girl was also the best at making this teacher aware of what she did best — namely, encouraging others.

The psychologist and her colleagues conducted studies of about 400 kindergarten and fifth-grade students, putting the children in various scenarios. In one scenario, adults complimented some kids on their abilities and others on their effort and strategies. The results were interesting: Children praised for intelligence were more likely to credit later failures to "low ability" and see that as unchangeable. The kids who were cheered for effort were more likely to feel that they just needed to try harder. By the third test, the "effort" group outperformed those praised for being smart, though both did equally well on the first test. Over 90 percent of the kids who were praised for being smart said that they'd choose an easy task over a harder challenge; three-fourths of those praised for effort chose the harder, learning task.

The message is clear: When a child makes an A on a test, it's of long-term benefit to say, "I know you've worked hard for that grade, not only on your homework but with your classroom habits, too. I'm proud of you for that."

Praise your kids for effort, not for their "smarts." Results will be better and lifetime habits will be formed, producing lifetime winners.

# If Only . . .

Surely, all of us will look back with some regret at the raising of our children. "If only I had taken time to attend the class play." "If only I had not spent all my energy on the job and pursuing my dream, I could have read more stories to my children." "If only I had realized that they would only grow up once, but that my job would always be there." "If only I had taken the time to counsel my children more." "If only I had been there to see my child at the piano recital or score the touchdown that won the game." "If only I had invested more time and resources in educational trips and a little less in hunting and golf equipment." "If only I had set a better example as far as drinking, drugs, and smoking are concerned." "If only I had realized what was really important."

It seems unfair that the years our families need us most are often spent in pursuit of financial success and security to the exclusion of the very people for whom we want the financial security. Many a parent is astonished at how quickly their children transform from child to young adult and what that transformation means in terms of the relationship. I can assure you that if you don't have an intimate relationship with your children while they are children, establishing one with mini-adults is difficult and awkward — but not impossible. Wise are the parents who understand in advance that the career climb is far less important than the children who need them.

Chances are good that you'll use the phrase "if only" many times before your life is over. However, I believe that if you change your course in time, you can avoid those "if onlys" and follow the advice that actor, lawyer, teacher, and writer Ben Stein gives in Volume 11, Number 3, of the *Executive Speechwriter Newsletter:*

✔ I am no longer interested in and don't have time for: anything concerning downsizing, what our balance of trade is, and anything having to do with celebrities and stars.

✔ I am interested in: whether I can get my son to do his homework; whether I can soothe him to sleep; whether I will be firm enough to give him a "sense of boundaries," yet not so strict that I scare him; whether I should allow him to snowboard without encouraging him to do anything that could hurt him.

✔ All of life is about opportunity costs. I could always be doing something else when I am with Tommy telling him a story. Usually, I could be writing something that gets published. Or I could be at my favorite restaurant, seeing my pals. But as I grow older, I realize that there is almost nothing that adds value to me or to my son or to my parents like being with them. Not just "quality time," but a lot of time. Nothing else seems terribly important to me at this point.

✔ I have no idea any longer what it means to be a "conservative." I know that for me, it means conserving my family, providing for them, protecting them, and leaving a legacy of my affection for my son. I can't control what's in the GOP platform, but I have a little control over what Tommy remembers of me and what a father is supposed to be. I can't have any impact on the debate about going back to the gold standard, but I can let my parents know how much I appreciate their sacrifices for me over the years.

Sounds like Ben Stein is well on his way to successful parenting. Apply what you have discovered here, and you will be a successful parent, too.

# Mending Your Relationship with Your Adult Children or Your Own Parents

Even if you look back with regret on the way you parented your young children, you don't have to let past hurts continue to damage your relationships with your adult children. If the relationship between you and your adult child — or between you and your own father or mother — is broken, the good news is that the relationship can be mended. The hard part is that you must initiate action that leads to forgiveness and reconciliation. Here's how.

I'm confident that many people who read these pages will say that they haven't spoken to their father or mother in years. In the event that your parent passed away before you had a chance to reconcile your relationship,

I encourage you to forgive him or her for any wrong that he or she may have done to you. If your parent is still living, I encourage you to make contact — either in person, by phone, or through the mail — and forgive him or her for anything he or she did to hurt you as you were growing up. (Now, don't just *tell* your parents that you forgive them; you have to actually *forgive* them.) The child isn't the only one who can initiate this contact; the parent can take the initiative, too.

You also need to ask your parent (or child) to forgive you for the part that you may have played in the breakdown of your relationship, and especially for your attitude toward him or her. I know that for many people, asking for forgiveness is extremely difficult. You may even need counseling to help you do so, but as my friend and fellow speaker Vicki Hitzges says, "One of these days, you will either say 'I wish I had' or 'I'm glad I did.'"

## Suicide prevention: Avoiding the biggest "if only" in the world

Most youngsters who take their own lives or attempt to take their own lives have never truly sensed love or warmth from an adult. This does not mean that their parents, grandparents, teachers, or others did not love them. It's just that the youngsters did not sense that love because, perhaps, they were never told of that love.

Seventy percent of all teens who commit suicide have alcohol in their bloodstream. That's a startling statistic, but perhaps equally startling is the fact that two-thirds of all fatalities on the highway are caused by beer-drunk drivers. So many teenagers never see alcohol as the truly deadly potion that, when used in excess, it can represent. Most teen suicide attempts also are from single-parent homes, and nearly 70 percent of all adolescent suicide attempts have experienced physical abuse or serious neglect within three months of the attempt. Eighty percent of all teen suicides are preceded by previous attempts, or else they have made overt threats of suicide.

Those frightening statistics are certainly not meant to place a "guilt trip" on any parent who has tragically lost a child to suicide. In most cases, we do not really know the exact circumstances leading up to what any person taking his or her own life perceives as being an unsolvable problem. But suicide is a permanent solution to a temporary problem. I believe that, as you read this book and learn to communicate with your spouse and your children, you will dramatically reduce the possibility of suicide in your own family.

As a parent, be on the lookout for signs that your child is troubled: drastic mood changes, a sudden loss of interest in school, the giving away of prized possessions — such as a favorite fishing rod or awards that are held dear. When teens start disposing of these things, an alarm should go off in your mind.

When your child's close friend is tragically killed or commits suicide, be particularly watchful and spend extra time with your teenager. Many times, the loss of someone dear to them makes them feel that they have no reason to live, and they subsequently attempt to take their own life.

Recently, a young man shared with me that he and his dad had been at each other's throats for years and that he hated his father. He took my advice, went to his father, and confessed his hatred. The young man told his father that he loved him and had forgiven him and asked his father to forgive him for his attitude toward him. The young man told me that he and his father shed many tears, embraced warmly, and are steadily building a great relationship.

Think about it this way: You have little to lose and a great deal to gain by giving my advice a try.

I have no way of knowing whether you are a wannabe parent, a parent with small children, or a "been there, done that" parent, but I know without a doubt that you have parents. Think for a few minutes about how they enriched your life. Consider how their input shaped you. What did they do that helped you to be a survivor? What made you strong? Did they influence your attitude? Are you proud of the values you have, and do you think of your parents when someone comments on your integrity or character? Yes, dear reader, you have much to be thankful for, and if your parents are living, I suggest that you share the things that came to mind as you asked yourself these questions.

If you're thinking, "Zig, you don't want to know what came to mind as I read those questions, and my parents don't, either," then I say to you: Give yourself a gift today. Call your parents and begin the forgiveness process now, while you still can. You'll be glad you did.

# Chapter 16

# Building Better Employer/ Employee Relationships

- ▶ Knowing what employers want
- ▶ Understanding what employees want
- ▶ Getting on the same side

*T*he concept of "You can have everything in life you want if you will just help enough other people get what they want" is hard-core and practical, yet it's also gentle, loving, and enormously effective. Throughout the book, I use examples to validate this point. The major objective of this chapter is to show you how this philosophy works for employers and employees.

## *What Employers Want*

I start with this question: Just what do employers want? I think it's safe to say that they want

- ✔ Loyal, productive employees
- ✔ A growing, profitable business
- ✔ The business to be as worry-free and trouble-free as possible
- ✔ The business to be a positive force in the community

How can employers accomplish these objectives? Only by having an organization of people who are happy and productive in their quest to acquire the things that they want. In order to find out what your employees want, you must *ask them.* If you decide that what your employees want doesn't matter because you're the boss, owner, or whatever and you're in charge, you're in for real disappointment — turnover will be extremely high, and productivity will be average.

## Turnover costs more than you may think

Turnover is tremendously expensive in today's marketplace. Competition for skilled, effective workers is intense. To run recruitment ads, interview and test candidates, hire new employees, and bring them up to speed is expensive, disruptive, and terribly time-consuming. And then you have to hope that the people you hire fit into the corporate or industry culture.

According to an article in the January 12, 1998, issue of *Fortune* magazine, for nine years, Merck and Company was voted the ninth most desirable company to work for in the United States. Merck achieved this lofty position by being employee-oriented and creating a work environment and philosophy that demonstrate care and concern for its employees. This approach enabled Merck to select the cream of the crop among the PhD graduates of the most

prestigious universities, which further increases their productivity and profitability. Thinking in terms of the employees' interests also enables Merck to provide the best products and services to its outside customers.

Merck and Company is so conscientious about its employees because it conducted a study and found that replacing a worker who resigns or is discharged costs the company one and one-half year's salary. That's an expensive price to pay for replacements! Merck and Company is a high-tech company, and most businesses don't require that much investment to replace a departed employee, but every business manager or owner I've talked with agrees that turnover is expensive.

# What Employees Want — and What Happens When Employees "Win"

As I explain in Chapter 1, most everybody wants the same eight basic things in life. People want to be

✔ Happy

✔ Healthy

✔ Reasonably prosperous

✔ Secure

People want to have

✔ Friends

✔ Peace of mind

✔ Good family relationships

✔ Hope that the future is going to be even better

Employees generally want the following things from their employers:

- ✔ Interesting work
- ✔ Appreciation for work done
- ✔ The feeling of being in on things

Now line up people's wants in life with their wants as employees and ask yourself: If employees get interesting work, appreciation for work done, and the feeling of being in on things, are they not happier, healthier, and more productive in their jobs, which legitimately justifies an increase in income? Most employees instinctively understand that employers do not *give* raises; an employee *earns* a raise by increasing productivity, which increases profitability. A raise is the employer's recognition of the contribution that the employee makes.

Going down the list, isn't it obvious that if employees are happy, healthy, and more prosperous and are appreciated and recognized, then they feel more secure? That sense of security ties them to their employers for a longer period of time, which reduces turnover.

Continue down the list: If employees are happy, healthy, prosperous, and secure, aren't they more likely to be stress-free, confident, and loyal? Those qualities attract friends, and having more friends gives greater peace of mind. Because what happens on the job has a direct bearing on family relationships, doesn't increased job satisfaction afford better family relationships? And having good family relationships improves their productivity on the job.

What employees do off the job plays a major role in how they do *on* the job.

Now put all these factors together, and employees have legitimate hope that the future is going to be even better than the present. Please understand that hope is the great activator. If a worker has no hope for his future in the company, he is far more likely to be unproductive and create more problems than if he believes that his job is a "lifetime home." It seems logical to me that if a worker feels that his place of employment is his home, then he's going to work to protect that home.

When employees have hope, even their language changes. They talk about "my" company, "my" boss, and "my" supervisor, instead of "the" company, "the" boss, or "that" supervisor. That change in language represents an important change in attitude, because in every business, the sales department isn't the whole company, but the whole company is the sales department. How employees feel and what they say on and off the job ultimately affect the profitability of the company.

What does the employer get from all this? For starters, the employer gets loyal, productive employees who are the foundation for every successful business — and the only major asset that most businesses have. Second, because the employees are happy, secure, healthy, relaxed, and more prosperous because of their increased productivity, the employer gets a growing, profitable business. The business may not be completely worry-free and trouble-free as a result, but bringing in profit greatly reduces those problems.

In the Introduction of this book, I point out that nearly 100 percent of counseling taking place today is due to relationship difficulties. Much of those difficulties originate in the workplace or marketplace. With the approach that I advocate here, the employer has fewer worries and needs to do less counseling and problem solving. When you put all these factors together, the employer also gets a fourth benefit, which is a business that is a positive force in the community.

Praise and reward on the job have a direct impact on an employee's attitude. This attitude directly affects the relationships at home, which affect the attitude of the employee when he or she returns to work — the boomerang effect.

# *An Approach That Gives Employees What They Want*

I recognize that employers can't always provide interesting work (something that all employees want), but by being fair, open, and accessible, you can help alleviate frustration on the job and increase employees' job satisfaction.

- ✔ **Take a sincere interest in your employees.** People who feel appreciated and respected are more likely to be loyal, happy, and productive. If they really believe that you have their best interests at heart and are interested in getting to know them, they are far more inclined to be dedicated to their work and are thus more productive.

- ✔ **Express appreciation for the work that your employees do.** The cheapest, most effective motivation going is a simple, pleasant "thank you" for a job well done. No, that doesn't include thanking employees for being at work on time and doing what they're expected to do — those "accomplishments" are part of the job. But at the end of the week, if they've done these things, a simple "It's nice to have you with us" or "Thank you for a good job" goes a long way toward reducing turnover.

✔ **Be specific when you praise employees.** Generalizations just don't work. Saying "I really admire the way you brought this account into line and kept the customer happy at the same time" is far better than saying "You did a good job with the Hilliard account."

✔ **Don't praise workers for doing an average or routine job.** Praising mediocrity leads the employee or associate to believe that they can get by with mediocre work. However, when they do outstanding work, your recognition and praise mean a lot.

✔ **When someone does an outstanding job, dwell on the fact that it really is outstanding and, if possible, let others hear your praise.** But keep in mind that praise goes only so far, and if an individual consistently does a great job, he or she needs more tangible recognition, such as a cash bonus, a day off, or dinner at a nice restaurant. This need for tangible rewards is especially true if the employee does an outstanding job building or retaining customers with superior service. Here's what the November/December 1995 issue of *Harvard Business Review* had to say on this subject:

"A discovery by Xerox shattered conventional wisdom: Its totally satisfied customers were six times more likely to repurchase Xerox products over the next 18 months than its satisfied customers. The implications were profound: Merely satisfying customers who have the freedom to make choices is not enough to keep them loyal. The only truly loyal customers are totally satisfied customers."

The moment people center their attention on service to others, they become more dynamic, more forceful, and harder to resist. How can you resist someone who's trying to help you solve a problem?

✔ **Communicate with your employees about what's going on in the company.** When employees feel that they are in on things, they don't have to rely on a grapevine that is generally fed by sour grapes. Then they feel better about the company, their jobs, and themselves.

# Building Employer/Employee Relationships through Training

How do you develop a mutually beneficial employer/employee relationship? One of the first things that you must do as an employer is to invest in training your employees — not just to do the job for which they were hired, but to prepare them for handling additional jobs as well. Providing this kind of cross-training is good business because if one or more employees are absent, productivity comes to a standstill unless someone else can handle the job and maintain productivity — especially in small companies.

# Motivation takes place when you accentuate the positive

According to Aubrey C. Daniels, PhD, and Neil Baum, M.D., in the August 1995 issue of the *Pacesetter,* too many businesses are managed in the negative rather than in the positive. They point out that managers often say to their staff, "Don't mention the competitor's product," or "Don't forget to make five cold calls this week," when they should be saying, "Emphasize the features and benefits of our services, and remember that making at least five calls on new prospects is a sure way to build your career."

"That which is recognized and rewarded is repeated" is a truism. If employees get attention through the use of the negative, they generally continue in that behavior. The good doctors point out that if employees receive positive reinforcement for behavior, they're likely to repeat those actions and that "Employees are not primarily motivated by money. Money will get them to show up, but once they have checked in or reported for duty, they are more influenced by other elements in their environment."

Bear in mind that people are different, so you need "different strokes for different folks." However, nearly everyone is motivated by positive attention from managers and peers.

Some respond to physical reminders, like a note or a bouquet of flowers. Others thrive on public recognition at a meeting. But some may be embarrassed if their names are called out in public and they're asked to come forward and accept their reward or recognition. That's why astute managers are sensitive to each person's personal preferences and understand that what makes one person tick may stop another's clock in its tracks.

The best way to show appropriate recognition is to get to know people and reinforce their positive performance with things that are important to them. Sometimes a card, a note, a fax, or verbal recognition for acquiring a new account or simply for maintaining such an upbeat, positive, cheerful attitude is the very reinforcement they need.

Keep in mind that when I talk about giving people the kind of reinforcement they need, I'm talking about motivation, not manipulation. In manipulation, you have only one winner — the manipulator. When only the manipulator wins, somebody else loses. With motivation, whether in the business world or as in your social or family life, if the other person wins, you win, too.

Preparing employees to effectively handle more than one job also improves employment security for the employee. Training truly is a win/win situation. With training, you add value to the individual; then the individual adds value to the company.

Unfortunately, many employers say, "Why should I train my employees and then lose them?" The answer is that the only thing worse than training employees and losing them is not training them and keeping them. You can measure exactly what training costs, but you have no idea what *not* training costs, because you don't know about all the business that you lose when your employees are irresponsible, ineffective, or have personality problems that run customers off. In any company, only a small percentage of the staff (25 percent in the case of Ziglar Training Systems) does the selling. However, everybody can cost sales, whether they are in accounting, shipping, customer service, or even reception — all these folks can, and do, have a direct impact on the business.

That's why the employer's objective should be to have each employee speak in terms of "my company" or "our company," not "the company." Every employer should work at getting everybody on the same page and having the employees feel that they have ownership in the company. Certainly, if the company goes belly up, every employee suffers!

Revered singer Marian Anderson said, "As long as you keep a person down, some part of you has to be down there to hold him down, so it means you cannot soar as you otherwise might."

# The Six Steps in Ensuring Employee Effectiveness

The "you can have everything in life you want . . ." concept applies so much to the training process because you train those people you consider valuable and you reprimand those you consider savable. When I say "reprimand," I don't mean "chew them out." The correction process should always include instruction and/or encouragement. Follow these steps:

1. **Make sure that the employee has a clear understanding of what you expect from him or her.**

   Bringing employees aboard, assigning them a new job, and expecting them to perform up to your standards, when they have no idea what those standards are, is unfair, unrealistic, and counterproductive. So make sure to communicate your expectations.

2. **Never leave new employees to fend for themselves on day one. The feelings of uncertainty and insecurity can be overwhelming. Also, always double-check that employees have the necessary skills for the jobs that you hired them to do by "walking" them through their duties.**

   You can expect a computer expert to be able to move from one software program to another, but even that individual can benefit enormously from a few moments spent with someone who's intimately acquainted with the program that your company uses. In short, you need to be certain that their skill level qualifies them to do the job you expect them to do, and if you find areas that need improvement, arrangements for the proper training can be made immediately.

### 3. "Inspect" to make sure that you're getting what you "expect."

This step is especially important for new employees, and it's useful on a periodic basis for all employees. The fact that you inspect doesn't mean that you don't trust your employees. This approach communicates that you're interested in what they're doing. Inspecting also gives you an opportunity to praise and encourage employees, and if their performance needs improvement, you have a marvelous opportunity to instruct them. This process enables you to take Step 4.

### 4. Set a standard for each employee to follow.

People need a way to gauge how they are doing. That's why quotas are set for salespeople and written job descriptions are a part of most new-employee information packets. An employee who knows the standard can strive to excel and produce above-standard accomplishments. They also have factual information that lets them know when they are doing substandard work.

Accepting substandard work is counterproductive because that's the standard that employees will follow in the future. The lower the standard, the less you get, and the more damage you do to the company and its employees. Habit quickly sets in, and low standards create the feeling that it doesn't really matter.

An often-overlooked positive aspect of setting standards is this example: When a job has gotten too big for one person to handle, an employee who strives to do well does not hesitate to ask for help when he or she needs it.

### 5. Keep in mind that failure is an event, not a person.

While hoeing our garden as a child, I learned an important lesson from my mother, who was a great leader and manager. She followed all the preceding steps: taught me how to do what she wanted me to do, demonstrated clearly, and assured me that she was going to inspect to make certain that I gave her what she expected. When she saw what I had done, she shook her head and said, "Son, for most boys, this would be all right. But my son can do better." She effectively met Step 6.

### 6. Praise the performer; criticize the performance.

My mother criticized the performance — which needed criticizing. Step 6 is one of the greatest management principles going. It clearly says to the employee, as my mother said to me, "Failure is an event — not a person. You failed in this task, Son, but you're not a failure in life. You're a good boy." In essence, that's the message the employer needs to convey to the employee. "You're too good a worker, you're too talented and skilled, to turn in work like this. You can do better. You always have. I'd appreciate it if you would give it another shot."

If you follow these six steps, your new employees begin their career with you on a positive, reassuring note. You create an atmosphere that says, "You are more than a number at this company. We want you to know everything you need to know to do the best job possible to ensure your continued job enjoyment and security. We want you to feel safe and relaxed because we care about you and how you function within our company. We understand that your contentment with your job directly affects your productivity, which affects our profitability and the security of everyone we work with. We *want* you to succeed in your job because you are an important team member."

# Improving (or Harming) Relationships through Language

The relationship between employer and employee, to an extraordinarily large degree, depends on not only the words that are said but also the tone of voice behind those words.

In the following story, you see that words can change — even save — lives:

Several years ago, I was conducting a four-hour seminar in Marion, Indiana, on a Tuesday night. When I returned home on Friday, I had received a letter from one of the women who had attended the seminar. She said, "Mr. Ziglar, I was there on Tuesday night, and I had just gotten back from a rafting trip in Colorado.

"It was truly one of the most magnificent experiences of my life. During the day we rafted down the river, and as the sun was beginning to set, we would pull off to a flat spot, build our campfire, and cook our dinner. After dinner," she said, "we would go up a few hundred more feet so we could get a better view. The rarefied air and the clarity were incredible! We could look at the stars and the moon. It was indescribable! When I looked at the magnificent universe, it was an awe-inspiring sight. The next morning we'd get up, go down to the streams, and watch the wildlife take their morning drink.

"The whole thing was so awesome that I thought of myself as being absolutely nothing and contemplated suicide." And then she said, "On Tuesday evening you quoted St. Augustine, who many years ago (in AD 399) said [and I paraphrase him], 'Man travels hundreds of miles to gaze at the broad expanse of the ocean. He looks with awe at the Heavens above. He stares in wonderment at the fields and the mountains and the rivers and the streams. And then he passes himself by without a thought — God's most amazing creation.'" She concluded her letter by saying, "When you quoted St. Augustine, I realized what I was." She finished on an upbeat note: "Yes, the right words really can build us up or tear us down."

Of course, words can be terribly destructive as well. The following paragraphs from an anonymous writer identify those types of words:

> "I am an office mystery. I'm never seen but I'm everywhere. I'm always on the job and often forecast important events. I make and unmake morals, reputations and cooperation, but I'm seldom blamed for my mistakes. I have no responsibilities, and I am one of the most powerful molders of opinion. I add humor and anger to the office, and I pass with the speed of sound. I am basic in human nature, and you must accept me. I grow right behind you. I am the office grapevine."

Employees and employers around the world suffer daily because of the speculation that goes on in the "office grapevine." People are fired for erroneous reasons, lives are permanently changed, and reputations are ruined. Sometimes the gossip is so prevalent that the truth is buried in its wake. Chaos, fear, and discontentment prevail where truth has fallen victim to the venom of gossip.

On a lighter note, two people were talking, and one said, "I hate to spread gossip, but I don't know what else you can do with it!" That little joke is kind of cute, but look at the serious side of it: You don't win friends and influence people by being a gossiper. Listening to gossip lowers your opinion of yourself. It lowers your opinion of the person who is spreading it and the person who is being discussed. You can't build permanent winning relationships on a foundation of wonder — "I wonder what that person's going to say about me when I get away from here?" And you can depend on it: That's what others are going to be wondering when you're spreading gossip. One of the best rules I've ever heard is, "Don't tell me something and then tell me not to tell somebody else. I've got such a lousy memory, I might forget that you told me not to tell. Oh, I'll remember the choice gossip, but I might forget that I'm not supposed to tell it."

If you won't say it *to* them, don't say it *about* them.

The way you put your words together can cause incredible pain, hurt feelings, and even destroy especially sensitive and tender people. For example: "How many times do I have to ask you for . . .?" "You *never* get it right!" "I don't have until Christmas!" "Why can't you . . .?" "You *always* . . ." "Which rock did you crawl out from under?" "Any idiot could . . ." "I don't know why I even put up with you!"

I hope that you didn't recognize yourself when you read that list of insults, but I believe that everyone has been subjected to at least one of those condescending statements or questions in their lifetime. Words like that devastate people, and they are totally uncalled for. If someone speaks to you that way, reject his or her words for what they are: the biased opinion of an insecure, dogmatic, prejudiced, uncaring person who is probably experiencing considerable pain himself or herself.

# Successful Business Relationships Start and End with Integrity

A strong force in the United States today is the movement to instill ethical behavior in the home, school, and business environments. Though I applaud the trend, I believe that this movement is putting the cart before the horse. The horse, in my opinion, is *integrity*. Integrity is who you are, a measurement of your character, and, consequently, the determining factor in your behavior. *Ethics* are the result of integrity. People of integrity breed an environment of trust, which is a marvelous foundation on which to build a thriving business and create that win/win situation between employer and employee.

Human nature being what it is, the person in the power position — namely, the employer — is often viewed with skepticism. Frequently, the employee feels that the employer has most of the benefits and that he or she has very few; the employee has heard promises before that have not been fulfilled. With this tendency toward skepticism in mind, integrity, which is important in all areas of life, is particularly important in the employer/employee relationship.

When the employer has integrity, he or she builds trust, and when employees trust their employers, they follow the right principles. Real leadership, according to Dwight Eisenhower, is getting other people to do what you want them to do because they want to do it. Employees want to do what employers want them to do when they trust their employers and their employers trust them.

Employees also have a responsibility to their employers in the integrity department. Significant sums of money are lost every year because employees dawdle away time at the coffee pot, borrow a few pens, mail a few personal letters, and make a few personal calls on the company's 800 number. Late arrivals and early departures by one employee can hurt the productivity of several people. Employees who take care of their company's best interests will have a place to work for years to come.

Yes, it takes everyone involved to make a company successful, and a company is the sum total of its workers, from the CEO to the cleaning crew. Each person's job is important, and each person has the power to make a positive or a negative difference. Whether you are in top management or you fill in part-time for a temporary service, you have a choice to make every day of the week. Choose to work with integrity. Choose to help create an atmosphere of peace, trust, and security. Choose not to participate in gossip or idle chatter that robs your company of your time. Choose to be a supportive part of the team that makes up your playing field — if you do, good things are almost guaranteed to come your way!

# Chapter 17

# Building a Character Foundation for Society

*E*veryone has goals for society — the world sure has plenty of problems! Obviously, I can't cover every societal goal in one chapter; racism, poverty, hunger, disease, war, and so on are issues that are just too big to tackle here. But in this chapter, I do point out what I think are the most important goals that we should set. I chose the topics of character, attitude, drugs, and teen pregnancy because I firmly believe that solving these problems will solve the other problems in our society. Think about it: With a character foundation, lying, cheating, and stealing are eliminated. Parents with character don't abuse or abandon their mates or children. Alcoholism, drug abuse, and drug dealing stop if everyone has a strong foundation of character, so crime, violence, and poverty decline dramatically, as do hunger, disease, and out-of-wedlock births. With character and the right attitude, the racism problem can be solved within a generation or two.

## Focusing on Character Education

The foundation upon which all permanent success is constructed is the character of the individual — including at the company, institution, or government level. Collectively, individuals make up society, and the success of any society is a reflection of the character of the individuals within that society. In the early years of United States history, over 90 percent of the educational thrust was along ethical/moral/religious lines, focusing on building students' character. In those early years, the country produced

George Washington, Thomas Jefferson, James Madison, James Monroe, Ben Franklin, John Adams, and so on. Very few people today believe that the current crop of leaders are anywhere close to what the fledgling United States produced in its developmental years.

I think that a good example of the importance of the character base and other qualities of success was when General Douglas MacArthur commanded the American occupation forces in Japan at the end of World War II. MacArthur knew that he needed to prepare the Japanese people to live in peacetime, but he also knew that a warlike nation can't be changed overnight, so he determined to make the changes through the educational system. He drew up a program for doing so and enlisted the aid of educators to implement it.

The obvious place to start changing the character and attitude of a society is in the home, but because they had lived under a military regime for so long, Japanese parents weren't as firmly rooted in these qualities as they needed to be to succeed in a nonwarlike world. So starting in kindergarten and going through high school, students attended courses emphasizing attitude, responsibility, commitment, positive thinking, enthusiasm, motivation, honesty, integrity, and so on for one hour a day. After 12 years of this instruction, when the young Japanese headed off either to college or to the workplace, they had a firm foundation in place and were ready to master the specific skills and gain the experience they needed to become productive in the world of business, industry, and government.

The results were truly spectacular. Japan had lost more of its young men than any other nation had lost in the last 100 years; its cities had been bombed and gutted by fires and atomic weaponry; and much of its food supply and raw materials had to be imported. However, in the 1950s, the Japanese became the number-one textile producer in the world; in the 1960s, despite having to import both iron ore and coal, they became the number-one producer of steel in the world; by 1980, they were the number-one producer of automobiles and electronic technology.

I believe that the Japanese were able to achieve these accomplishments because of a team effort among government, business, and education and because their young people learned the foundational qualities of character, integrity, morality, and positive mental attitudes.

## *Bringing values back to mainstream society*

In modern American society, which is much freer than the Japanese society of the 1940s, we can't mandate that character, integrity, morality, and positive mental attitudes be taught for an hour each school day, but we *can* sell the concept to school systems around the country and around the world. More and more people are recognizing that character is the key to a healthy, thriving society, that some values are absolute, and that society has a great need and responsibility to teach at an early age the benefits that go with this approach to life. Fortunately, many individuals and organizations are working hard to bring the values system back into mainstream America.

Some people argue that you can't legislate morality, and the qualities I'm talking about definitely carry moral implications. But actually, society has always attempted to legislate morality. Virtually everyone agrees that murder is immoral, so we've passed laws against it. People agree that stealing is immoral, so we have laws against theft. People agree that rape and other violent acts are immoral, so we've passed laws against them. Yes, those laws are broken on a regular basis, but for the most part, folks agree that these activities are immoral and should be illegal. Without these laws, anarchy would exist.

## Finding integrity in the business world

I'm sure that you, like me, prefer to do business with ethical individuals and companies. Whether you're dealing with a doctor, lawyer, mechanic, butcher, or baker, you're far more comfortable and trusting when you know that the other person is going to treat you right. When you find businesspeople who are ethical, you recommend them to your friends and relatives and give them your business. The December 9, 1989, issue of the *Wall Street Journal* carried an article on "Golden Rule companies" (meaning companies that operate on the concept that you treat others like you want to be treated) that pointed out that these companies grow faster, make more money, and have better return on equity.

Dr. Millard MacAdam, in his book *Intentional Integrity,* tells one of my favorite stories about the benefits that value-driven business leaders experience. This one came out of the Johnson&Johnson Tylenol tragedies.

As you may recall, several deaths occurred in 1982 and 1986 as a result of someone putting cyanide in Tylenol capsules. Because of Johnson&Johnson's respected position and company credo that said, "Never offer for sale any product that might prove to be a hazard to a person's health," the company pulled Tylenol off every retail shelf in America without hesitation. Johnson&Johnson would not jeopardize the health of even one person, and though there was no doubt that virtually all the literally tens of millions of capsules that were pulled were perfectly safe, the executives felt that the integrity of the company demanded a removal of all those capsules from store shelves. The cost was enormous, but Johnson&Johnson's credibility was instantly restored, and the company later produced tamper-proof containers as well as tamper-proof Tylenol tablets. In a matter of weeks, its business was better than ever.

## Is it fair?

Several years ago, one of our salespeople was told by a teacher that, when asked, he shared with his students the alternatives in a given situation, but he didn't tell them which alternative was right and which was wrong. Our salesman asked, "What if a person makes a mistake and breaks a law? Do you think we should punish that person?" The teacher responded, "Yes." Our salesman then asked, "Is it fair to punish someone for breaking a law if we have never taught that person that breaking the law is wrong?"

Albert Einstein believed that human beings must have clear standards of right and wrong in order to realize their potential. "The most important human endeavor," said Einstein, "is striving for morality in our actions. Morality is what gives beauty and dignity to life. Following our animal instincts is not enough. Without high standards of right and wrong, men cannot live together in peace and friendship."

Most people agree with Einstein's approach. Unless firm character-based teaching is in place, human nature doesn't lead in the right direction. Most of us are self-serving in our endeavors, and if something isn't identified as being wrong, we generally follow the course of action that brings us the most immediate rewards.

MacAdam wrote in his book, "High-integrity companies driven by high ethical standards for conduct are far more successful financially over the long term. I believe the same holds true for individuals, their families and their careers."

## Putting good news at the forefront

Knowing the value to society of character, integrity, morality, and a positive attitude and knowing that societies can't thrive without those qualities, doesn't guarantee that everybody in the world is going to adopt these values and teach them in schools or abide by them in business and government. However, this idea is so critical to the solution to modern societal problems that everyone needs to promote it as a solution. One way to do so is to embark on a letter-writing and call-in campaign, urging newspapers, radio stations, and television stations to put good news on the front page and bad news in the center of the paper or newscast.

For example, think of the impact of having the daily paper run one good-news event — an unsung hero story, a company that went out of its way to be a good corporate citizen, a church or charitable organization that is reaching out to solve problems — on the front page every day. Think of what could happen if just one article of this nature appeared every day on the front page of every paper. The merits of hard work, accepting responsibility, and living with integrity would permeate society. That's the way — and the only way — that we're going to build the foundation that is a must for solving societal problems and moving to the place we need to be.

# Building the Right Attitude

An example of the kind of good-news story that I proposed in the preceding section appeared in a column by Cal Thomas in the *Dallas Morning News* on May 10, 1997. (This story was originally reported in a *60 Minutes* segment.) He writes about Rob Carmona, executive director of Strive, telling 91 unemployed New Yorkers in the basement of a Harlem housing project some truths that can make a difference in their lives. Carmona is a role model who knows whereof he speaks. He's been in prison and was addicted to drugs, but then he turned his life around and founded Strive.

The story opens as a man named Steve Berlack tells his audience, "You might type 100 words a minute and know every computer program that ever came out, but if you're a jerk, you aren't gonna get a job! It isn't your skills that are keeping you from succeeding; it is your attitude."

The training in Strive is basic training. Participants find out how to smile, not smirk; to give a businesslike handshake, not the handshake of the street; to maintain eye contact with an interviewer; to wear shoes that can and must be shined. They're even shown how to walk, sit, and style their hair. People who whine or make excuses for not measuring up are told that the expectation to behave in this manner is the reality of the working world. They're told not to expect others to do for them what they are unwilling to do for themselves.

Strive isn't a do-good, feel-good encounter group. The language is tough, the expectations are high, and the results are impressive. In the past 12 years, Strive has put more than 15,000 people into real jobs — not government make-work — and has done so at a fraction of the cost of government efforts and with a far greater success rate.

The beauty of Strive is that it's funded entirely with corporate and charitable donations and is not just for people on welfare but also for anyone who is poor and out of work. Graduates of Strive frequently shed tears of joy when they get jobs for the first time in their lives. More than three-quarters of all Strive graduates find work in New York and in the four other cities where Strive has expanded. In three weeks, Strive turns around the lives of some of the hardest-core unemployed. Instead of thinking failure and victimization, they begin thinking that they can succeed — and they do.

## Is attitude important?

Survey after survey and study after study reveal that, far and above, the number-one attribute that employers look for in an employee is a good attitude. As a group and as individuals, employers believe that if a person has the right attitude, they can teach that person the specific skills that he or she needs to function well in the job. However, if the person has the wrong attitude, almost regardless of how many other good qualities he or she has, employers expect that person to create problems within the organization and negatively impact the productivity of other team members.

The question that employers instinctively consider is this: Is this person's attitude worth catching, or is it one to avoid? If it's one to avoid, you can be sure that individual won't be on the job for long — or won't be hired at all.

## An attitude adjustment

At long last, people are moving the "right," or positive, mental attitude out of the feel-good, "oh, you would be so much happier if you put on a happy face" soft-skill training realm. Now, teaching the importance of attitude is considered foundational to success training. Ask yourself these questions, and you quickly see how having a good attitude can affect your success in all areas of life:

✔ What is your attitude toward yourself? Your spouse? Your children? Your parents? Your employer or employees? Your fellow students? Your neighbors? Your job? Your opportunity? Your responsibilities?

✔ If you could, would you do something to improve your attitude in any or all of these areas?

✔ Are you willing to help others to improve their lives by helping them to improve their attitudes?

If you answered yes to these questions, you are a true team player and an asset to society. Start helping today by writing letters to your local newspaper and radio stations. Contact your school districts and encourage them to add courses that teach morality, values, attitude, and so on. You can influence others and make a positive difference in society.

Being a team player is definitely an attitude component. Here's one of my favorite examples to prove the point: 44 players who played football at Notre Dame were on the 1997 roster of the National Football League, and 36 players from Penn State were on the rosters of NFL teams that year. All told, nearly 1,600 players were on the roster of NFL teams in 1997; 80 of those players were from those two schools. That means that slightly over 5 percent of all players in the NFL came from just two schools, despite the fact that hundreds of schools have football programs. Why?

Many reasons help to account for this situation. Traditionally, these two teams have built a reputation of winning football and, consequently, are able to attract high-quality high school athletes to attend those universities — but many schools have fine histories, reputations, and so on. However, one thing is different about Penn State and Notre Dame: They are the only two major schools that don't put the names of their players on the jerseys.

Players are identified only by their numbers. We all pay lip service to the idea that "individuals score points but teams win games," but these two institutions support the concept by demonstrating their complete belief that it really is the *team* that wins the game.

Granted, you have to have great individual talent in order to play on a major college team. You have to have even more talent to make the roster of an NFL team, so you know that the individual players have that ability. But when great players with individual ability become team players and work toward winning games rather than scoring individual points with their special assignments, their value to the team goes up dramatically.

When we recognize that basically all honest people with good intentions are on the same side, we can work together more effectively and have a much better, more livable, loving society.

# Looking at a Couple of Specific Issues

You can't tackle all the societal issues at once, but everyone can do something to make society better. In this section, I take a look at two issues that I think we can do something about that will have a significant impact on society right away. Substance abuse — the use of drugs, legal and illegal — and teenagers having babies have a tremendous effect on society, and we *can* help to reduce the occurrences of both.

## Winning the war on drugs — legal and illegal

Legal drugs (tobacco and alcohol) kill well over half a million Americans each year. Illegal drugs kill approximately 30,000 Americans each year. Both kinds of drugs cost society incalculable amounts of money through

- ✔ Accidents
- ✔ Illnesses — whether life-threatening or the kind that result in days lost from work
- ✔ Family or marital breakups
- ✔ Child and spousal abuse
- ✔ Increased taxes to care for drug abusers and their families, who often end up homeless or on welfare

✔ Diversion of money and attention from mainstream education in order to accommodate the special educational needs of children harmed in the womb by drug use

✔ Increased taxes to pay for more police protection due to drug-related robberies and murders

If we can first stop the growth in drug use and then steadily reduce the usage, we can save hundreds of thousands of lives and billions of dollars each year. Solving the drug problem involves a dramatic change of attitude:

✔ We must believe that we can solve the drug problem, and we must marshal parents, school officials, government officials, and civic leaders to work toward that goal.

✔ We must change our vocabulary. "Casual" or "recreational" illegal drug use doesn't exist; there is only "criminal" drug use (if the drugs are illegal, the use of them is criminal). After that name is attached, youngsters and their parents will get the idea that using illegal drugs is breaking the law, a serious offense, and is not "in," "cool," or smart.

✔ We must understand that we will never be able to completely stop the flow of illegal drugs across U.S. borders. Consider this: One of the most prevalent places to find drugs is in jails and prisons. If we can't keep drugs out of a small, armed camp, believing that we can keep them out of a country that has thousands of miles of borders and even more thousands of miles of airways just doesn't make sense. We should make every effort to keep drugs out of the country, but we must accept that we have to deal with the user, not just the dealer.

With a change in attitude and vocabulary and an acceptance of our limitations in the drug war, we can begin to make real progress in defeating drugs. But truly solving the drug problem takes ambitious reforms. In the following sections, I suggest some steps to take to break the hold that drugs have on American society. Obviously, if these steps work in the United States, they can work around the world!

### Advertise the downside of legal drugs on TV

Television advertising, which is so effective that companies pay up to a million dollars for a 30-second commercial on Super Bowl Sunday, can be used to show the negative aspects of drinking alcohol and smoking cigarettes.

Tobacco companies have sold cigarettes as a way of being "in" for years, using print ads that imply that smoking makes you glamorous, healthy, and cool. Instead of that kind of false advertising, we can create both print and TV ads depicting elderly people coughing furiously and showing their nicotine-stained fingers and teeth, their wrinkled skin, and the ashes on their clothing. When tobacco-negative ads were run in California several years ago, the impact was so dramatic that the tobacco industry, using all its political muscle, fought to get those ads stopped.

Alcohol ads can depict stumbling drunks making complete idiots of themselves, clearly showing that the drunks are struggling to get out to the sidewalk because they are sick to their stomachs and about to throw up. The ads should bear the caption "This is fun?" Graphic? You bet! Then we can remove all pro-alcohol ads from television. When Sweden took these steps, alcohol consumption went down 20 percent, proving that this strategy does work.

### Reward drug informants

I read that officials in Los Angeles seized 20 tons of cocaine because a local citizen was suspicious of the truck traffic in his neighborhood and called to report it. Over $12 million in cash was recovered.

A reward system would encourage everybody to be on the lookout for situations like this one. I suggest establishing a national hot line with an 800 number (1-800-A-REWARD, for example). When anyone observed drug activity, he or she could call this number. The national drug enforcement people could then contact local law enforcement officers to follow through and investigate. Under the same anonymity afforded CrimeStopper reporters, the informant could be given a reward and remain anonymous.

I propose rewarding the informant with the first $10,000 in recovered cash and cash raised from the sale of seized valuables. Reward the informant with 50 percent of everything recovered from $10,000 to $50,000, and 25 percent of all monies or valuables recovered over $50,000. Using this plan, the $12 million cash recovery would have netted the informant over $3 million! Incentives like this would encourage citizens from all walks of life to turn in drug dealers via the national hot line.

### Increase cigarette taxes to pay for reforms

Instead of gradually escalating the tax on cigarettes, I think that we should make a huge increase with real shock value. I propose that we immediately place an additional $3 tax on each package of cigarettes. Currently, tobacco companies sell roughly 5 billion packs of cigarettes each year. This tax would promptly reduce that number and, because virtually all beginning smokers are young, would also dramatically reduce their numbers. Most young people simply can't afford $5 or so for a pack of cigarettes.

The additional tax would raise well over 10 billion dollars each year. The money could be used in the following ways:

- To subsidize tobacco farmers and retrain them for new professions.

- To convert tobacco warehouses and cigarette manufacturing plants to manufacture goods that benefit and serve humankind.

- To build homes in low-income districts for drug-, alcohol-, and tobacco-free families (or those who are willing to go into a sustained substance abuse treatment program to eliminate those problems).

Well-known drug authority Forest Tennant, M.D., has said that when society solves the tobacco problem, it will have solved the drug problem — which means taking a huge bite out of crime and untimely deaths.

### Lead by example

Teaching kids about the negative effects of drug use, both legal and illegal, is especially important. As parents and role models, we need to overcome the hypocrisy of lecturing kids on the evils of drugs while sipping cocktails and smoking cigarettes. Kids know that spending billions of dollars to keep illegal drugs out of the country, and then spending more billions advertising legal drugs that kill over half a million Americans every year, just doesn't make sense. Consistent leadership from parents and role models is the key.

People do follow examples. In November 1996, my wife and I celebrated our 50th honeymoon. We invited a large number of people to attend a reception at which we served no alcohol. One of our close friends heads a large organization and had always served alcohol at his conventions, even though he doesn't drink. However, when he saw how much fun everyone had at our party without having to put up with anybody drinking too much, or getting overly friendly with somebody else's spouse, or getting sick, he decided that a no-alcohol policy was a good idea for his company and has not served alcohol at his conventions since then. Not surprisingly, his people have had even more fun without alcohol than with it — there are no embarrassing incidents.

### Make young lawbreakers pay the price

Youngsters are often caught, lectured, and released several times for smoking pot, drinking, and otherwise engaging in self-destructive, antisocial behavior. As a result, the problem escalates. I propose to make 30 days' confinement at home and school the mandatory sentence for a youngster's first arrest for drug use or possession. As soon as school is out for the day, these first-time offenders would have to report for a two-hour work assignment involving manual labor: cleaning up slum areas, cutting yards for senior citizens, and so on. These tasks would produce blisters and consume their after-school energy. Next, they could spend one hour learning the benefits of being drug-free and one hour improving their education. The functionally illiterate kids could be taught by the literate kids, which would prepare both sets of youngsters for a better life ahead.

At the end of 30 days, they would have served their time, and if they didn't get arrested again for any drug-related violation, their records could be purged. If they were arrested a second time, they would spend the four weekends of the month in jail; the rest of the time they would follow the procedures I already recommended, except that once each week they would have to attend a Narcotics Anonymous or an Alcoholics Anonymous meeting to get better acquainted with folks who are long-term addicts and to discover the impact that drugs have had on their lives.

### Make non-users the winners

Because education and public awareness are "must-have" weapons to be used in the war, I suggest that schools sponsor song-writing contests to educate and alert young people to the dangers of drugs. Songs for the contest must carry the theme "I will never smoke, drink, or do drugs." Award prizes at the district, state, and national levels. In each school district, the writer of the winning entry and the school itself would receive a cash award. The winner, his or her parents, the teacher who helped the student enter the contest, and the principal would receive a trip to the state capital to have dinner with the governor. The winning song in each district could be played many times on local radio stations, and both the school and local papers could make a big deal of the contest.

Because this contest would create interest and controversy over whether the best song really won, several entries in addition to the winning song could also be played on local radio, and people could debate about why "song number two was the best" or "song number seven was best of all." Many young people are talented and extremely creative, and in the process of writing the songs, the kids and the community would become familiar with the hazards of doing drugs and the benefits of staying sober.

This approach gives winners positive publicity — a refreshing change from the negative publicity about drug arrests, drunk driving, and so on. The objective is to make everyone aware of the dangers of drugs and to shift the focus from users being losers to non-users being winners.

## Keeping kids busy after school

Another step in solving societal problems is keeping non-working kids busy, particularly after school. Many kids go home to an empty house and spend two to four hours alone before their parents get home.

This idle time can create problems — kids aimlessly cruising, doing drugs, drinking, engaging in sexual activity, and so on. To solve the problems, we could open up classrooms and athletic facilities that are not in use for team practice to students who attend that school. People from the business community could volunteer their time to teach kids some of the lessons that life after school requires — how to get a job, set and reach goals, build winning relationships, develop the qualities necessary to succeed in life, develop and maintain the right mental attitude, and build a character foundation. In life after school, those qualities are extraordinarily important.

Scout troops could use open classrooms in a very effective way. Kids who get into scouting move up the success ladder in life at a rate that is much higher than the national average; according to a 1995 Harris Poll, young people who spend five years in scouting are nearly two and a half times as likely to finish college and nearly twice as likely to earn more than $50,000 a year. Ninety-four percent of them say that the values they gained in scouting influenced them all their lives.

## Teaching abstinence, not "safe sex"

A major problem today is teen pregnancy, with babies being born to teenage mothers who are ill-prepared to give them the care and support they need. Virtually all these children, along with their mothers, end up living at or below poverty level, and the impact on their lives is almost entirely negative. In my opinion, "safe sex" education is partly at fault for the rise in teen pregnancy. I believe that we must teach kids sex education that is truly sex education, not a how-to course.

Ideally, parents should teach their own kids about sex, but if the parents don't have the inclination, the know-how, or the patience and love required to do so appropriately, other available sources are extremely effective. Dr. Diana Richard, in conjunction with Focus on the Family (a family-friendly organization with a daily radio program heard weekly on 1,400 radio stations), conducted research and discovered that in schools where "safe sex" is taught, teenage pregnancy rates are substantially higher than in schools where abstinence is taught.

For example, Elayne Bennett, wife of Bill Bennett, the former Secretary of Education and drug "czar," teaches a program in inner-city Washington, D.C., called Best Friends. This program teaches abstinence, and it's been reported that the rate of pregnancy is less than 3 percent for the kids who attend. (During one two-year stretch, not a single pregnancy occurred in the group of kids who attended Best Friends.) In a similar neighborhood, another program used the "safe sex" approach, and the pregnancy rate is said to have been over ten times as high.

## Getting Society in High Gear

Finally, to get society in high gear, every member of society needs to understand the role that he or she can play in societal wellness. Setting an example of morality, integrity, and character is a good place to start. Keep in mind that one person — you — can make a difference.

Author, speaker, and leadership expert John C. Maxwell says that, over a lifetime, the average person directly or indirectly influences 10,000 people, either for good or bad. In short, you can be a hero!

# Part V
# Moving Onward and Upward

The 5th Wave                    By Rich Tennant

"The pay's not great, but where else can you get a retirement plan that will last for eternity?"

## In this part . . .

The key to success is relationships, and improving the relationships in your life is the central purpose of *Success For Dummies*. In this part, I show you how to incorporate the relationships you have into your grand plan for success. I also show you how habit-forming success can be!

# Chapter 18

# You'll Never Walk Alone

## In This Chapter

▶ Understanding that there's no such thing as a "self-made man"

▶ Getting a start from your parents

▶ Inviting your teachers, mentors, employers, and friends to join the team

▶ Ensuring that you'll never be alone

▶ Using lonely time to do great things

*O*ver the years, I have realized that I really am not alone. Incredible sources of strength and help are all over the place — I just have to use them. Sometimes those sources come to me, but often I have to seek them out. Frequently, the people who help me are part of a team effort, and I may never meet them. For example, the products that my company sells have to be produced, manufactured, packed, shipped, serviced, financed, and so on. All the people involved are looking after my interests — making sure that I'm not alone — yet many of them are unknown to me. Obviously, every one of them is vitally important, and I am grateful for what they do.

I think of the huge Peter Lowe International seminars in which I participate. The seminar features only ten speakers, but several hundred people work behind the scenes — the increasingly important security people, the salespeople who sell the tickets, the marketing staff that creates the ads, the ushers who show people to their seats, and the organizational staff that coordinates it all. In short, literally hundreds of details must be taken care of in order for the speakers to be able to do their thing in the most effective way. Putting on one of these seminars really is a team effort, and each speaker is far from alone.

A team is behind virtually every successful endeavor. Although the shooter makes the basket, that shooter isn't going to have an open shot if the four other players on the basketball court don't do their jobs. The head coach directs the overall operation of the team, but without assistant coaches and trainers, he or she wouldn't have time to teach the players the game and make sure that each one is doing his or her job.

One of my delights in life is being able to talk with my children and get advice from them. I recently talked with my son Tom about a speaking engagement in Panama. I was hesitant about whether I should accept the invitation. From a scheduling vantage point, I knew that accepting the engagement may not have been wise; however, I didn't know what the international implications of establishing an operation in Panama would be. Tom, who is our president and CEO, has a much better grasp on the overall operations of our company than I do, and he advised me that accepting the invitation to speak in Panama wasn't a good move at the requested time. Having that kind of input is reassuring.

When I lost my oldest daughter Suzan to pulmonary fibrosis in May 1995, I truly discovered that I am never alone. The outpouring of love, understanding, and compassion was, at times, almost overwhelming. I didn't know that so many people care so much — for me, my daughter, and my family. Friends and even total strangers wrote, called, sent flowers, and contributed to charities in her memory. Friends and pastors supported our family during Suzan's hospital stay and for weeks and months after the funeral. Doctors and nurses were kind and patient with us through every step of the journey that none of us wanted or knew how to take. A father is never more helpless than when he is losing a child — I couldn't have made it through that ordeal without my heavenly Father and my friends and family.

All these examples from my everyday life show that I certainly am not alone. Chances are about 4,000 to 1 that neither are you.

# Realizing How Many People Contribute to Your Life

A moment's reflection may be all you need to realize that no one is truly "self-made." You are influenced directly and indirectly by many, many people throughout your lifetime, each of whom adds a brick to the building of your life, even if only in a small way. In most cases, the individual who claims to be self-made either hasn't really thought about what he or she is saying or has a considerable ego problem. More than just a grain of truth lies in the statement that "the problem with the self-made man is that he has a tendency to worship his creator." Or, as they say back home, "He's got the big head." People afflicted with this "disease" seldom are popular and even more rarely are able to move to the top and realize their potential.

To help you understand just how many people you have to thank for who you are, what you've done, and what you will be in the future, I encourage you to put this book down, get out a sheet of paper, and start making a list of all the people who have made an impact on your life. As you search your memory bank, you'll probably be amazed at the number of people who have influenced you. Making this list is an important step. I hope that you take that step now.

If you have trouble making your list, read the following sections, which explain the roles of some of the most important people in your life.

## Parents play a major role

Your parents, if they were there to raise you, had the greatest influence on your life. Research shows that when a mother is able to hold her baby immediately after birth, the bond between them is stronger and far more likely to continue to grow than when that experience is delayed. Whether mother and baby are able to bond immediately affects the physical and emotional health of the baby in a substantial way. Feelings of love and security are established early. Children who have parents who love, care for, and protect them gain enormous psychological and physiological benefits.

In the first months of life, a child hears either the language of love, care, and protection or the language of neglect or even, tragically, abuse. Soft, gentle words and sweet lullabies, sung as only a parent can, have a soothing effect and a positive bearing on a child's self-esteem. On the other hand, words with sharp edges delivered in a demanding, uncaring, dogmatic tone of voice also begin to set a tone and establish fear, bewilderment, distrust, and anger in the child.

The language that very young children hear has another important effect. Whether positive or negative, the words children hear repeatedly are the words they pick up and use with their own children, spouses, colleagues, neighbors, and friends later in life.

Although my mother was burdened with a heavy workload (keep in mind that she had 12 children), I can remember that she frequently sang as she did household chores — cooking, washing dishes, making beds, quilting, and churning milk to produce butter. Her loving, supportive, upbeat nature had a huge impact on my life, and I'm truly grateful that I was able to start my life's journey with her. In short, I did not start alone.

## Teachers play a role

My memory of my first-grade teacher on my first day of school is painful and unforgettable. We had recently moved from the country to Yazoo City, Mississippi. Going from our little farmhouse in the country to that "huge" school with high ceilings, maps and pictures on the walls around the room, and a long blackboard in front — all fascinating sights for me — was a major change in my little world. Mrs. Dement Warren had a long pole with a hook on the end for pulling down the maps that hung above the blackboards. As she was teaching, I was busy looking around the room. Suddenly, I felt the sting of that pole on my knee and heard the sharp admonition to pay attention. The physical sting was unpleasant, but the embarrassment of the encounter was far worse.

It took me a long time to forget that introduction to the educational system. As a matter of fact, I didn't understand "the rest of the story" and what Mrs. Warren ultimately meant to me until long after I became an adult. As a first-grader, I had nearly all the childhood diseases — mumps, measles, and whooping cough — and missed four months of school. I have no doubt that I would have failed first grade had Mrs. Warren not taken it upon herself to come out to my house. She came not once but twice weekly to bring me up to speed with what the class was doing and to give me my assignments for our next session.

Had she not done that, I would have been drafted out of high school into World War II in 1945. Instead, I enlisted in the V-5 program of the Naval Air Corps in January 1944. The program permitted me to wait until July 1 to enter the service. Initially, I was scheduled for 12 months of college before starting flight training, but the war was winding down and the need for pilots no longer existed, so I received 20 months of college education.

I seriously doubt that I would have been able to go to college had I not had that chance to get into the V-5 program; the economy and our family circumstances were such that I never even imagined being able to attend college. What Mrs. Warren did impacted my entire life. One of my deepest regrets is that she died before I fully appreciated and understood the significance of what she had done for me. Mrs. Warren really did help to ensure that I didn't "walk alone."

## Many others play a role

Obviously, other people from many walks of life help to make sure that you never walk alone. The following sections describe some of those folks.

### Friends

From childhood, you begin to form friendships, and your ability to form friendships develops as you grow older. The happiest and most successful people seem to have a wide range of friends from many different walks of life. (See Chapter 13 for information about developing friendships.) I've been particularly fortunate in that I have many friends with whom I've been close for 30, 40, and even nearly 50 years. They are an integral part of my life and are one of the reasons I am truly never lonely. Even though on occasion I am alone, as are you, I know that those friends are a part of me and that a phone call or a visit from me is always welcome.

### Mentors

The need for mentors is growing in this complex world. Few people have the time to acquire through research and reading all the information and techniques that they need to be successful. For that reason, mentors in more than one area are certainly helpful. I've been privileged to have resources in the three major disciplines — namely, the physical, the mental, and the spiritual. I periodically call my mentors in these specializations and ask them questions.

At least once a week, I talk to someone about the areas of life in which I have deep interest. I encourage you to network and make friends with people you respect and trust, people who can guide you down the pathways that you travel in life. For example, the person you work for can give you invaluable information on how to reach the level of success that he or she has attained. Your job is to seek out such information, listen carefully, and apply it to your own life.

If someone approaches you and asks for your guidance, give him or her the kind of help that you've been given. *Being* a mentor is every bit as important as *having* a mentor. When you give freely to others, asking others for help when you need it is less difficult, and seeing the people that you mentor progress enriches your life.

### Authors and speakers

My most reliable sources of information, because they're available at my discretion and I don't have to depend on someone else's timetable, are the authors I read and the speakers I listen to while I'm in my car. I can't even begin to adequately describe all the resources that are available in this department. The library is chock-full of marvelous books; bookstores offer them at bargain prices. You can tap into the minds of the wise people of today as well as those of old. When you're with these men and women through their spoken and written words, you certainly are not alone.

### Spiritual leaders

Spiritual leaders — ministers, priests, rabbis, and so on — are in a marvelous position to make significant contributions to your life. What they teach can keep you from being lonely. When a crisis strikes, no one is better prepared to help you handle it than your spiritual leaders. They have a foundation of spiritual knowledge to help you find the answers that you seek, and they can help you regain hope when all seems hopeless. No person is more alone than the one who feels hopeless, and no person sees a brighter light than the one coming out of the darkest hole of hopelessness. Having a spiritual leader doesn't guarantee that you'll never feel despair, but it does guarantee that you don't have to go through the darkest times alone.

## This man was lonely

A man went to the top of the Empire State Building in New York City to jump off and kill himself. When he got to the top, he discovered that it was fenced in, so committing suicide there was impossible. He decided to jump off the Brooklyn Bridge instead. On the long walk to the bridge, he had time to do more thinking. He decided that if even one person smiled at him on the way, he would consider life worth living and not take his own life. The question is, if you had been one of the people he passed that day, would you have smiled at him and saved his life?

I recognize that the question is rhetorical. But wouldn't it be tragic if the person looking for a smile was your mate, your child, your parent, your brother or sister, your neighbor, or maybe someone you work with or exchange hellos with? A simple word of encouragement or an indication that you know of another person's difficulties and are concerned can make a big difference in that person's life. In the process of encouraging others — whether with a smile, a friendly greeting, or a humorous, encouraging thought — you yourself benefit. So give a little something to someone who's in need. That person will no longer feel lonely, and neither will you.

# Being the Kind of Person Who Is Never Lonely

In the next few pages, I share with you some basic lessons through my favorite method of teaching — stories and parables. These stories demonstrate that, even though you may be alone from time to time in terms of human contact, you need never be lonely. Applying the principles brought forth in these stories to your own life guarantees you friends and contacts that can make your life much more pleasant and far more fun.

## Make friends by being a friend

The best way to ensure that you are never truly alone is to do something like the gentleman in the following story did.

A man bought a new television set. The neighbors gathered one Saturday to help him put up the antenna. Most of them had only the simplest tools, so they weren't making much progress. Then one of the neighbors who was new on the block appeared with an elaborate tool box. The box contained everything needed to get the antenna up in record time. As they all stood around congratulating themselves on this piece of good luck, they asked the new neighbor what he made with such fancy tools. The new neighbor smiled and answered, "Friends, mostly."

What a marvelous example! Wouldn't it be wonderful if everyone thought in terms of making friends by doing such simple acts? You may well say that you need to be an electrician, a mechanic, and a carpenter to make friends the way this man did, but if you do, you just missed the point. He bought those tools to take to the neighbors on special occasions so that *they* could use them.

The best way to make friends is to be friendly. You can start with a simple smile, a cheerful hello, or a word of encouragement. Dropping an uplifting note in the mail to someone can lift spirits and lessen burdens. You can have an amazing impact when you engage in a simple, thoughtful, kind act. Your benefit is that you'll never be alone. You'll draw friends like honey draws bees.

## Be there when others need you

At 6 feet, 2 inches and 275 pounds, Daniel Huffman was quite a football player. He was the team co-captain and a star defensive tackle on his high school team, and his dream was to be a football hero at Florida State University. Daniel lived for football, but something else entered the picture, changing forever his chances of winning a football scholarship and playing at Florida State or in the National Football League.

According to the October 27, 1997, issue of *People* magazine, Daniel lived with his grandparents from age 12 on, and he and his grandmother, Shirlee, had a closer-than-usual relationship. He and Shirlee discovered that they had a real affinity for reading, writing, and each other. But Daniel's beloved grandmother desperately needed a new kidney. He drove her to the hospital for dialysis three times a week, and while he waited for her, he read about diabetes and her condition. He found out that people die every day because of donor organ shortages.

As the weeks turned into months, Daniel watched Shirlee change. She lost her enthusiasm. When he took her home after dialysis, she slept for ten hours. Her decline bothered Daniel deeply. As her condition worsened, Daniel realized that he had to do something, so he volunteered to give her one of his kidneys. Her initial response was "Absolutely not!" But he persisted, and he finally persuaded her that donating his kidney was what he wanted to do.

The operation was an immediate success. The change in Shirlee was remarkable: Her energy, enthusiasm, and zest for life returned. Daniel was thrilled.

Daniel's unselfish sacrifice cost him the chance to play football. However, when accepting an award at Walt Disney World for being the Most Courageous Student Athlete of the Year, Daniel mentioned that he was a huge Florida State Seminoles fan. By "coincidence," Florida State coach Bobby Bowden was at the ceremony. Bowden arranged to get Daniel a full scholarship and gave him a position on the team as a trainer.

Florida State's head trainer, Randy Oravetz, says that Daniel is an inspiration to the team. His zeal and enthusiasm for working with the team are fabulous. Daniel is thrilled beyond belief to be working with Coach Bowden, one of the real coaching geniuses in college football today. I'll be surprised if, in the future, Daniel Huffman doesn't end up coaching at one of the major U.S. universities. In the meantime, he's living life to the fullest and couldn't be happier.

You may have heard the saying "Bread cast upon the waters often returns buttered." Shirlee made sure that Daniel wasn't alone when he needed her, and Daniel made sure that Shirlee wasn't alone when she needed him. Daniel did give up a great deal, but the joy he received from his beloved grandmother's renewed zest for life was full compensation for his unselfish act. Working directly with Coach Bowden was the butter on the bread he cast on the water.

## *Be a friend by encouraging*

If you're a golf fan, you may remember that John Daly won the British Open in 1995. What you may not know is that some unsung heroes were involved — tour players Corey Pavin, Brad Faxon, Bob Estes, and Mark Brooks and a caddy. None of these four players made the playoff that Constantino Rocca made necessary when he sank a 65-foot putt on the 17th hole to tie Daly.

Golf analysts speculated that Constantino's putt had shifted the momentum and that in all probability he had snatched the title out of Daly's hands. They wondered whether Daly would be able to recuperate and respond to what had happened. That's when Pavin, Faxon, and Estes, along with Brooks and the caddy, stepped forward to encourage John Daly.

All five men assured Daly that they believed he was going to win. Brooks gave Daly a distance card that measured the exact distances from every spot on the course (Daly had misplaced his), and the caddy helped him read those tricky British greens. Put all that help together with the fact that Daly was playing unusually well that day, and you have the reason why Daly won the British Open. Yes, Daly got all the publicity and all the money, but the question is, had those people not been behind the scenes, would he have won the British Open? Personally, I doubt it. The encouragement of others makes a tremendous difference in what you're able to do. Daly felt good about winning, and Pavin, Faxon, Brooks, Estes, and the caddy also felt good.

The message here is to be an unsung hero by making sure that someone else isn't alone at a critical time. Because of the way the wheel of life turns — "what goes around comes around" — being there for someone else improves your own chances of not being alone in a critical situation. After all, the measure of a human being isn't the number of servants he or she has, but the number of people he or she serves.

## Do the right thing

Many people believe that the 1996 U.S. Amateur Golf Championship was one of the most exciting and dramatic golf events of the year. Playing in the finals (which consisted of 36 holes in one day) were Steve Scott and Tiger Woods. At the end of the first 18 holes, Steve was well ahead. However, on the last 18, Tiger clawed his way closer and closer to the top. On the green of the final hole, Steve, one up, was putting first because he was farther from the cup. Tiger's ball was in Steve's putting line, so Tiger spotted his ball a clubhead's length away and marked it. Steve putted and missed.

If Tiger sank his next putt, the match would go into sudden death. Tiger carefully circled the green, viewed every possible angle, and had lined up to putt when Steve reminded him that he hadn't moved his ball back to the original spot. After making the correction, Tiger sank the putt. Tiger won the match in sudden death, giving him an unprecedented third straight U.S. Amateur Championship and catapulting him into the pro ranks with an unheard-of $60 million in guaranteed endorsement fees.

Had Steve not reminded Tiger to respot his ball correctly, and had Tiger then putted from where it lay, Tiger would have been penalized two strokes and lost the championship. Steve would have won the championship, but he would have lost something far more valuable: his integrity. I believe that Steve Scott's integrity will ensure that he is never lonely or alone.

## Have compassion

"Two wrongs don't make a right" is one of the "sentence sermons" that my mother used to preach to me when I was a child. The second wrong is often an act of revenge, done in retaliation for the first wrong. Many people carry revenge and hatred in their hearts because wrongs were done to them and they want to get even.

## These men are together — not alone

A movement sweeping the United States is bringing about remarkable societal changes. Promise Keepers, an organization put together by former University of Colorado football coach Bill McCartney, is filling football stadiums around the country with men of every race and creed, seeking solutions to family, racial, and social problems. Promise Keepers calls men to be accountable for all their actions. Speakers from all walks of life repeatedly tell the men of Promise Keepers that they must meet their family responsibilities and that they must be financially and emotionally supportive of their mates and children.

Based on what I saw at the two Promise Keepers meetings I attended at Texas Stadium, I'm convinced that Promise Keepers can help alleviate the racism problem in the United States. I observed scores of men — African-American, Caucasian, Latino, and Asian, to name a few — weeping as they walked forward, arm in arm, to become Christians and accept their responsibility and be servant leaders. Many were seeking reconciliation, and white men frequently asked their African-American brothers for forgiveness.

I've talked individually with many Promise Keepers and have had an extended conversation with Coach McCartney. I looked into his eyes; I listened to his heart. I've never met a man more genuinely concerned about accepting responsibility and seeking forgiveness as the best way to solve racial problems. He meets with African-American pastors at a luncheon before each Promise Keepers event, listening, answering their questions, and asking forgiveness. He recognizes that a great deal of bitterness and anger exists between African-Americans and Caucasians, but instead of just talking about the problem, he and thousands of Promise Keepers are actively working toward a solution.

McCartney began months ago to urge those men who couldn't go to the Promise Keepers' Stand in the Gap event in 1997 to send a member of another race to Washington. Hundreds of people who couldn't attend sent others to Washington. That's another reason the movement is successful. Here's an example: A member of the Ku Klux Klan who attended Stand in the Gap event returned home, destroyed his Klan garments, sought out an African-American acquaintance, asked him for forgiveness, and invited him to attend church with him. Now, neither one of these men — or any of the other Promise Keepers — is alone.

For example, the captain of the U.S. cruiser *Vincennes* made an honest but horrible mistake on July 3, 1988, when he used a missile to shoot down an Iranian airliner, killing all 290 passengers. The captain of the *Vincennes* erroneously thought that his ship was under attack by an F-14 Iranian fighter. Needless to say, a hue and cry went up all over the world.

Not everyone in the U.S. felt remorseful about the tragedy. Many people carried vivid memories of the cruel treatment of the Americans who had been held hostage in Iran. They felt that having shot down the Iranian airliner "served them right," discounting the fact that the victims had nothing to do with the government's conduct or the people who made the decision to take Americans hostage.

In the midst of all this controversy, President Ronald Reagan sought to compensate the Iranian victims' families. Polls revealed that most Americans opposed his actions. But when reporters confronted Reagan with the idea that making such payments would set a bad precedent and send the wrong message, Reagan replied, "I don't ever find compassion a bad precedent."

How true. That kind of thinking is why Reagan has so many friends and why today he is never alone.

# Capitalizing on Lonely Times

Somebody once said that success without adversity is not only empty, it is not possible. One of my favorite observations is that the only way to the mountaintop is through the valley — in most cases, a series of valleys. For example:

- One of the greatest books ever written, *Pilgrim's Progress,* was written by John Bunyan during his imprisonment in Bedford Jail.

- Daniel Defoe wrote *Robinson Crusoe* in prison.

- After he fell from favor with the queen, Sir Walter Raleigh wrote his *History of the World* during a 13-year prison sentence.

- The great poet Dante worked and died in exile, but his contributions to humanity during that time were immeasurable.

- Miguel de Cervantes, who wrote *Don Quixote* in a Madrid jail, was so poor that he couldn't even buy paper for his writing; instead, he used scraps of leather.

- John Milton did his best writing while blind, sick, and poor, and Ludwig van Beethoven composed his greatest music after he went deaf.

Instead of complaining about their cruel fates, these people took advantage of the opportunities they had. I have little doubt that they were lonely during these difficult times in their lives, but the works they produced in their loneliness enabled millions of people to never feel alone. Their writings inspired others to live more fulfilled lives.

# The best way to never be alone

C.S. Lewis writes in the book *Mere Christianity:*

"The rule for all of us is perfectly simple. Do not waste time bothering whether you 'love' your neighbor; act as if you did. As soon as we do this we find one of the great secrets. When you are behaving as if you loved someone, you will presently come to love him. If you injure someone you dislike, you will find yourself disliking him more. If you do him a good turn, you will find yourself disliking him less."

# Chapter 19

# Success Is a Habit

*A*ny sports fan recognizes that athletes sometimes get in a "zone," when everything goes their way. For a golfer, the ball may bounce left onto the putting surface instead of right into the bunker. A football defensive lineman may throw up his hands just high enough to tip the quarterback's pass, deflect it, catch the ball, and return it for a touchdown. A batter may step to the plate and hit the ball just an inch inside the line for a home run instead of a long foul ball.

Other times, everything that can go wrong does go wrong. The golfer's ball hits an unseen object and, instead of bouncing straight onto the green, careens sharply to the left and into the water. The quarterback throws a perfect pass, but the ball slips through his receiver's hands and into the arms of the defensive back. The pitcher throws a great breaking fastball only to see the batter hit a broken-bat single.

One thing is sure, though: If you play any sport long enough, you know what to expect most of the time. And when you combine that knowledge with "the breaks" — good and bad — you're going to be more successful than the person who has less experience, because you will make more of the right decisions.

The same things happen in the business world. Those folks who make the right decisions seem to get all the good breaks. The new product is an instant hit. The advertising campaign, though a little off-the-wall, is exactly what the product needs to bring it to life. The new salesperson who doesn't seem to fit the mold turns out to be the most productive salesperson in the company's history. A favorable report by a business analyst drives the company stock up seven points in one day. In short, things just go right.

The reason for the seemingly large number of "good breaks" is *expectancy*. Even though you are "born to win," you still must *plan* to win and *prepare* to win. Then and only then can you legitimately *expect* to win. Expectancy is a key word in this chapter.

# Achieving Success by Expecting Success

When you plan and prepare carefully, you can legitimately expect to have success in your efforts. When you recognize and develop the winning qualities that you were born with, the winner you were born to be emerges. When you plan and prepare to make a sale, for example, you can legitimately expect to make a sale. Although not all your expectations are going to come to pass, you give yourself an infinitely better chance of succeeding by taking the proper steps. Regardless of your goal — losing weight, making more sales, furthering your education, earning a promotion, saving money for a new home or an exotic vacation — you can expect to achieve your goal if you plan and prepare for it.

You also need to understand that the path from where you are to where you want to be is not always smooth and straight. The reason for the twists and bumps is simple, and it has nothing to do with you. It has more to do with the fact that not everyone is as interested in your success as you are. Some people may accidentally hinder your efforts; others who are in competition with you and have little or no integrity may try to sabotage your efforts.

Keep in mind, though, that when you hit those roadblocks or even reversals, your character, commitment, and attitude are the determining factors in your success. You need to carefully review your plan of action, seek wise counsel, and be particularly careful to feed your mind good information. An optimistic, positive mind is far more likely to come up with creative solutions than a mind that dwells on setbacks and difficulties.

Particularly concerning your long-range plans, I strongly suggest that you carefully reread this book's section on persistence in Chapter 3. When you understand the benefits of persisting, your patience is likely to increase, and patience is one thing that all long-term success requires.

# Knowing That Success Begets Success

Success truly does beget further success. My younger brother, Judge Ziglar, was one of the most phenomenal "streak" salespeople I've ever seen. He would get on a roll when he just *couldn't* miss a sale. I saw him make more than 20 sales in a row — which, in the direct sales world, is phenomenal. After he got those first two or three sales under his belt, he expected to make the fourth and fifth, and after that he was really on GO. Momentum built, and success for him became a habit — one that all salespeople love.

As another example, when you successfully reach a weight-loss goal, you gain confidence that you can also succeed in, say, getting your closet organized. That success convinces you that you can plan a little better and never be late again. That success persuades you that if you really want to, you can make an A in biology or acquire the skills you need to remain competitive in this highly technical world.

Success means succeeding in every area of your life. Concentrate first on succeeding in one area; the confidence and momentum that you build in the process lead you with more surety and confidence into the next area. When you succeed in one area, you'll be amazed at how that success transfers over to other areas.

# Making Success Happen through Repetition

When you watch NFL games, you frequently hear analysts say that repetition is the key to successful execution. If the quarterback doesn't throw enough passes in practice, he'll never really get into the flow of a pressure-filled game. Constant repetition also establishes the habit of doing all the little things exactly right. Every teaching pro in golf understands that a golfer who doesn't have a swing that can be repeated consistently isn't going to win on the PGA Tour. Again, analysts frequently say, "There's a swing you can repeat over and over." The swing is simple, but the golfer hits the ball in exactly the same way every time. It gets to be a habit that he or she repeats automatically, even under intense pressure.

If you find out what brings you success and repeat that process regularly, you can enjoy success in any endeavor. For example, start your day in a positive way by listening to upbeat music, doing something nice for someone else, or reading something that brightens your day. Make it a habit to smile at and pleasantly greet the first three people you meet each day, and the rest of the day will be much easier. Make it a habit to keep your promises and show up for work and social commitments on time, every time. Make it a habit to learn something new and apply it every day. Repeating these actions over and over may be tough initially, but as they become habits, they quickly become fun — and profitable in every area of your life.

# Being, Doing, and Having

One of my favorite phrases is "You've got to be before you can do and do before you can have." In short, you have to be a person of character and do the right things, and then you can have the things you really want.

To make the "be, do, have" theory valid, believable, and usable on your part, look at some examples in your own life:

1. **Take a sheet of paper and draw two vertical lines to make three columns.**

2. **At the top of the left-hand column, write** Be; **in the middle column, write** Do; **and over the last column, write** Have.

3. **In the right-hand column, list all the things that you really want in life, whether it's an education, good family relationships, a beautiful new home, a fancy luxury car, a trip around the world, better health — you name it.**

4. **Work your way down the center column of the page, identifying the things that you have to do in order to have the things listed in the right-hand column.**

   As a brief, simple example, say that you want a successful marriage. To do so, you must be willing to share your innermost thoughts and concerns with your mate. You must carry more than your share of the workload, encourage your mate when he or she is down, and defend your mate against criticism. You need to remember special occasions (which go beyond birthdays, Valentine's Day, and anniversaries). Be particularly helpful when your mate is having a "down day," is not feeling well, or has had a tough time on the job. Apply the philosophy that "you can have everything that you want out of this marriage if you just help your mate get what he or she wants." Everybody's list varies, because each of us has unique needs, beliefs, and interests. However, the formula remains the same.

5. **Go to the left-hand column and identify what you have to *be* in order to *do* so that you can *have*.**

   To have a successful marriage, some of the things that you must be are faithful, attentive, loving, caring, helpful, empathetic, encouraging, persistent, committed, kind, thoughtful, considerate, and responsible. Not having all these qualities at this moment is okay, because they're all skills, and skills can be developed.

Regardless of what you want to have — whether it's a better education, more sales, a beautiful home, closer relationships with your children, or a handicap of ten on the golf course — you can use this basic formula. Just look at what you have to do in order to accomplish that objective, and then examine yourself and determine what kind of person you have to *be* in order to *do* so that you can *have*.

# Choosing Success

In a lifetime, you make literally millions of choices. Most choices, after you make them a few times, become ingrained in you. You know from past experience what works for you, so you repeat the process. You only get into trouble when you *don't* get good results but keep doing the same things over and over again. It may seem hard to believe, but many people operate that way.

You literally can opt to be happy or miserable by the choices you make. If you choose to be happy, you need to explore what *makes* you happy. Identify whether happiness is a sense of accomplishment when you make an A in school, achieve a specific weight-loss goal, make a difficult sale, complete a mini-marathon, win over the sourpuss at the checkout counter, or whatever. Accomplishments make you feel good, and you're happy as a result. After you determine what makes you happy, choose to do those things.

People who are unhappy are generally unhappy because they think that other people should be doing things *for* them. From time to time, people say to me, "I want to thank you for making me successful." But I can't accept credit for making anyone successful, nor do I accept responsibility for causing anyone to fail. I am responsible *to* people but not *for* them. And that credo also applies to you.

People who choose to follow the success procedures I offer (which I've validated psychologically, theologically, and physiologically) get good results. But, to be honest, I give those principles to several hundred thousand people each year, and by no stretch of the imagination do I believe that all of them follow those principles and become successful. I do believe that people of good character who follow these procedures are far more successful than they otherwise would be. However, following or not following my suggestions is their choice, so if they follow the procedures and are successful, they are the ones who did it — not me.

On the other hand, if they say, "I attended your seminar, read your books, and listened to your tapes, but none of it worked for me," I have to question whether they actually followed the principles carefully, whether they followed those principles believing that they would work, or whether they followed them with the idea that "I'll do it, but I know it's not going to work." That's one of the reasons I'm careful to emphasize that the right mental attitude needs to go behind each procedure you follow.

Success is a choice in all areas of life; that's why I deal with the physical, the mental, the spiritual, the financial, the personal, the family-related, and the career-related in this book. I touch all the bases, make suggestions, and give instructions that, when followed with the right mental attitude, enable you to be more successful in each area of your life. Whether you follow those instructions is up to you. I believe that, as you explore each area of life, if you concentrate on your area of greatest need, your chances of succeeding in that area go up substantially. Then, as you look at the wheel of life in Chapter 7 and bring all the spokes into focus, you can choose to be successful in every area.

Speaker Earl Nightingale once said that "success is the progressive realization of a worthwhile goal." I can expand on that statement to say that success is progress you can enjoy every day as you pursue your objective of getting more of the things that money can buy and all of the good things that money can't buy.

# Remembering That Experts Can Be Wrong

According to legend, Wilma Rudolph was repeatedly told by her doctors that she would never walk. However, her mother told her that she would. Fortunately for sports fans and those who enjoy studying the lives of people who overcome adversity, Wilma chose to believe her mother, and therefore she maintained the right mental attitude. She won three gold medals in track and field events in the 1960 Olympics and set the world's record for the women's 100-meter dash in 1961. Wilma Rudolph won the most important race of her life when she decided to compete with herself at each step. The man in the next story was too young to make that choice.

For 32 years, Bernie Lofchick has been my closest friend. When his son David was born, 30 doctors diagnosed the baby's condition as cerebral palsy. They unanimously agreed that David would never be able to walk, talk, or count to ten. Bernie and his wife, Elaine, decided that they would keep trying. They managed to get an appointment with Dr. Meyer Pearlstein in Chicago, reputed to be the world's foremost authority on cerebral palsy. Pearlstein, after giving David a complete examination, gave the Lofchicks real hope — along with specific directions.

Bernie and Elaine chose to listen to the last doctor and follow his advice. Today, 39-year-old David Lofchick is a healthy man, happily married with two beautiful daughters and a son. He's a successful businessperson with a long career ahead of him. David, his wife and children, and many others benefited because Bernie and Elaine chose to keep looking until they found that 31st doctor and believed him.

Please don't misunderstand: Sometimes conditions really are impossible. But I wonder how many people have been relegated to a lower rung on the ladder of health — and life itself — because they believed that first opinion.

The message? Choose to keep looking and stay optimistic. Who knows, maybe the solution to your problem is right around the corner! As Ralph Waldo Emerson said, "A believer is never disturbed because other people do not yet see the fact which he sees."

# Overcoming Adversity

At this stage of your life, you may have experienced more downs than ups, so I want to conclude this chapter with an uplifting story. The following tale is about a man who has been subjected to tremendous racial prejudice, has had serious bouts with alcohol, and has struggled much of his life, yet in many ways he epitomizes what I've been talking about in this chapter.

Gordon Thayer was born in Wisconsin on March 14, 1945. His parents had divorced, and life was difficult for a single mother with three children. For a brief time, Gordon lived on the Lac Courte Oreilles Ojibwe reservation with his grandmother, who spoke only the native tongue and practiced much of the native way of life. His life with her during those early years gave him some of his fondest memories, such as going to Sunday school and Vacation Bible School at a reservation mission church — and also memories of some of the hardest times of his life. As he says today, little did he realize that seeds were being planted that would shape his life in later years.

Gordon started getting into trouble with the law in his teens and eventually was placed on probation. When he violated the provisions of his probation, the court gave him the option of going to a boys' reformatory or joining the military. In 1962, after dropping out of high school and with a court mandate over his head, he joined the U.S. Air Force.

After completing basic training, Gordon volunteered for the elite Pararescue unit, which was used for special missions during both wartime and peacetime. At that point, he was tired of the failure of his early life and decided to give it all he had. He passed the admissions standards, which gave him a boost because the selection process is extremely rigorous — only 180 members of the entire Air Force are in the unit at any given time. The Pararescue logo is an angel holding a globe in her hands with the motto, "That others may live."

A few years after his Pararescue training, Gordon was sent to Thailand and Laos during the Vietnam War to fly rescue missions into North Vietnam jungles to recover downed U.S. pilots. He said that one of his first missions was to rescue a pilot under heavy fire. "As I helped him into the 'Jolly Green Giant' chopper," he recalled later, "the guy said I was like an angel to him." On another mission, his helicopter was shot down in a heavy firefight. Even though he was drenched in aviation fuel, his life was spared.

Gordon spent a total of eight years in the military and received his high school diploma while in the service. He also enrolled in a few college classes and was honorably discharged from the military in 1970 with the rank of sergeant. He is highly decorated, having received the Silver Star, two Distinguished Flying Crosses, several Air Medals, and other awards. However, his alcohol addiction overshadowed his valor.

After his discharge, Gordon continued to drink heavily. He attended college in northern California but dropped out and moved back to the Midwest when his father passed away. He returned to school at the University of Minnesota for a time and eventually moved back to his reservation in Wisconsin. He was elected to the tribal council in 1977 and to the chairmanship in 1979, and he served in that capacity until 1984.

Despite his leadership role, the deadly grip of alcoholism continued to take its toll on Gordon's life. His long drinking binges came more frequently, and he began to lose the respect of friends, colleagues, and family. He recalls one incident in 1981 when, after several weeks of drinking, he returned home sick and tired. At the end of his rope, he cried out to God in loneliness and desperation because he wanted to quit drinking and could not do so on his own. Gordon says that God heard his prayers and brought him back to the little mission church on the reservation where he had been 31 years earlier. The same pastor who had been there when he was a child led him out of alcoholism and into a new life as a Christian.

Gordon was determined to change his life. In his Pararescue days, he was trained not to be a quitter; therefore, he would not quit. He thought, "If God's promises are for real, then mine to Him must be real." With God's help and his own commitment, he had the tools he needed to get back on his feet. He had great leadership abilities and other skills that he had been using in the wrong ways. He started focusing on the opportunities that would enhance his life, opportunities that had always been there but had been dimmed by alcoholism.

In 1984, Gordon resigned his chairmanship of the tribe after winning the prestigious Bush Foundation Leadership Fellowship Award for his outstanding accomplishments as tribal chairman. In 1986, he received his master's degree in Administration/Management and shortly there-after went to work for the Bureau of Indian Affairs in Minneapolis. Although the job was difficult and humbling, he discovered some things about himself and about life during this period that prepared him beautifully for the work that lay ahead. In 1992, Gordon resigned his position with the Bureau of Indian Affairs and founded the American Indian Housing Corporation. In 1996, the American Indian Housing Corporation opened Anishinabe Wakiagun (translated as "The People's Home"), a $4 million permanent residence for homeless, chronic alcoholic Indian men and women. It is the first home of its kind for Indian people in the United States.

Today, Gordon is one of the hardest-working, most committed, and most motivated people I know. He and his wife, Sheila, also direct Overcomers Ministry, which he founded in 1988. The objective of Overcomers is to go into reservations in the U.S. and Canada, where alcohol abuse is prevalent, to start Christian-based leadership programs and to develop a Christian recovery program for people who are struggling with alcohol addiction.

Gordon says he has realized that God has a divine plan for his life, and he feels that utilizing the tools that he has been given to fulfill his plan is up to him. He says he now realizes that God used his Vietnam experience to "help me in my ministry role, fighting the battle of alcohol that afflicts our native people." He says that he does what he does "so that others may live."

From my perspective, this man overcame enormous difficulties, fought against the odds, and came out a winner. Gordon is totally committed to serving his people, and in the process, he is benefiting not only them but himself and his family as well. He is reaching down and helping many to stand up because he has "been there and done that," and he has a heart for helping his fellow human beings.

# Part VI
## The Part of Tens

The 5th Wave — By Rich Tennant

"Don't laugh – it's added 30 yards to his drive."

# In this part . . .

No ...*For Dummies* book is complete without a Part of Tens — a section of the book that gives you lists of quick tips and tidbits in groups of ten (or so). In this part, I include inspirational and motivational stories of successful folks, ideas for your grand plan for success, and benchmarks of success — standards that you can adopt for your life to help you become successful.

# Chapter 20

# Ten (Or So) Benchmarks of Success

. . . . . . . . . . . . . . . . . . . . . . . . . . . . . . . . . . . . . . . . . .

## In This Chapter

▶ How to know that you've achieved success — or what you need to aim for

. . . . . . . . . . . . . . . . . . . . . . . . . . . . . . . . . . . . . . . . . .

*I*n my book *Over the Top,* I identify what I think is "The Top": the benchmarks of success. With permission from Thomas Nelson Publishers, I reprint those benchmarks here and explain how you can put them to work.

# Understanding That Failure Is Just an Event

*You are a success when you clearly understand that failure is an event, not a person — that yesterday ended last night, and today is a brand-new day.*

There's a difference between failing at a project and failing in life. Missing a sale is one thing; being a failure as a salesperson is yet another. Failing to reach a specific goal is one thing; being a failure in life is entirely different. Think about it: Most success stories you hear validate that most people who "make it big" experience several failures on their way to the top. Every day is an opportunity to start over, and every failure can be a learning experience that prepares you for success. You can let failure teach you or beat you — the choice is yours.

# Knowing That a Success Doesn't Make You and a Failure Doesn't Break You

*You are a success when you know that a success (a win) doesn't make you and that a failure (a loss) doesn't break you.*

A single event — scoring the winning goal, acing a difficult course, getting a promotion — can catapult you to a more successful future. And, admittedly, failing to reach a coveted objective can negatively impact your future. But you must understand that failure is an *event* and that success is a *process*. Each event is important, but don't build your future on a single event or allow your future to be destroyed by a single failure. Instead, acknowledge what happened and give each event the recognition that it deserves. If the event is a success, build on it; if it's a failure, learn from it and go full speed ahead. (You can find out more about this process in Chapter 19.)

# Making Friends with Your Past and Seeing Bright Things in Your Future

*You are a success when you have made friends with your past, are focused on the present, and are optimistic about your future.*

You can use your past as a stepping stone to the future, or you can use it as a stumbling block to negatively impact that future. To be successful, you must accept that you have to make friends with your past if you're going to live up to your potential. Your past is important because it has brought you to where you are; however, your past is not nearly as important as the way you see your future. The way you view your future determines your thinking today; your thinking today determines your performance today; and your performance today determines your future. Understanding that connection enables you to learn from your past, which is the best way to make your future even better.

# Filling Yourself with Faith, Hope, and Love

*You are a success when you are filled with faith, hope, and love and live without anger, greed, guilt, envy, or thoughts of revenge.*

What you put into your mind determines your outlook on life. Your outlook determines your output, and your output determines the outcome. With that in mind, choose to attend motivational seminars or worship services; read optimistic, upbeat, uplifting books; and listen to inspirational tapes. These things fill your mind with the right kinds of thoughts. When you put faith, hope, and love into your mind, you get the same things out of your mind. And when faith, hope, and love come from your mind, you're able to overcome adversity and live free from the negative impacts of anger, greed, guilt, and envy.

# Thinking of Your Responsibilities Rather Than Your Rights

*You are a success when you are mature enough to delay gratification and shift your focus from your rights to your responsibilities.*

In a society that focuses on getting everything immediately, many people get every little thing they want right now, which prevents them from getting the important things that they really want later in life. Don't worry about "rights." Maturity says, "I can wait for something this insignificant in order to achieve worthwhile objectives later." Choosing to accept and meet your responsibilities now is the best way to have the things that are important to you later.

For example, in 1947, I met an auto mechanic who had developed a passion for the new step-down Hudson automobile. He gave up soft drinks, hot lunches, fishing, athletic events, movies, vacations, and day trips to save every dime for his dream car, which cost nearly $2,000. A little over 14 months later, the car was his. He was elated and felt that those little sacrifices were nothing compared to the enjoyment and satisfaction he gained from finally owning his dream car.

# Standing for What Is Morally Right

*You are a success when you know that failure to stand for what is morally right is the prelude to becoming a victim of what is criminally wrong.*

Years ago, Edmund Burke observed that the certain way for evil to succeed is for good men to do nothing about it. When you tolerate brutality, crime, spouse and child abuse, drunk driving, drug dealing, and so on, it's just a question of time before you yourself become a victim. Your greatest failing occurs when you do nothing.

# Being Secure in Who You Are

*You are a success when you are secure in who you are, so you are at peace with your Creator and in fellowship with others.*

It's true that you've got to be *be* before you can *do* and *do* before you can *have*. A humble confidence in who you are enables you to be at peace with your Creator, which is the prelude to being in fellowship with other people. If you're not secure in who you are, Chapter 6 can start you on your way to finding out, and if you don't like who you find, Chapters 10 through 17 can help you improve yourself, one goal at a time.

# Gaining Love and Respect from Enemies and Friends Alike

*You are a success when you have made friends of your adversaries and have gained the love and respect of those who know you best.*

It has been said that we should be proud of our enemies because we're the ones who made them. Because you made those enemies (in most cases) through your actions and attitudes, you can often make friends of them by reversing those actions and attitudes. Doing so not only enables you to deal effectively with your enemies, but in the process you also earn love and respect from the people who know you best for what you have done.

# Understanding That Happiness Comes from Doing Things for Others

*You are a success when you understand that others can give you pleasure, but genuine happiness comes when you do things for others.*

In our pleasure-seeking "Hooray for me, to heck with you, what are you going to do for me today?" world, you find that others can temporarily give you a measure of enjoyment and pleasure. However, as story after story in this book indicates, happiness is yours when you encourage, build, and befriend other people.

# Giving Hope, Love, and Encouragement to Those in Need

*You are a success when you give hope to the hopeless, love the unlovable, and are pleasant to the grouch, courteous to the rude, and generous to the needy.*

The character-building that comes from lending a hand to someone in need can lift you to unimagined heights. It's easy to be kind to those who are kind to you, but when you go the extra mile with those who are rude or those who are in need and cannot repay your kindnesses, you bring out the best in yourself. Your feelings of accomplishment and self-worth enable you to climb higher and faster.

For example, I was thrilled when a friend invited my son Tom and me to be his guests for two days of golf at the famed Augusta National golf course. It was truly one of my most pleasurable experiences. However, that pleasure pales in comparison to the happiness I experienced when a young bartender whom I had talked to about Christ decided to join me in my Christian faith. Today, the young man is the pastor of a growing church, is happily married, and has two beautiful children.

# Forgiving Those Who Have Wronged You

*You are a success when you can look back in forgiveness, forward in hope, down in compassion, and up with gratitude.*

Until you forgive someone of wrongdoing, that individual remains in control of your thoughts and actions. Until you extend that hand of forgiveness, you concentrate on the problems of the past. After you extend forgiveness, your burden lightens, and you can move forward with excitement and put yourself in a position to help the helpless. Therefore, you can look up with gratitude, which is a key to happiness.

# Being a "Servant Friend"

*You are a success when you know that the greatest are those who choose to be the servants of all.*

In today's world and marketplace, you repeatedly hear about "servant leadership," where the leader, owner, manager, clerk, and so on see themselves in the role of serving internal or external customers. This approach to customer service, and winning people to your way of thinking and doing business by being their servant, makes sense. Extending a helping hand in a "what can I do for you?" manner, rather than a "what can you do for me?" manner, is a philosophy that really works. This approach clearly separates you from a fair-weather friend who is always there when he needs you; as a servant friend, you are there when your friend is in need.

# Recognizing and Using Your Talents

*You are a success when you recognize, confess, develop, and use your physical, mental, and spiritual abilities for the benefit of others.*

Recognizing who you are is a prerequisite to using the qualities and abilities that God created in you. When you know who you are, your potential for doing great things explodes.

# Serving God Well

*You are a success when you know that you have been a good and faithful servant of the Creator of the universe.*

Benjamin Franklin once said that only two things are certain: death and taxes. (Sure, some people avoid taxes.) I believe that when you make your appearance before your Creator and own up to what you did and believed in your life, you will either say, "I wish I had listened and obeyed," or, "I'm glad I did." The choice is yours.

# Chapter 21
# Ten Successful Individuals

*In This Chapter*

▶ Drawing inspiration from people who have risen from rags to riches

▶ Understanding that success involves much more than your bank account

*N*o book on success would be complete without several genuine success stories. This chapter gives you a place to return to as often as you need to be inspired. All the individuals you can read about overcame the odds to reach the level of success that they achieved. Some of them never could have dreamed dreams as big as their real-life success became, but they started on a journey toward success and found it. I hope that this chapter gives you the courage to start your journey or, if you're already on your way, to continue it with added zeal!

## *Dave Anderson: Against All Odds*

Dave Anderson is a Native American. His dad is an enrolled member of the Choctaw Nation; his mother is an enrolled member of the Lake Superior Band of Lac Courte Oreilles Ojibway Tribe. Dave, now 44, was born in Chicago, Illinois.

At age 18, Dave heard the tapes of a speaker who encouraged him to believe that he could be successful beyond his wildest dreams. The speaker saturated Dave's mind with optimism, positive thinking, and the idea that he could make something of his life. Dave was told that his past was not important; what he did in the *present* would determine his future.

By age 19, Dave had started a wholesale florist business with money borrowed from his dad. However, he needed more money than his dad could secure. With his newfound confidence, Dave was able to convince a banker to entrust him with a loan. By age 21, he was selling to Sears, K-mart, and nearly every retail florist in Chicago.

Then something happened to Dave Anderson that frequently happens to people who enjoy success early in life: He became a know-it-all, got cocky, and by age 26 lost everything and went bankrupt. Dave knows what it means to dig in the couch cushions to find change to buy milk for his kids. He knows the heartbreak of having to sell his wife's jewelry to pay the rent. He knows how it feels to stand outside McDonald's, waiting for everyone to leave, trying to decide which counter person looks approachable enough to ask for the hamburgers that have been cooked but not sold.

At that time, Dave remembered that he had experienced a sample of motivation and had bought into the notion that when you feed your mind the pure, the clean, the powerful, and the positive, exciting things happen. So he got out his tapes and started reading inspirational books again. For a time, he made a living making and selling Indian jewelry of silver and turquoise. Although he filled out the paperwork to go on unemployment and stood in line several times, he always backed out at the last minute and rededicated himself to pushing even harder to find work. Dave says that even though he went bankrupt, he never lost his dream of being a success someday.

As I sat across the counter in a fast-food restaurant talking with Dave Anderson, I found it hard to believe that this gentle, confident, humble human being had endured the difficulties he had. I had met him 17 years earlier when he attended, along with many members of his tribe, our three-day "Born to Win" seminar. I was intrigued as he talked about going to Toastmasters to learn how to speak in public and being scared stiff — his first 30-minute speech was over in five minutes.

However, Dave felt quite strongly that if he was ever going to succeed, he had to learn how to speak in front of people. He bought an inexpensive mirror and kept it in his basement. When everyone was out of the house, he would read books aloud to himself for hours. He practiced shaking hands with himself. He even taped himself giving make-believe speeches.

Dave's commitment, persistence, and thirst to prepare himself for the future paid off. In 1982, at age 29, he was hired as CEO by his tribe, the Lac Courte Oreilles Ojibway, to head up their various business operations, which were losing more than half a million dollars a year.

Within three years, the tribe's gross sales improved from $3.9 million to $8 million, and they received recognition from President Reagan's Commission on Indian Reservation Economies for their achievement. In 1985, Dave was recognized for a lifetime of outstanding achievement by the Bush Foundation as a Leadership Fellow. In 1986, he received a master's degree from Harvard University, even though he didn't have an undergraduate degree.

Today, this once-bankrupt Native American who scrounged for coins in his sofa and accepted leftover hamburgers from a fast-food restaurant has founded two highly successful restaurant companies that have been recognized as the "hottest concept in America" by *Nation's Restaurant News*. His persistence paid off in another way, which excites him the most: He has created more than 15,000 new jobs and has donated more than $6 million to charities.

Dave told me that he is living the American dream. But he also wanted to make clear that it wasn't easy. As with all successful people (and that probably includes you), he experienced frustrations, and at times he really wanted to give up. Going bankrupt and having to reestablish himself was tough and humiliating. He's had to go through treatment to quit drinking, and, as he puts it, "I've done some things in my life that I have not been proud of." Some people wonder why, with all the good things he's done, he tells stories about the bad things. Dave's explanation is simple: "I believe that if I hadn't experienced the rougher side of life, I would not be where I am today."

Dave also pointed out that when he was working only to promote his own status, he kept failing. However, he says, "My whole life changed the day I realized that I could not do it by myself and that I needed something stronger in my life." That day came, he said, "when I surrendered myself to God and said, 'You take control of my life and you guide me. This isn't about Dave Anderson anymore.'" He points out that taking Dave Anderson out of the picture was one of the hardest things he ever had to deal with. He had to let go of his ego, and when he did, a big change took place.

Today, Dave's whole motivation is to make a difference in his community, especially the Native American community. In 1997, he has set aside more than $1 million as seed money to start a life-skills boot camp for Native American youth. This camp is based on developing hope for disadvantaged youth with spirituality as the foundation.

It's difficult to sum up Dave Anderson because Dave is, in my opinion, just getting started. Let me emphasize that, regardless of your circumstances, remember what Dave has gone through: He went from losing everything to where he is today. Failure really is an event, not a person.

# Steve Bacque: From Homeless to "Entrepreneur of the Year"

Steve Bacque repeated the first grade because he couldn't read. He was put into special education classes but was still unable to keep up academically. However, he was passed from one grade to the next, and because all learning is sequential, he fell further and further behind. Even making the effort to keep up became harder and harder for Steve.

Unfortunately, everyone of importance in his life — teachers, classmates, friends, and family — told him that he was stupid. "When you fail most of your tests in most of your classes, you begin to believe that you *are* stupid," he said.

Steve couldn't achieve in the academic arena and was only moderately successful at sports, so he tried his hand at business. He loved horses, so starting a horse-drawn carriage service seemed natural. But the business failed because he "did everything wrong." He mismanaged his money, had his truck repossessed, was evicted from his apartment, and found himself homeless.

Steve spent six months in a shelter and wound up in New Jersey, where he met and married the woman who changed his life. She encouraged him to return to school, where he was diagnosed with dyslexia, a learning disability in which words are scrambled during reading and writing, making written communication difficult. The college helped him with his dyslexia but said that he would never be able to realize his academic dreams. To cap off his difficulties, the most devastating event in his life occurred: the death of his infant son, Paul Joseph.

One heartbreaking part of this tragedy for Steve was that his son would never experience the simple things that children do, such as play with toys. Perhaps that was the motivation behind Steve's next step, which was to design toys for children. A native Texan, Steve had always loved the West and cowboys. One day, he made a trick lasso and then began to refine it into a safe toy — the type of toy he felt that Paul Joseph could have played with. With this endeavor came a vision that became Steve's obsession: creating safe toys for children. This mission helped him work through his grief.

In November 1991, Steve started a one-man-operation toy company in his basement, making Western-theme toys. Those cowboy toys caught on, and the company grew quickly. In 1992, Steve was recognized for his achievement by receiving the First Annual Small Business Success Award. His creative, nonviolent (no guns were included in his inventory), educational cowboy toys, made by people with disabilities, won him the Excellence Award for the Most Inventive Toy. In 1993, Steve won the highly prestigious Entrepreneur of the Year Award, sponsored by Merrill-Lynch, *Inc. Magazine*, and Ernst & Young, for being socially responsible.

Because of his own difficulties in life and the double appeal of hiring the disabled and creating toys that his own son would have enjoyed playing with, Steve Bacque became enmeshed in doing things for others. The philosophy that "You can have everything in life you want if you just will help enough other people get what they want" emerged. By giving jobs to persons with disabilities, he helped others to circumvent their limitations, just as he was trying to conquer his own. In 1994, by securing venture capital financing and setting up an export business, his vendors grew from specialty-shop owners to mass-market chains worldwide, and his toy line grew to include more than 60 products.

In 1995, Steve sold his company to one of the largest toy companies in the world and remained with them in a management position until early 1997. He wrote his first book and also writes columns in several magazines on running a successful business. He has his own radio business talk show and is a sought-after public speaker.

When you ask Steve how he went from being homeless and a terrible student to being a successful businessperson, he tells you that the answer lies in his deep-rooted faith. He believes that to be truly successful in every aspect of life, your life must be centered around and founded in God. Steve constantly reminds himself of the words from the Bible: "What does it profit a man if he gains the whole world and loses his own soul?"

Faith, hard work, and persistence are powerful factors in success. Though he was discouraged, Steve never gave up on himself. It's ironic that the death of his son, the most devastating event in his life, provided his inspiration and drew out of him the commitment and desire to do something that benefited others and, in the process, benefited himself.

# Doug Blevins: How Did He Do That?

Doug Blevins is the kicking coach for the Miami Dolphins in the National Football League. He has this job despite the fact that he has spent his life flat on his back in bed or enthusiastically tooling around in his wheelchair. Doug has never taken a step or kicked a ball, yet he's one of the most successful, highly motivated people you'll ever see.

The question is, how did Doug become a successful coach in the most highly competitive branch of football in the world? The credit starts with his parents. They raised him to believe that he could accomplish incredible objectives if he believed that he could, set them as goals, studied, and worked hard at accomplishing those objectives. As a child, Doug's goal was to coach in the NFL.

How did Doug learn how to coach, having never kicked a football? Never having kicked has turned out to be an advantage, because he never imposes his own techniques or experiences on a player. Early on, he studied intently the techniques of the most successful kickers. At Doug's request, Ben Agajanian, who was working with the Dallas Cowboys, sent him all the material that he had on successful kickers, including videotapes. Doug invested countless hours intently watching videos of the best kickers in professional football. As a result, he was able to detect the slightest flaws when a kick went wide, fell short, or never got airborne enough to keep from being blocked. More important, he carefully studied every detail of what happened when the kick was good. Over a lengthy period of watching those kickers, Doug was able to identify the techniques that were the most effective — not for any specific kicker, but for kickers in general.

Doug had an opportunity to coach at the high school level and was an instant success. Next, he wrote to Miami Dolphins coach Jimmy Johnson and sent him reports and concepts that he had developed as a coach of kickers. Johnson was thoroughly impressed and invited Doug for an interview. At that point, Johnson had no idea that Doug had been wheelchair-bound all his life. This fact obviously made zero difference to Johnson, who is results-oriented. He invited Doug aboard to be his kicking coach, which is really incredible, since it's almost unheard of for a coach to jump straight from high school coaching to the National Football League.

It's important to note that there are things Doug cannot do — that is, run and kick. However, he recognizes that he can think, study, plan, prepare, and expect. Because he does all those things, he has become the successful kicking coach for the Miami Dolphins that he is today. The same process enables you to be more successful, too. I encourage you to take this powerful message and apply it in every phase of your own life and to emphasize it with your kids.

# *Larry Carpenter: The American Dream*

Larry Carpenter is from a down-to-earth, hard-working, dedicated family of strong faith. He is the oldest of four sons and has been a responsible citizen all his life. His parents taught him the wonderful character qualities just mentioned. At age 13, he was mowing lawns with equipment that he purchased with money he earned himself. His father's business, while steady, was struggling, so at age 15 Larry went to work with his dad to help the family.

After high school, Larry went to work in a machine shop during the day and worked with his father in the evenings and on weekends. As he put it, he was "twisting wrenches on trucks and cars," which was a hard way to earn a living. However, this experience gave him insight into the selection of his long-term goals.

Larry was blessed with an optimistic and happy outlook on life, but he was not always greeted at the machine shop with enthusiasm because he was "different" from the others. He had ambition, was driven, and accepted responsibility. After working there for a while, he asked what it would take to receive a promotion. At that point, he was entrusted with a special assignment that enabled him to go in and out of the shop with a degree of freedom and make decisions. In addition, a good friend persuaded him to take specialized training courses that most formal educational institutions do not provide — for example, they do not teach people how to set and reach goals, build winning relationships, get a job, develop the right attitude, develop the qualities of success, and build a character foundation.

Armed with his credit card and his Toyota with 150,000+ miles on it, Larry attended a seminar and went home loaded with excitement and the tools to learn many of the other things that he needed to know. In 1983, he came to Dallas with one goal: to work for the Zig Ziglar Corporation. However, we persuaded Larry to pursue his college education instead of working part-time with us and going to school part-time. He enrolled at Dallas Baptist University and on his first day on campus met Lisa Michelle Coats. Today, she is his wife and the mother of their three beautiful boys.

Larry's next step before graduating from college was to move to Oklahoma and sell books door-to-door for the Southwestern Book Company. He had a rough beginning, but by the end of the summer, with a lot of determination, hard work, and learning everything he could about selling, he finished fourth out of over 2,000 first-year salespeople.

Always on the lookout for learning opportunities in the business world, Larry worked his last three semesters with Herschel Forester in outdoor advertising. Forester became a mentor and good friend to Larry and was tremendously influential in his climb to success. Larry finished his four-year degree in three years and did so with a 3.2 grade point average. He also served as president of the Student Government Association, served as vice president of the business club, and was nominated into "Who's Who in American Colleges and Universities."

Larry Carpenter is probably the most consistent, enthusiastic goal-setter I've met. He keeps meticulous records, uses his goal planner, and knows exactly where he is in his goals at any given time. After graduation, Larry's goal was to sell billboards, and he accepted an offer from a sister company of the Red Roof Inns motel group, Red Roof Interstate. This job took him away from his wife in Dallas to St. Louis, Missouri.

Larry spent considerable time in St. Louis and saw tremendous opportunities for his business there, yet he hesitated to move because Lisa loved her job in Dallas so much. Eventually, Lisa suggested that they move from Dallas to St. Louis and begin his new company. She observed, "If we succeed, history will be written, and our family will forever be thankful. Even if we fail, we can always come back to Dallas and do what we've been doing." Larry pointed out that in those few short moments Lisa gave him permission to fail. She was saying that it was okay to go for this new goal and "If we failed, she would still love me, believe in me, and trust me to get us back into the ball game of life."

In St. Louis, Larry worked temporarily with a company on a 50 percent partnership basis. For many reasons, the arrangement did not work out, but instead of letting the experience discourage him or make him bitter, he took the valuable lessons that he had learned and let them make him *better*.

Because finances were tight, Larry did the selling, the manual labor, the proposals, and so on for his fledgling company. He was badly in need of capital, but three banks turned him down. One bank finally agreed to lend Larry $40,000 for one billboard, but at high interest.

Eighteen months following the birth of their twin boys, Adam and Alex, Larry and Lisa were blessed with their third son, Luke. By then, their little rented house was beginning to get tight, but Larry believed in delayed gratification, so they spent only what they had to on themselves and put everything else back into the business. Larry points out that their success did not come from his financial genius; they had to operate that way in order for the company to remain in the black, so they continued to live on a fixed budget. He felt that his goal to be a good provider did not leave room for status-seeking symbols such as a big house or an expensive car. He says that status is "when people buy things they can't afford to impress people they don't like."

Larry's goal for his first five years in business was to own and operate 30 billboards; in just two years, he did that. His life goal was "to know that my wife and three sons would be taken care of" if anything ever happened to him. He wanted to provide an ongoing income stream, and that's what the billboards did.

Larry's next goal was to own and operate 60 billboards in the next three years. He accomplished that goal in two years and went over the 100 mark in 1996. Today, at the ripe old age of 39, Larry and Lisa own and operate 137 advertising billboards in Dallas and St. Louis. Their company's market value is in excess of $5 million, and their monthly cash flow is incredibly exciting. They still live modestly on a conservative budget and put the extra cash into funding new growth.

Many people think that the fast lane is a fun lane; believe in big houses and cars, luxurious vacations, and so on; and consider Larry's lifestyle boring. Just before I started to write Larry's story, I talked with Lisa for a few minutes. She had been out at the shallow little lake in their front yard, watching the boys fish and having a wonderful time. Later, I talked with Larry, who explained that he had finished work early that afternoon so that he and his family could spend a beautiful evening together. I don't recall knowing a man more content, more excited about life, more grateful for his family, or more in love with his wife. His faith is strong, his health is good, and his future is bright. He's a real American success story.

The wonderful thing about Larry Carpenter is that he has accomplished his achievements by applying old-fashioned principles that work for anyone: He made a commitment, set his goals, accepted responsibility, pursued his faith, worked hard, lived with integrity, and used his money wisely. Today, if he chose to do so, he could retire for the rest of his life. What's even more significant is that if he lost every dollar he's acquired over the years, he would still be a successful man because what he's got, money can't buy.

# Truett Cathy: The Picture of Success

From my perspective, if you look up the word *success,* you should see a picture of Truett Cathy. Here's a man who is successful in every area of his life.

Truett is the founder, chairman, and chief executive officer of Chick-fil-A, Inc., an international chain of fast-food restaurants with nearly 800 locations in shopping malls, supermarkets, airports, and hospitals; on university campuses; and in free-standing units. Over the years, he has been recognized in every possible way, from the Horatio Alger Award to countless awards from both local and international business communities.

Truett's road to success hasn't been easy. He and his brother, Ben, started in the restaurant business in 1946 just after World War II ended. They had to scrounge for building materials and had to make a deal with a larger restaurant to sell them food because the food they needed was scarce. They even had to go directly to farmers to get the amount of beef they needed for their small Dwarf House restaurant.

Truett says that when he opened the business, he and Ben had to do a little of everything, from preparing the food to serving to cleaning up. Business was good, and from the very first, they turned a profit. Truett made closing on Sunday an unbreakable policy, and, although he's missed out on some mall locations, he still believes that his employees should have Sundays off to honor God. He remembers his own childhood, when Sunday gave him relief from work and school, and he wants his employees to enjoy the same benefits. This policy may be one of the reasons that Chick-fil-A has the lowest turnover in the fast-food industry.

Truett's upbeat, optimistic lifestyle, with his ever-present faith and his belief that every problem has a solution, has been the foundation upon which he has built his business. He believes that the financial success of his business is a result of his actions, rather than the goal of his life.

The success of Chick-fil-A has not been one long string of victories, however. In 1982, the company experienced a serious financial downturn. Truett took it personally. He asked God to show him what he had done wrong and pledged that he would do whatever it took to change that situation. He did not accept his salary that year so that none of his people would have to take a cut in pay. Next, he did what any good corporate executive does: He asked his family and staff for help. He also recognized the primary importance of being right with God. The executive committee held meetings away from the office and formed Chick-fil-A's corporate purpose statement, which brought renewed focus on being a positive Christian witness to the public. Within six months, the company rebounded with more than a 40 percent increase in sales.

Today, Truett doesn't have to work, but he and his wife of 50 years believe that God has called them for a higher purpose. Truett is active in his church, having taught a Sunday school class of 13-year-olds for the last 40 years, and has created a scholarship fund that has enabled him to give more than $13 million in scholarships to promising restaurant employees. His goal is to help those who work for him to realize their own dreams.

Perhaps the thing that moves Truett most today is his work with children, which he somehow manages to do on top of a steady work schedule. He owns and runs 11 WinShape Foster Care Homes caring for some 100 kids. He also provides 120 scholarships to Berry College in Rome, Georgia. One of Chick-fil-A's latest ventures is to sponsor an annual golf tournament for the Ladies Professional Golf Association, the Chick-fil-A Charity Championship, benefiting WinShape Foster Care Homes, and the Chick-fil-A Peach Bowl which have raised nearly $750,000 for WinShape.

It's often said that "what you see is what you get." In the case of Truett Cathy, you get a great deal more than you see. He is a modest, unpretentious individual. His humility, hard work, faith, commitment, and passion for loving kids and doing something for them, combined with his dream of making a difference in the world, make him truly one of the most remarkable people I know. He and his wife, Jeannette, make a marvelous team, and he will be the first to tell you that without her love, support, and encouragement, Chick-fil-A would not be where it is today, and neither would he.

# Dave Hurley: From Shack to Mansion

I have always been accused of being a "flag-waver." When I met Dave Hurley, my flag-waving activities grew even more vigorous. Dave's is truly a rags-to-riches story that can happen only in a free-enterprise system.

Dave's family was not the motivational tool that led him to his position of prominence in the sales profession. His father was obsessed with the survival of his children and gave them few, if any, privileges. His mother suffered from severe manic depression. This, as he puts it, made for a less-than-positive start in life, particularly as a teenager. When Dave was told that he couldn't go to his high school prom, he joined the Marine Corps to escape the discipline at home. Dave made it through a stint in Vietnam, marrying soon after his return to the United States.

Dave had a tremendous desire to better himself. The problem was that he had no direction and not a clue as to what he could or should do. He worked in a toy factory earning $1.50 per hour (which, even in 1970, was a pauper's wage). In his terms, poor was three steps up from his social status. He and his new bride lived in a $30-a-month two-room house with electricity in only one room and no plumbing or running water. He got a new job in a quarry, and every day he carried home from the quarry ten one-gallon jugs filled with water.

At that point, an event occurred that changed Dave Hurley's life. A salesman (who was anything but professional) selling waterless cookware stopped by Dave's house. He carried a can of beer to the house, deposited the can in the front flower bed, and smoked five cigarettes in the process of selling Dave a $400 set of cookware that appealed to Dave because he had no running water.

Dave purchased the cookware with a postdated check for $38.95 and a promise to pay $15 each month until the balance was paid. He then walked the salesman out to his long Fleetwood Cadillac. To say that Dave was impressed is an understatement. He asked the salesman if he was hiring, and the guy laughed and said no. However, Dave had gotten a glimpse of what life can be like when one has the right opportunity. He made 12 long-distance calls until finally he convinced the salesman that he should at least consider hiring him. When the salesman told Dave that he would have to buy his own samples for $300 cash, he figured that he had gotten rid of him. However, he did not know Dave Hurley.

Dave pawned everything of value he had and showed up at the salesman's house on the appointed Saturday morning. Flabbergasted, the guy rummaged around in his garage through repossessed sets of cookware, some of which had eggs still stuck to them. The order pad was mildewed and smeared with ink, but Dave was too excited to really care. He felt that he now had a chance in life.

Monday afternoon at 4:00, after he finished his stint at the quarry, Dave showered, put on his only suit, and headed down the streets of Anna, Illinois, banging on doors. Dave had what I call "intelligent ignorance." He did not know that he could not sell without being trained, and he didn't realize that he faced an almost impossible task. All he knew was that he was excited about a chance in life, and he proceeded to sell 11 sets of cookware before the following Saturday, when his boss showed up to train him. Out of those first sales, two women wanted to pay cash, but Dave didn't know how to write the order because the only experience he'd had was the way he purchased his own set, so he required them to buy exactly as he had. The guy who hired him was stunned when Dave showed him the 11 orders. Dave still had to sell one more set in order to retrieve his valuables from Charlie's Pawn Shop.

Yes, Dave was off to a fast start, but as is often the case, an excited salesperson starts with such a passion and belief in the product that he transfers that belief to prospects who buy without fully understanding why they're buying. When his "trainer" saw that he had already sold 11 sets of cookware, he packed up and left, saying that Dave was already trained, and wished him luck. After two more weeks of moderate success, Dave quit his salaried job to devote all his time to selling. In the meantime, he upgraded to a small, used mobile home that had plumbing and electricity.

Then the struggle began. Working in a depressed area, combined with the reality that everything depended on the commissions he received from sales, he struggled desperately. He worked hard and learned more about his product, but with each missed sale, he lost a little of his enthusiasm, and the going got tougher and tougher. Combine all this with the fact that the guy who had hired him took advantage of his naïveté and paid him a fraction of what was fair on each sale he made. Things were so bad that Dave briefly considered going back to the quarry.

In order to survive, Dave took a part-time job selling insurance. He was immediately successful and won a trip to the insurance convention in Las Vegas, where he "accidentally" bumped into Don Christianson, an executive with West Bend, the manufacturer of the cookware that Dave sold. When Don heard Dave's name, he got excited because Dave had set some records, and Don assumed that he was there for the West Bend convention. Doors were opened at this "chance meeting": The distributor was retiring, and Don offered Dave the chance to take over the distributorship — actually a simple paper transaction involving no money. With renewed enthusiasm, Dave went back and sold better than ever at a higher rate of commission.

The journey to the top, however, was still a long, hard climb. For nearly ten years, Dave did not see himself as capable of teaching others and sharing the opportunity with them. In the midst of his struggles, he picked up some training tapes by a former cookware salesman and started listening to them every time he got into his car. Now, to go with his incredible desire, drive, and determination, he had direction and training. That combination has produced spectacular results.

Today, Dave Hurley owns the largest cookware distributorship in the nation, the third largest in the world. His organization produces millions of dollars of sales annually, and in September 1997, it experienced its first million-dollar week. Dave personally sells in excess of a million dollars every year and has several salespeople who earn in excess of a quarter-million dollars each year.

Long ago, Dave moved out of that two-room rented house and built a beautiful new home close by, just to show his neighbors who had laughed and said that he would fail. He also owns a home in the mountains of north Georgia and a home in Florida, where he enjoys his 51-foot yacht and his family. If he chose to do so, Dave could spend 365 days a year on that yacht because, in the last ten years, he has achieved financial security.

You'll probably never have a chance to meet and come to know Dave Hurley. That's too bad, because if you did, regardless of your status, you would be convinced that if Dave Hurley can do what he's done with his start in life, surely you can do more with yours.

# Clint Lewis: Man on a Mission

Clint Lewis is a state-champion wrestler, taught wrestling for eight years, has his own radio program, received the Unsung Hero Award, and has been interviewed on *Good Morning, America,* as well as by numerous local papers and *USA Today.* He is a musician who has written original songs and is currently in demand as a speaker, particularly in schools but more and more often in the business world. His hobbies include rock climbing, skydiving, bungee jumping, golf, darts, and tandem bicycling. He is also blind.

Clint is an inspiration to those who have had the privilege of getting to know him. I met him via telephone a couple of years ago and saw him while I was on a speaking engagement in Salt Lake City. He has since attended our "Born to Win" seminar in Dallas, where I really got to know him. However, it wasn't until he sent me a cassette recording of one of his speeches that I came to appreciate his incredible talent as a professional speaker.

Clint is downright funny. He tells an amazing story about playing a softball game (he admits that he's a lousy hitter) that is one of the most entertaining stories I have ever heard. However, hidden beneath his humorous one-liners and his "facts of life" demonstration of courage and humor is a message that can inspire anyone in need of inspiration — and that includes everyone from time to time. Clint Lewis is truly remarkable because it is impossible to detect any sense of self-pity in him. A couple of years ago, Clint completed a 7,000-mile bus tour with his dog, Libo, just to show the people who had hired him to speak that he was completely independent and could do things on his own. He has a strong mission in life; his goals are clearly identified. He reaches out to help the truly handicapped and those who are not fortunate enough to have been gifted with what he has.

Coming from a loving and supportive family with a mother who was a marathon runner, a father who was a wrestler who finished fourth in state competition, and a brother who finished first in the state as a wrestler, this self-taught musician and optimist spreads cheer and a marvelous attitude wherever he goes. Clint laughingly says that when he started wrestling, his little sister, Shaela, provided the practice he needed, and he used her to perfect some of his moves. Apparently, it worked, because as a ninth-grader he finished first in state competition in his class.

I chose to include this young man, who was born in 1969, in this chapter because I believe that for sheer inspiration and an all-around good time, he's one of the neatest guys I've ever been around. He inspires school kids and adult audiences alike. He really is an "unsung hero" and a marvelous role model for those who see him in action. It's inspiring to watch a young man who, despite the fact that he lost his sight, did not lose his vision.

# Mamie McCullough: The "I CAN" Lady

Mamie Claire Darlington was born on a sharecropper's farm, the youngest daughter of six girls and three boys. Her father died in 1942, leaving a widow who could neither read nor write with nine children under 17 years of age.

"Miss Mamie," as she is affectionately known by people all over the United States, tells the story of growing up "pore." That's different from being poor, she says; "pore" is when you would need a substantial raise to qualify for the "poor" category. They lived off the "hard road" in a condemned house that they bought for $250 and took ten years to pay off. The house never had paint or running water, and all the windows had been knocked out. Later, the family purchased a prefabricated shell home, which they paid for in monthly installments of $27.68.

Mamie got her education in Dixie, Georgia, attended the Baptist Church, and worked in the fields for neighbors who paid her $2.50 for a 14-hour day. She did just about everything during those tough years. She played on the basketball team and started selling *Grit* magazine under the name of her brother, Joe Darlington, since in those days girls couldn't sell magazines. Tragically, starting at age 5, she was abused by "friends."

When she graduated from high school, she worked for two years before deciding that she needed more education. With encouragement from her older sister, Martha, she rode a bus for 36 hours to get to Brownwood, Texas, to attend Howard Payne University. Knowing Miss Mamie today, it's difficult even to imagine that when she arrived in Brownwood, she didn't know that you majored, minored, or paid to go to college. After she registered for a bachelor of arts degree in business administration and secondary education, she was summoned by the finance department and was dismayed to learn that the tuition was $598.

When Mamie went to see Dr. Guy Newman, the president of Howard Payne, to explain her withdrawal from school, she experienced a remarkable invitation: Dr. and Mrs. Newman invited her to live in their home. Dr. Newman was the first person ever to tell her that she was bright. The college permitted her to work out her registration costs, and four years later, after holding down four jobs in college in order to pay her way through, she graduated in 1963. Her college honors were Future Teacher of Tomorrow and Best Dressed. She worked for a local businessman as secretary/office manager, apartment manager, and hotel/motel manager until 1968.

In 1968, Mamie Claire Darlington was married and divorced within five months. Incredibly enough, this beautiful woman of unshakable faith and undying optimism moved back to south Georgia to "sit on her mama's front porch and die." The next two years were incredibly tough. She was depressed, devastated, empty, and alone. Then she was asked to teach school and found her true love in education. She married Don McCullough in 1971 and her first child, Patti, was born on March 9, 1973; Brian arrived on April 8, 1975, and Jennifer Ann was born on September 12, 1976. Mamie continued teaching and started selling Mary Kay Cosmetics part-time, first as a consultant and then as a director. She also taught Sunday school while looking after her family. She was — and is — a busy lady.

Mamie McCullough created a course for high school students called "I CAN," based on my book *See You at the Top.* The results were phenomenal. Her philosophy was simply that if you teach kids to act right, they will do right. This course has since reached more than 3 million kids. In 1978, Miss Mamie became one of the first female high school principals in the state of Georgia. As one of the board members expressed it, "She was not certified, but she was certainly qualified." She displayed love and concern for her students and teachers and implemented "tough love" mixed with common sense and compassion.

In 1979, when her mother died, Mamie accepted our offer that she and Don come to Dallas and work with us. After several years, Don died suddenly of a heart attack, leaving Mamie to raise the three children alone. It was a sad and trying time, but Mamie had learned what it takes to be more than just a survivor. She went on to form Mamie McCullough and Associates and has literally been going "like a house afire" ever since. She is much in demand as a speaker, doing seminars addressing not only educators around the country but business people as well. She has also written several books, including *I Can, You Can, Too; Get It Together and Remember Where You Put It; Mama's Rules for Living;* and *Rules for Success.*

I've had the privilege of meeting some truly remarkable people, from the heads of major corporations to presidents of the United States. However, I've never met anyone who has overcome as many obstacles and who had so many "excuses" to fail. Raised under dire financial circumstances, abused as a child, abandoned as a bride of five months, widowed with three small children — these things would be all some people would need for a lifetime pity-party. Despite all these things, however, Mamie is one of the most giving, loving people I've ever known.

Mamie's home has been open to countless people who spend weekends with her as she encourages, teaches, and inspires them. Her children are an unqualified success — sound ethically and morally, with their heads squarely on their shoulders and their eyes looking to the future. One of the major reasons Miss Mamie is so effective is that she believes with all her heart that "I CAN" and that you can, too. The way she says it makes you believe that she's right.

# David Sun and John Tu:
# The Good Guys Win

David Sun and John Tu, two immigrants from Taiwan, are extraordinarily successful "good guys." The neat thing is that these men recognize that their success comes as a result of having great people working with them. They are modest and unassuming, yet their net worth is approximately $900 million each.

An article in the December 17, 1996, issue of the *Dallas Morning News* tells their story of generosity, gratitude, commitment, and love. For example, when the account manager at the computer software company that the two men own had no money for funeral expenses for her mother, Tu and Sun picked up the tab. Ever sensitive to the demands of their employees' jobs, they responded in a unique way when the Web page manager attended a grueling trade show in Germany. Tu suggested that the manager spend a few days recuperating at the company's expense in Paris and London. When another coworker casually mentioned a childhood dream of owning a Jaguar someday, Sun spontaneously gave her his.

Incidents like these are a large part of the reason that these men have been so successful. Perhaps the most amazing thing occurred, though, when Tu and Sun, who are the cofounders of Kingston Technology Corporation, announced a $100 million bonus package for their 523 employees. Tu and Sun had just received $1.5 billion as a windfall from selling 80 percent of the company. The heartfelt gratitude of their employees was obvious as they embraced Tu and Sun in tears, many of them saying, "You've changed my life." Strange as it may seem, they weren't talking about money — or certainly not just about money.

What the employees were really saying was that working for models of generosity, compassion, and fairness had made them better human beings. Some of them still shed a tear or two when they talk about their bosses' essential goodness. Tu and Sun are embarrassed and a little bewildered by all the media attention their bonuses have attracted. Because family has a strong impact on our thinking, our actions, and our lives, it's not too surprising to learn that these men credit their mothers with teaching them the value of friendship over maximum profits. Tu asked, "Don't you think the happiest thing in life is sharing?" Good question. He then expounds on it by saying, "We're so lucky, David and I. We feel we owe these people here more than they owe us."

Their lives have not always been easy. Tu, who is 56, was born in China. When civil war broke out, the family fled to Taiwan, where his father worked censoring films with Communist themes. His mother's advice to him was "Don't bring flowers to those who have plenty. Bring coal to them who need heat in the winter."

Sun, 46, is a Taiwan native whose father abandoned his wife and four small children when Sun was 5. "Money isn't the only thing," his mother, a high school biology teacher, told Sun. "Treat people right; then they will help you when you need it." Let me point out that this is another way of saying, "You can have everything in life you want if you will just help enough other people get what they want."

These two men immigrated to the U.S. in the late 1970s and met in California. They made their first fortune when they sold a company they founded. After the 1987 stock market crash, they founded Kingston, which makes add-on memory modules for personal computers. Today, according to *Forbes* magazine, Kingston is among the 500 largest private companies in the United States, with sales in the neighborhood of $2 billion. Tu and Sun say that their generosity makes good business sense. "If you put people first, the bottom line will follow," Tu said.

# Chapter 22

# Ten (Or So) Things to Incorporate into Any Success Strategy

. . . . . . . . . . . . . . . . . . . . . . . . . . . . . . . . . . . . . . . . . . .

### In This Chapter

▶ Take a do-it-now, "hustle" approach to life

▶ Have a character base — the only one that supports long-term success

▶ Evaluate risks and take the best ones

▶ Be a time-miser

▶ Communicate effectively — both verbally and nonverbally

▶ Have a thick skin

▶ Be an optimist and a good-finder

▶ Learn to be obedient so that you can learn to lead others

▶ Know that courage upholds all the other qualities

▶ Be intolerant of immoral behavior

▶ Develop a sense of humor

▶ Form winning habits

. . . . . . . . . . . . . . . . . . . . . . . . . . . . . . . . . . . . . . . . . . .

*O*f course, every success strategy is different — you have to find the approach that works for you. But nearly all successful people share more than just a few of these characteristics. In this chapter, I outline those characteristics that you should incorporate into your success strategy.

## Hustle

On the way to becoming successful, people who make it and make it big are almost without exception ambitiously dissatisfied with the status quo. They understand that where they are is part of the process of getting where they want to be, and they don't dally around. They have specific objectives in mind, get busy seeking them, and work hard. They hustle.

The 40-hour work week, in most cases, does not suffice for those who want to climb the corporate ladder or build their own business while maintaining a balanced life with family and friends. Another thing that these people invariably do is to give up some of the things that are not only not productive but also detrimental. I'm speaking of the countless hours squandered in front of the television set or engaged in nonproductive chatter at a bar on the way home. People who are serious about their success show it in the things they do and don't do.

Recently, I needed a new cassette recorder. Because I liked the one that I had been using, I walked into the store that sells them, held up my recorder, and asked if they had another one. The manager said, "Yes," turned to the young man standing beside him, and asked him to get one for me. The young man headed for the rear of the store *very* slowly. He returned even more slowly — so slowly that I had to line him up between two shelves to make certain that he was moving. (I exaggerate only slightly.) If this young man continues to take this approach to life, he's going to find himself unemployed much of the time and working in minimum-wage jobs the other part of the time.

I make this statement because I worked in a grocery store as a youngster. From the beginning, my boss taught me to hustle. If I wasn't hustling while I ran to get something for a customer, my boss would call out, "Come on, boy! A dollar is waiting on a dime!" meaning that the customer was really my employer, and if I was going to keep my job with that employer, I had to hustle.

# Character

Another factor that belongs in every success strategy is character. It has been said that character is "what you do in the dark." Character is "the ability to carry out a good resolution long after the excitement of the moment has passed," said the late Cavett Robert. Sometimes life throws tough situations at you, but there's a difference between being tough and being hard. Author Joe Batten, whose book *Tough-Minded Management* is a classic, puts it this way:

> "Granite is very hard, but you can take that slab of granite and hit it with a hammer and it will shatter. However, you can take a piece of leather, which is tough, and you can hammer and hammer and while it will make little dents in it, little damage is done despite all of the hammering."

Batten is saying that you should be tough, not hard, when you're attacked. You mustn't be a pushover, but you also need to be compassionate, gentle, and flexible, particularly on procedure (as opposed to principle).

## Good news about hard work

In most cases, you don't have to worry about working too hard. According to a well-known psychiatrist, people who work extremely hard in a productive way rarely complain of exhaustion. People who are bored with their jobs, frustrated about their futures, worried about their marriages, or troubled about their finances burn up more nervous energy than someone who's working extremely hard in a fulfilling assignment. Those who are emotionally spent are far more likely to complain of chronic tiredness.

Sometimes you have to be particularly tough when it comes to protecting your character. Young people today especially need to consider this. There was an enormous amount of discussion in the last U.S. presidential campaign about whether a person's private life has any bearing on his or her effectiveness as a public servant. Basically, the question being asked was "Is character really that important?"

What disturbs me most about this discussion is that young people may be led to assume that if the highest-ranking politicians do not believe that character is important, then they should not believe that it's important, either.

Define character for your children. Explain that the way they feel about themselves is dictated by the character they exhibit in their daily lives. If you can help them see the connection between internal feelings and external behavior, the choices they make will reflect more and more character as they mature.

# Risk-Taking (Not Gambling)

Gambling is very different from risk-taking. My *1828 Noah Webster Dictionary* says that risk is a "pushing forward, a rushing." It is "to be bold and hearty." Gambling is a far more hazardous undertaking. For example, an article I read revealed that if you play the dollar slots at a casino every day for two months, the odds are 2 trillion to 1 that you will lose $1,000 before you win $1,000. That's not gambling; that's highway robbery! If you play the other person's game long enough, you're going to lose.

But the reality is that people who refuse to take risks are definitely going to lose. If you refuse a new promotion because you're not sure that you have the skills to do the job, you probably will be passed over when other chances for advancement open up. If you're afraid of rejection, you won't risk being the initiator in friendships, and you'll miss out on one of life's greatest treasures. If you put all your money in an interest-bearing savings account instead of a CD or stocks so that you can always get to it, you'll never realize the income that you could have if you'd just taken a risk.

Farmers, for example, certainly take a risk when they plant their crops. They invest a considerable amount of money in the endeavor, yet they're at the mercy of the weather, the economy, the condition of the soil, the labor supply, and so on. But the farmers would be committing financial suicide if they did not take risks and plant their crops. Every aspect of life involves some degree of risk-taking, but that doesn't necessarily mean that life is dangerous. It simply means that there's a chance that things are not going to work out as you plan. For that reason, you need to carefully lay your plans, as explained in Chapters 6 and 7 of this book. Also, read about the lives of the successful people I talk about in Chapter 21. You'll discover that they are risk-takers — but not gamblers.

# *Time-Miserliness*

One year contains 525,600 minutes. Unfortunately, multitudes of people waste a high percentage of those minutes. Those who enjoy a balanced success — success in their personal, family, business, spiritual, physical, and financial lives — however, are the ones who most effectively utilize their time. Both the successful and the not-so-successful have exactly 1,440 minutes in every day of their lives. Needless to say, they use that time in vastly different ways and get vastly different results.

Proper time management is a must for every person who aspires to be successful. Time is your most important, and certainly your most consistent, commodity; you get the same amount each day. When you let those moments and hours slip away, they're gone forever. The question is, how do you more effectively use your time?

I encourage you to record what you do each day for a week. Break the day into 30-minute segments and note what you do during those 30 minutes. In most cases, you'll be astounded to spot an hour or even two hours each day when you accomplished little of value. Going through this process makes you aware of the incredible amount of time that slips through your fingers in 5-, 10-, and 15-minute increments.

The first step in developing more effective work habits is to set realistic goals. Next, you need to take advantage of the time you have. Herbert Hoover wrote a book in the time he spent waiting in railroad stations. Noel Coward wrote his popular song, "I'll See You Again," while caught in a traffic jam. You have just as much time as Leo Tolstoy had when he wrote *War and Peace*. You have just as much time as Thomas Edison had when he invented the light bulb.

# The best time-saver is to do it now

One of life's ironies is that we somehow find time to do things over when we didn't have time to do them right the first time. Yes, my tongue is slightly in my cheek, but when it gets down to the absolutely gotta-do-it-right time, most responsible people do exactly that. Had they invested a few more minutes initially, they may have saved themselves the time and trouble of doing it over.

The problem is that they figure, "I'll do it when it becomes absolutely necessary. I'll make that service call when I absolutely have to." By then, the customer may be so unhappy that satisfying the customer takes three times as much time and effort. "I know I'm running out of gas, but I'm in a hurry, so I'll make it a point to fill up when I get out of this heavy traffic." We all know the end of that story, don't we?

Sometimes, when someone demands something of us, we respond rebelliously, "I'll do it when I'm good and ready!" Don't do it "when" — do it now!

I have observed that people who make and use to-do lists and take advantage of "two-fers" get the maximum benefit from their time. What is a two-fer, you ask? Here are a couple of examples:

- ✔ I never get in a line without something to read. I probably salvage an hour a week of reading time by using this strategy.

- ✔ In my car, I almost always listen to cassette recordings that inspire and inform me. I get to my destination in the same amount of time, but I arrive better prepared for life's opportunities. This is a classic two-fer. Mary Kay Ash of Mary Kay Cosmetics, Wallace Johnson, cofounder of Holiday Inns, and W. Clement Stone of Combined Insurance all told me that they regularly listen to cassette recordings in their cars. You may not have time to be a bookworm, but you *can* be a tapeworm.

Be prepared to make the best use of your time and take advantage of life's two-fers by having reading and learning materials handy.

Each day is important, and the way you use it determines just how important it will be to those who follow in your wake. So use your time wisely, because a lack of time is not the problem — having a sense of direction and using your time wisely are the critical factors.

# Nonverbal Communication: Saying a Lot without Saying a Word

In addition to speaking and writing, you communicate with your facial expressions and body language. Have you ever heard anyone ask, "Are you okay?" and been surprised when they said that you looked worried, tired, sad, unhappy, and so on, because you thought that you were hiding your problems pretty well? Surely you've seen people who look so dejected, with their heads hanging, shoulders sagging, and feet dragging, that you wanted to go over, ask them what was wrong, and offer to help in any way. You "felt" their pain just by looking at them. When the words that come out of your mouth don't match the expression on your face or the stance of your body, it confuses the person with whom you are trying to communicate. Consider these examples:

✔ When you shuffle papers on your desk while an associate or employee is telling you something, you communicate that what you're doing is more important than what the other person is saying. When you look the associate or employee in the eye and nod or shake your head as that person talks to you, you communicate that you're listening intently and that what's being said is meaningful to you.

✔ When, as a manager, you keep your door closed, you communicate that you do not want the employees you are paid to manage to bother you. An open-door policy encourages openness and makes you approachable, which makes you part of the team you are in charge of leading.

✔ When a factory superintendent keeps his office at the back door next to the parking lot and leaves the door open, he communicates to workers that he's open to them and interested in what they have to say. When his office is up front and the door remains closed, he communicates an entirely different message.

All kinds of communications deliver scores of messages — some of which are not intended. For example, people who are consistently late communicate that they believe their time is more important than the time of the person who has to wait. Most people can forgive an occasional slip, but those who are perennially late lose friends and influence in the process.

Yes, what you communicate does make a difference. Consider what your actions and expressions communicate, and make the necessary changes.

# Thick Skin

One of the most important success strategies is developing a thick skin to the barbs that come your way — some deserved, some not. How do *you* deal with criticism? Do you lose your cool, become defensive or angry, or blow off steam? Admittedly, you can go in those directions, but they serve no constructive purpose.

I like Jay Leno's approach. When he replaced Johnny Carson on *The Tonight Show,* Leno took some heat. Critics compared him unfavorably to Carson, and from all that criticism, people thought that he was in big trouble and that his stay as host would be short-lived. Fortunately, Leno never really worried. In fact, he kept a stack of unpleasant reviews on his desk for inspiration. One critic said, "Too many soft questions." Another said, "He's being too nice." These unkind words didn't bother Leno, though, because they were written in 1962 and were directed at Jack Paar's replacement — "an awkward nobody named Johnny Carson."

You can depend on it: Anybody who does anything of significance, regardless of the field of endeavor, is going to be criticized. The way the successful ones handle that criticism is a big part of their success.

# Obedience

Another trait that you need to incorporate into your success strategy is old-fashioned *obedience.* I recognize that, in our society, that word is not only "foreign" but also considered demeaning by many people. Yet I believe that this concept is extremely important. One of the first principles of leadership is to understand that before you can become a leader, you must learn to follow — which means that you must learn to obey.

Once, in an airport, I saw a teenager wearing a T-shirt with the slogan "I obey no one." I couldn't help but feel sorry for the young man, because if he meant that literally, he will never be able to lead anyone, either. Look at it this way: 175 of the CEOs of Fortune 500 companies are former United States Marines, and 26 U.S. presidents served in the military. This is a phenomenal percentage of successful people who moved into the top ranks in the political world as well as in the business world.

These people succeeded partly because of what they learned in the military. Before they learned to lead, they learned to obey. From the moment boot camp starts, drill sergeants drill obedience into the troops. They do not have the option of challenging or questioning; they simply are disciplined to obey whatever command is issued. Colin Powell, who arguably is the most highly respected person in the United States because of his exemplary life — his climb from swabbing the floors in a Pepsi plant to moving into

ROTC and then to the highest level of command in our military forces as Chairman of the Joint Chiefs of Staff — stated that the military puts everybody on the same level. Recruits learn from the very beginning that they have a job to do, and they are required to conform to the standard in order to accomplish their objective.

Similarly, in the corporate world, somebody is ultimately responsible for final decisions. Those people who play by the rules and learn to obey place themselves in the best position to learn how to command or lead the organization to higher levels.

# Courage

Most people have watched with envy as some simple idea produces notable results and brings fame and fortune to its originator. Haven't we all heard somebody say, "I thought of the same thing several years ago and never did anything about it!"

Philosopher Alfred North Whitehead observed: "Almost all new ideas have a certain aspect of foolishness when they are first produced. The history of science is full of examples. Copernicus said the earth revolves around the sun. Louis Pasteur said disease is caused by microscopic creatures called 'germs.' Newton spoke of an invisible force called 'gravity.' These scientists could have been top comedians in their day just by standing on a stage and reciting their theories. The acceptance process that accompanies many new ideas was best summed up by William James. He said, 'First, a new theory is attacked as absurd. Then it is admitted to be true, but obvious and insignificant. Finally, it is seen to be so important that its adversaries claim they themselves discovered it.'"

Many people go through life without the courage to stick their necks out, even a little bit, to get ahead. When I was a young man starting my career, I remember one Saturday morning sitting on our front steps, resting between shots at finishing my yard duties for the day, when the mailman came by. It was hot, and he was sweating. We exchanged pleasantries, and I asked him how he was doing. I will never forget his response: "I only have 12 more years of doing this, and then I can set this bag down, never to pick it up again." I commented that it sounded like he didn't like his job. He said that he literally hated every day on the job and every step he had taken, but he had come this far and was going to tough it out for 12 more years to get his retirement.

I was torn as to whether lack of courage or just plain fear kept him from getting a job doing something else, but I've often pondered how a man could dedicate his working life to something he absolutely hated. It seems that, with a little courage, he would have stepped out shortly after he realized that his future was not going to be what he wanted for himself.

When you have courage, you follow through on your vision. I think of all the immigrants who have come to America because they had a vision. They gave up a great deal in order to make the trip. Not only did they have a vision, but the vision also had them. Without courage, the vision would never have become reality.

Yes, courage is on display every day, and only the courageous wring the most out of life. The next time you're confronted with a decision, weigh it carefully and consider heavily the right thing to do. Then summon the courage to do what's right. You'll be glad that you did.

# Intolerance

Intolerance, too, must be incorporated into a workable success strategy. One of the greatest disasters of our time is the universal acceptance of the word *tolerance* as a virtue. Tolerance is lauded from the big and little screen to the print press — we mustn't be judgmental; we must be tolerant of other people and their points of view.

Actually, everyone should be intolerant of many things. For example, should a person be tolerant of child abusers, wife abusers, or groups that preach hate and violence? Should people really be tolerant of a person's right to say and do *anything* they believe is right?

I believe that the problem is the confusion between "tolerance" and "an open mind." My mind is open to people and ideas until it becomes obvious that the people or ideas are immoral, unethical, or illegal. For example, I would not defend the rights of pedophiles, and I hope that your tolerance level for them is also zero. I would be tolerant of a pedophile's right to a fair trial, but intolerant of his or her right to continue to abuse children.

I sincerely hope that you, too, are intolerant. I encourage you to keep an open mind. Be tolerant of the rights of others to believe what they believe, but if what they believe violates divine or human laws, I encourage you to be intolerant.

# A Sense of Humor

Your success strategy should include humor. The health benefits of a good, hearty laugh have been well established. The relief from tension that laughter brings is significant. And humor's impact on others is usually positive because everyone enjoys being around pleasant, optimistic people who get real enjoyment out of life.

One of my favorite anecdotes is the one about going to the recreation center to do my exercising and weight lifting. I frequently point out that I had to cut down on the weight lifting because I was bulking up, and many people thought that I was on steroids. As a general rule, this story gets quite a good laugh when you're over 70 and tell it. However, if a young, husky, 30-year-old were to use this example, it would not be funny. Instead, it would sound like his ego had gotten the best of him.

Humor also helps to build winning relationships, because all of us like to be around people who are fun. In the business world, people with a sense of humor are better liked — and, everything else being equal, management promotes people they like. Persons with a good sense of humor don't take themselves overly seriously. I love the story of the lady who was talking to a salesperson on the telephone and, after a few minutes, said, "Oh! You're trying to sell me something! Thank goodness! I thought you were trying to collect for all that stuff I've already bought!" A good sense of humor just comes in handy.

# Winning Habits

Winning habits are the best friends you can have, particularly in the business world. Look carefully at what an anonymous writer said about habits:

> "I am your constant companion. I am your greatest helper or heaviest burden. I will push you onward and upward or drag you down to failure. I am completely at your command. Ninety percent of the things you do might just as well be turned over to me, and I will be able to do them quickly and correctly. I am easily managed, show me exactly how you want something done and after a few lessons I will do them automatically. I am the servant of all great people and, alas! of all failures as well. I am not a machine, though I work with all the precision of a machine, plus the intelligence of a man. You can run me for profit or run me for ruin — it makes no difference to me. Take me, train me, be firm with me, and I will place the world at your feet. Be easy with me and I will destroy you. Who am I? I am Habit."

In the business world, good work habits lead to promotions and job security. Arriving at work and completing assignments on time, being courteous and conscientious, returning phone calls promptly, and going the extra mile are all habits that lead to success. Remember, when you do more than you're paid to do, the day will come when you're paid more for what you do.

Good habits must be grabbed firmly and with a strong commitment. That decision, reinforced by your will to take action on your commitment regardless of how you feel at the moment, produces marvelous results in an amazingly short period of time.

# Chapter 23

# Ten Motivational Gems — Plus One

. . . . . . . . . . . . . . . . . . . . . . . . . . . . . . . . . . . . . . . . . . . . . . . . . .

## In This Chapter

▶ Stories that lift you up — and make you think

. . . . . . . . . . . . . . . . . . . . . . . . . . . . . . . . . . . . . . . . . . . . . . . . . .

*1* believe that the following 11 stories contain some extraordinarily valuable lessons. I encourage you to discuss them one at a time with your family, staff, friends, or classmates, or any time you get together with others. They make for a wonderful, short, inspirational meeting and fit virtually any occasion.

## To Give Is to Receive

This little story from the publication *Cheer* demonstrates the importance of teaching children, by example, the value of giving:

"When I was a small child my grandfather often took me with him on Saturdays to do the weekly shopping. On one of these outings, we walked by a house with a fenced-in yard. The fence was covered with the most beautiful roses I had ever seen. I stopped to gaze at them and smell their glorious scent. Wonderstruck, I declared my amazement. 'Grandpa, aren't they the most beautiful flowers you've ever seen!' Then a voice came floating out from the front porch of the house. 'You may have one, dear. Pick any one you like.' I glanced first at my grandfather, who nodded, then back to the elderly woman rocking on the front porch. 'Are you sure, ma'am?' 'Yes, my dear.'

"I quickly chose a full red rose. Thanking her, I told her how lovely her whole yard was and turned to go. She spoke again. 'I grow the flowers for others to enjoy. I can't see them, you know. I'm blind.' I was stunned. I knew this generous woman was special even then. Later, I realized she had given me much more than a rose. To this day, I try to live her example — to give something to others so they might be happy, regardless of what you yourself get from it."

The blind woman was sharing, which is one of the greatest formulas for happiness that anyone can employ. Agnes Wylene Jones, who tells this story, and others who passed by the woman's house had been the instruments that the blind woman used to make herself happy. I can only imagine the joy that she received when a small child — or, for that matter, an appreciative adult — expressed delight at receiving such a lovely, unexpected gift.

If you take this approach to life, you'll be happier and, according to psychologists, healthier — which means that you'll enjoy other benefits that make life easier for you.

# A Kind Word Can Give Direction

When our youngest daughter, Julie, was in grade school, her teacher confidentially shared with us that she was a sweet, lovable child with an outgoing personality and would do well in life because she made friends easily and genuinely loved others. However, she cautioned us not to expect too much from Julie academically because she would probably always be a C student, with perhaps an occasional B. Of course, we never told Julie about the conversation, but inwardly, we at least partially bought that idea.

For her first nine school years, the Cs and occasional Bs appeared on Julie's report cards, and we "understood" that was the best she could do. We always told her that her grades were fine, that they were acceptable. The second semester of Julie's ninth-grade year, she contracted mononucleosis and missed nine weeks of school, fully one half of the semester. Today, she credits that illness with teaching her how to study and become an A student. Julie was so afraid of failing and being held back a year that she studied almost constantly. For the first time in her life, she made As and Bs in everything . . . *except* math.

I tell you this because one night many years later, I called Julie, and her husband, Jim Norman, answered the phone. When I asked to speak to her, he started laughing. I asked him what was funny, and he responded, "She's not here; she's teaching Diane her basic algebra."

This struck both of us as funny because all her life Julie had been saying to herself and anyone who would listen, "I can't learn math, I can't learn math." However, when she reentered college at age 30, she discovered otherwise. She explained that her problem was that she tried so hard to understand how math worked that she had never carefully learned the formulas. When she did that, math became another subject that she could handle.

She also informed me that a government professor told her she was a lot smarter than she thought she was, and his words had a tremendous impact on her. Julie learned that, with diligent effort, she could learn anything she wanted to know.

Today, Julie is the editor of my books and daily newspaper column. I mention this not only because I'm proud of and grateful for my daughter, but because it makes a critically important point for you. Like her, you are probably much more capable than you think you are, and all you need is a word of encouragement and some direction. The good news is that you hold what you need in your hands right now. I encourage you to take the suggestions and directions in this book seriously and expect good — even great — things to happen.

Keep this little bit of wisdom in mind: Anything I can do, I can do better.

# Be at Risk of Succeeding

Several years ago, Carl Hugebeck was teaching a course in character education in the small Texas town of Bastrop with truly outstanding results. He wrote me a letter that contained some significant statements, explaining, "These kids are 'at-risk,' so I reminded them that because they live in America, lifelong education and self-improvement are available and they can make them a reality."

Hugebeck pointed out that his students had difficult backgrounds and lived in some almost impossible situations that are not conducive to creating optimistic, enthusiastic, goal-oriented kids. However, that's exactly what they were. Hugebeck said, "I tell them that they are definitely 'at-risk.' If they keep doing what they're doing, they will be 'at-risk' of graduating, going to college, meeting their ideal mate, prospering, and enjoying the type of life God intended them to have."

Interesting, isn't it, how a man who loves kids can give their lives a whole new direction with the turn of a phrase? Hugebeck instinctively knows that, with character as a foundation, students really are "at-risk" for getting a good education, followed by a good job, a loving mate, and a wonderful future. Isn't it too bad that we don't have dozens of Carl Hugebecks in every school teaching that, by doing the right thing, students are "at-risk" of being successful?

Now take this thought into the adult world and install it in today's businesses, large and small. If only employers would make available "at-risk" training for employees, telling them that if they show up enthusiastically on time, prepared to do a good day's work, they are "at-risk" of creating job security for themselves. They are also "at-risk" of getting advancements, "at-risk" of being able to purchase a nice home, and "at risk" of building a secure future.

As a matter of fact, everyone is "at-risk." The neat thing is that you can choose to take the risk and make your life productive, rewarding, and exciting.

# Change Your Opinion of Yourself

Several years ago, a young couple from Utah attended our three-day "Born to Win" seminar. The husband was an All-America football player, destined to be a number-one draft choice in the NFL before he was injured during his senior year of college. He's a handsome guy and an outstanding speaker. The wife was a beauty queen — lovely, wonderfully personable, and a sweet individual. When you see them, you think, "Now, they really do go together."

At this particular seminar, we had a memory expert teaching people how to remember names. One hundred people were in attendance, and the expert conducted a test, giving two points to each participant for every first and last name he or she got correct. In that test, the wife finished number one in the class with 199 out of a possible 200 points. We handed out a small recognition award, and when she stepped up to receive it, she broke down weeping. She confessed to the class, "All my life I thought I was dumb, and in this past hour and a half I learned that I am a very bright person, capable of learning anything I really want to know."

This story makes a strong point: There are a lot of good memory books and techniques that you can use to substantially improve your memory. All personal growth — but especially memory improvement — does wonders for your self-image and confidence, which are extraordinarily important in this ever-changing world. Every time you take a step forward by learning something of value, you improve your picture of yourself. Because that picture determines your performance and your performance determines your future, the daily acquisition of knowledge and skills is a marvelous way to ensure your future.

# Conflict Resolution

Most people are familiar with Indian expressions such as "burying the hatchet" and "smoking the peace pipe." Here's a story of how children from the Seneca tribe settle disagreements:

If two Seneca boys got into a serious squabble, their mother would say to them, "Go and set up your sticks." The boys would know exactly what this meant. They were to go some distance from the lodge and set up three sticks in a tripod form. Then they had to leave the quarrel with the sticks for one moon (or month). At the end of that time, the position of the sticks would determine who was right. In the meantime, the boys would go back to their play, leaving the sticks to settle the quarrel.

They may have agreed that if the sticks leaned toward the rising sun at the end of the moon, Running Deer was right; if they leaned toward the setting sun, Flying Squirrel was right. If the sticks had fallen down, neither of the boys was right. Because of wind and rain, the sticks almost always fell down. More often than not, the boys could not even remember why they had set up the sticks — thus the quarrel was settled easily.

Thank you, Mabel Powers, for your article in *Cheer* sharing an intriguing example of a sensible solution to everyday squabbles. Shakespeare would say that, in most cases, these quarrels are "much ado about nothing." If we walked away and agreed to discuss the issue at a later time, even on another day, our tempers would cool, logic and reason would take over, and problems would be resolved amicably.

My grandmother took a similar approach. When heated discussions took place, she would say firmly, "Let it sit." Take this approach to settling squabbles, and life becomes much simpler and more rewarding.

# Praise Gets the Desired Results

It pays to be a good-finder — finding good things to say about a person or a situation. This anecdote that I read somewhere says a lot:

> Not long after moving with her husband to a small town, a woman complained to a friend about the poor service at the library. On her next trip to the library, however, the librarian had set aside two best-sellers for her and a new biography for her husband. The librarian also seemed genuinely happy to see her. Later, the woman reported the curious changes to her friend. "Did you tell her how poor we thought the service was?" she asked. "No," her friend admitted. "As a matter of fact, I told her that your husband thought she had a terrific collection of biographies, and that you thought she was very talented at selecting new books to order."

This is one of many examples illustrating that people respond more positively to sincere compliments and praise than to criticism and condemnation. When you think about it for a moment, you realize why. In this case, criticism would have indicated that the librarian either didn't know how to do the job or didn't care about doing a good job.

Most of us "get our dander up" when we're criticized like that. We consider the judgment unfair; we grow defensive; and, as a result, we build a wall that makes open communication difficult. A friendly gesture removes the barrier, and a change of attitude is the outcome. When you change attitudes, you can change the world — at least your world. And that's a step toward changing somebody else's world. That approach can make everyone's life easier and more fulfilling.

# Be Slow to Judge

Thank you, Jim Gillon, for sharing this story in the monthly publication *Cheer:*

"It was cold and blustery, as it had been for a month. The weather had been good for our business in the grocery store, but some of the customers were getting on our nerves — particularly one little old lady. She was new in the neighborhood, but everyone soon had problems with her. She always needed help to find items, was constantly returning things, complaining, and seemed to do anything else she could think of to irritate us.

"As I went to open the store, our pesty customer was making her way across the parking lot, practically dragging a bulky old bag. 'Oh, no, what is she up to this morning?' I asked one of the cashiers. 'Probably bringing back the items we had to hunt for her yesterday,' he said. I angrily watched as she slowly made her way to the store.

"'Excuse me, sir,' she said while tugging at my arm. 'Is there a place in back to plug in my crock pot?' 'What?' I said very rudely. 'I made some stew for your people, and the pot needs to be plugged in so it will be warm for lunch.'

"I didn't know what to say. Very embarrassed, I helped her to our coffee room. While she was putting her things on the table, I thought of all the terrible things we had said about her. None of us really knew her, but we had been quick to talk badly about her. After she was out of the store, I went back to the coffee room. On top of her crock pot was a hand-printed message: 'For the employees, from one who always needs help.' That was wrong. We were the ones who needed help."

There's a reason that everyone seems to be familiar with the saying about taking the log out of your eye before trying to remove the speck from your brother's eye. Humans seem to be critical by nature. Looking for the whys and trying to understand a person who irritates you or is "hard to get along with" is a learned and conscious behavior. Choose to give the person who gets under your skin the benefit of the doubt, and you'll never suffer the humbling experience that the man in the grocery store did. Besides, going out of your way to be nice to someone makes you feel great!

# Small Kindnesses Seem Huge When Received by the Grateful

This story is old and has been told many times, but it is so poignant and says so much that it always carries a timeless message:

Shortly after the end of World War II, Europe was in ruins. Perhaps the saddest sight was the little orphaned children, starving in the war-torn streets. Early one chilly morning in London, an American soldier was making his way back to the barracks. Turning the corner, he spotted a little boy of six or seven, standing with his nose pressed to the window of a pastry shop. The hungry boy stared in silence as the baker kneaded dough for a fresh batch of doughnuts. The soldier pulled his Jeep over, got out, and walked quietly to where the little fellow was standing. Through the steamy window, he gazed at the mouth-watering treats. The soldier's heart went out to the child, so he asked, "Son, would you like some of those?" Startled, the little boy peered up at the tall American and cried, "Oh, yes, sir, I would!" Quietly, the soldier stepped inside, bought a dozen doughnuts, and exited into the London fog. Turning to the child, he smiled, held out the bag, and said simply, "Here you are." As he turned to walk away, he felt a tug on his coat. He stopped and smiled back at the boy, only to hear him ask, "Mister, are you God?"

Obviously, the soldier was not God, but he was a genuine unsung hero. He was an encourager who demonstrated to a child that there are kind and compassionate people in the world. I have a feeling that the child never forgot that unknown soldier who helped to fill the emptiness in his life.

Take this story to heart: Be an unsung hero. Do a simple deed regularly and often. You never know how far a simple gesture or a kind word planted in the grateful heart of a child will take that child.

# Success Is What You Make It

On Saturday, May 3, 1997, I had the privilege of attending a Special Olympics event with my family. My granddaughter Elizabeth participated in two races and won a silver and a gold medal. Her coach was every bit as excited as she was, but for a different reason: Elizabeth had stayed in her own lane from start to finish, a feat she had been unable to achieve until the day of her victory. Victory comes in many forms at the Special Olympics.

When we entered the stadium, we were surprised to learn that many of the 1,500 participants train all year for these competitions. The opening ceremonies, complete with color guard, masters of ceremonies, salute to the flag, "The Star Spangled Banner," and performances by a well-coordinated Coppell High School drill team, were spectacular to watch. However, the most moving sight was the opening parade. Many emotions were displayed, but the main one was the sheer delight of so many of the athletes: their smiles, the jumping up and down, the way they hugged each other, and the enthusiasm displayed with their crowd-pleasing performances.

One young man could do cartwheels. After the first one, the crowd asked him to do another, and he responded with exuberance. A second young athlete was a natural-born cheerleader who beckoned the crowd to stand up, cheer, and show enthusiasm.

The master of ceremonies reminded us that, just 30 years ago, experts believed that no mentally challenged person would ever be able to swim the length of an Olympic-size swimming pool or run a mile. But then he rightly observed that they did not measure the hearts or the souls of these athletes.

What would happen if we all used the same percentage of our ability that these special athletes use of theirs? Seeing the athletes' commitment gave hope to those who were present that day. Remember, those who give hope to others are generally filled with hope themselves. Give hope to others, and you will be rewarded in more ways than you can imagine.

# Encourage Yourself

One of the most moving experiences of my life took place on September 13, 1997, when I was in the process of autographing books. The line was long and the people there were excited, but one lady had such a compelling expression on her face that I knew I had to listen carefully to what she had to say.

She shared with me that when she got the self-talk card that was included in one of my audio tape programs that she had purchased, she couldn't even read the list of qualities that she was supposed to claim. Throughout her life, she had been so beaten down by her family, and most recently by her husband, that it was impossible for her to believe that she had the character and success qualities that I identified. It took two or three weeks of listening to the tapes to build herself up to the point where she could look herself in the eye and claim that she was an honest, intelligent, goal-setting person.

Even then, she could claim only two or three of the words. But she kept listening until the day came when she got all the way to the tenth word on the list. At that point, she was convinced that she was a person of genuine worth. She was so overwhelmed with joy and gratitude that she literally slumped to the floor and cried for several minutes.

Her feelings of inadequacy and worthlessness had frequently left her with no energy; she never realized that her low self-esteem was a result of the abuse of others toward her. Over the next few weeks, she continued to claim additional qualities until she could go through the entire list of 60-plus positive qualities. As a result, her demeanor and attitude changed dramatically. She started standing up straight, smiling, and even laughing. Then something truly fascinating happened.

Her husband watched her new attitude emerge and, realizing that something dramatic was happening in her life, decided that if claiming the qualities of success made such a dramatic difference in her, maybe claiming the qualities could do the same for him. He started the process of claiming the qualities, and he, too, started to change. "He especially changed in the way he treated me," the woman told me. "Today we're getting along better than ever and are happier than we've ever been." The first part of her conversation was interrupted by tears. She was very emotional. In the last part of the conversation, as she talked about the changes in her husband and their relationship, she started to smile.

The most important opinion you have is the opinion you have of yourself, and the most important conversations you will ever have are the conversations you have with yourself. The list of qualities contains the statements, "I am kind, gentle, affectionate, passionate, loving," and so on. The reality is that you cannot consistently, consciously claim all those qualities and abuse others at the same time. That's what caused the change in her husband.

If you would like a copy of that self-talk card, just send a stamped, self-addressed envelope to this address:

> Ziglar Training Systems
> 2009 Chenault #100
> Carrollton, TX 75006

I hope you will, because if you combine this self-talk procedure with the information in this book, it will enrich — and maybe even dramatically change — your life, as it did for the woman in this story.

# People Need a Purpose to Live

Joseph P. Klock tells this story in the November/December 1993 issue of *Personal Selling Power* magazine:

A group of refugees was about to flee a war zone by hiking over some of the most rugged terrain in their country. As they were about to leave, they were approached by a frail old man and a sickly mother who carried an infant. The leaders of the group agreed to take them along with the understanding that the men would take turns carrying the baby, but that the mother and the old man would have to make it on their own.

Several days into the journey, the old man fell to the ground, saying that he was too exhausted to continue and pleading to be left behind to die. Facing the harsh reality of the situation, the leaders of the group reluctantly decided to do just that and started on their way.

Suddenly, the young mother placed her baby in the old man's arms, told him that it was his turn to carry the child, and walked away with the group. It was several minutes before she allowed herself to look back, but when she did, she saw the old man stumbling along the trail with the child in his arms.

This story shows that when a human being is given a new purpose in life, a wellspring of strength, courage, and persistence comes along with the goal — often where none had existed before. People who are too tired, discouraged, or fearful to go on are often suffering from lack of motivation, which is to say that they've either lost sight of their purpose or need to find a new one.

Chapters 6, 7, 8, and 9 of this book are designed to help you find your purpose in life and begin to set goals to achieve that purpose. If you look around, you can find many goals in your life. Each goal often brings with it the energy, courage, creativity, and stamina necessary to reach it. Fortunately for the old man in this story, his new purpose found him — but it's rare to be so fortunate. You must find your own purpose and then stick to it. After all, a life (yours!) depends on it.

# Index

*(continued)*

# A Free Subscription to Ziggets Weekly

Time and money: Two big obstacles that block our paths to success. For years at Ziglar Training Systems, we've heard business people and other professionals say that they could be more successful "If only we had more time . . ." and "If money wasn't an issue . . ." With those two obstacles out of the way, all of us can achieve greater success.

We've eliminated those two obstacles at Ziglar Training Systems, and now there are no more "ifs"!

Now, there are Ziggets!

Say what?

Say *Zig-gets!* They are key points of information folded into a bite-sized training program exclusively developed by Ziglar Training Systems. Ziggets are easy to implement and they provide solutions and improvements that can be applied in every business environment.

Perhaps best of all, Ziggets are *inexpensive* and *time-sensitive.* A self-taught Zigget lesson can be absorbed in under 30 minutes . . . and for less than the price of a good haircut!

We don't promise that one Zigget will lead you to more success, although it might. However, we know that if you implement all 48 Zigget lessons, you're bound to achieve greater success. Not even a good haircut can promise that!

Ziggets come in six different modules covering the following subjects: Sales, Marketing, Team Development, Management, Customer Service, and Personal Development. Why these six subjects? Because our research told us that these are the six subjects that nearly everyone in business wants to know more about.

Each Zigget module includes eight different lessons related to the subject matter of that module. In all six modules, there are a total of 48 lessons . . . just about enough to absorb one lesson per week. That's less than 30 minutes a week. Less than $15 per lesson. It's even less money when you consider that you can use the same Zigget to train the people you employ, manage, or mentor.

Now here's some really exciting news. To help you absorb and implement Ziggets, we'll give you a free subscription to our Ziggets Weekly newsletter. You subscribe by visiting www.zigziglar.com. Not yet online? Then write the words *Ziggets Weekly* on your letterhead and fax it to **972-991-1853**.

Along with your first Ziggets Weekly, you'll receive information about how you can own a set of Ziggets. If you can't wait that long, then call **800-527-0306** and we'll give you the scoop.

# Notes